JOSEPH BANKS: A LIFE

PATRICK O'BRIAN's many books include the Jack Aubrey and Stephen Maturin novels about the British Navy during the Napoleonic Wars, described in *The Times Literary Supplement* as "a brilliant achievement", several volumes of short stories, a biography of Picasso, and distinguished translations of Simone de Beauvoir, André Maurois and Jacques Soustelle.

By the same author

BIOGRAPHY

Picasso

NOVELS

Testimonies
The Catalans
The Golden Ocean
The Unknown Shore
Richard Temple
Master and Commander
Post Captain
HMS Surprise
The Mauritius Command
Desolation Island
The Fortunes of War
The Surgeon's Mate
The Ionian Mission
Treason's Harbour
The Far Side of the World
The Reverse of the Medal

TALES

The Last Pool
The Walker
Lying in the Sun
The Chian Wine

ANTHOLOGY

A Book of Voyages

Patrick O'Brian

JOSEPH BANKS

A Life

COLLINS HARVILL
8 Grafton Street, London W1
1988

Collins Harvill
William Collins Sons and Co Ltd
London · Glasgow · Sydney · Auckland
Toronto · Johannesburg

BRITISH LIBRARY CATALOGUING IN PUBLICATION DATA

O'Brian, Patrick
Joseph Banks: a life
1. Banks. *Sir* Joseph 2. Scientists – Great Britain – Biography
I. Title
581'.092'4 Q143.R3

ISBN 0-00-272340-9

First published by Collins Harvill 1987
This edition first published by Collins Harvill 1988
Reprinted 1988

Printed and Bound in Great Britain by
Hartnolls Limited, Bodmin, Cornwall.

for Mary, with love

CONTENTS

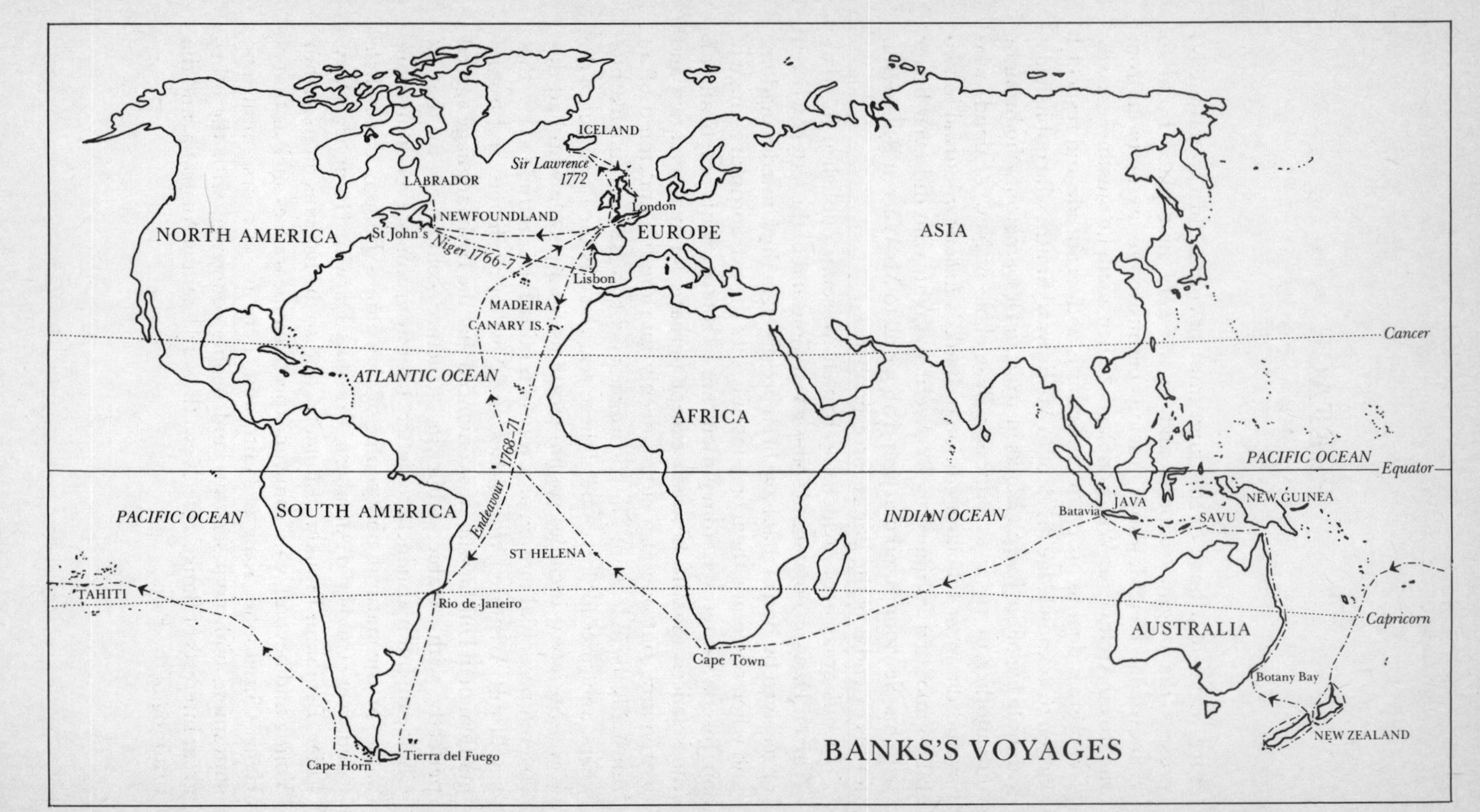

BANKS'S VOYAGES

PREFACE

THE writer of a book of this kind must of course turn to those who possess the original papers, and in the very first place I am to acknowledge Her Majesty's gracious permission to use material from the Royal Archives at Windsor Castle. Then again he must necessarily owe a great deal to his predecessors: it is with gratitude and respect I hasten to acknowledge my debt to Mr Edward Smith, who published a valuable life of Sir Joseph Banks in 1911; to Dr Cameron, who brought out another in 1952; to Professor Beaglehole of New Zealand, who produced a most scholarly edition of Banks's *Endeavour* journal in two fully annotated volumes; to Dr Averil Lysaght, who did even better with his Newfoundland diary; and above all to Mr Warren R. Dawson for his calendar of the Banks correspondence.

In this great book, which the British Museum published in 1958, Warren Dawson condensed some seven thousand of the letters written or received by Banks that have been preserved in the United Kingdom; and when one reads them one not only sees the extraordinary range of Sir Joseph's interests, from agriculture to zoology with practically all the sciences that lie between except perhaps for mathematics and astronomy, but one also enters deeply into the life and mind of an unusually likeable man. The correspondence covers something like fifty years, and since for forty-one of these years he was the President of the Royal Society it includes communications from people who had discovered perpetual motion or a way of finding the longitude at sea that would put Aristotle, Archimedes and Newton to shame, and from a gentleman in Dublin who was convinced that the Irish language agreed perfectly with Arabic, while its structure conformed to that of Chaldean; but it also includes letters to or from almost every illustrious name in the natural philosophy of the time – Buffon, Cavendish, Condorcet, Cuvier, d'Alembert, Erasmus Darwin, Humphry Davy, Euler, Benjamin Franklin, Linnaeus, and so the list runs on to Arthur Young and beyond, with some unexpected appearances such as that of Henri Christophe, King of Haiti; and there are of course ministers, statesmen, high civil servants and people concerned with the other great interests of Banks's life, Kew, the settlement of Australia, and the draining of the Fens.

The gathering of all these letters was a most prodigious task, for although Banks had kept everything in the most exact order, both in London and at Revesby Abbey, his country house in Lincolnshire, they were dispersed after his death. He had no legitimate children, nor I think any surviving natural child, and in his will he asked Sir Edward Knatchbull, a nephew by marriage and one of his executors, to look through the papers in his room in Soho Square and the passage next to it, to select those that had to do with Lincolnshire and his estate there (these were to be sent to Revesby), those which were of interest to the Royal Society and the Mint (which were to be sent to those bodies), and the foreign correspondence, bound or unbound (which was to go to the British Museum), and to burn the rest.

But there must have been some confusion, for although Sir Edward did give the Museum the bound part of the foreign correspondence, nothing ever reached the Royal Society or the Mint; and when eventually Mr Dawson Turner, FRS, an East Anglian banker and a botanist of high standing, undertook to write a life of Banks, he was never lent more than a small proportion of the whole correspondence, which Warren Dawson estimates as something above fifty thousand letters – and perhaps as many as a hundred thousand. Some no doubt had been burnt in 1820, but long after that period there are still references to ninety volumes of letters at Sir Edward's house in Kent. Mr Turner did however have twenty-seven volumes at Yarmouth, where he lived, and these he had copied, mostly by his two daughters; but after about twelve years, when he was over seventy, he felt that he would not be able to write the biography as he had conceived it, and he sent the letters back; with remarkable delicacy he added the copies too, in case after his death they might fall "into the possession of any one who might be distasteful to Sir Edward Knatchbull or who might so use them as might not do honour to the memory of Sir Joseph Banks".*

In time, no suitable biographer having been found, the papers came into the hands of Lord Brabourne, Sir Edward's son, who offered them to the Keeper of Manuscripts at the British Museum for £250, which the Keeper thought too much. In the same year, 1884, the New South Wales government bought a large number having to do with Australia, and in 1886 those that Lord Brabourne still retained were sold by auction, fetching very little money and going all over the world, sometimes to serious libraries, sometimes to autograph collectors. In 1919 and 1929 the great mass of papers that had remained at Revesby suffered the same fate; but very fortunately the twenty-three bound and

* Warren Dawson, *The Banks Letters*, XXVIII.

indexed volumes of the Dawson Turner copies had somehow come into possession of the British Museum's Department of Botany as early as 1876, so that when Warren Dawson began his enormous task first of finding and cataloguing and then of calendaring the correspondence he had a respectable body of material at hand. Respectable that is to say in bulk and general fidelity; less so in textual accuracy. Banks had a highly personal approach to writing, with a fine disregard for convention in the use of capitals, spelling, and punctuation; but unhappily almost all his editors and copiers, including the Miss Turners, have seen fit to put him right.* As Warren Dawson says, "This method of presentation may convey the purport of the letter to the present-day reader, but it completely effaces all the characteristic mannerisms of the writer", and wherever possible I have gone back to the originals.

Warren Dawson, of course, ranged far beyond the Dawson Turner copies; indeed it is said that to the two thousand of these copies that he used he added no fewer than five thousand from elsewhere, and quite apart from his own important collection he lists more than a hundred sources from which he gathered the scattered leaves; but then, having travelled and searched in sometimes very remote libraries, he had to decipher what he had found. When Joseph Banks was young he wrote a round, unformed hand, quite easily legible apart from its strange use of capitals and so on, but with age his writing grew steadily harder to make out, and even one so accustomed to it as Warren Dawson found that "the letters written in the last years of his life, when physical infirmity also made itself felt, are often very difficult to read". For those less steeped in Banks the difficulty starts much earlier, and there is one word in an important letter of 1794 (printed on page 310) that I still cannot make out, though I have tried to catch it by surprise ever since the Yale Library was kind enough to send it to me; and it is not impossible that my transcripts may sometimes be mistaken.

The many other writers who have helped me are most gratefully acknowledged in sequence as their books, articles or letters are cited: the acknowledgements do not take the form of footnotes but rather of references, chapter by chapter, at the end of the book.

And finally it is a great pleasure to record the kindness of the Royal Society, in whose splendid library I met with so very much help; while in the Botany Library of the British Museum (Natural History), which is reached by passing through a long passage lined in part with Banks's own herbarium itself, I met with even greater kindness, guidance and

*Usually on the grounds of "making it easier for the reader", who is presumably rather backward.

advice, because there I asked for more. The British Library and the London Library, the lion and the unicorn without whose support scholarship could scarcely stand, were naturally of essential importance; and indeed I may say that I never turned to any learned society, any library or any scholar without receiving the most generous and disinterested assistance.

Chapter 1

ORIGINS, EDUCATION, BOTANY

JOSEPH BANKS was born in London on 15 February 1743, and even before he possessed a Christian name the world learnt a good deal about him from the list of births in *The Gentleman's Magazine*:

Feb 2 The Lady of Isaac Hill, Esq; deliver'd of a Son.
5 Lady of Col. Sabine – of a Son & Heir.
12 Lady Conway – of a Son.
15 The Lady Petre, Relict of the late Ld Petre – of a [blank]
Wife of Wm Banks, Member for Grampound, Esq; – of a Son.
17 The Princess of Orange, – of a Princess.

In the first place the baby was important enough to be mentioned: only seven others were thought worthy of print in that month. In the second his father was obviously a wealthy man, since his constituency was a notoriously rotten borough whose fifty-odd electors had to be well paid for their votes. And in the third the editor did not think that the mother should be described as Mr Banks's lady but only as his wife.

It is easy to exaggerate the importance of this last point – the usage was by no means rigid – but the distinction, though perhaps unintended, does in fact suit the position to a certain extent. The Bankses were a recent family, a good example of English social mobility: William's grandfather, the first Joseph Banks (1665–1727) and the first of his name to rise to any prominence, was an attorney. This was not a very glorious calling – Pope's "vile attorneys, now an useless race" come to mind – but it was one that in able hands could prove more profitable than most; and Joseph Banks I was exceptionally able. He was born at Giggleswick in Yorkshire, the son of Robert Banks, who was either a lawyer or a soldier (the evidence is conflicting); and at the age of sixteen he was articled to a busy, thriving attorney in Sheffield. He was diligent and hard-working and before he was forty he was managing several important estates on his own, spending part of the time at Sheffield and part of the time at his country house at Scofton in Nottinghamshire, not far away.[1]

He was rising fast in his profession. In December 1701 for example[2] the Right Honourable the Lady Mary Howard of Worksop, Mother and Guardian of the most Noble Thomas Duke of Norfolk Lord of the Manors of Ecclesfield, Cowley and Hansworth in the County of York sent Greeting in our Lord everlasting to all Xtian people to whom these presents should come and gave them to know that reposing especial trust and confidence in the skill and fidelity of Joseph Banks of Sheffield she appointed him steward of the Court Barons and Copyhold Courts of the said manors.

In August 1705 the Duke confirmed the appointment and in October of the same year yet another Duke, his grace of Newcastle, entrusted his manors of Mansfield, Clipstone and Edwinstone to the same hands. The Duke of Leeds followed suit.

Banks's professional activities took him to Yorkshire, Nottinghamshire (among other things he was Register of Sherwood Forest, an appointment he owed to the Duke of Newcastle, Lord Lieutenant of the county), Derbyshire and Lincolnshire. He was very well acquainted with the estates in those parts and with the financial position of their owners – like many attorneys he arranged loans – and in 1709 he made his first great purchase, the Holland estate in south Lincolnshire, an immense tract, mostly of fenland, near the mouth of the river Welland, that cost him £9900. This however did not exhaust his purse: when he married Mary Hancock, the daughter of a dissenting minister, in 1689, he had £400 with her, but now that he had a daughter of marriageable age he was able to give her a fortune of £10,000, Sir Francis Whichcote, a Lincolnshire baronet, being her husband. Then a little later his son, Joseph Banks II, who was born in 1695, also came to be married; it was an advantageous match with the heiress of William Hodgkinson, a wealthy merchant and mine-owner of Overton in Derbyshire, and for his part Joseph Banks I not only settled much of his Holland estate on his son but also installed the young couple at Revesby Abbey, which he bought in 1714, the year of their marriage. Although it was 1715 before he could take full possession, this was far and away the most important and most profitable of all his transactions. The Abbey had been founded by the Cistercians in Stephen's reign; it stood on the southern edge of the Wolds where they give way to the fenland, and since Henry VIII's time it had passed through various hands, coming eventually to the Howards, who built the great house in about 1670, setting it at some distance from the monastic ruins. Banks made his purchase in troubled times, when Whigs and Tories were very strongly opposed, the Protestant succession by no means a certainty, and the Jacobite rising of 1715 clearly foreseeable; this may help to account for the remarkably low price of £14,000 for the house, the lordship of the manor and the two thousand acres that were concerned in this particular sale; much more land was added later.

If Joseph Banks I had relied on peace and quiet and a safe tenure he was right. George I and his supporters remained firmly in power, and Banks himself was elected to Parliament for Grimsby in the Whig interest, and afterwards for Totnes, probably (since the seat was in the gift of the Treasury) through the influence of his great neighbour Lord Lindsey, whom George I made Duke of Ancaster.

He settled down to life in the country, buying still another series of manors called the Marsh Estate, actively improving the fenland, and delighting in Revesby. But it was here that he met his death in 1727; while he was climbing about among the rafters of a new wing he fell, and the infected wound proved fatal.

He left the memory of "a pleasant, very facetious companion",[3] and like many lawyers he was something of an antiquary. His bust stands in Revesby church, a commanding figure with a double chin; and if one makes abstraction of the elaborate full-bottomed wig it is possible to see a likeness to his famous descendant, particularly in the Wedgwood cameo of about 1780. He died before he had time to carry out all his kindly intentions, but his son Joseph Banks II carefully observed his wishes, rebuilding the church (some of the material seems to have come from the Cistercian remains; but the whole was replaced by a Gothic structure in 1891), building almshouses on Revesby green for ten farmers who had grown poor through no fault of their own, and setting up a foundling hospital in London: he also gave John Norton, believed to be Joseph I's natural son and left out of the will by mistake, £300.

Joseph II was member for Peterborough during part of one parliament, but he does not appear to have taken any real interest in politics. On the other hand he was chosen a Fellow of the Royal Society in 1730, which, though it was of much less significance than it became in his grandson's day, nevertheless suggests the probability of some intellectual interests, if no more. He had eight legitimate children. The eldest boy, Joseph III, was looked upon as the heir of Revesby, but he died before his father, whereupon the second boy, William (our Sir Joseph's father) took his place. This William, born in 1721, was a barrister; as second son he had succeeded to the Overton estate of his maternal grandfather and had therefore taken the name of Hodgkinson; but now he reverted to Banks and, primogeniture being what it was, he increased very much in importance, so much so that it was quite natural for him too to buy a seat in Parliament. In 1741 he married Sarah Bate in the chapel of Burleigh House (her sister had married the Earl of Exeter, which explains the chapel: they were both wealthy heiresses). The next child, Elizabeth, ran away with James Hawley of the Lincoln-

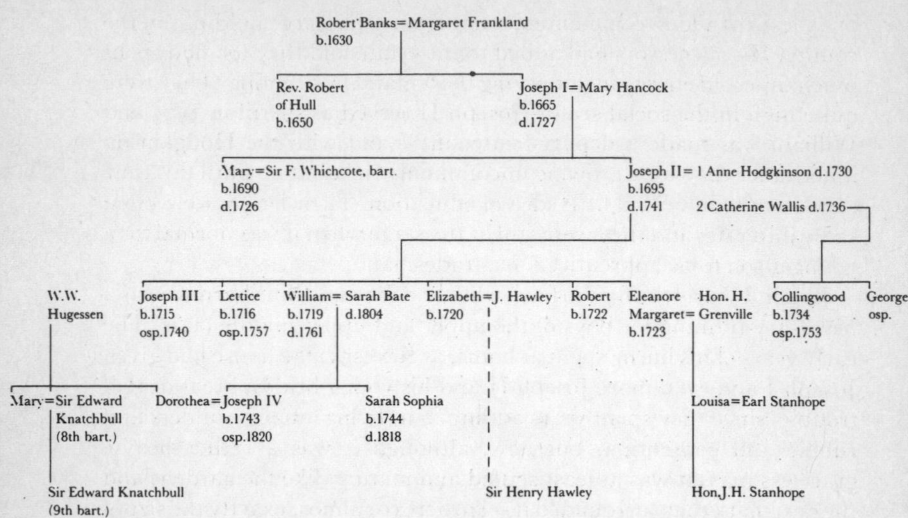

SIR JOSEPH BANKS'S ANCESTORS, based on J.W.F. Hill, *The Letters and Papers of the Banks Family of Revesby Abbey* (Lincoln Record Society, vol.45, 1952), and continued to show the eventual heirs of his estates.

shire family, and by marrying him established a link that eventually carried some of the Banks land to that family. The next, Robert, was bound apprentice to a Bristol merchant; but William relinquished the Hodgkinson estate in his favour, it returning to Joseph IV at Robert's death. The next was Eleanore Margaret, a famous beauty, the "Peggy Banks" of Horace Waipole'ꜱ letters, who married the Hon. Henry Grenville: her daughter Louisa married Lord Stanhope, also of Lincolnshire; and this was another connection that affected the inheritance of the estate.

By 1743, when Joseph Banks IV, our Joseph Banks, was born to William and Sarah, the family had been established in the county for nearly thirty years. It was not a great while as these things go (their neighbours the Dymokes of Scrivelsby had been King's Champions since 1381), but they had been exceptionally well introduced. Joseph I had early formed a professional connection and then a friendship with Lord Lindsey, the head of the great Bertie family of Lincolnshire, and in 1715, the year the Bankses came to live at Revesby, Lord Lindsey was not only given his dukedom by the new king but was also confirmed in his office of Lord Lieutenant, so his kindness counted for a very great deal. Then again by the time of his death Joseph I had become the lord of no less than fourteen manors, apart from other large holdings in the county. His successors had added to the estate and they too had spent much time and energy in improving the fenland by draining. They were quite high in the social scale – Joseph II served as sheriff in 1735 and William was made a deputy-lieutenant – and with the Hodgkinson inheritance they were growing uncommonly rich; but up until this time they seem to have had little idea of education. Their letters were often sadly illiterate; and they were still at the stage when it was normal for a younger son to be apprenticed to a tradesman.

Joseph IV was the first to have what had for some time been seen as a necessary training for boys of the upper and upper middle class. The early years of his life he spent at home, at Revesby; the house had given Joseph I and even more Joseph II and his young bride a great deal of trouble, since they spent years adding to it, living among builders and rubble and contention, but now, although it was a rather heavy, graceless mass it was at least settled and mature, like the gardens and the deer-park that surrounded it – 340 acres or almost exactly the size of Hyde Park in London. In addition to this there were vast woods behind, vast fens in front, quantities of horses in the stables, cricket on the village green, and almost unlimited water for one fond of fishing.

Young Joseph Banks was very fond of fishing, as he was of most country pursuits, and this must have been very like Paradise. It is true that a private tutor came to give him lessons, but they seemed to make little impression upon his mind, which was no doubt one of the reasons that a more regular education was decided upon.

In 1752, when Joseph Banks was nine, his father sent him to Harrow, to the Free Grammar School of John Lyon at Harrow. Although by this time the process by which the free scholars were edged out and their building taken from them was well under way, the place was still quite recognizable as the foundation John Lyon had contemplated: a school in which thirty (later forty) boys belonging to the parish could be educated at no cost to their parents, while two might go on to Oxford and two to Cambridge with modest scholarships. But in his simplicity the Elizabethan yeoman had not seen that the clause by which he allowed the schoolmaster to increase his stipend of thirty pounds a year by taking in some paying pupils from elsewhere, "foreigners", was tantamount to the introduction of a flock of cuckoos into his nest – slow-growing cuckoos, it is true, but powerful ones and casuistical too, since they presently found that John Lyon did not really mean that his school should be for poor boys at all, and that Free was to be understood as Paying.[4]

The transition from grammar school to public school, both in the modern sense, was in progress at Harrow, but when Banks arrived something like a quarter of the boys were still free scholars: it is impossible to give an exact figure, since the records are imperfect, but in 1721, when the school numbered 140, or slightly more than in 1752, there had been the full complement of forty. Yet on the other hand by 1752 the foreigners, the paying boys, already included a Scottish duke, an English peer and a baronet, presently to be joined by an Anglo-Irish earl, for this was in Dr Thackeray's reign. Thackeray had been at Eton both as a boy and a master, and with the governors' approval he had at once set about introducing Etonian ways. It is said that he was no great scholar, but in other respects he was a man of remarkable powers, for not only did he change the nature of the school, setting it firmly in the new mould, but he combined his duties with those of archdeacon of Surrey and chaplain to Frederick Prince of Wales; he also had sixteen children; and perhaps it was the multiplicity of his occupations that prevented him from seeing that an unscholarly boy in the lower school was making no progress.

Nine seems pitifully young to go to a public school, even in the eighteenth-century sense; but Banks was by no means the youngest at Harrow. One of his better-known contemporaries, Samuel Parr, who became the "Whig Johnson" and an eminent Latinist, went when he was five. Parr was typical of the older Harrow; he was a local apothecary's son and a free scholar, and he went on to Emmanuel College, Cambridge (though to be sure his allowance was so small that he could not stay up long enough for a degree). And there were other children scarcely older than little Parr. This was possible because at that time Harrow still retained John Lyon's system of school dames, village women who looked after the very little boys and taught them reading and scripture. But though they were no doubt kind, and although Samuel Parr and the great Orientalist William Jones flourished under their care, neither they nor the masters could make anything of a scholar out of Joseph Banks. He was an exceedingly active boy, much given to play, and no persuasion could keep him to his book; although he was by no means a fool he never learnt to spell, nor did he ever master the use of capital letters or punctuation; his Latin left much to be desired, and he knew no Greek at all. In 1756, when he was thirteen, his father took him away and sent him to Eton.

There was much to be said against Eton: it lay in low, damp, unhealthy ground rather than upon a salubrious hill; in many respects it was more like an ill-managed bear-garden than a school; and even then there were people who felt that Etonians spent more time than was necessary in thanking God that they were not as other men. But with all its faults it was not in a state of transition. Eton had settled into its "public school" stride at least as early as the seventeenth century and in any case from the very beginning its founder, Henry VI, had laid down that as well as the seventy poor and indigent scholars there should be as many as twenty commensals "sons of noblemen and special friends of the College" and an indefinite number of other commensals who were to dine at the third table in Hall with the choristers and scholars.

In 1756 the Collegers, or most of them, still slept in the Long Chamber that had been provided for them in the fifteenth century, and the two sorts of boys, the Collegers and the fee-paying Oppidans, the descendants of the commensals, lived reasonably well together. The unscrupulous rapacity, not to say the downright dishonesty, of successive provosts and fellows had already deprived the Collegers of much of the food and many of the benefits intended by the founder, but the boys had not yet been so reduced that their Long Chamber was a byword for squalor, cruelty, bullying and sexual immorality, notorious to such a degree that candidates for election were hard to find and a scholar was looked upon as an inferior being: that belonged to the later part of the century.[5]

Long Chamber can never have been a comfortable berth for the half-starved little boys, the fags, even when the Lower Master lived at the far end of it, within earshot of their screams; but in Banks's time College was still regarded as a reasonably desirable place for one's son; apart from anything else there were the closed scholarships to King's College, Cambridge, and the possibility of becoming a Fellow of Eton, even the Provost, both places being reserved, at least in theory, for former Collegers and members of King's. Somewhat earlier than this, Robert Walpole's father, a wealthy man but with a keen eye for a job, falsified his son's age to get him in; and it was not considered extraordinary that the particular friend of Charles James Fox (nearly contemporary with Banks) should be a Colleger named Hare, the son of a Winchester apothecary.

Banks came to Eton at a fortunate time. Dr Barnard had been the headmaster for some years, coming after a disastrous person who believed that respect, Latin, and even Greek could be driven into boys with a birch. Barnard was no great flogger, though he was an admirable disciplinarian; he was also an uncommonly amiable man,* at ease in

* There is a pleasant anecdote of Dr Barnard in Thraliana. "To return to Mr Pepys. He told me one Day a comical Thing concerning his quitting Eton School: Dr Barnard under whom he was

any society, particularly that of Windsor Castle, and he succeeded in bringing the school's numbers up to 522, more boys than had ever been seen before and more than were ever to be seen again in the eighteenth century. The school, then, was flourishing; and although the same could hardly be said for the other and originally more important side of Henry VI's foundation, the splendidly endowed chantry in which Mass should be said for the soul of Henry V and eventually for that of the founder, it nevertheless existed, living on in spite of the Reformation and many other crises, providing comfort for the provost and fellows if for nobody else. They were not a strikingly distinguished body of men at this time, but they were there, a visible link with an ancient past, giving a certain air of learning and even of civilization.

In the middle of the eighteenth century Eton could do with all the civilization it could come by. Until 1747 the school had the custom of chasing a ram (supplied by the butcher) and beating it to death with clubs made for the purpose; but, and here I quote from Christopher Hollis's *Eton, a History*, "It was a few years after this [1730, when the Duke of Cumberland had joined in the fun] that the ram broke loose from the hunt, ran up the High Street over Windsor Bridge and through the market with the boys in hot pursuit until eventually they caught it and beat it to death. This was disapproved of not because of the public killing or of the cruelty to the ram but on the curious grounds that the exercise might make the boys too hot and thus endanger their health. Therefore for the future, as a reform, the ram was hamstrung and made to hobble round and round School Yard with the boys in pursuit and beating it until it was dead."

But though the ram was abolished before Banks's time there was still badger baiting, bull baiting, bear baiting, cock fighting and – why not? – small boy baiting. William Pitt, the first Lord Chatham, who was there from about 1720 to 1726, said that "he had scarce observed a boy who was not cowed for life at Eton; that a public school might suit a boy of turbulent, forward disposition, but it would not do where there was any gentleness"; and many, many other witnesses could be brought to show that in a rough and often cruel century Eton and public schools in general were also rough and often cruel.

Yet there was another side to it. Gray, Horace Walpole, Richard West and their friends can hardly be said to have had turbulent,

educated, had it seems a way of talking to the Boys who were taking Leave of him at once so tender and so full of Admonition that many of them had been known to shed Tears at parting – says Pepys to his Companion who went home the same Day, I dread going up to the Doctor, I am afraid of being made to cry, – believe me replies his Friend I am more afraid than You – for I have the Misfortune to *cry loud*."

forward dispositions, nor were Gray or West devoid of gentleness; yet they looked back on their schooldays with pleasure.

No doubt a very great deal depended on a boy's house, and no doubt Banks fell lucky. He was of course an Oppidan, and at that time the Oppidans were divided among thirteen houses, ten kept by Dames and three by Dominies: none of these housekeepers, female or male, had any teaching duties at all; their function was to provide board and lodging. Housemasters in the modern sense there were none, for although some assistants were allowed to have a few boys living with them this was not the same thing at all, and the domestic authority that they later came to possess was then exercised by the Dames alone. And in the nature of things a kind, attentive Dame with plenty of inherent authority ruled over a happy house.

But even if Joseph Banks had chanced upon an overworked, harassed, inept Dame incapable of keeping the rougher, more brutal boys in order, it is probable that he would have come through fairly well. He was not a sensitive plant; he was thoroughly used to public school life and he was not given to any offensive degree of application; he was big for his age, uncommonly strong, active and brave – some years later he showed remarkable courage when he was faced with angry cannibals in the Antipodes. Then again he was quite good-looking, and generally speaking people liked him, particularly when he was young. Even though he was not of a particularly aggressive disposition, and even though there was a fair amount of gentleness in his nature, Eton suited him: he made many friends, and in a tolerably extensive view of his correspondence I have not found him say an unkind word about his time there.

Yet on the other hand he did not suit Eton. At least he did not suit Eton particularly well, and there were complaints that he was not profiting from his education as much as he should. These complaints were certainly justified, for as Lord Brougham, the son of one of Banks's school friends, observed in his *Lives of Men of Letters and Science who Flourished in the Time of George III*, "My father . . . always said that his friend Joe cared mighty little for his book, and could not well understand any one taking to Greek and Latin." Though indeed when one considers the official education offered by the school it is difficult to see how any but a gifted boy, already well grounded in Latin and Greek, could possibly have profited from it. Masters were few and their classes were intolerably big: Dr Barnard took the whole of the sixth and fifth forms as a single division of more than a hundred boys, and he led them through Homer or Virgil in one part of a fair-sized room while in the rest of it, under other guidance, the remove and the fourth form were going through Virgil or Homer. When a couple of hundred boys are gathered together under one roof there is bound to be a certain amount of din: even under such a devoted flogger as Dr Keate somewhat later "the boys occupied their time by singing songs and choruses", and this cannot have helped reflection. Things were much the same in Lower School, where the first, second and third forms met, except that some of the voices were higher pitched. It was no doubt great fun, particularly for the undetectable boys at the back, but it did not bring them forward very fast nor was it much use to them in their other tasks. For quite apart from the formal lessons, prayers, roll-calls and the like, the upper boys were required to produce three exercises a week: an original theme in prose of not less than twenty lines, a copy of verses of not less than ten elegiac distichs and five or six stanzas of lyrics on the same subject – all in Latin, of course, except that the sixth formers were to hand up one of their copies in Greek hexameters.

It is probably true to say that unless he were exceptionally endowed no boy, unhelped by anything but the official teaching in class, could perform these exercises and still have time for cricket, the river, fives, or bowling his hoop. But many boys came to Eton bringing their own tutors with them, while most of the assistant masters taught boys privately; and a great deal of the real learning took place outside Upper or Lower School. There was of course a large quantity of hack verse in the common domain, and exercises could also be bought or begged; but as far as real learning was concerned the tutor was generally of the first importance. This was certainly the case with Banks, who owed what classical acquirements he ever possessed to Edward Young, an assistant master, under whom he did at least learn to spell Latin a good deal better than ever he spelt English and to write a reasonably grammatical piece of Latin prose. Mr Young wrote a long letter[6] to Joseph's father at Revesby on 6 February 1757 beginning

Sir

I have received the Favour of your letter, and am very glad Master Banks was detained by nothing worse than the Badness of the Roads and weather. I began indeed to be afraid he was kept at home either by his own or your Illness; being well satisfied you would not suffer him to be absent from School so long without some very substantial Reason. I will take care to explain the Affair to Dr Barnard and Dr Dampier according to your desire.

It gives me great pleasure to find You think Master Banks improved. To be able to construe a Latin Author into English with Readiness and Propriety is undoubtedly no less necessary than to be able to turn an English

> one into Latin. They ought indeed to go hand in hand together. And I hope we shall by degrees bring Master Banks to a tolerable Perfection in the former; tho' the Point, which I have hitherto been chiefly labouring, is to improve him in the latter, because of his great Deficiency in that Respect when He came to us.

Then, after a piece about the difficulty of parsing Greek without some knowledge of Greek grammar, the importance of the fourth form, and attention to one's book, Mr Young asks Mr Banks to

> take the Trouble to write to Him, to show the great Necessity there will be for Him to exert particular Diligence at that Time; and I will likewise take all Opportunities of inculcating the same to Him. For You can't but be sensible that there is a great Inattention in Him, and an immoderate Love of Play . . . which we must endeavour to get the better of in some degree, or it will be a constant Obstacle to his Improvement. This sometimes occasions Quarrels between us; tho' in other respects we agree extremely well together; as I really think Him a very good-tempered and well disposed Boy.

At just about this time an artist painted a portrait of Master Banks; it hung at Revesby for a great while, but when the Abbey was demolished it came down to the Hon. Mrs Clive Pearson and it is now at Parham Park, together with the splendid Reynolds. The picture is attributed to Lemuel Francis Abbott, though an eminent connoisseur once suggested to me that it might be one of Zoffany's earliest works in England – the dates would just fit – and a connection of this kind would go some way to explaining Banks's very surprising notion of taking Zoffany with him in the *Resolution* on Cook's second great voyage. But whatever his name, the painter was evidently a most accomplished man, and the impression the work gives of being a big picture is by no means due only to its considerable size of some seven feet by four and a half. On the upper left-hand part of the canvas there is the base and the first three or four feet of one of those prodigious columns so usual in seventeenth- and eighteenth-century pictures together with the inevitable curtain in great folds across the corner: the background is a fine cloud-swept sky. And in front of this high drama, on quite another plane of reality, sits a slim, thoughtful, very pleasant-looking boy in fawn-coloured breeches with one white-stockinged leg stretched out across the foreground, making a good diagonal, a fawn waistcoat, a frilled and ruffled shirt and a green coat with gilt buttons; his auburn hair falls over his shoulders on either side and it comes low over his forehead, but it does not look in the least affected. He is sitting rather sideways in a brass-studded leather chair with his left elbow on its back and his right hand resting on a print that in its turn lies upon a cloth-covered table which also holds some books and plants. Beneath it there are half a dozen dim folios, and to the boy's left, on the floor, stands a fair-sized and most prophetic terrestrial globe. His face is turned almost to the spectator, but he is looking down, obviously in thought, deep thought.

The "good-tempered and well disposed" side of Mr Young's pupil is certainly there, but there is no trace of the great inattention, nor yet of the immoderate love of play, for a great change had come over Joseph Banks. He had not suddenly acquired a taste for Virgil, Horace or Tully; he had not become a classical scholar; but he had become a botanist, and the print under his right hand in the picture is in fact a botanical print. The moment of his change – one might almost say of his vocation – was clearly marked and abrupt, and once it had occurred his strong natural intelligence at last had something to feed upon. Latin and Greek had not been a nourishment that his mind could assimilate, and Latin and Greek were virtually the only subjects taught at Eton – taught, furthermore, in a pronunciation that guaranteed incomprehensibility abroad, whereas an Irishman or even a Scot could prattle away from Poland to Peru. It is true that on holidays the younger boys had two hours of writing and arithmetic, while the fifth form learnt geography or algebra; and of course French, dancing, fencing and drawing could be taken as extras outside school hours, though it does not appear that Banks ever learnt them (he possessed no word of French at any time, nor could he draw), and had it not been for botany his mind might never have blossomed at all.

The story of his conversion is contained in a Hunterian Oration delivered to the College of Surgeons on 14 February 1822 by Sir Everard Home, a friend of Banks's and a surgeon himself. The relevant passage runs:

> When fourteen, his tutor had, for the first time, the satisfaction of finding him reading during his hours of leisure. This sudden turn, which his mind had taken, Sir Joseph explained to me in the following manner; one fine summer evening he had bathed in the river as usual with other boys, but having staid a long time in the water he found when he came to dress himself, that all his companions were gone; he was walking leisurely along a lane, the sides of which were richly enamelled with flowers; he stopped and looked round, involuntarily exclaimed, How beautiful! After some reflection, he said to himself, it is surely more natural that I should be taught to know all these productions of Nature, in preference to Greek and Latin; but the latter is my father's command and it is my duty to obey him. I will however make myself acquainted with all these different plants for my own

> pleasure and gratification. He began immediately to teach himself Botany; and, for want of more able tutors, submitted to be instructed by the women, employed in culling simples, as it is termed, to supply the Druggists and Apothecaries shops, paying sixpence for every material piece of information. While at home for the ensuing holidays he found, to his inexpressible delight, in his mother's dressing room, a book in which all the plants he had met with were not only described but represented by engravings. This, which proved to be Gerard's Herbal, although one of the boards was lost and several of the leaves torn out, he carried with him to school in triumph; and it was probably this very book that he was poring over when detected by his tutor, for the first time, in the act of reading.
>
> He now exulted over his former preceptors, being not only independent of them, but in his turn, whenever they met with a new plant, told them its name and the qualities ascribed to it.

In parenthesis I may say that I do not believe in the literal truth of Banks's reflection nor in his exulting. Both are contradicted by everything one learns from his correspondence and his journals, but they may well be characteristic of Home, who left no pleasant reputation behind him: indeed, the *DNB* directly accuses him of having "destroyed Hunter's manuscripts after utilizing them".

From now on his life had an aim, and it was not botany alone, though that remained his chief love and delight, but the whole range of natural philosophy short of mathematics. Lord Brougham says, "My father described him as a remarkably fine-looking, strong and active boy, whom no fatigue could subdue, and no peril daunt; and his whole time out of school was given up to hunting after plants and insects, making a *hortus siccus* of the one, and forming a cabinet of the other. As often as Banks could induce him to quit his task in reading or in verse-making, he would take him on his long rambles; and I suppose it was from this early taste that we had at Brougham so many butterflies, beetles, and other insects, as well as a cabinet of shells and fossils."

During the remaining years of Banks's time at Eton his herbarium grew, but so did his resistance to Greek, which became something of a legend; he kept out of serious trouble however and in any case the remaining years were cut short. A little after his seventeenth birthday he was at Revesby, and there he was inoculated with smallpox, that being the somewhat dangerous means of immunization against the disease before the discovery of vaccination: the first inoculation did not take, and by the time the whole thing was over and he was well again his parents did not think it worth while sending him back to school. He went to Oxford instead, his name being put down on the books of Christ Church as a gentleman-commoner at the end of 1760.

A little while before this Gibbon had spent "fourteen months at Magdalen College; they proved the fourteen months the most idle and unprofitable of my whole life". His remarks about the university, so admirably and so memorably expressed, have coloured the general view ever since: the idle, port-drinking fellows, the worthless tutors, the dissipated, neglected undergraduates are sometimes held up to be wholly typical of mid-eighteenth-century Oxford. Yet Gibbon was only sixteen when he was expelled; he had been as unprepared as he was unsuited for university life; and he was particularly unfortunate in his tutors. Port was certainly drunk and there were certainly idle dons, while a good many undergraduates undoubtedly played the fool; but there was another side to Oxford. A university whose press brought out Hyde's *Historia Religionis Veterum Persarum*, Chandler's *Marmora Oxoniensia* and Heath's *Notes on the Greek Tragedians*, to name only a few of the books published in Banks's time, and which contained Blackstone, Warton and Lowth, to mention only three of the dons, could not be described as a hive of drones. No one can deny that the examinations were often ridiculous (this was of course long before the day of the honours degree) or that there were professors who thought it no part of their duty to teach; yet on the other hand when the Chancellor's Latin Prize was instituted "a prodigious number of men"[7] entered, and when the set subject was electricity, Christ Church was expected to win; and even Gibbon admits that "Under the auspices of the late deans, a more regular discipline has been introduced, as I am told, at Christ Church; a course of classical and philosophical studies is proposed, and even pursued, in that numerous seminary; learning has been made a duty, a pleasure, and even a fashion; and several young gentlemen do honour to the college in which they have been educated." Furthermore, when Banks fetched Israel Lyons from Cambridge to act as a private tutor in botany he lectured to as many as sixty pupils ("with great applause" says Nichols in his *Literary Anecdotes*) – sixty voluntary, paying pupils in a university that probably did not possess a thousand solvent undergraduates, and this at a time when science, apart from mathematics and astronomy, had little standing.

Dr Sibthorp, who held the Sherardian chair of botany, was one of the professors who did not teach, or who at any rate did not lecture, perhaps regarding his chair as a place for research rather than one from which he should read out information available to all literate students since the invention of printing; but although he may not have been a distinguished botanist (Robert Brown, correcting Brougham's memoir, observed that of his botanical activities "there is nothing to be said"[8]) he did bring up a most distinguished son, the author, or at least the prime collector and designer, of the splendid *Flora Graeca*. He was not at all opposed to Banks's idea of finding a teacher: indeed, he gave him a letter of introduction to John Martyn, the Professor of Botany at Cambridge, an unusually learned and enterprising man, who produced Israel Lyons the younger, the son of Israel Lyons the elder, a Polish Jew who kept a silversmith's shop and who gave private lessons in Hebrew.

It was perhaps typical of the age that the younger Lyons (he was only four years older than Banks) should have been so much esteemed not only by the Professor of Botany but also by the Master of Trinity and other notable men at Cambridge. It is true that he had been devoted to botany from childhood and that he had already published *A Treatise of Fluxions* which impressed mathematicians, but a later, more snobbish century might well have kept him down. Mid-eighteenth-century society was intensely conscious of rank – noblemen had extraordinary privileges – but in some ways it was much more democratic than ours. Joseph Ames, for example, began life as an apprentice plane-maker and went on as an ironmonger all his days, yet because of his skill as an antiquary he became a Fellow of the Royal Society and the colleague of some of the highest in the land; the Musical Small-Coals man had very grand friends indeed; and one could cite many more instances. Professor Martyn himself had lived by his pen, translating French botanical works and contributing to the *Grub Street Journal* at intervals of collecting plants until he managed to get to Emmanuel College at the age of thirty and so to the chair of botany.

Banks's journey was successful: he brought Lyons back to Oxford and the mathematical botanist did very well there. How much of this success was owing to Banks's position and how much to his personality one can but guess; but there is no doubt that Banks was a most amiable young man. He had a great number of friends of all ages; and some years later Reynolds painted a portrait of him that shows why he was so generally liked. It is a particularly brilliant Sir Joshua: I remember how it stood out on a wall of perfectly respectable paintings at an exhibition at Sotheby's in 1983, and how much I was struck by the sitter's face – a timeless and entirely human face that happened to be in the context of the 1770s but that might just as well have belonged to the days of Aristotle or Pliny or Darwin, the face of an eager, intelligent, disinterested enquirer, the kind of face that might be seen in the Royal Society today, if there were any Fellows under thirty. This painting too shows Banks sitting at a table, turned slightly from it to face the viewer; but now he is on the other side and it is his left hand that is upon a sheaf of papers, while the terrestrial globe is behind him. He is wearing a dusky-red fur-lined coat and a brown waistcoat, and again his eyes are directed downwards, in thought. He is of course no longer the slim, handsome boy of the first portrait, but although the waistcoat does betray an incipient paunch, there is no hint of the massive, black-browed, dewlapped, important and authoritarian Bull of Revesby (as those who disagreed with his views on draining the Fens called him)[9] that he was later to become, at least in outward appearance.

As for his position at this particular time, in 1760, he was like Gibbon a gentleman-commoner, one of that "pert and pampered race, too froward for controul – privileged prodigals" denounced by an angry correspondent in the *Gentleman's Magazine*.[10] These people were not as pampered as noblemen (a category that included the *nobiles minorum gentium*, knights and baronets) who might wear gold tassels and gowns of any colour they pleased – Lord Fitzwilliam of Trinity Hall walked about in a pink one, adorned with lace – but in a university that still had servitors and that still made them aware of their inferior station, a gentleman-commoner in his velvet cap and silken gown was a person of some consequence. He was necessarily richer than the ordinary undergraduate and this gave him much more freedom; he could easily pay the fines for cutting lectures or meals in hall, for neglecting matins or vespers (twopence a time) or St Mary's on Sunday (a shilling if detected), and, as the angry correspondent calculated, he could buy absolute liberty for about thirteen shillings a week. He was fairly sure to have influential connections, and he might even have church livings in his gift now or in the future; he was, potentially, a man of some weight.

This became more obviously the case with Banks in 1761, when his father died. The Bankses were not a long-lived race – Joseph III died at twenty-five, Joseph II at forty-five and Joseph I at sixty-two – yet even so, and despite the fact that his health had been poor for some years, William Banks's death at the age of forty-two was unexpected.

The Lord of the Manor of Revesby, Member of Parliament for Grampound and Deputy-Lieutenant for Lincolnshire remains a shadowy figure; he was no doubt a most attentive landlord and his chief interest in life was the draining of the Fens, but in later years Joseph, his son, wrote an account of his end in which there is no mention of kindness given or received, no emotion of any kind, and it is possible that they were not very good friends.

One certain result of William Banks's death was that his son, on reaching the age of twenty-one, would come into estates in Lincolnshire, Staffordshire, Derbyshire and Sussex yielding six thousand pounds a year. This was not quite the "ten thousand a year and a deer-park" that accompanied the ideal husband up until quite recent times, yet it was still a great deal of money; what is more, there were already deer at Revesby, and with high farming and improved drainage coming in the fenland estate was eminently improvable. There is not much point in trying to establish any simple figure by which this six thousand could be multiplied to give the modern equivalent, but a few comparisons may give a certain sense of its value. Philip Miller, the very highly skilled gardener in charge of the Chelsea Physic Garden, a man whom Linnaeus called "not only a prince of gardeners but a prince of botanists", had fifty pounds a year. Mr Peregrine Langton lived in a handsome country house on two hundred a year, employing two manservants and two maids and keeping a carriage and three horses (he was, it must be admitted, an admirable manager; but there was no meanness, says Boswell, no skimping). Dr Johnson's three hundred a year kept him in London, together with the blind Mrs Williams and her maid, Francis Barber and his wife Elizabeth and her child, a Mrs White, Miss Carmichael, the widowed Mrs Desmoulins, and at least to some extent Mr Levett, while at the same time he maintained a cousin at Coventry and shared the cost of keeping another relative in a private madhouse. At the same period Lord Shelburne, who lived as splendidly as anyone, told the Doctor "that a man of high rank, who looks into his own affairs, may have all that he ought to have, all that can be of any use, or appear with any advantage, for five thousand pounds a year", a figure confirmed by Mrs Thrale who speaking of her husband in *Thraliana* said "If he got but 2/6 by each Barrel [Thrale brewed 80,000 of them] eighty Thousand half crowns are 10,000 pounds and what more would mortal Man desire than an Income of ten Thousand a year – five to spend, & five to lay up." A farm labourer might earn twenty-five pounds, counting his extra money for harvest and haysel; an ordinary seaman in the Royal Navy had nineteen shillings a month; and Lieutenant James Cook, being in command of the *Endeavour*, had the unusually large sum of five shillings a day.

Values and prices, together with the extremes of wealth and poverty, have changed so much in these few generations that one is often puzzled; but in this case there is no sort of doubt that six thousand a year, with no income tax to pay, was a most desirable sum.

There were of course very much richer men – some of the coal-mining dukes were enormously wealthy* – just as there were men of very much

* Lady Mary Coke says that the Duke of Marlborough had £50,000 a year, even without any coal.

higher social standing; yet even so, most people would probably have placed Joseph Banks well up among the top five per cent.

Some young men, after a decent period of mourning, would have borrowed money to be repaid when they came of age, and would have run rather wild. Joseph Banks did not do so: he was in regular residence at Christ Church throughout 1761 and 1762 and for most of 1763. It is usually said that he then went down, but the college records (quoted by Professor Beaglehole in his edition of the *Endeavour* journal) show him in residence for twenty-one weeks in 1764 and for a little while in 1765.

Like many of his kind he took no degree, but there is no doubt that he worked hard, if only at botany. Much of this sobriety was owing to his love for plants – for natural philosophy in most of its forms – and for the congenial company at Oxford; but a glance at John Russell's portrait of Mrs William Banks will convince most people that she had a good deal to do with it.

Not only does the picture show a strong-minded, determined woman, but we also learn from Banks himself that she was above ordinary weaknesses: in a letter to an unknown correspondent quoted by Bowdler Sharpe[11] (who I am afraid improved the writer's English) he said, "I have from my childhood, in conformity with the precepts of a mother void of all imaginary fear, been in the constant habit of taking toads in my hand, and applying them to my nose and face as it may happen. My motive for doing this very frequently is to inculcate the opinion I have held, since I was told by my mother, that the toad is actually a harmless animal; and to whose manner of life man is certainly under some obligation as its food is chiefly those insects which devour his crops and annoy him in various ways."

Strength of mind and the habit of command can, it is said, be found in women of modest means; but money does seem to foster these qualities and it may not be irrelevant to observe that Mrs Banks, together with her sister the Countess of Exeter, was the co-heiress of the wealthy Thomas Chambers of London.

After her husband's death she left Revesby for the time being and moved to Chelsea, taking Turret House, an elegant Queen Anne building with an immense arcaded court in Paradise Row, just by the Physic Garden, which in those days, before the embankment, ran right down to the river – indeed, the Society of Apothecaries, to whom the garden belonged, had their bargehouse at the bottom, together with those of the Tallow-Chandlers and the Vintners, the Thames being still an important thoroughfare, crowded with boats, and reasonably full of fish.

At that time Chelsea was still green with fields; there were market gardeners and nurserymen too, and it was also quite a fashionable suburb. Lord Orford lived close to Turret House – his father, better known as Sir Robert Walpole, had built an immense greenhouse in his garden – and when Lord Sandwich, an old friend and fenland neighbour of the Bankses, returned to office in 1763, he spent much of his time in Chelsea. And apart from friends and acquaintances of this kind, Mrs Banks, who like her daughter Sophia was a deeply religious woman, had the Moravian Brethren half a mile up the river, in the splendid Lindsey House at the far end of Cheyne Walk, beyond what is now Battersea Bridge and what was then a ferry. Lindsey House had belonged to the Lincolnshire Berties, now Dukes of Ancaster, but in 1750 it was bought by Count Zinzendorf for the Moravians, a religious community originating in Bohemia and ultimately deriving from Hus that sent missionaries to the West Indies, Greenland and North America. Some of these missionaries were interested in botany, and they gave Joseph Banks specimens from Labrador that are still to be seen in his herbarium, now housed in the Natural History Museum.

But there were of course many, many more North American plants in the Physic Garden, just over the way. The man in charge of the establishment was Philip Miller, who succeeded his father in 1722; he was a very able man indeed, and in the forty-eight years of his reign he increased the number of plants from one thousand to five thousand, having correspondents and fellow collectors in many parts of the world. He was a friend of Linnaeus himself, who said of his well-known *Gardener's and Florist's Dictionary* "Non erit lexicon hortulanorum sed botanicorum", in spite of the fact that Miller, whose mind had been formed by Tournefort and Ray, did not fully adopt the Linnaean system or nomenclature until his eighth edition, in 1768, thirty-two years after their first meeting. (Banks, coming to botany well after the publication of the *Systema Naturae*, the *Fundamenta Botanica* and the *Genera Plantarum*, was a Linnaean from the start; and although he would occasionally use an earlier, much longer name, his taxonomy was entirely based on the sexual system.)

It appears that in his old age Miller became so positive and froward that the Apothecaries dismissed him, but at the time when the Bankses were living in Chelsea he was a highly respected figure, the head of a famous garden and eventually a Fellow of the Royal Society, sometimes serving on the council: Joseph Banks could not have had a better neighbour and guide; and after Miller's death (in poverty, alas) Banks bought his herbarium, so that something tangible remained.

Lord Sandwich was also something of a botanist, but his interest in the sexual system was of a very much wider nature: in earlier days he had been a member of Sir Francis Dashwood's Hellfire Club at Medmenham Abbey together with John Wilkes, among others, and he had the reputation of being a sad rake. But in the eighteenth century this would hardly have been held against him to any serious extent; it would certainly not have made him unpopular. Yet unpopular he was, in spite of having been an excellent First Lord of the Admiralty from 1748–51, helping Anson carry through some most important reforms, so that when the Seven Years War broke out in 1756 the Navy was reasonably well equipped to fight it. The trouble was that in 1763 he was made First Lord again and then almost immediately afterwards one of the two principal Secretaries of State, being succeeded at the Admiralty by Lord Egmont (who gave his name to Port Egmont in the Falklands and thence to the Port Egmont hen, *Stercorarius antarcticus*, the southern skua); and as Secretary of State he was much concerned with the prosecution of Wilkes, his former playmate. Wilkes, an unusually disreputable, unusually charming and learned man and a member of parliament under Pitt's leadership, was refused various posts, including that of ambassador to Turkey; he therefore joined the opposition, badgering the ministry in a newspaper called *The North Briton*. In the forty-fifth number he attacked George III's message to parliament: he was arrested on a general warrant and clapped into the Tower. This was in 1763. The judges held that as a member he was immune from arrest and that in any case general warrants were illegal. Wilkes had the appearance of an oppressed martyr; he was already popular and his victory made him even more so; in his glee he reprinted number forty-five, but at the same time he struck off a few copies of a more or less obscene *Essay on Woman*, written by his friend Thomas Potter, the son of the Archbishop of Canterbury. The ministry took proceedings at once: Wilkes was expelled from the House and condemned in the King's Bench on the charge of publishing an impious libel. And since he was not in court to receive sentence (he was recovering from a wound received in a duel) he was outlawed. A good deal happened after this, but the main point is that he was elected member for Middlesex (a popular constituency with hundreds of voters) again and again, his supporters roaring "Wilkes and liberty", and again and again the House refused to let him sit. Eventually he did return to Parliament: he also became Lord Mayor of London, one of the few Lord Mayors ever to have edited Catullus and Theophrastus and to have been an outlaw. Throughout the whole affair Sandwich appeared as the enemy of the immensely popular if somewhat demagogic Wilkes: Sandwich was witty, intelligent, and good company, but he was no match for the brilliant Wilkes and his great host of supporters, some of them highly literate and with newspapers and caricaturists at their command – no match, that is to say, in a public controversy of this kind. It was above all held against him that he should have brought the *Essay on Woman* before the House of Lords, complaining of improper notes attributed to the Bishop of Gloucester, as though he were a Moravian missionary rather than a former member of the Hellfire Club. The idea seemed to be that if a man had once frequented a group of dissolute companions then he must support those companions for ever after, however much their political ideas might have diverged. The prosecution and the persecution of Wilkes were hopelessly mismanaged by a succession of ministries, but nearly all the odium fell on Sandwich. He was nick-named Jemmy Twitcher, after the character who betrayed his friend Macheath in the Beggar's Opera; and indeed he was so much disliked that when his amiable mistress Martha Ray was shot dead outside Covent Garden theatre by the Rev. Mr Hackman, a rejected lover, his unpopularity actually increased.

At Turret House however quite another face of things was seen. Sandwich was not only good company, but like Joseph Banks he was devoted to fishing. They had fished together in the Fens, and now they fished together in the Thames and the Serpentine. In fact Lord Brougham says that they formed a plan for suddenly draining that sheet of water, not for mere fun but in order to learn more about the nature of the fishes – Sandwich had been a Fellow of the Royal Society since 1740. This particular plan fell through, but others they made did not, and upon the whole it may be said that Lord Sandwich was a very good friend to Banks.

In 1764 Joseph Banks came of age and he entered upon his landed estates, which, with agriculture and stock-raising and rural economy, provided one of the great interests of his life. He also established himself in a house of his own in London, and here, where he was entirely his own master, it was much easier for him to invite people, to come and go, and to entertain. Until he adopted a filing system in 1776 he did not keep many letters, or at least few have survived, and the dates of his earliest meeting with some of his friends is necessarily a matter of conjecture; but to this period must belong his introduction to the Bishop of Carlisle, Dr Morton of the British Museum, Dr Watson, Mr West, joint-secretary to the Treasury, and the Rev. Mr Kaye, the gentlemen who proposed him for membership of the Royal Society. He also became acquainted with Thomas Pennant (and later, by means of Pennant, with his much more amiable friend Gilbert White of Selbourne and Gilbert's brother Benjamin, a publisher and bookseller at the Horace's Head in Fleet Street), with the Hon. Daines Barrington, John Lightfoot the botanist, and in some ways the most important of all, Daniel Carl Solander.

Solander,[12] the son of a parson, was born in 1733 at Piteå, an uninviting place in Swedish Lapmark, on the Gulf of Bothnia, about eighty miles south of the Arctic Circle. Linnaeus passed through Piteå on his tour of Lapland the year before Solander was born, and the first thing he saw was two beheaded Finns and one quartered Lapp, exposed after their execution for murder; and speaking of the region in his diary he said "Never can the priest describe Hell, this is much worse; never can the poet describe Styx, as this is much uglier."

In 1750, when Solander was seventeen, he was sent to Uppsala university, where his uncle was Professor of Jurisprudence: the eighteenth-century torpor, so usual in European universities, does not appear to have spared Uppsala, but new life had been stirring for some years, and in 1750 Linnaeus had the chair of botany, while Wallerius had that of chemistry and Rosen von Rosenstein that of medicine. Linnaeus was by far the most famous of the three: not only was he a passionate and very highly gifted botanist, but he was working at an unusually favourable time. The Societas Regia Litteraria et Scientiarum (which had financed the Lapland journey of his youth) and the Royal Academy of Science were active and influential; the court was well-inclined (the king and queen both had splendid natural history collections, which Linnaeus catalogued; for although he was famous primarily as a botanist, his investigations covered all the three kingdoms of nature), and there were many people who were willing and even eager to learn about botany, a science less forbidding than chemistry or medicine. Of course botanists had been writing about their subject from the time of Theophrastus on, and quite recently John Ray and Joseph Pitton de Tournefort had produced admirable taxonomies, yet they had been known to few but specialists and now they were swept away by the Linnaean system – so much so that the general opinion, fully shared by Linnaeus though not by all botanists, was that the *Systema Naturae* and his other publications had brought order out of chaos. Linnaeus classified by stamens and pistils, and by observing their various arrangements one could identify the plant, an absolute prerequisite for any meaningful discussion: the system was artificial in that it ignored natural affinities, but it was accessible and clear; it worked, and it held the field until the days of A.-L. de Jussieu and A.-P. de Candolle, while his binominal nomenclature is with us still. Yet perhaps even more important than his publications was the fact that Linnaeus was an inspired teacher and that he raised both the study and the status of botany to heights unknown before his day. It is said that in ordinary times Uppsala had five hundred undergraduates; when he held the chair of botany the number rose by a thousand. He filled his students with his own passionate love of the subject, and many of them, travelling to remote parts of the world, have had the plants they discovered named after them, so that a botanical catalogue is not unlike a list of Linnaeus's pupils – Tärnstrom, Kalm, Osbeck, Lagerström, Sparrman, Alströmer, Thunberg at once come to mind, and there are many others. This century, opening wide to science, was the time for immortality; yet it is an odd kind of immortality, too, for one does not always remember that Volta and Ampère were living men, nor that it was Linnaeus and his friends who placed their contemporaries Magnol, Dahl and Alexander Garden in the botanical firmament with an "ia" added to their names.

It is small wonder then that Solander, having studied classics and law for a while, wished to move over to the scientific side and join Linnaeus's numerous band of disciples. Linnaeus had stayed with Solander's parents at Piteå during his Lapland journey and he persuaded them to let the youth make the change and read for a medical degree.

The great man did not regret his intervention: Solander had a remarkable aptitude for natural philosophy and he soon became one of Linnaeus's favourites, both as a student and a person. As early as 1752 he helped his master in the cataloguing of the royal collections as well as those of Count Tessin: some time later he made two botanical journeys of his own, the first into the Kjöllen range north-west of Piteå and so over into Norway, and the second in the Torneå basin in Lapland. He also published *Caroli Linnaei Elementa Botanica*, a shortened version of the system; and he indexed the sumptuous great catalogues and saw them through the press, acting as the professor's right-hand man. Indeed, the two were so close that Linnaeus, who had four handsome daughters, hoped that in time Solander would become his son-in-law and his successor. Solander was also his choice when his correspondents Peter Collinson and John Ellis asked him to send a student to England. Collinson was a wealthy Quaker merchant trading with North America, an ardent botanist who had brought many American plants to England, and a Fellow of the Royal Society: he wanted a skilled young man to catalogue his garden according to the Linnaean system. Ellis was also a Fellow and a botanist with interests in the West Indies (he was agent for Dominica) and the Orient (he published *Directions for bringing over Seeds and Plants from the East Indies*), but his great love was zoophytes, particularly the corallines, upon which he was an authority. He was also a very sensible man in other directions, and he advised Linnaeus to tell Solander to improve his English before coming over.

As it happened Solander had plenty of time to do so, since illness and bad weather and the fact that the Seven Years War was in progress put off his departure for more than a year, and when he arrived in 1760 he spoke the language remarkably well. In any case he was, like so many Swedes, an excellent linguist: his Latin was of course fluent, since it was the medium of instruction at Uppsala, and he also knew German and Dutch.

Linnaeus had asked Ellis to take care of "my beloved pupil", and both Ellis and Collinson did so. Solander could not have had a better introduction to the English world of natural philosophy in general and of botany in particular. His early letters to Linnaeus, often accompanied by seeds and plants from English naturalists, or books, such as the *Flora Anglica* in which William Hudson, sub-librarian at the British Museum, had adopted the sexual system, show that he had soon met a great many people, including Philip Miller of the Physic Garden and J. Empson of the British Museum, G. Brander, FRS, a director of the Bank of England and also connected with the Museum, Richard Warner the botanist, George Edwards, FRS, the author of a valuable *History of Birds*, and Sir William Chambers the architect (a Swede by birth) who had just finished the pagoda in the royal gardens at Kew – a significant mixture of Fellows of the Royal Society, people belonging to the British Museum, and great men owning great gardens or closely concerned with them. He had also travelled over much of southern and south-western England, viewing the country, its plantations and its gardens, or, when he was with John Ellis, its shores, its zoophytes, sponges and sea anemones.

He was well received, not only because he was Linnaeus's pupil and because he was well introduced but because he was himself amiable. Sir James Smith, who eventually bought Linnaeus's vast collections, founded the Linnean Society, and compiled *A Selection from the Correspondence of Linnaeus*, said of him that "he was esteemed . . . for his polite and agreeable manners, as well as his great knowledge in most departments of Natural History". And some time later Fanny Burney called him "very sociable, full of talk, information, and entertainment", while Mrs Thrale said "The Men I love best in the World are Johnson, Scrase, and Sir Philip Jennings Clerke. The Men I like best in the World are Burney, Solander, and the Bishop of Peterborough", and Sir Charles Blagden, later secretary of the Royal Society and a close friend of Banks and Solander for many years spoke of him as "the mildest, gentlest, most obliging of men".

He was no less dear to Linnaeus, who arranged for him to have the chair of botany at St Petersburg in 1761 and who the next year offered to name him as his successor at Uppsala. After some hesitation Solander declined both offers: he had decided to stay in England.

There was no communication between Solander and Linnaeus from the autumn of 1762 until 1768, and this breach is sometimes attributed to the marriage of Linnaeus's eldest daughter Elizabeth Christina to a soldier. Dr Rauschenberg, who has made a deep study of Solander, does not believe the explanation, and certainly it does seem a little strange, since Solander never appears to have taken any interest in women at all.

However that may be, Solander certainly began to cut his ties with Sweden: he was a most indifferent correspondent all his life, but now he quite stopped writing to his widowed mother as well as to Linnaeus.

At this period his friends were busily trying to get him a post at the British Museum, which had opened in 1759 and which was struggling along with high ideals and an income of nine hundred pounds a year. Many friends were concerned, since in the eighteenth century as much influence as possible was required for even a modest official appointment; and it is said that Collinson went so far as to ask Lord Bute to speak to the King. These solicitations were successful, and Solander joined the meagre staff in February 1763. The appointment was modest enough, in all conscience, yielding rather less than sixty pounds a year, and at first there was no working-place apart from the public rooms; but the work itself was interesting, and Solander was ideally suited for it: he spent his days classifying, describing and cataloguing plants, insects, mammals, birds, fishes, reptiles, fossils and indeed almost anything that could be said to belong to the realm of natural philosophy and therefore to possess an inherent order that was susceptible of being brought to light. This eventually included the rather sparse collection of objects from the Pacific brought home by Commodore the Hon. John Byron, RN (the poet's grandfather, known in the service as Foulweather Jack) after he had sailed round the world in that fine copper-bottomed ship the *Dolphin*, a voyage more remarkable for its rapidity (a mere twenty-two months) than for any discoveries in the South Seas. But this is to anticipate, since the *Dolphin*, having taken possession of the Falklands in 1765, did not reach home until 1766.

Before this time, that is to say in 1764, Banks and Solander had become acquainted, as it was natural that they should, having so many friends and so many interests in common. In these earliest years, however, the acquaintance did not develop into that close friendship which was to be so important to both men in later times: Banks was much taken up with Revesby and his other estates – farming was, after all, a form of applied botany – with Oxford and with settling into independent life. And, since the war was now over, he was also much engaged with those friends who had been concerned with the fighting and who had now come home.

Chapter 2

NEWFOUNDLAND AND LABRADOR

MOST PEOPLE would agree that a man can be judged by his friends, by the company he keeps; and it may well be that to see him in the round one needs the indirect light shed upon him by his associates. Joseph Banks was a complex being as well as a sociable one and his many friends ranged from the somewhat rakish Lord Sandwich to the Bishop of Carlisle and to James Lee, the Hammersmith nurseryman. Perhaps the most amiable of them was Constantine John Phipps: he and Banks had been at Eton together and they shared many of the same interests, though Phipps was somewhat more concerned with animals than with plants; but Phipps left school early to go to sea with his uncle, Captain the Hon. A. J. Hervey, then in command of HMS *Monmouth*, a seventy-gun ship of the line. In her Phipps took part in the blockade of Brest, when Captain Hervey kept the sea, often in appalling weather that blew the rest of the fleet into Torbay or Plymouth Sound, for nearly six months without a break. By 1763, when the Seven Years War came to an end and Phipps was nineteen and a recently promoted lieutenant, he had borne a hand in the taking of Belleisle off the coast of France, in the taking of Martinique and St Lucia in the West Indies, and in the protracted, arduous, bloody siege and eventual storming of the great Moro Castle, which led to the surrender of Havana. It also led to prize-money of about £750,000, which pleased the soldiers and sailors until they found that the general and admiral in charge were to have £122,697 10*s* 6*d* each while the private was to be content with £4 1*s* 8½*d* and the seaman with £3 14*s* 9¾*d*. However, when Captain Hervey, now in the *Dragon*, 74, was on the way home with Admiral Pocock's dispatches, he took a French West Indiaman worth £30,000, which must have been some consolation.

Yet although Phipps was no doubt happy to receive his share, which would have been about £2,000 or some thirty years' pay, he certainly did not need it as much as most junior lieutenants. His father had great estates in Yorkshire that had come into the family by a complicated series of successions from that Duke of Buckingham and Normanby who married an illegitimate daughter of James II, estates which had belonged to the Sheffield earls of Mulgrave, the duke's ancestors, for a great while, so that when Mr Phipps senior was raised to the peerage in

1767 he too chose Mulgrave for his title, a title that his son Constantine inherited some years later.

In 1766 however Constantine had neither a title nor yet a ship; like so many of his fellows in time of peace he was a half-pay lieutenant, thrown on the beach. But he was a most ardent sailor, and given his zeal, outstanding competence and outstanding connections, it was not surprising to find him entrusted with a naval mission to Newfoundland in that same year. Nor was it surprising that Banks should undertake to go with him, both of them travelling in HMS *Niger*.

The Treaty of Paris, ending the war in 1763, had transferred Canada, among many other territories, to Great Britain, but it had left France certain fishing rights on the Banks, and in the season very large numbers of French fishermen mingled with the English, Spanish and Portuguese. There was continual disagreement, and serious trouble was prevented only by the presence of a small naval force, based on St John's. The *Niger*, a thirty-two gun frigate commanded by Sir Thomas Adams, was part of this force, and she sailed from Plymouth on 22 April 1766, with the wind at east-north-east.

The captain of a man-of-war might carry friends if he chose, so long as he fed them himself – Commodore Keppel, for example, took the young Joshua Reynolds to the Mediterranean in 1749; and many captains had young ladies for company – but Banks was not aboard as the captain's guest and his presence certainly had a great deal to do with his friendship with Lord Sandwich, who had been First Lord of the Admiralty some time before and who was to be First Lord again some time later, just as his equipment owed much to his acquaintance with Solander, that experienced Lapland naturalist.

The *Niger*, of course, did not sail as early as might have been wished, but this allowed Banks and Phipps to botanize round Mount Edgcombe, where among other things they found wild madder, *Rubia angelica*, and stinking gladwin, *Iris foetidissima*, in peculiar abundance, and deadly nightshade, *Atropa belladonna*, among the rocks; and they observed swallows for the first time that year. They thought they had found the radical leaves of the field eryngo, *Eryngium campestre*, but were not quite certain. Yet when at last the delays were over and the wind came fair, the *Niger* set off at a splendid pace, so that by noon the next day they were well out into the Atlantic, twelve leagues beyond the Scillies.

The first few days yielded little but seaweed, a young shark that did not stay to be fished up, and some shoals of porpoises; then the freshening breeze made Banks so ill that he could not write. It does not appear that Phipps was seasick, but whether or no, they were both well and active by the end of April: both, for although Phipps was an ardent sailor, he, like his uncle and so many other naval officers, was no mere seaman. Not only was he a capital astronomer and mathematician, but he was as eager as Banks to haul a jellyfish aboard, identify a sea bird or trail a fine-meshed net for plankton: indeed, it is to the somewhat older Phipps that we owe the first scientific description of the polar bear, *Thalarctos maritimus* (Phipps) and the ivory gull, *Pagophila eburnea* (Phipps), both of them encountered in a voyage to the far north in which he was accompanied by the fifteen-year-old Nelson, who also attempted to collect a bear.

Perhaps the best way of dealing with their crossing and with Banks's journeys in Newfoundland and Labrador is to give large extracts from the journal he kept. A paraphrase might in some ways be clearer and easier to read, but the journal brings one directly into touch with Banks; it also serves as an introduction to his style, which is at first a little disconcerting. Some editors have improved him, making him write more like a Christian, but it seems to me that one should not alter a text and except for the occasional silent correction of an obvious slip of the pen I give Banks unchanged. Yet it must be admitted that printing his manuscript just as he wrote it has disadvantages: cold print differs essentially from a page written by hand, and its inhuman precision makes Banks's way of writing seem wilder and more outlandish than it really is; for when one reads his papers, particularly his correspondence, one soon grows used to the rather flourishing letters that may or may not be capitals, and one's eye, helped by vague flecks and dashes of the pen, readily supplies the wanting stops, which is harder to do in the formality of print. The result is that to begin with the printed page gives the impression of someone not very wise nor very highly educated speaking at a breakneck pace, rather like Miss Bates or Flora Finching; but one soon gets accustomed to it; one soon sees the strong good sense beneath the strange exterior; and even if at times one does stumble for a moment, it is at least a genuine Banksian obstacle that interrupts one's course.

The journal from which I quote is in Adelaide, in the library of the South Australian Branch of the Royal Geographic Society of Australia, and it was edited with the utmost scholarship and with infinite pains by the late Dr Averil Lysaght. She provided a great deal of background material, valuable notes and identification, and when the scientific names of plants or animals have changed she gave the modern versions. With her publishers' permission I have made the freest use of her splendidly illustrated book *Joseph Banks in Newfoundland and Labrador, 1766: His Diary, Manuscripts and Collections*, and if I have not also transcribed her scientific names or notes it is because I wish to give the pristine Banks; but the zoologist or botanist concerned with North American fauna or flora must certainly turn to Dr Lysaght and her constellation of expert advisers.

This chapter, then, will be written by Joseph Banks, with short connecting pieces and an occasional footnote on some particular eighteenth-century usage that may not be quite familiar, such as penguin for auk or blubber for jellyfish. It will begin with the first entry for the month of May 1766, and it will be printed as Banks wrote it except that I leave out the numbers referring to the plants and animals collected whenever they do not form a kind of punctuation: some entries will be silently omitted, but even so I hope that what is included will give a balanced picture of the whole, which, in its two manuscript volumes, runs to about 22,000 words.

May 3 Today a calm fish'd with a landing net out of the Quarter Gallery window. Caught sea weed, Fucus acinarius, with fruit like Currants on slight Footstalks & Common Knotted Fucus, Fucus Nodosus also two species of what the seamen call Blubbers the one roundish and Transparent with his Edges a little Fringed the inside is hollow adornd with 4 little Clusters of Red spots within the Transparent substances Possibly Eggs from the Center Proceeds 4 feelers spotted from their bases with Longish Red Spotts and each Edged on the upper side with 2 thin Membranes the other is Conical and hollow the outer Part Transparent the inner coverd by a thin Coat of Reddish Purple which Runs up beyond the top of the Hollow Part in a line not unlike the footstalk of some Fruit the Bottom Edge seems to be broke by some accident

4 today being also very fine the business of fishing is Continued we now took what we hope will Prove a compleat Specimen of No (1) it has a large Crenated Fringe round the Lower Edges we also took another Fragment much like that taken yesterday within each of the Broken ones was an appearance which we supposed to be of an Insect devouring it

one Part of this morn the sea was Coverd with small Transparent Bubbles which we supposed to be the spawn of some insect or fish as they were full of small Black specks

we also took another insect of a very Peculiar appearance his Case is triangular with a very Sharp Point of a Transparent substance not unlike very thin Glass the insect within is of a Colour not unlike New Copper

6 Yesterday & today hard Gale of wind with Frequent and some heavy Squalls Carried away Main top Mast Myself far too sick to write

7 This Morn Weather much more moderate a number of Birds are about the ship which the seamen call Penguins Gulls Shearwaters one species of

them with sharp tails Puffins and Sea Pigeons* we could not get any of them tho we took Pains we Comforted ourselves however being told that we should meet with them all upon the Coast at Present they are a sign that we are upon the Banks

8 Birds Continue today in great abundance especially Puffins and Sea Pigeons at twelve Sound & find 75 fathoms Birds Continue at 6 sound again 50 fathoms Let down our fishing Lines but Caught nothing at ten tonight for the first time we see an Island of Ice the night is Hazy but the Sky clear no moon the Ice itself appears like a body of whitish light the Waves Dashing against it appear much more Luminous the Whole is not unlike the Gleaming of the *Aurora Borealis* When first seen it was about half a Mile ahead it drives within ¼ of a mile of us accompanied by several small flat Pieces of Ice which the seamen call field Ice which drives very near us and is Easily seen by its white appearance not unlike the Breaking of a wave into foam.

Soundi upon th Banks

Island o

9 This Morn Seven Islands of Ice in sight one Very Large but not high about a League from us we steer very near a small one which from its Transparency & the Greenish Cast in it makes a very Beautiful appearance two very Large Cracks intersect it Lenghways and Look Very Like mineral Veins in Rocks from its Rough appearance the Seamen Judge that it is old Ice that is what formed the Winter before Last In the course of the Day we steer still nearer to another Island which appears as if Layd Strat: Super Stratum one of White another of Greenish at – Past five this afternoon we made NFLand a quantity of sea weed Part of which I fish'd up 3 or 4 Species with my Landing Net tonight we stand of with too little wind to Carry us in

10 this morn a Mist accompanied with Frost which hung our Rigging Full of Ice Continues till about twelve when we see Land again but so little wind that we cannot make it tonight This Even Fish with Landing net take 9 specimens of a singular Kind of Blubber which abounds here tis transparent with 2 or three Reddish lines in the middle tis octangular Each angle being adornd with an undulated red line which serves for the Basis of a fin Longitudinally Stretched upon it which it moves with a quick undulatory Motion it is so tender I have little hopes of Preserving it as it Floats in the sea at Pleasure puts out two Antennae sometimes to a distance of a foot or more, but upon being taken they constantly draw them up & do not shew the Least appearance of them.

11 this Morn quite Calm took a large Float of Long stalkd sea Belts in the Roots of which were a Small sort of Star fish about 3 got into St Johns on the 20th day of our Voyage

12 this morn went on shore found the Spring very Little advanced but hope its approaches will be quick as it is warmer than I Ever felt it at this time in England the Country is Coverd with wood fir is the only tree which can yet be distinguished of which I observed 3 sorts (1) Black Spruce of which they

* Black guillemots.

Make a liquor Calld Spruce Beer (2) white Spruce & (3) weymouth Pine no large trees of any Species Possibly so near the Town they are Constantly cut down on the Trees and Rocks were 3 or 4 species of Lichens, Lichen Pascalis, Lanatus, ? Hirtus, & under them the Leaves of many rare northern Plants of the Club Mosses 3 sorts, a small plant whose Blossoms have 5 Stamina Mosses 3 sorts Bryum Hornum, or Purpureum, one of which is quite new to me – too sorts of Bird were taken today one the Black Cap Parus ater, the other an american thrush with a ferrugineous Breast Possibly described by Catesby insects were few Cimex lineatus water Bugs in Abundance one Carabus granulatus

Neighbourhood of St Johns

13 Walk out Fishing this Morn Took great plenty of small Trouts, Salmo saw a small Fish in the Brooks Very like English Stiklebacks, Gasterosteus Aculeatus, in the way took a small Bird something Between a yellow hammer & a Linnet

15 Walkd this day to a Small Lake north of the Town found in the way another species of Club moss, Lycopodium complanatum, a Shrub with ten Stamina, Andromeda Calyculata, which grew by the side of the Lake – upon a stoney Soil in great abundance a Kind of Moss, Bryum, with Pendant heads in our way home we Killd a musk Rat, Fiber Moscatus in Kitty Vitty Pond

16 This day wind very high NW went into the Harbour with the Traul Took Lobsters, Cancer gammarus Common crab, Cancer, Spider d^{o}, Cancer araneus, Sculpen, another Sort of D^{o}: Cat fish, a Shell of the Scallop Kind One of the Muscles Sea Urchin, Echinus, another Kind of the Spatagus tribe, Echinus, Starfish, Asterias, a . . . two sort of Sea weed Soldier crab, Cancer diogenes

19 Set out on foot to get as far into the Countrey as Possible Soon after We set out began to snow Continued all the day but did not Cover the Ground deep Enough to hinder our Observing Several Plants a Kind of Bilberry in full Blossom a kind of Juniper with white Berries, The Larch, Pinus Larix, which is here calld Juniper & which is said to make better timber for shipping especially masts than any tree this Countrey affords & a species of Moss with Bending heads and fine golden footstalks, Bryum N^{o}: 19

20 Continues to Snow all this day Which Confines us within doors at a small Town Calld Petty Harbour the Snow so incessant that we have not an opportunity to Stir out to make the Least Observation

Petty Harbour

21 Snow Lies now four & five feet deep upon the Ground & the Air looks so Hazey that we think it Prudent to Return upon the Rocks & Barrens (for so they Call the Places where Wood does not Grow) we find that the wind had drifted the Snow Very thin we observe Some few Plants Fir Moss, Lycopodium Selago, Rhein Deer Moss, Lichen Rangiferinus, A Kind of Horned Liverwort, Lichen, a Plant that has very much the Appearance of Crow Berries, Empetrum of which I have only got the female which has 10 Stigmata.

25 Snow Very near gone Walk out to day gather the Male Blossoms of a Plant resembling duch myrtle which like it grows in Bogs & watery Places also a sort of Cyperus which grew upon the same flat but not in so wet a situation & a Kind of Black Liverwort growing upon dry tops of the Barrens the weather grows very mild many Plants are in Bud.

For the rest of the month Banks and Phipps collected plants and birds with the same zeal, although the weather was upon the whole unpleasant, with fog and rain; however, it improved in June.

June 1 This Even very Fine walk'd out Gatherd Currants, Ribes, some Lichens which seemd to be only Varictics of English species & abundance of Water Mnium, Mnium aquaticum, the Female of which has Stellate Heads I have not seen any with dusty ones as they are in England the men of the ship brought me some Large Specimens of a Kind of Stone Coral which is found Fossil in Many Parts of England by the Name of Honeycombstone another man brought me the shell of a tortoise which he told me he got in the Archipelago and that it was found there in fresh water a ship Came into harbour from which I procured specimens of a shell fish calld Glams of a Peculiar use in the fishery as the fishermen depend upon them for their Baitts in their first Voyage to the Banks at that time of the Year the fish feed upon them & Every fish they take has a number of them in his Stomach which the Fishermen take out & with them Bait for others the fish itself is Remarkable as it is far too large for the shell which is so little adapted to Cover its inhabitants that Even when the fish is taken out the sides will not Close together a boy brought me two shells

6 Walkd out to day gatherd some of the Northern English Plants which grow here Every where not Coveting high Land tho indeed we have seen no high Land here (1) the Little dwarf Honeysuckle, Cornus Herbacea, said to grow upon the cheviot hills which part Scotland from England (2) alsinanthemos, Trientalis Europaea & (3) the stone Bramble, Rubus Saxatilis, also some Common English Plants as (4) (5) sorts of Rush grass, Juncus Campestris, Juncus Pilosus (6) Black Carex, Carex strata, (7) vernal grass, Anthoxanthum odoratum, (8) Black headed Bog rush, Scirpus Caespitosus, (9) sundew with round leaves, Drosera rotundifolia, & several more which I mention in my Catalogue – of English Plants Some Plants also of this Country a (10) Kind of Alder, Betula, differing very little if at all from the English sort a beautiful Kind of (11) Medlar, Mespilus Canadensis?, a Kind of cherry, Prunus, which however is so Scarce here that I have got very few Specimens. I have not seen above 2 Plants of it neither in Blossom but at a few Extremities it differ very little if at all from our English garden cherry

7 Today shooting Killd 3 small Birds Probably varieties of the Gold Bird as there is but little difference between them chiefly the want of a black spot on the head, Foemina? N^{o}: 10, & a small Bird N^{o}: 11 which seems to be scarce here as I have seen it only this once.

8 Walk out this day Gatherd a Species of Solomons Seal, Convallaria Racemosa
11 this day at 12 set sail for Croque.

Here a few lines about Newfoundland may help to set Phipps' and Banks's journey in its historical context. John Cabot, sailing from Bristol, discovered the island in 1497, claimed it for Henry VII and brought back an account of the extraordinary fishing – his men had only to let down baskets and cod swam into them. Throughout most of the sixteenth century English, French, Spanish Basque and Portuguese ships came to the Banks in the summer, and they carried home immense quantities of dried and salted cod; but no one stayed there for the winter. In 1583 Sir Humphry Gilbert sailed for St John's with five ships and founded the first British colony in North America; but that same year he was lost at sea. James I encouraged settlement, yet progress was very slow, partly because of raids by the French from Canada and partly because of opposition from the shipowners, who wanted to retain a monopoly of the fishing and who therefore induced government to pass restrictive laws. Indeed, successive governments were very hard on the Newfoundlanders: in 1713 the ministry that negotiated the treaty of Utrecht gave the French the right of fishing and drying their cod from Cape Bonavista northwards and so down the western side of the island as far as Rich Point; and even when the French had been beaten again in the Seven Years War and Canada taken from them, they were given back the islands of St Pierre and Miquelon together with these same fishing rights.

However, by the end of the war, in 1763, Newfoundland had some eight thousand permanent inhabitants, and with the French threat gone at least for the time, the authorities, headed by the Governor and Commander-in-Chief, Commodore Hugh Palliser of the Royal Navy, were filled with energy; and among other things James Cook, then a master in the Royal Navy, carried out a most painstaking and accurate survey of the coasts and harbours between 1763 and 1767, including part of the coast of Labrador, which, right up to Hudson's Strait in the icy north, had been added to the colony.

This was largely Eskimo country, and the government hoped that relations with them would be more successful than they had been with the Beothuks, the original Red Indian inhabitants of Newfoundland. At this point Europeans and Indians were killing one another on sight, and since the white men had firearms and the red men had none there was no question which side would win in the end. By Banks's time there were said to be about five hundred Beothuks living in the most retired parts of the island, as far as they could get from the fishermen; by 1829 they were totally extinct.

The official attitude towards the Eskimos was quite different. For some years the Moravian Brethren, so well known to the Bankses, had been in contact with them, and the Moravians' influence was regarded as entirely good. If they had been Jesuits the official view of their activities might not have been the same, but the Moravians had been legally recognized as "an ancient Protestant Episcopal Church" and their settlements in Labrador were actively helped and encouraged, since apart from anything else the missionaries told the Eskimos in their own language that King George loved the Innuit; he was like a father to them, and when they obeyed the Governor it was the same as if they were being obedient to the King.

In 1765, the year before Banks's voyage, the *Niger* had taken four Moravians to Chateau Bay in Labrador, where two were made to stay (much against their will – Adams was an autocratic captain and by no means a scrupulous one) and two went much farther north in the schooner *Hope*, commanded by Lieutenant Candler, RN, who was to survey and chart the coast. One of *Niger*'s tasks in 1766 was to take Phipps up to Croque (it is now usually spelt Croc), a small bay and harbour in the north-west part of the island, well within the Frenchmen's fishing zone, where he was to set up the building that in his jovial way he called Crusoe Hall and where he also planted a garden. The frigate was then to sail north, crossing the Strait of Belle Isle to Chateau Bay in Labrador, where her Marines and some civilian workmen were to make a regular fortification, a blockhouse and stockaded fort "for the Protection and Encouragement of His Majesty's Subjects to carry on the Fisheries on the Coast, for the Security of their Boats and Fishing craft and Tackle from being Stolen or destroyed by the Savages of the Country or by Lawless Crews resorting thither from the Colonies".

> June 13 this Morn at 7 anchor in Croque harbour after a very favourable Passage Walk out gather a species of Bilberry, Vaccinium mucronatum, a species of Orchis, Ophrys, a Beautifull Plant described No: 5, Uvularia Amplexifolia, another of the Hexandria Class No: 6 another No: 7 which is of the Pentandria Class tho both Calyx and Corolla are divided into 6 Laciniae water Ranunculus several sorts of Lichens two sorts of Mosses This morn Experienced a Very Extraordinary Transition from Cold to Heat The air at 5 in the morning while we were at sea being so Cold that with the great Coat buttoned I was forced Every moment to Come down to the Fire at seven we came into harbour in ½ of an hour were set on shore where the weather was as hot or hotter than Ever I knew it in England I lament much

Croque

not having noted the Difference by Thermometer but hope for future opportunities

14 This day still Extremely Hot spend most of our time working in the garden go out however in the Evening Find (1) a Kind of Bramble, Rubus Arcticus, (2) a Kind of Meadow Rue, Thalictrum alpinum, (3) Dwarf Birch, Betula Nana, (4) 2 Varieties of a Beautifull Plant Possibly our English Birds Eye one of which had flowers of a Clear white the other Blueish (5) in the woods found one tree only of Takamahaka in the Evening went out Fishing had no sport at all at the harbours mouth tho there seemd to be abundance of Small Trout saw no signs of Large ones Killd today a Kind of Mouse, Mus Terrestris, which Differs scarce at all From the English Sort but is Rather Larger & his Ears Extreemly Broad

16 Walkd today from the watering Place to Crusoe hall Mr Phipps's Habitation of which more when it is finished at Present give him his due he works night & day & Lets the Mosquetos eat more of him than he does of any Kind of food all through Eagerness in the way to him I found Moon wort, Osmunda Lunaria, a Kind of Grass a Plant which seems of the Carex kind dioecious but found only males a Kind of Cuckow flower

18 Walkd out shooting today Killd nothing but found a Plant which I thought had been Peculiar to Lapland, Diapensia Lapponica, it grows however but in one spot & there was only a single Plant of it Wooly Mouse Ear, Cerastium alpinum tomentosum, a small Flower Like a daizy, ?Erigeron ?Philadelphicum, a species of Moss, Bryum, a small nest Nidus, was brought to me by the Master Carpenter who Declard he saw a bee fly out of it When he took it a species of stone which appears white from a great distance Mr Ankille brought me in a species of Owl, Strix ?Ulula, he had shot My servant shot a bird quite Black Neither of which I can find Describd

19 This Morn we had intelligence that a white Bear with two cubbs had been seen on a hill above St Julians a Party was raisd to go in search of her of which I was one but we returnd without success Just as we returnd a shallop with the master of board was Setting Sail to Examine some of the Harbours
Inglie to the southward I got on board in hopes of some opportunity of Gathering Plants or Collecting insects that night we arriv'd at Inglie* in the Mouth of Canada Bay 11 Leagues to the southward of Croque but so late that I had not an opportunity of Collecting any thing the next morn Wind blew to hard for our Vessel to

20 Attempt getting out which gave me an opportunity of Examining a small Island above the Harbour which I found Loaded with Plants I had not seen before in a Wonderful manner . . .

Banks lists a score of them, including one with "a beautiful Yellow Flower growing on the tops of dry hills a Kind of Anemone in Company with it": he also observes that there were half a dozen English vessels

* Englée.

fishing there and near twice that number of French; "the French indeed have almost the Sole Possession of the Fishery in this Part of the Island Many Harbours (St Julians for instance) not having so much as one Englishman in them they seem to Value & Encourage the trade more than we do sending out infinitely Larger ships and Employing more hands in the Trade." The next day they looked at two other harbours, Wild Cove and Hilliard's Arm, where Banks found a most Elegant Plant with red Flowers.

> 22 here we slept tonight the next morn Early set out for Conche with the wind Directly in our teeth here we found a bad harbour Exposd to both sea and wind only one Englishman & 3 or 4 french were fishing here the Englishman complained grievously of the french hindering him from taking bait by denying him his Proper turn with the Seine while they were fishing and mooring bait boats on the ground where the fish were usualy Caught he told us that if Proper Precautions were not taken mischief would certainly Ensue as the french sent out arms allowing two Musquets to Each Bait boat he had intelligence during this Voyage that the French Carreid on an illicit trade with the Esquimaux indians tho Probably not Countenanced by Government as one ship only had been seen Engaged in it Precautions will be taken this fall to find what ship it is if she ventures to attempt it again this night at 3 o'clock came to the ship very Compleatly tired as we had not Pulld off our Cloaths since we came out nor lodgd any where but in the aft Cuddy of our boat.

After a few more shattering trips of this kind, in which he kept his notes on small pieces of paper so that his book might not be looked into by "Every Petty officer who chose to peruse it" – the only note of ill-humour in the whole journal, in spite of his frequent and very bad seasickness, the cold, and the discomfort and promiscuity of shipboard life – after a few more trips of this kind, Banks came down with

> a fever which to my great misfortune Confined me the greatest Part of that month [July, 1766, for which there are no entries at all] to the ship incapable of Collecting Plants at the Very season of the Year when they are the most Plentifull Some few indeed I got by the Diligence of my servant who I sent often Out to bring home any thing he thought I had not got He also shot several birds for me But My situation far too weak and dispirited by my illness to Examine Systematically any thing that was brought has made my Bird tub a Chaos of which I Cannot Give so good an account as I could wish & has left many Blanks in my Plants which I fear I must trouble my good freinds in England to fill up.
>
> As soon as my health was sufficiently Established to be allowed to go on shore I employd my time in Collecting insects & the remainder of the Plants

which ought to have been Collected through the month of July and insects tho I was baffled by Every Butterfly who chose to fly away for some time till my strength returned & which it did in an uncommonly short time & I thought myself able to take another Boat Expedition to the Island of Belleisle de Grois for which Place I set out about the 1st or 2nd of this month [August] & was repayd for my Trouble by the acquisition of several Valuable Plants & the sight of a wild Bear who was seen about 4 Miles above Conche into which harbour we were forc'd by Contrary winds

August 6 But Successfull as This Expedition was in itself in its Consequences it was much the Contrary as Several Plants were left at Croque some not in Perfect order for Drying others which as I could every day Procure were Left For the Present Least they should take up time Better employd in Visiting Places I had not seen since my Illness upon my arrival at Croque I found the Ship under orders to Sail without Delay for Chatteaux Bay which the Next morning august 6th She did & met with as Strong a gale of Wind as She Could have feard had she saild at the worst time of the Year which however She weatherd it out Extremely well & on the 9th arrivd at Chatteaux where she Found the Zephyr Captn Omyny & the Wells Cutter Captn Lawson which Last She had sent from Croque before her.

In this trip I for the first time Experienced the happiness of Escaping intirely the seasickness which had so much harrassd me always before in the Least Degree of Rough Weather which I attributed in Great measure to my having been so much at sea in Boats which by being so much more uneasy than the Ship made me less Sensible of her motion.

Here we have remaind Ever since the Ships Company Employd in Assisting in the Building of a Block house in which a leuftenant & 20 men are to be Left in the winter to Defend the winterers & Protect the fishery for the Future from the Indians

The Country about this Place tho much more Barren is far more agreeable than Croque here you may walk for miles over Barren Rocks without being interupted by a Bush or a tree – when there you Could not go as many Yards without being Entangled in the Brushwood it abounds also in Game Partridges of 2 sorts Ducks teal in great abundance But particularly at this season with a Bird of Passage Calld here a Curlew from his Great Likeness to the smaller sort of that Bird found in England their Chief food is Berries which are here in Great abundance of Several Sorts with which they make themselves very near as fat & I think tho Prejudicd almost as good as our Lincolnshire Ruff & Reve

Curlews came here August 9

about a week after the Curlew The Green Plover made its appearance tho not in near so great abundance feeding like him upon Berries!

Charadrias Pluvialis

For most of August Banks abandoned the day-by-day chronicle and wrote in a far more general way: he speaks of the finding of an immense amount of whalebone, carefully buried long ago on the nearby Eskimo

Island but now so old as to be utterly decayed, "scarce distinguishable from Birch Bark", and of a few boat expeditions, one to St Peter's Bay,

> where we found the Wreck of a Birch Bark Canoe a sign Probably that some of the Nfland Indians Live not Very far from them tho as Yet we Know nothing of them. Nfland Indians
>
> This Subject Leads me to say Something (tho I have as yet been able to Learn Very little about them) of the Indians that inhabit the interior Parts of Newfoundland and are supposed to be the original inhabitants of that Countrey they are in general thought to be very few as I have been told not Exceeding 500 in number but why that should be imagind I cannot tell as we Know nothing at all of the Interior Parts of the Island nor Ever had the Least Connextion with them tho the french we are told had
>
> The only Part of the Island that I have heard of their inhabiting is in the neighbourhood of Fogo where they are said to be as near the coast as 4 miles
>
> Our People who fish in those Parts Live in a continual State of warfare with them firing at them whenever they meet with them & if they chance to find their houses or wigwams as they call them Plundering them immediately tho a Bow and arrows & what they call their Pudding is generally the whole of their furniture.
>
> They in return Look upon us in exactly the same Light as we Do them Killing our people whenever they get the advantage of them & Stealing or Destroying their nets wheresoever they find them
>
> The Pudding which I mentioned in the Last Paragraph is our People say always found in their hutts made of Eggs & Dears hair to make it hang together as we put hair into our mortar and Bakd in the Sun our People beleive it to be Part of their Food – but do not seem Certain whether it is intended for that or any other use They are said to fetch Eggs for this Composition as far as fung or Penguin Island ten Leagues from the nearest Land.
>
> They are Extreemly Dextrous in the use of the Bows and arrows & will when Pressed by an Enemy take 4 arrows 3 between the Fingers of the Left hand with which they hold the Bow & the fourth notchd in the string & Discharge them as quick as they Can draw the bow & with great Certainty
>
> Their Canoes by the Gentlemans account from whom I have all this are made like the Canadians of Birch Bark sewd together with Deers sinews or some other material but Differ from the Canadians Essentially in that they are made to shut up by the sides Closing together for the Convenient Carriage of them through the woods which they are obligd to do on account of the many Lakes that abound all over the Island.
>
> Their Method of scalping to is very different from the Canadian they not being content with the Hair but skinning the whole face at Least as far as the upper Lip
>
> I have a scalp of this Kind which was taken from one Sam Frye a

Sam frye fisherman who they shot in the water as he attempted to swim off to his ship from them they Kept the Scalp a year but the features were so well Preservd that when upon a Party of them being Pursued the next summer they Dropd it it was immediately Known to be the scalp of the Identical Sam Frye who was Killd the year before.

So much for the Indians if half of what I have wrote about them is true it is more than I expect tho I have not the Least reason to think But that the man who told it to me beleivd it & had heard it all from his own people & those of the neighbouring Planters & fishermen

It is time that I should give Some account of the Fishery both French & English as they differ much in their methods of Fishing and have Each their Different merits the Englishman indeed has the advantage as he catches considerably a larger quantity of Fish and his Fish fetch more money at Foreign markets being better Cured.

This Banks did, conscientiously and at some length, following the whole process through from the catching by handline to the heading and gutting, the splitting, the salting, the washing out of the salt, the drying, the sweating and the drying again; and coming to the end of the English way of fishing he says

Lastly Let us remember their Train Oyl for by that name they distinguish it from Whale or Seal Oyle Which they Call Fat Oyle which is sold at a Lower Price being only usd for the Lighting of Lamps than the train oyl which is usd by the Curriers They make it thus they Take a half tub & boring a hole Through the Bottom Press hard down into it a Layer of Spruce boughs upon which they Lay the Livers & place the whole apparatus in as sunny a Place as Possible as the Livers Corrupt the Oyl runs from them and strains itself clear through the Spruce Boughs is caught by a Vessel set under the hole in the tubs bottom

So much For the English Fishery I shall now mention the methods of the French which are Different from ours in some of which as I said before they Excell us but more in their neatness & manner of Carrying on Business among their People than in any Superiority in Point of Curing

Their Boats are not much more than half as Large as ours much more Clumsily Built & Less adapted for sailing

Yet on the other hand their officers had talents of no common order:

The Seconde or mate of the French ships the Major or surgeon occasionaly the Captain are the People who split the Fish by which means it is never Carelessly or ill Done as is too often the Case among our People where splitting is done by the Common People the too first of these officers are not qualified for their office unless they can sing which they Do to amuse the People who occasionally all join the chorus the whole time of their Splitting

I remember Coming into a french Stage & hearing Voi amante as agreeably sung as Ever I heard it by the Major & seconde the first of whoom had a remarkably good voice

These Officers being of some Consequence among the People & commonly going Pretty well Dressd have an Ingenious way of Keeping themselves Clean in the Dirty operation of Splitting they have a Case made of Bark to Cover them from their chins to their heels which Constantly stands over their Stools in the splitting table into this they Creep & Putting on sleeves & Large woolen gloves split the fish in a manner without touching it

Their Oyl they also make in a much neater manner than we do if neatness is an excellence in so nasty a thing they certainly excell us much theirs is all straind through a thin Cloth not unlike the Canvas that Ladies work Carpeting upon strechd on the upper side of a Vessel made with Poles Placd in the shape of a Pyramid Reversd under which is Placd a trough for the receiving it as it strains out

After having said so much about Fishing it will not be improper to say a little about the Fish that they catch & of the Dish they make of it Calld Chowder which I believe is Peculiar to this Country tho here it is the Cheif food of the Poorer & when well made a Luxury that the rich Even in England at Least in my opinion might be fond of It is a Soup made with a small quantity of salt Pork cut into Small Slices a good deal of fish and Biscuit Boyled for about an hour unlikely as this mixture appears to be Palatable I have scarce met with any Body in this Country Who is not fond of it whatever it may be in England Here it is certainly the Best method of Dressing the Cod which is not near so firm here as in London whether or not that is owing to the art of the fishmongers I cannot pretend to say Salmon & herrings we also have in Plenty but neither of them near so rich & fat as they are in England Halibuts are the only fish common To both places in which this Country Excells

He goes on to speak of birds from the culinary point of view, curlew, golden plover, ducks and teal, geese and partridges:

these are all good to Eat but Some birds there are that I must mention tho they have not that Excellence Particularly one Known here by the name of Whobby he is of the Loon Kind & an Excellent Diver but Very Often amuses himself especially in the night by flying high in the air and making a very Loud & alarming noise at least to those who do not know the Cause of it as the following circumstance will shew

In August 1765 as Commodore Paliser in the Guernsey a 50 gun ship Lay in this Harbour Expecting the Indians one Dark night in a thick fog the Ships Company were alarmed by a noise they had not heard before Every one awoke Conjecturd what it could Possibly be it came nearer & nearer grew louder & louder the first Lieuftenant was calld up he was the only man in the Ship Who had Ever seen the Esquimaux immediately as he heard the noise he declard he rememberd it well it was the war whoop of the Esquimaux who were certainly Coming in their Canoes to board the Ship & Cut all their throats the Commodore was aquainted up he Bundled upon Deck orderd ship to be cleard for Engaging all hands to Great Guns arms in the Tops Every thing in as good order as if a french man of war of Equal Force was within half a mile Bearing down upon them The Niger which Lay at some Distance from them was haild & told the indians were Coming when the Enemy appeared in the shape of a Troop of these Whobbys swimming & flying about the Harbour which From the Darkness of the night they had not seen before all hands were then sent down to Sleep & no more thought of the indians till the Nigers People came on board next morning who will Probably never Forget that their Companion Cleard Ship & turnd up all hands to a flock of Whobbies

Banks returned to his earlier diary form on 2 September to record a most surprising fish:

This day a Halibut was brought aboard so large that his dimensions I fear will appear incredible in England the first I took with my own hands therefore I can venture to affirm them Exact They are as follows

From the Tip of his nose to the end of his Tail	6ft	11 inches
Breadth from fin to fin	3	10
Thickness of his solid Flesh By running a priming wyer through		8¼
Breadth of his Tail	2	0½
Lengh of the Fin next his Gills	0	10
he weighd		284 lb

which was only 14 lb Less than an Ox Killd for the ships Company the Day he was weighd which was not till near 24 hours after he was Caught so he may fairly be said to have weighd as much as the Ox had he not been wasted as all fish do considerably by Keeping.

After this he gives a receipt for spruce beer and apart from a note on 6 September "Curlews gone" he returns to a general narrative, of which these are extracts.

We were told by the Old Salmoneer that there were Owls there as big as Turkies he indeed gave us the Claws of one which I take to be the Strix Bubo of Linnaeus tho I was never Lucky Enough to See one of them the whole time of our Stay nor any of the Shipps Company tho they were Eternally Employd at cutting wood for the Fort in temple Bay

As an Excuse for my not Stirring More from home while at this Place I mention an escape I had on the Second of this month when mere accident Preservd my Life I set out with the Master of our Ship on a Cruise to the

Northwards meaning to Cruise along shore for a week or ten days where no vessel that we Knew of had Ever been we were both Extreemly fond of the Plan & Pushd out of Chatteaux with a foul wind in an open Shallop by way of putting ourselves in a fair winds way we with difficulty Turnd the Lengh of Castle Island when the wind Coming right ahead we agreed it was impossible to go any farther & we Put back into Esquimaux harbour to stay till the next morn in hope of change of wind we had Scarcely made our Boat fast along side of a snow* there when it began to Blow Very hard and that night Came on a most severe Gale of Wind which Destroyd an infinite number of boats Everywhere the French Particularly whose boats are smaller than ours are said to have lost an hundred men & three of their Ships Drove on shore a brig of Captain Derbys at Isle Bois a little down the Streights was Beat all to Peices this totaly Destroyd our scheme to the northward Sir Thomas being after that very Careful of Letting the boats go out & indeed as the blowing Season was Come in I was Easily Persuaded that I was safer on board the Niger than in any Boat in the Country

About the latter End of this month Partridges Became much more Plenty then they were before Possibly they Came from the Norward Mr Ankille while Shooting in the neighbourhood of St Peters Bay saw by his account at Least 100 in one Company while he was making up to them to have shot at them an Eagle made a stoop among them & Carried of one the rest immediately took wing & went off I should mention here that tho I have not been able to Procure an Eagle from the Scarcity here are two sorts one of which we had a young one who got away is the Chrysaetos of Linnae the other I apprehend to be a Canadensis but I never could see him but upon the Wing

Just before we Left this Place the Sergeant of marines belonging to York fort brought me a Porcupine alive it is quite Black except the Quills which are Black & white alternately about the size of an English hare but shorter made after sulking for three or four Days he begins to Eat & I have great hopes of Carrying him home alive

Early in October the *Niger* left Labrador for Newfoundland, putting in at Croque, where Banks went to see the garden that Phipps had planted.

This is a very Strong Vegetable mould which with the Quickness of Vegetation in the Climate had such an Effect on many of our English Seeds that they Run themselves out in stalk Producing little or no fruit Pea haulm we had 11 feet high & as thick as my finger which Produced scarce anything Beans ran till they could not support their own weight & fell without Producing a Pod Probably from the ignorance of the gardener we Left behind who did not Know the Common Practise Even in England of

* A snow was a vessel very like a brig but with a third mast (or sometimes a horse) just abaft the mainmast for the trysail.

> Cutting of their tops Cabbage & Lettuce Throve surprizingly as did our Radishes & small Sallet carrots & Turnips which especially the Last were remarkably Sweet The Coldness of our nights made it necessary to Cover our Onions with Hammocks we left them also till the Very Last but when we got them tho they were very small they were very good

The garden had thriven, upon the whole, in spite of the fieldmice, and so had the poultry, in spite of the weasels and goshawks; but Banks could not really love the place:

> Croque tho tolerably Pleasant now was intolerable in the Summer on account of its heat & the Closeness of its situation confind on all sides by woods & no place but the Ship Free From mosketos and Gadflies in Prodigious abundance we had only one Clear walk on a morass a little above the Gardens but there you could not Long walk dry shod Sr Thomas & I were both Very Ill here especially me who at one time they did not Expect to recover I know not whether that gave a disgust but we both Joind in Pronouncing the Place the Least agreable of any we had Seen in the Countrey

Banks then gives an account of the seal fishery and goes on

> Octr 10th After this Short Stay at Croque intended only for filling Water & getting on board the Produce of the Gardens & Poultry we Saild for St Johns on the 10th & arriv'd there on the 13th without any Particular Transaction During our Passage Here we found the Greater Part of the Squadron under the Command of Mr Palliser in the Guernsey whose Civilities We ought to acknowledge as he Shewd us all we could Expect we all Felt great Pleasure in Returning to Society which we had so long been deprivd of St Johns tho the Most Disagreeable Town I Ever met with was For some time Perfectly agreable to us I should not omit to mention the Ceremonies with which we Celebrated the Coronation which happened whilst we were there the Guernsey was Dressd upon the Occasion & if I may compare Great things with small Looked Like a Pedlars Basket at a Horse race where ribbons of divers Colours fly in the wind fastend to yard wands stuck around it after this we were all invited to a Ball Given by Mr Governor where the want of Ladies was so great that My Washerwoman & her sister were there by formal invitation but what surprized me the most was that after Dancing we were Conducted to a realy Elegant Supper Set out with all Kinds of Wines & Italian Liqueurs To the Great Emolument of the Ladies who Eat & Drank to some Purpose Dancing it seems agreed with them By its getting them such Excellent Stomachs

The Governor's ball was given on Saturday, 25 October 1766: on the morning of Monday, 27 October, James Cook arrived in HM Brig *Grenville*, the vessel in which he had been surveying so much of the coast of Newfoundland and Labrador since 1764. The *Niger* did not sail until the following Wednesday (Banks says Tuesday, but he was writing this part of his journal from memory, whereas Cook's log, a daily record of events, gives the later date, which is surely more probable) and although there is no evidence of their having met, naval etiquette required Cook to call upon Commodore Palliser and Sir Thomas Adams, and once he was aboard the *Niger* it is scarcely possible that he and Banks should not at least have exchanged a how do you do. Banks, however, though a zealous botanist, was no seer; his journal makes no mention of the encounter but goes on

It is very difficult to Compare one town with another tho that Probably is the Best way of Conveying the Idea St Johns however Cannot be Compard to any I have seen it is Built upon the side of a hill facing the Harbour Containing two or three hundred houses & near as many fish Flakes interspersed which in summer time must Cause a stench scarce to be supported thank heaven we were only there spring & fall before the fish were come to the Ground & after they were gone off

For dirt & filth of all Kinds St Johns may in my opinion Reign unrivald as it Far Exceeds any Fishing town I Ever saw in England here is no regular Street the houses being built in rows immediately adjoining to the Flakes Consequently no Pavement offals of Fish of all Kinds are strewd about The remains of The Irish mens chowder who you see making it skinning and gutting fish in Every Corner.

As Every thing here smells of fish so You cannot get any thing that does not Taste of it hogs Can scarce be Kept from it by any Care and When they have got it are by Far the Filthyest meat I ever Met with Poultry of all Kinds Ducks geese Fowls & Turkies infinitely more Fishy than the Worst tame Duck That Ever was sold For a wild one in Lincolnshire The Very Cows Eat the Fish offal & thus milk is Fishy This Last Particular indeed I have not met with myself but have been assured it is often the Case

While we remaind here I Employd some of my Time in searching for Plants but the Season was so far advanced that I could find none in Blossom by the Leaves & remains indeed I discovered that there were several here different from any I had seen to the northward the Leaves of Some I Collected but many were so far destroyd by the Cold that Even that was Impossible so that there remains a feild for any body who will Examine this And the more southern Part of the Island but I have Vanity enough to beleive that to the northward not many will be found to have Escapt my observation

On the 28th of Octr we Left St Johns in our Passage to Lisbon where we arrived on the 17th on the fifth of Novr we had a very hard Gale of Wind of the Western Islands* which has almost ruind me in the Course of it we Octr 28

* The Azores.

> shipp'd a Sea which Stove in our Quarter & almost Filld the Cabbin with water in an instant where it washd backward & forward with such rapidity that it Broke in Peices Every chair & table in the Place among other things that Suffered my Poor Box of Seeds was one which was intirely demolish'd as was my Box of Earth with Plants in it which Stood upon deck

This disaster may to some degree account for Banks's rather cross and censorious remarks about Portugal, where the *Niger* stayed for some weeks before going home, and about the Portuguese, who had no notion of gardening or of planting trees. ". . . their Taste in Gardening is more trifling than Can be Conceivd a Pond Scarce Large Enough for a frog to swim in the Sides of Which are lind with Glaz'd tiles and which has two or three fountains in it about as thick as a quill is their Greatest Ornament this with a few Close Walks of Myrtle and Vines & a Statue or two Placed on awkward Pedestals at the Entrance of the Walks make a Place that People are Carried to See." But these few pages were written as a set piece, not in the true, day-by-day diary form that shows Banks at his best; and in any case they give a somewhat false impression, because in fact when he was not disapproving of Portuguese gardens and Popish magnificence he had quite a good time, becoming a member of the local natural history society and meeting English and Portuguese botanists, some of whom remained his friends for life.

Yet even if the loss of his seeds and some of his plants did combine with Portuguese cooking to depress his spirits for a while they certainly revived quite soon, for in spite of the storm, in spite of his long illness, and in spite of the shortness of his time in Newfoundland and Labrador, he reached home in January 1767 bearing specimens or exact records of at least 340 plants, 91 birds, many fishes and invertebrates, and a few mammals, including the porcupine, that at least began the voyage alive. He possessed the beginnings of a herbarium that was soon to become famous, together with a nascent reputation that was soon to enable him to take part in one of the most interesting voyages ever made by a natural philosopher; and in his absence he had been elected a Fellow of the Royal Society, a body of men who could appreciate his energy and his disinterested love of science at their true value.

Chapter 3

THE ROYAL SOCIETY: SOLANDER: THE *ENDEAVOUR* VOYAGE

THE ROYAL SOCIETY of which Banks became a fellow in 1766 was a body of some 360 ordinary and 160 foreign members. It had increased greatly in size since the days when Wren, Boyle and a few of their friends discussed "the founding of a Colledge for the promoting of Physico-Mathematical Experimentall Learning", and if it had not increased proportionately in reputation this may be put down to the fact that men like Newton, Hooke and Halley are not to be found in every generation and to the ease with which candidates were elected: a wealthy Englishman was almost sure of success, particularly if he was also a peer, and so was a reasonably well recommended foreigner. Banks himself, though full of zeal for botany, had published nothing; and Lord Sandwich's scientific zeal was confined to fishing, though indeed he was well disposed towards men of science and he was in a position to support their projects.

Yet with all its faults the Society was still a most respectable institution – the list of 1768, the first in which Banks's name appears, does show 46 lords temporal or spiritual, but a peerage does not necessarily make a man a fool and in any case there were 339 other members, including Henry Cavendish, Daines Barrington, Pennant, Priestley, William Hamilton (Nelson's friend) and perhaps more surprisingly Joshua Reynolds, while among the foreigners appeared such names as d'Alembert, Buffon, Euler, Linnaeus, Montesquieu and Voltaire.

From the earliest days some part of the public had made game of the Society for weighing air, dissecting fleas and so on, and even in the 1760s many people thought entomology a pursuit unworthy of a grown man; but also from the earliest days the government had taken advantage of that pool of science, asking the Royal Society to supervise the observatory at Greenwich, for example, and to give advice on a great many subjects, such as that change in the calendar which lost us eleven days, never to be recovered; and on being informed somewhat later that Venus would pass over the face of the sun in 1761, so that with due attention the sun's parallax might be determined, to the great advantage of navigation, the ministry turned to the Society once again.

The reply was that observations of this rare phenomenon would indeed be of great value, and the Rev. Nevil Maskelyne was sent to St Helena, while Mason and Dixon (the same who traced the line between Maryland and Pennsylvania) went to the Cape of Good Hope. But at the critical moment clouds lay thick over St Helena; the weather was little better at the Cape; and the astronomers were obliged to console themselves with the reflection that there would be other transits in 1769 and 1874.

Banks, though as ardent a natural philosopher as any of his colleagues, was not much concerned with stars; in his surviving letters of this period there is not the least sign of any interest in transits, past or present. His immense energy was directed to having his specimens from Newfoundland and Labrador painted, to setting up house in New Burlington Street with his sister, Mrs Banks remaining in Chelsea, to travelling about south-western England and Wales, to making new acquaintances and to consolidating older friendships.

He was particularly fortunate in his painters. Georg Ehret, a friend of Linnaeus, had been brought forward in England by Sir Hans Sloane, Dr Mead and the Duchess of Portland; he was now at the head of his profession and he figured at least twenty-three of Banks's flowers, most delicately painted on vellum. Many of the animals (animals in the widest sense) were painted by an amiable, conscientious, highly talented young man from Edinburgh, Sydney Parkinson, who was introduced to Banks by James Lee the nurseryman. The others were painted by Peter Paillou: he too was a gifted man, but little seems to be known of him except that he was connected with Thomas Pennant.

Pennant in his turn was connected with Banks's journeys in the south and west, since one of them was directed towards Downing, his house in North Wales. Pennant was nearly twenty years older than Banks, and he had published the first part of his *British Zoology* as early as 1766: it has already been observed that Pennant knew Daines Barrington, the lawyer, antiquary and naturalist, and that both knew Gilbert White, whose enchanting *Natural History of Selborne* takes the form of letters to them; but it is worth repeating because both White and Banks, who could rarely have been deceived by even a half-seen bird or plant, were at least in some cases incapable of fine discrimination where their friends were concerned. Banks eventually got rid of the invasive, self-seeking Pennant, but there were others he endured all his life.

A far more important and increasing friendship was that with Solander, who was now firmly established at the British Museum, but who in spite of working hard still had time to survey the Duchess of

Portland's wonderful collections, to attend the meetings of the Royal Society, of which he too was a Fellow, to help Banks catalogue his American plants, to dine out pretty often, and at least to contemplate a visit to Downing.

There can be little doubt that it was Solander's growing influence that led Banks to form the plan of going to Uppsala to study under Linnaeus and even to push on and travel in Lapland. After a tour in the west country (where he was "almost bit to death" by gnats at Glastonbury) he wrote Pennant a letter which contained this passage:

> "What will you say to me if I should be prevented from paying my respects to you in N: Wales this year tho I so fully intended it nothing but your Looking upon it with the Eye of an unprejudiced nat: Historian can bring any excuse to be heard with Patience Look then with Zoologick Eyes & tell me if you could blame me if I Sacraficed every Consideration to an opportunity of Paying a visit to our Master Linnaeus & Profiting by his Lectures before he dies who is now so old that he cannot Long Last."[1] [Banks was twenty-four, Linnaeus sixty.]

The visit to Downing was not in fact put off: Banks went there in the late summer, together with his eminent colleague William Hudson of the *Flora Anglica*. It is possible that Pennant, who was no great admirer of Linnaeus ("his work too superficial except in botany – little opinion of him as a zoologist") may have poured cold water on the scheme, but if he did so Banks obviously remained undamped, for in a letter of January 1768, when Banks was travelling from Chester to London, a letter from Pennant spoke of his going "thro all the perils of snow and ice, a good foretaste of your Lapland Journey".[2] And other correspondence of the time speaks of it as quite settled.

From Pennant's letters it is clear that Banks meant to take Parkinson with him as a draughtsman on his northern journey. But in the event the voyage they made together was one of greater consequence by far.

Well before 1769 the Royal Society, and particularly Dr Maskelyne, now the Astronomer Royal, had begun to prepare for the coming transit. In 1766 they determined to send observers to various parts of the world and to invite Father Boscowitz of Pavia to be one of them; in 1767 the President, Lord Morton, was in correspondence with the unhelpful Spanish ambassador about the astronomer's journey to California; in the same year, having discarded California, the Society decided on three places for their observers, Hudson's Bay, the North Cape, and a suitable island in the Pacific; and probably in the same year they drew up the following undated memorial, the Council approving and signing it on 15 February 1768.

> To the King's Most Excellent Majesty. The Memorial of the President, Council and Fellows of the Royal Society of London for improving Natural Knowledge Humbly sheweth –
>
> That the passage of the Planet Venus over the Disc of the Sun, which will happen on the 3rd of June in the year 1769, is a Phaenomenon that must, if the same be accurately observed in proper places, contribute greatly to the improvement of Astronomy on which Navigation so much depends . . .

The memorial also showed that apart from the ships needed to carry the observers the expedition would cost four thousand pounds, which the Society did not possess, and it ended:

> The Memorialists, attentive to the true end for which they were founded by your Majesty's Royal Predecessor, the Improvement of Natural Knowledge, conceive it to be their duty to lay these sentiments before your Majesty with all humility and submit the same to your Majesty's Royal Consideration.

The memorial was presented at the right time and to the right monarch. King George III was no more than thirty, and although his political education may have been deplorable, he was full of energy, enterprise, and good intentions; there were certainly unofficial discussions both before and after the formal memorial, but the request was granted, and fully granted, as early as March 1768.

Once the expedition had been decided upon, the Admiralty moved with surprising speed: Sir Edward Hawke, the admiral who "did bang Mounseer Conflang" in Quiberon Bay in 1759, taking or sinking five of his ships and running more aground, was then First Lord, and he was accustomed to brisk action. In March 1768 the Navy Board was directed to find a suitable vessel; the Royal Society was firmly told that the claims of Mr Dalrymple, a distinguished hydrographer with much experience of the north-western Pacific in the East India Company's service whom it put forward as principal observer, to direct the voyage were "entirely repugnant to the regulations of the Navy"; and Mr James Cook, the former surveyor of the coasts of Newfoundland and Labrador and a master in the Royal Navy, was sent for, commissioned as a lieutenant on 5 May and given the command. (In passing it may be observed that masters in the Royal Navy, a race long since extinct, were responsible for the navigation of the ship: they were relics of a time when sailors did the sailing of a man-of-war and soldiers, commanded by gentlemen, the fighting: although they usually began as midshipmen and although they messed in the wardroom or gunroom, they were only warrant officers, and as masters they had reached the highest point in their career. Lieutenants, on the other hand, were commissioned officers, to whom all masters were subordinate in command, and they might be promoted to commander, to post-captain and thence by seniority to the various grades of admiral. It was quite rare for a master to be given a commission, and the only cases that come readily to mind are those of Mr Bowen, who handled Lord Howe's flagship so well on the Glorious First of June, and the unfortunate Mr Bligh of the *Bounty*.)

The Royal Society bowed to Hawke's decision: they too knew Cook quite well, for not only had he published admirable sailing directions for the regions he had surveyed but he had also contributed his accurate observations of the 1766 solar eclipse to the Society's *Philosophical Transactions*; and since Dalrymple refused to go except in command, thus leaving the main scientific post vacant, they asked Cook to come and see them. After a short interview on 5 May 1768 the Council appointed him the Society's chief observer of the transit, allowing him £120 a year for victualling himself and the second observer, Charles Green of Greenwich, undertaking to produce "such a gratuity as the Society shall think proper" (it turned out to be a hundred guineas), and to provide two telescopes, a quadrant, a sextant and some other instruments.

Then on 20 May Captain Wallis brought the *Dolphin* home from her second voyage round the world, this time with news of Tahiti, which its discoverer, reaching it a few months before Louis-Antoine de Bougainville, had named King George's Island, and with a song that ended

> Then we plow'd the South Ocean, such land to discover
> As amongst other nations has made such a pother.
> We found it, my boys, and with joy be it told,
> For beauty such islands you ne'er did behold.
> We've the pleasure ourselves the tidings to bring
> As may welcome us home to our country and king.
>
> For wood, water, fruit, and provision well stor'd
> Such an isle as King George's the world can't afford.
> For to each of these islands great Wallis gave name,
> Which will e'er be recorded in annals of fame.
> We'd the fortune to find them, and homeward to bring
> The tidings a tribute to country and king.[3]

Since the island was well within the southern zone that Dr Maskelyne had laid down as the best for observing the transit ("any place not exceeding 30 degrees of Southern Latitude and between the 140th &

180th degrees of longitude west of your Majesty's Royal Observatory in Greenwich park"), the Society wrote to the Admiralty on 9 June asking them to agree that Tahiti should be the place for the observation. The letter continued "Joseph Banks Esq[r], Fellow of the Society, a Gentleman of large fortune, who is well versed in natural history, being Desirous of undertaking the same voyage the Council very earnestly request their Lordships, that in regard to Mr Banks's great personal merit, and for the Advancement of useful knowledge, He also, together with his Suite, being seven persons more, be received on board of the ship, under command of Captain Cook."

The news of Tahiti may possibly have increased Banks's desire to go on the voyage, but it was quite certainly not the first cause. Just when the Pacific displaced Lapland in his mind is not clear, but the idea was firmly implanted before the *Dolphin*'s return, and it may have arisen when the memorial was under discussion – when it became apparent that there was a real likelihood of a ship's being sent to the Great South Sea.

Their Lordships had no objection to the Society's request, and on 22 July their secretary directed Cook to receive "Joseph Banks Esq and his Suite consisting of eight Persons with their Baggage, bearing them as Supernumeraries for Victuals only, and Victualling them as Barks Company during their continuance on board."

This is the official sequence of events; but there is no doubt that private arrangements preceded the public announcements both with regard to Banks and Cook. Cook had earned golden opinion at the Admiralty, and it is probable that this command, so admirably suited to his talents, was intended for him as soon as it was decided upon; Captain Hugh Palliser, his friend and patron from the beginning, had great influence with the Navy Board (he was Comptroller in 1770) and it is therefore not surprising that a north-country cat, or to be more precise a Whitby collier, the kind of vessel in which Cook had learnt his calling, was chosen for the expedition, perhaps at Cook's suggestion. This is not to imply that the *Endeavour* was not the most suitable for the purpose – she was – but only to emphasize the fact that Cook and his friends were intimately acquainted with that suitability, not always evident to those whose service had been confined to men-of-war. And it is quite clear that Banks knew he would be a member of the expedition long before his formal acceptance in July. Lord Sandwich was not only a friend of long standing and a fellow member of the Royal Society, but he also formed part of the government and in a few months he was to return to the Admiralty (where he had many friends) as First Lord: he was therefore ideally placed for those unofficial contacts that can give an early assurance of success even in the present century. Besides, as early as April 1768 Pennant was urging Banks to take umbrellas, both the fine silk kind and the strong oilskin kind, as well as oilskin coats; and in any event a satisfactory suite of eight persons, all willing to go to the ends of the earth, with no certainty of return, could hardly be gathered together in a few weeks: still less could Banks and Solander have accumulated all the equipment that Ellis described in a letter[4] to Linnaeus – equipment that was said to have cost ten thousand pounds. "No people ever went to sea better fitted out for the purpose of Natural History, nor more elegantly. They have got a fine library of Natural History; they have all sorts of machines for catching and preserving insects; all kinds of nets, trawls, drags and hooks for coral fishing . . . All this is owing to you and your writings." There was however one remark in the letter that Sandwich or any other friend of Banks's with long experience of the world would have read with some uneasiness: "After . . . their observations on the transit of Venus they are to proceed under the direction of Mr Banks, by order of the Lords of the Admiralty, on further discoveries of the great Southern continent . . ."

Whether this was a mistake on Ellis's part or whether Banks or possibly Solander had been boasting or had even been facetious about who was to direct whom there is no telling. What is certain is that on 30 July 1768 the *Endeavour* dropped down the river from Gallions Reach (she had been fitting in Deptford Yard) and anchored in the Downs; Cook joined her there, having received his orders, and sailed for Plymouth on 8 August. He had a tedious passage down the Channel, but six days later he was able to send an express to London, telling Banks and Solander to come directly.

On 15 August, the day the message reached him, Banks was at the opera with Miss Harriet Blosset, a ward of the Hammersmith nurseryman James Lee. Horace de Saussure, the Swiss botanist and physicist, met them there and went back with them to sup at the Blossets' house, he being acquainted with the family. He speaks of them as being engaged, of Miss Blosset's being desperately in love and of Banks drinking heavily to hide his feelings, since he was to leave the next day. Yet since Banks could not speak a word of French, as Saussure points out, there was no communication between them, and Saussure's testimony[5] would not be worth recording but for the fact that it is confirmed by others. Not only was the matter taken up in ill-natured squibs and scandal-sheets when Banks returned famous from the voyage, but Beaglehole quotes two letters from Daines Barrington to

Thomas Pennant in the Turnbull Library at Wellington in New Zealand, the first of which reads in part "Upon his arrival in England he took no sort of notice of Miss Blosset for the first week or nearly so at the same time that he went about London and visited other friends and acquaintances. On this Miss Blosset set out for London and wrote him a letter desiring an interview of explanation. To this Mr Banks answer'd by a letter of 2 or 3 sheets professing love &c but that he found he was of too volatile a temper to marry."

The interview took place, and although the account, which Barrington received from a lady, is confused, it was obviously very painful ("Miss Bl: swoon'd &c") but no marriage came out of it; yet later, to quote Dr Lysaght, "the Blosset family was rumoured to have withdrawn with a substantial sum of money from Banks [Lee 1810] to console her for all the knitted waistcoats with which she had sought to enmesh him."

But this is to anticipate: on 16 August 1768 Banks and Solander set out for Plymouth – the "suite" was already there – and they arrived on the twentieth. The *Endeavour* had taken in all her stores; the shipwrights and joiners had finished their work on the gentlemen's cabins; the ship had been brought out into the Sound; and if the wind had been kind Cook would have sailed the next day. But instead of weighing his anchor, he was obliged to let go another because of gales and thick weather, while the "gentlemen" (this was Cook's term for those of his passengers who were not servants) had nothing to do but contemplate their vessel through the pouring rain.

Although her captain no doubt loved her, she was nothing much to look at, being only a rather small cat-built bark, a north-country collier: to a sailor the *cat* part of her name meant that she was built in the northern way, remarkably strong, and that she was distinguished by a narrow stern, projecting quarters, a deep waist and no ornamental figure on the prow, while the *bark* part implied that she was smallish, square-sterned, and without headrails – that is to say she did not have that elegant cut-away dip in front through which the bowsprit rises that was so marked a feature of the contemporary men-of-war and larger merchantmen, but ended prosaically in a point, and rather a blunt one at that. Logically enough most barks were also bark-rigged, carrying square sails on the fore and main masts and fore-and-aft sails on the mizen. But to the seaman this was not at all a necessary consequence, and in fact the *Endeavour* was square-rigged on all three.

Her bows were bluff; she was wall-sided, with no handsome inward slope or tumblehome; her homely lines made it clear that she would be slow and her flat bottom meant that she would not be a very weatherly ship – that she would find it difficult to claw off a lee shore. But her flat bottom and her straight sides gave her wonderfully roomy holds – she had eighteen months' stores aboard – and a shallow draught; and if she was slow her great strength of construction meant that she was also sure: at least as sure as any vessel could hope to be on the sea, that wholly unreliable element. She was one hundred and six feet long and twenty-nine feet two inches at the widest; she drew fifteen feet abaft with six months' stores, she gauged 368 tons, she carried ten four-pounder carriage guns and twelve swivels, and her complement numbered eighty-five, including a dozen Marines under a sergeant.

Although she was a king's ship, wearing a pennant at the main, she had obviously been built for the coal or timber trade and she must have looked a commonplace, shabby little object in Plymouth Sound among all the regular men-of-war. But there was nothing commonplace or shabby about her captain, although he too had spent his early days at sea carrying coal and wood: James Cook was a big, unusually good-looking man with a strong, determined face, and he would have stood out even on a particularly distinguished quarterdeck; he had all the marks of a seaman, and from everything one hears or reads, all the seaman's amiable qualities: courage, resolution, modesty, and the gift of being good company, as well, of course, as great professional abilities and natural authority. Yet like Cochrane or Sir Francis Chichester he did not go to sea until he was relatively old. Cook was born in 1728 and as a boy and a youth in Yorkshire he helped his father, a farm labourer, at the same time getting a little education at the village school; and when he was seventeen he was apprenticed to a grocer at Snaith, not far from the port of Whitby. Eighteen months of grocering was all he could bear however and in 1746 he went to sea in a Whitby collier, the strangely named *Freelove*, plying the difficult and often very dangerous sea between Newcastle and London. Other ships followed and a great deal of sea-time, and in 1752 he became mate of the *Friendship*, also belonging to Whitby. In 1755 war between England and France became almost certain, and although it was not declared until the next year, press warrants were already out: the Navy had to be manned, if necessary by force. Cook's ship was in the London river, the most likely place to be taken, and after some hesitation he decided to volunteer, "having a mind to try his fortune that way", and entering of course as a foremast hand. His first ship was the *Eagle* of sixty guns.

He did uncommonly well, finding an appreciative captain who changed his rating from able seaman to master's mate: this was not a rank held by warrant, still less by commission, but strictly a rating, like that of midshipman. Yet it did bring him aft to the quarterdeck in an officer's uniform, messing with the surgeon's mates, the other master's mates and the senior midshipmen. Then Captain Hugh Palliser took over the *Eagle*: he at once distinguished Cook and encouraged him, and in 1757, having passed the necessary examination at Trinity House, Cook was given a warrant as master of the *Pembroke*, also of sixty guns. The war now took him to Canada, where he did better still; among other things he sounded and charted the St Lawrence both above and below Quebec, a very risky and technically arduous undertaking opposite the French positions but one essential for the capture of the city. For the rest of the war Cook was on active service in the *Pembroke* and in Lord Colville's flagship the *Northumberland*; and when peace came his service – his surveying, charting and sounding in American waters – was hardly less uncomfortable and perilous; but at least he did have more time to devote to mathematics and astronomy, and now, in his fortieth year, he was acknowledged to be the fittest man in the Navy to lead the present expedition.

His officers too were a picked, seamanlike set: what is more, Lieutenant John Gore had already sailed round the world in the *Dolphin* with Byron and again with Wallis, while Molineux, the master, and his two mates Pickersgill and Clerke had also made this most recent circumnavigation. The senior lieutenant, Zachary Hicks, and the surgeon, William Monkhouse, were both men of great experience; and the midshipmen were grown youths with several years of sea service, with the one exception of Isaac Manley, who was then twelve but who reached the age of eighty-one, dying an admiral of the red. Banks and Monkhouse (whose younger brother was one of these midshipmen) were old acquaintances, for they had been shipmates in the *Niger*: though perhaps one should write Munkhouse, since that was how he signed his will, one of the many wills written aboard the *Endeavour*, and rightly written, since so many were called for. Of the original gunroom, only Gore came home; and of Banks's followers, six died out of eight.

These followers consisted of Sydney Parkinson; Herman Spöring, a Swede who had lived for some years in London as a watchmaker and for the last two as Solander's clerk and who now acted as secretary as well as draughtsman; and Alexander Buchan, an artist who was to deal with landscapes and figures. There were also four servants, Peter Briscoe, who had been to Newfoundland with Banks, and young John Roberts, both of them from the Revesby estate, and two black men, Thomas Richmond and George Dorlton.

There was also Dr Solander, of course, though he cannot be described as one of Banks's followers. He was more in the nature of a guest, and his presence should have been explained earlier. Quite early in 1768, when Banks was actively preparing for this prodigious voyage, Lady Monson invited him to dinner; among others she had also invited Solander, who had a considerable acquaintance in London by this time. The conversation turned upon Banks's opportunity of enriching science and becoming famous, and Solander, leaping to his feet, proposed himself as a fellow-adventurer.[6] Nothing could have pleased Banks more: he agreed, at his persuasion the Admiralty agreed, the British Museum agreed, giving Solander leave of absence; and now he was sitting here in Plymouth, waiting for the wind to change.

All these people, as well as Mr Green the astronomer and his suite of one, and the bark's company, ninety-four souls as well as Banks's two dogs, the ship's cat, and a goat that had already been round the world with Wallis, were to fit into a vessel just over a hundred feet long, not all of whose meagre length was usable space by any means. It is difficult to see how they did it at all, even with the Navy's rule of fourteen inches for a hammock and one watch perpetually on deck; it was accomplished however, yet only at the cost of making the people live on top of one another in the promiscuous fashion usual in the heavily manned ships of the Royal Navy. But in this case the promiscuity was even worse, for even the most favoured, even the captain himself, had to share the great cabin, and not only with Banks and Solander but also with those of the draughtsmen who happened to be working on any of the innumerable forms of life that could be collected on land, skimmed from the surface of the sea, fished up from its depths, or shot down from the air. This cabin was about fifteen feet by twenty, and ordinarily it would have been kept strictly for the captain, with a sentry at the door to guard his invaluable privacy.

Seamen learn very early that discord in a confined space can soon reach horrible proportions and they put up with their shipmates' little ways remarkably well; but a considerable proportion of the *Endeavour*'s people had none of this long training in forbearance, and it is not the least of the many wonders in this very long, very crowded voyage that no one murdered any of his companions.

It was not that the bark was manned by saints: far from it, indeed. Cook, though fairly mild by contemporary standards, quite often had to flog his men for drunkenness and, in Tahiti, for stealing the nails that would purchase fornication; some of the officers were perfectly willing to shoot hostile natives, using the lethal ball rather than small-shot; and the midshipmen were rough by any standard. Orton, the captain's clerk, messed with them, and one day when the ship was off the east coast of Australia and he, being apt to drink, was lying in an alcoholic coma, they cut the clothes off his back and then cropped his ears. It is little wonder that Gilbert White, writing to Pennant not long after Banks's departure, should say, "When I reflect on the youth and affluence of this enterprising Gent: I am filled with wonder to see how conspicuously the contempt of danger, & the love of excelling in his favourite studies stand forth in his character. And tho' I admire his resolution which scorns to stoop to any difficulties: I cannot divest myself of some degree of solicitude for his person."

Rough the people were and comfortless their dwelling, yet upon the whole the *Endeavour* was a happy ship. Almost all the credit for this obviously lies with Cook: although he was a taut captain his officers and men liked him so much that they stayed with him – familiar names are found again and again in his later voyages. Yet the curious sweetness of Banks's character that his tutor had recognized at Eton and the social talents that had already made Solander so popular in London must have had some share in the matter, if only because they did not send an exasperated captain out on deck, seeking whom he might devour.

It would be a very wild exaggeration to say that no cross words were ever uttered during the *Endeavour*'s three years' circumnavigation, yet apart from a disagreement between Banks and the surgeon over a girl in Tahiti and a somewhat acid remark about turtling on the Great Barrier Reef ("Myself went turtling in hopes to have loaded our long boat, but by a most unaccountable conduct of the officer not one turtle was taken") there is no trace of them in Banks's journal.

This journal has many points in common with the one he kept in Newfoundland; there is the same firm attitude towards spelling, capital letters and punctuation, the same objectivity, and, showing through the whole, the same true devotion to natural philosophy. Naturally it is a very much longer book, something in the nature of 250,000 words filling two fat quarto volumes; and in the course of it one can see the author maturing. He did become a truly remarkable letter-writer in later years, and there are passages, particularly when he pauses for reflection, that foreshadow his manner at its best. It is an exceedingly valuable day-by-day account of the *Endeavour*'s voyage, and it is necessarily a portrait of Banks, though at a certain remove; it also has the great virtue of immediacy, and no one has ever questioned its perfect truth. Yet it has its drawbacks. The journal is not unlike one of Alice's books "with no pictures and no conversation": Banks was as it were a voyaging eye, and this eye was turned perpetually outwards. He no doubt had an inner life, but he almost never mentions it, and the book is even more objective than the earlier one: in Newfoundland Phipps possessed a certain being: he was at least devoured by mosquitoes. Banks's shipmates in the *Endeavour* are scarcely mentioned; even his close friend Solander (always referred to as Dr Solander or the Doctor) is but a faint ghost, and Cook is scarcely more substantial. And William Green the astronomer, whom Banks must have seen every day on that exiguous quarterdeck for more than two years, might not have existed until he died in Java. It was the same with the others, officers and men; yet Banks liked them and was liked by them. In some ways dogs are even more intimate companions, particularly on a voyage; but it is not until quite late in the journal that Banks happens to refer to his greyhound, while the bitch Lady who slept on a stool in his cabin is never mentioned at all until her sudden fatal seizure only a week from home, though it would have been strange if they had not walked about with him in every land they visited. Some of this reticence arose from the fact that the journal was not a private diary but a record meant to be read by others. His sister would copy it as she had copied his others; it would circulate among his friends, and Phipps would have an example for his splendid nautical library. Yet it is perhaps allowable to wish that Banks had been a little less reserved – that he had occasionally been a little more domestic as it were, speaking of their daily life at sea, the dinners he and his shipmates must have shared, and giving us something of their conversations, characters and amusements.

The journal itself, the original version written by Banks, is in the Mitchell Library in New South Wales, and in 1962 it was edited with the most scrupulous scholarship and copious notes by Dr J. C. Beaglehole of the Victoria University of Wellington, the same gentleman who edited Cook's journals in four volumes and a portfolio, published by the Hakluyt Society in 1955, upon which I have also drawn. The *Endeavour* journal was handsomely brought out in two illustrated volumes by the Public Library of New South Wales in association with Angus and Robertson as the first part of the State's memorial to Sir Joseph Banks, and it is with their permission that I make the following extracts.

My plan is to give the entries just as Banks wrote them, leaving his scientific nomenclature and his rendering of Polynesian words as they stand, keeping notes to the minimum. Obviously some connecting material must be supplied – much more than in the case of the Newfoundland journal – and from time to time it may be as well to quote from Cook's own account to show particular incidents from another point of view, but otherwise the essence of the two following chapters is pure Banks.

August 1768 Plymouth

25 After having waited in this place ten days, the ship, and everything belonging to me, being all that time in perfect readyness to sail at a moments warning, we at last got a fair wind, and this day at 3 O'Clock in the even weigd anchor, and set sail, all in excellent health and spirits perfectly prepard (in Mind at least) to undergo with Cheerfullness any fatigues or dangers that may occur in our intended Voyage.

26 Wind still fair, but very light breezes; saw this Even a shoal of those fish which are particularly calld *Porpoises* by the seamen, probably the *Delphinus Phocaena* of Linnaeus, as their noses are very blunt.

27 Wind fair and a fine Breeze; found the ship to be but a heavy sailer, indeed we could not Expect her to be any other from her built, so are obligd to set down with this Inconvenience, as a necessary consequence of her form; which is more calculated for stowage, than for sailing.

28 Little wind today; in some sea water, which was taken on board to season a cask, observed a very minute sea Insect, which Dr Solander describd by the name of *Podura marina*. In the Evening very calm; with the small casting net took several specimens of *Medusa Pelagica*, whose different motions in swimming amus'd us very much: among the appendages to this animal we found also a new species of *oniscus*. We also took another animal, quite different from any we have Ever seen; it was of an angular figure, about 3 inches long and one thick, with a hollow passing quite through it. On one end was a Brown spot, which might be the stomach of the animal.

Four of these, the whole number that we took, adherd together when taken by their sides; so that at first we imagind them to be one animal, but upon being put into a glass of water they very soon separated and swam briskly about the water.

29 Wind foul: Morning employd in finishing the Drawings of the animals taken yesterday till the ship got so much motion that Mr Parkinson could not set to his pencil; in the Evening wind still Fresher so much as to make the night very uncomfortable.

30 Wind still foul, ship in violent motion, but towards Evening much more quiet: Now for the first time my Sea sickness left me, and I was sufficiently well to write.

31 Wind Freshend again this morn; observ'd about the Ship several of the Birds calld by the seamen Mother Careys chickens, *Procellaria Pelagica* Linn. which were thought by them to be a sure presage of a storm, as indeed it provd, for before night it blew so hard as to bring us under our Courses,* and make me very sea sick again.

But this was not to last; they had almost crossed the Bay of Biscay, and

* Foresail, mainsail and mizen.

early in September they passed Cape Finisterre, sailing into calm seas that among many other things provided a salp, a creature not unlike a mollusc, which "was possest of more beautiful Colouring than any thing in nature I have ever seen, hardly excepting gemms. He is of a new genus and calld   of which we took another species who had no beauty to boast, but this which we called *opalinum* shone in the water with all the splendor and variety of colours that we observe in a real opal; he livd in the Glass of salt water in which he was put for examination several hours; darting about with great agility, and at every motion shewing an almost infinite variety of changeable colours. Towards the evening of this day a new phaenomenon appeard, the sea was almost coverd with a small species of Crabbs *Cancer depurator* of Linnaeus, floating upon the surface of the water, and moving themselves with tolerable agility, as if the surface of the water and not the bottom was their Proper station."

By this time the bark had settled down into the routine of a long voyage, the Royal Navy's routine; for although the *Endeavour* might not look much like a king's ship she was run in strict man-of-war fashion, as precise in the little bark of which Cook was the commander as ever it had been in sixty-gun line-of-battle ships in which he had been the master, the unchanging pattern of her days and nights punctuated by bells and and bosun's pipes, her upper decks scrubbed and swabbed at dawn, her hammocks piped up at seven bells in the morning watch, hands piped to breakfast at eight bells, lower decks cleaned, and then at midday the ceremony at which all the officers and midshipmen took the sun's altitude and the master reported noon and the latitude to the officer of the watch, whereupon the officer of the watch, stepping across the quarterdeck and taking off his hat, reported it to the captain, who would reply "Make it twelve, Mr —", thus formally and legally beginning the nautical day. Immediately after this eight bells was struck and the hands were piped to dinner, just as they would be piped to supper in the evening and then to quarters; while a little later still hammocks would be piped down, the watch set, and the order of the night would begin. And this very long-established form of communal life was repeated indefinitely: except in times of extreme crisis its groundwork never varied: and it is this continual near-repetition, day after day, more than a thousand entries in the log as the degrees crept by, that gives a sense of the immense length of the *Endeavour*'s voyage – a sense that no abridged account, with its merely factual statement of weeks, months, and years, can give with anything like the same force.

Banks and Solander lived on the periphery of this well-knit traditional community, and they might have had a sad time of it; but sailors are friendly creatures upon the whole, and although Cook was a firm disciplinarian he never made any difficulty about unimportant things: the *Endeavour* carried a longboat, pinnace and yawl, but Banks also had a lighterman's skiff of his own, and he could have it hoisted out whenever the operation did not hold up the ship's progress, and this he did with great profit during the calms that followed until 7 September, when

> The wind was now fair and we went very pleasantly on towards our destined port, tho rather too fast for any natural Enquiries, for my own part I could well dispence* with a much slower pace, but I fancy few in the ship, Dr Solander excepted, are of the same opinion, tho I believe Every body envyed our easy contented countenances during the last Calm, which brought so much food to our pursuits.
>
> 8 Blew fresh today, but the wind was very fair so nobody complaind, nor would they was the wind much stronger, so impatient has the Calms and foul wind made every body; by the reckoning we were off Cape St Vincent so shall soon bid adieu to Europe for some time.
>
> 10 Since the northerly wind began to blow it has not varied a point, the Sea is now down and we go on pleasantly at the rate of about 6 Knotts; could any contrivance be found by the help of which new subjects of natural history could be taken Dr Solander and myself would be Quite happy, we are forc'd to be content; three days are now passd since any thing has been taken or indeed seen, except a stray turtle who swam by the ship about noon, but was left far behind before any instrument could possibly have been got to hand.

On 12 September Madeira came in sight and that night the *Endeavour* anchored in Funchal Bay. As soon as the ship had been given pratique the next morning, Cook, with his usual kindness, sent Banks and Solander ashore; here they were received with equal kindness by the English consul, who provided them with beds, permits, guides, horses and everything necessary for a rapid and determined exploration of the island, an exploration very much helped by the presence of Dr Thomas Heberden, a resident physician, a fellow member of the Royal Society and, though this was not his main interest, something of a botanist (they named *Heberdenia excelsa* after him). They only had five days, and one of these was largely wasted, to their fury, by a courtesy-visit from the Governor, but even so they collected 18 fishes and 246 plants (including cryptogams), in spite of the fact that in September nearly everything but the vines had died down. Banks also had time to make some remarks about the people (exceedingly idle, exceedingly con-

* In the older sense of "deal indulgently with".

servative), the wine (ill made, ill cultivated, and carried on men's heads in goatskins), the friars and their admirable hospital, and the nuns (civil, but wonderfully talkative); yet although he sounds a little censorious and No-Popery, it is clear that he enjoyed himself very much indeed, as well he might, having seen the banana in great abundance, the guava, the pineapple, the cinnamon tree and the mango.

On 18 September they sailed away, the light airs carrying them south and presently allowing them to catch "a most beautifull species of Medusa, of a colour equaling if not exceeding the finest ultramarine; it was described and call'd *Medusa azurea*." Then in 30°7′N, 15°55′W they saw the Dry Salvages; and two days later they were called up very early in the morning to be shown Tenerife a great way off. "While we were engagd in looking at the hill a fish was taken which was describd and called *Scomber serpens*; the seamen said they had never seen such a one before except the first lieutenant, who remembered to have taken one before just about these Islands; Sr Hans Sloane in his Passage out to Jamaica also took one of these fish which he gives a picture of, Vol I, T. 1. f. 2."

Off the Canaries they picked up the north-east trade wind, and on 25 September Banks wrote in his journal:

> Wind continued to blow much as it had done so we were sure we were well in the trade; now for the first time we saw plenty of flying fish, whose beauty especialy when seen from the cabbin windows is beyond imagination, their sides shining like burnished silver; when seen from the Deck they do not appear to such advantage as their backs are then presented to the view, which are dark colour.
>
> 26 Went as usual and as we expect to go these next two months; flying fish are in great plenty about the ship. About one today we crossed the tropic, the night most intolerably hot, the Thermometer standing all night at 78 in the cabbin tho every window was open.

Their expectations were justified; the trade wind bowled the *Endeavour* along towards Brazil at seven knots, a very fine pace for her, and although this put an end to Banks's boating, there were often birds in the rigging and there were always, of course, the traditional sharks. The first of a long series was taken on 29 September:

> About noon a young shark was seen from the Cabbin windows following the ship, who immediately took a bait and was caught on board: he proved to be the *Squalus Charcharias* of Linn and assisted us in clearing up much confusion which almost all authors had made about that species; with him came on board 4 sucking fish, *echineis remora* Linn. who were preserved in spirit. Notwithstanding it was twelve O'Clock before the shark was taken, we

made shift to have part of him stewd for dinner, and very good meat he was, at least in the opinion of Dr Solander and myself, tho some of the Seamen did not seem to be fond of him, probably from some prejudice founded on the species sometimes feeding on human flesh.

Day after day the north-east trade carried them southwards, not leaving them until 3 October, when the *Endeavour* reached latitude 12°14′ and the northern edge of the doldrums, the uncomfortable, oppressive zone of calms and squalls between the north-east and the south-east trades. The zone varies in position and width, and sometimes it was so broad and so windless that ships spent weeks or even months in getting across; this year however it was comparatively narrow – too narrow for Banks's liking, for the doldrums provided him with wonderful opportunities for fishing, collecting and bathing – and they picked up the south-east trade well north of the equator on 17 October. A fine brisk breeze, but it brought a certain amount of unhappiness: in the first place Banks "trying as I have often (foolishly no doubt) done to exercise myself by playing tricks with two ropes in the Cabbin I got a fall which hurt me a good deal and alarmed me more, as the blow was on my head, and two hours after it I was taken with sickness at my stomach which made me fear some ill consequence." He survived however and on 20 October he could write "Quite well today, employd in describing and attending the Draughtsmen." But only the next day "the cat killed our bird *M.Avida* [a wagtail that had been captured in the rigging] who had lived with us ever since the 29th of Septr intirely on the flies which he caught for himself; he was hearty and in high health so that probably he might have livd a great while longer had fate been more kind." And then the day after that "Trade had got more to the Southward than it usually has been, which was unlucky for me as I proposed to the Captain to touch for part of a day at least at the Island of Ferdinand Norronha, which he had no objection to if we could fetch it: that however seemd very uncertain." Uncertain it was, alas, and the island had to wait for Darwin sixty-four years later; but there were whales, and there was the equator, which they cut on 25 October, with the usual ceremonies. Those who had not crossed before were required either to submit to being ducked three times from the yardarm or to pay a forfeit in rum or wine; Cook, Banks and Solander paid up, but a score of men and boys were dipped. All this was very cheerful and in the purest tradition, but what was a little unusual was that the names of the dogs and cat were down in the list. Banks may have compounded for his dogs, a greyhound and a nondescript bitch, but whether the cat paid or submitted does not appear.

South of the equator they sailed into a wonderfully luminous sea, luminous in itself and luminous in its inhabitants – luminous jellyfish, luminous crabs, luminous barnacles, several of which they caught, finding them to their delight to be new species and even new genera. Southward still day after day, and Cook knew very well that the coast of Brazil lay no great way to the westward; he had no chronometer to fix his longitude, but in Dr Maskelyne's recently completed lunar tables he had the next best thing, and he was one of the earliest scientific navigators to sail with them. Indeed, as Banks recorded on 8 November:

> At day break today we made the Land which Provd to be the Continent of S. America in Lat. 21.16; about ten we saw a fishing boat who told us that the country we saw belonged to the Captainship of Espirito Santo.
>
> Dr Solander and myself went on board this boat in which were 11 men (9 of whom were blacks) who all fished with lines. We bought of them the cheif part of their cargo consisting of Dolphins, two kinds of large Pelagick Scombers, Sea Bream and the fish calld in the West Indies Welshman, for which they made us pay 19 shillings and Sixpence. [It was enough for the whole ship's company.]
>
> Soon after we came on board [*Endeavour*] a Sphynx* was taken which proved to be quite a new one, and a small bird also who was the *Tanagra Jacarini* of Linn; it seemd however from Linnaeus's description as well as Edwards's and Brisson's that neither of them had seen the Bird which was in reality a *Loxia nitens*.

Now with varying breezes Cook took the *Endeavour* down the coast until 13 November, when "This Morn the Harbour of Rio Janeiro was right ahead about 2 leagues off."

As Banks said in a letter he wrote to Lord Morton, the President of the Royal Society, "On the 13th of this Month we arrivd here having saild up the river with a very light breeze and amusd ourselves with observing the shore on each side coverd with Palm trees a production which neither Dr Solander or myself had before seen and from which as well as every thing else which we saw promis'd ourselves the highest satisfaction." But their promises were fallacious; with all the delights of a new flora and a new fauna within their reach they met with little but the bitterest frustration. It has been said that the Portuguese viceroy did not believe the *Endeavour* was a king's ship, and that he supposed she was some kind of a pirate or smuggler; at all events he forbade anyone but the captain and the hands needed for watering and victualling to go ashore. Cook told him that the bark had to be given a heel to clean her

* A hawk-moth.

sides and that it would be very unpleasant for people to live aboard in such conditions, and he reminded him of his predecessor's traditionally kind and helpful reception of Byron in the *Dolphin* only a few years before; but neither this nor the repeated memorials that Cook and Banks sent his Excellency had any effect. The ship might victual and water, but her people were not to go ashore; and guards were placed to enforce the order.

"Your lordship", said Banks in another part of his letter, "can more easily imagine our situation than I can describe it all that we so ardently wishd to examine was in our sight we could almost but not quite touch them never before had I an adequate Idea of Tantalus's punishment but I have sufferd it with all possible aggravations three weeks have I staid aboard the ship regardless of every inconvenience of her being heeld down &c. &c. which on any other occasion would have been no small hardships but small evils are totaly swallowd up in the Larger bodily pain bears no comparison to pure in short the torments of the damnd must be very severe indeed as doubtless my present ones Cannot nearly Equal them."

In spite of the very real danger of violence and imprisonment if nothing worse, Banks or his servants did in fact slip ashore occasionally and collect for a few hours, and he was able to botanize among the fodder brought for the livestock and the greenstuff brought for the bark's company; but his list did not amount to more than about three hundred plants – very miserable poverty indeed when compared with the prodigious wealth only a few hundred yards away.

It is pleasant to know that on 7 December, when the *Endeavour* sailed and when they were at last free of the viceroy and his troublesome guardboat, they "immediately resolved to go ashore on one of the Islands in the mouth of the harbour; their ran a great swell but we made shift to land on one called Raza, on which we gatherd many species of Plants and some insects. *Alstromeria salsilla* was here in tolerable plenty and *Amaryllis mexicana*, they were the most specious plants; we stayed till about 4 oClock and then came aboard the ship heartily tired, for the desire of doing as much as we could in a short time had made us all exert ourselves in a particular manner tho exposd to the hottest rays of the sun just at noonday."

This entry is followed by a long, conscientious but understandably jaundiced account of Rio gathered from those who like Monkhouse the surgeon were allowed to visit the town, but then Banks's energy seems to have dwindled; as the *Endeavour* sailed into the cooler seas south of the tropic of Capricorn his journal amounted to little more than a couple of lines a day, generally saying that the wind was fair, sometimes that it was foul.

> December 17 Wind foul, blew rather fresh, so the ship heeld much which made our affairs go on rather uncomfortably.
> 18 Calm at night, wind to the northward; we began to feel ourselves rather cool tho the thermometer was at 76 and shut two of the Cabbin windows, all of which have been open ever since we left Madeira.
> 22 This morn quite calm. [Pilot whales appeared] When they were gone Dr Solander and myself went out in the boat and shot one species of Mother Careys chickens and two shearwaters, both proved new, *Procellaria Gigantea* and *sandaliata*. The Carey was one but ill described by Linnaeus, *Procellaria fregata*. While we were out the people were employed in bending the new set of sails for Cape Horn.
> 25 Christmas day; all good Christians that is to say all hands got abominably drunk so that at night there was scarce a sober man in the ship, wind thank God very moderate or the lord knows what would have become of us.

By that time the *Endeavour* was well down in the South Atlantic, in cold waters immensely rich in all forms of life from plankton to whales, and now they began to see much greater numbers of birds, petrels of many, many kinds, shearwaters, albatrosses of several species: for in the new year they were coming into a new world entirely.

> January 1769
> 1 New years day today made us pass many Compts, and talk much of our hopes for success in the year 69. Many whales were about the ship today and much sea weed in large lumps but none near enough to be caught.
>
> In the Evening rather squally; the true sea green colour upon the surface of the water was often to be seen now between the squalls, or rather under the black clouds when they were about half a mile from the ship. I had often heard of it before but never seen it in any such perfection, indeed most of the seamen said the same, it was very bright and perfectly like the stone calld aquamarine.

They paid for their pretty sea, however: they were in the latitude of the Falklands at this point (indeed, Banks hoped they might land there) and the wind began to blow strong and cold – their first real touch of antarctic weather with its enormous gales and monstrous seas. Magellan jackets made of thick wool were served out to all hands, and Banks put on thick trousers and a flannel jacket and waistcoat. Seals and penguins appeared, and Banks thought it probable that he had seen a black bird described by Linnaeus as *Procellaria aequinoctialis*, but he could not quite make out the colour of its bill. Everyone was agreed that "the ship during this gale has shewn her excellence in laying too remarkably well, shipping scarce any water tho it blew at times vastly strong; the seamen in general say that they never knew a ship lay too so well as this does, so lively and at the same time so easy."

For the next few days the weather was kinder; the *Endeavour* sailed south among seals, albatrosses, dolphins and diving petrels, and then Banks wrote in his journal

> 11 This morn at day break saw the land of Tierra del Fuego, by 8 O'Clock we were well in with it, the weather exceedingly moderate. Its appearance was not near so barren as the writer of Ld Ansons voyage has represented it, the weather exceedingly moderate so we stood along shore about 2 leagues off, we could see trees distinctly through our glasses and observe several smokes made probably by the natives as a signal to us. The captain now resolved to put in here if he can find a convenient harbour and give us an opportunity of searching a country so intirely new.

Because of foul winds and the furious tides that drove the ship out of the strait Le Maire between Staten Island and Tierra del Fuego three times, this could not be done until 14 January, when Banks and Solander went ashore for four hours while Cook stood on and off, there being no holding ground for an anchor. They found about a hundred plants, all of them "new and intirely different from what either of us had before seen", as well as the antiscorbutic Winter's bark, wild celery and scurvy grass. But the next day was much better; they anchored in the Bay of Good Success after dinner and made contact with the timid but quite amiable natives: "Dr Solander and myself then walked forward 100 yards before the rest and two of the Indians advanc'd also and set themselves down about 50 yards from their companions. As soon as we came up they rose and each of them threw a stick he had in his hand away from him and us, as a token no doubt of peace, they then walked briskly towards the other party and wavd to us to follow, which we did and were receivd with many uncouth signs of friendship. We distributed among them a number of Beads and ribbands which we had brought ashore for that purpose at which they seem'd mightily pleased." The journal goes on:

> 16 This morn very early Dr Solander and myself with our servants and two Seamen to assist in carrying baggage, accompanied by Msrs Monkhouse and Green, set out from the ship to try to penetrate into the countrey as far as we could, and if possible gain the tops of the hills where alone we saw places not overgrown with trees. We began to enter the woods at a small sandy beach a little to the westward of the watering place and continued

pressing through pathless thickets, always going up hill, till 3 o'Clock before we gained even a near view of the places we intended to go to. The weather had all this time been vastly fine much like a sunshiny day in May, so that neither heat nor cold was troublesome to us nor were there any insects to molest us, which made me think the travelling much better than what I had before met with in Newfoundland.

Soon after we saw the plains we arrived at them, but found to our great disappointment that what we took for swathe was no better than low bushes of birch about reaching a mans middle; these were so stubborn that they could not be bent out of the way, but at every step the leg must be lifted over them and on being plac'd again on the ground was almost sure to sink above the anckles in bog. No travelling could possibly be worse than this which seemd to last about a mile, beyond which we expected to meet with bare rock, for such had we seen from the tops of lower hills as we came: this I particularly was infinitely eager to arrive at expecting there to find the alpine plants of a countrey so curious. Our people tho rather fatigued were yet in good spirits so we pushd on intending to rest ourselves as soon as we should arrive at plain ground.

We proceeded two thirds of the way without the least difficulty and I confess I thought for my part that all difficulties were surmounted when Mr Buchan fell into a fit. A fire was immediately lit for him and with him all those who were most tird remained behind, while Dr Solander Mr Green Mr Monkhouse and myself advancd for the alp which we reachd almost immediately, and found according to expectation plants which answerd to those we had found before as alpine ones in Europe do to those which we find in the plains.

The air was here very cold and we had frequent snow blasts. I had now intirely given over all thoughts of reaching the ship that night and thought of nothing but getting into the thick of the wood and making a fire, which as our road lay all down hill seemd very easy to accomplish, so Msrs Green and Monkhouse returnd to the people and appointed a hill for our general rendezvous from whence we should proceed and build our wigwam. The cold now increasd apace, it might be near 8 O'Clock tho yet exceedingly good daylight so we proceeded for the nearest valley, where the short Birch, the only thing we now dreaded, could not be ½ a mile over. Our people seemd well despite the cold and Mr Buchan was stronger than we could have expected. I undertook to bring up the rear and see that no one was left behind. We passd about half way very well when the cold seemd to have at once an effect infinitely beyond what I have ever experienced. Dr Solander was the first who felt it, he said he could not go any farther but must lay down, tho the ground was coverd with snow, and down he laid notwithstanding all I could say to the contrary. Richmond a black Servant now began also to lag and was much in the same way as the dr: at this Juncture I dispatched 5 forwards of whom Mr Buchan was one to make ready a fire at the very first convenient place they could find, while myself with 4 more staid behind to persuade if possible the dr and Richmond to come on. With much persuasion and intreaty we got through much the largest part of the Birch when they both gave out; Richmond said that he could not go any further and when told that if he did not he must be Froze to death only answerd that there he would lay and dye; the Dr on the contrary said that he must sleep a little before he could go on and actually did full a quarter of an hour, at which time we had the welcome news of a fire being lit about a quarter of a mile ahead. I then undertook to make the Dr Proceed to it; finding it impossible to make Richmond stir left two hands with him who seemd the least affected with Cold, promising to send two to releive them as soon as I should reach the fire. With much difficulty I got the Dr to it and as soon as two people were sufficiently warmd sent them out in hopes that they would bring Richmond and the rest; after staying about half an hour they returnd bringing word that they had been all round the place shouting and hallowing but could not get any answer. We now guess'd the cause of the mischeif, a bottle of rum the whole of our stock was missing, and we soon concluded that it was in one of their Knapsacks and that the two who were left in health had drunk immoderately of it and had slept like the other.

For two hours now it had snowd almost incessantly so we had little hopes of seeing any of the three alive: about 12 however to our great Joy we heard a shouting, on which myself and 4 more went out immediately and found it to be the seaman who had wakd almost starvd to death and come a little way from where he lay. Him I sent back to the fire and proceeded by his direction to find the other two, Richmond was upon his leggs but not able to walk the other lay on the ground as insensible as a stone. We immediately calld all hands from the fire and attempted by all the means we could contrive to bring them down but finding it absolutely impossible, the road was so bad and the night so dark that we could scarcely ourselves get on nor did we without many Falls. We would then have lit a fire upon the spot but the snow on the ground as well as that which continually fell renderd that as impracticable as the other, and to bring fire from the other place was also impossible from the quantity of snow which fell every moment from the branches of the trees; so we were forc'd to content ourselves with laying out our unfortunate companions upon a bed of boughs and covering them over with boughs also as thick as we were able, and thus we left them hopeless of ever seeing them again alive which indeed we never did.

In these employments we had spent an hour and a half expos'd to the most penetrating cold I ever felt as well as continual snow. Peter Briscoe, another servant of mine, now began to complain and before we came to the fire became very ill but got there at last almost dead with cold.

Now might our situation truely be calld terrible: of twelve our original number were 2 already past all hopes, one more was so ill that tho he was with us I had little hopes of his being able to walk in the morning, and another very likely to relapse into his fitts either before we set out or in the course of our journey: we were distant from the ship we did not know how far, we knew only that we had been the greatest part of a day in walking it through pathless woods: provision we had none but one vulture which had been shot while we were out, and at the shortest allowance could not furnish half a meal: and to compleat our misfortunes we were caught in a snow storm in a climate we were utterly unacquainted with but which we had reason to beleive was as inhospitable as any in the world, not only from all the accounts we had read or heard but from the Quantity of snow which we saw falling, tho it was very little after midsummer: a circumstance unheard of in Europe for even in Norway or Lapland snow is never known to fall in the summer.

17 The Morning now dawnd and shewd us the earth coverd with snow as well as all the tops of the trees, nor were the snow squalls at all less Frequent for seldom many minutes were fair together; we had no hopes now but of staying here as long as the snow lasted and how long that would be God alone knew.

About 6 O'Clock the sun came out a little and we immediately thought of sending to see whether the poor wretches we had been so anzious about last night were yet alive, three of our people went but soon returnd with the melancholy news of their being both dead. The snow continued to fall tho not quite so thick as it had done; about 8 a small breeze of wind sprung up and with the additional power of the sun began (to our great Joy) to clear the air, and soon after we saw the snow begin to fall from the tops of the trees, a sure sign of an approaching thaw. Peter continued very ill but said he thought himself able to walk. Mr Buchan thank god was much better than I could have expected, so we agreed to dress our vulture and prepare ourselves to set out for the ship as soon as the snow should be a little more gone off so he was skinnd and cut into ten equal shares, each man cooking his own share which furnished about 3 mouthfulls of hot meat, all the refreshment we had had since our cold dinner yesterday and all we were to expect till we could come to the ship.

About ten we set out and after a march of about 3 hours arrivd at the beach, fortunate in having met with much better roads in our return than we did in going out, as well as in being nearer to the ship than we had any reason to hope; for on reviewing our track as well as we could from the ship we found that we had made a half circle round the hills, instead of penetrating as we thought we had done into the inner part of the countrey. With what pleasure then did we congratulate each other on our safety no one can tell who has not been in such circumstances.

It scarcely seems believable that later the same day Banks, "considering our short Stay & the Uncertainty of the weather" as the master put it in his journal, asked for a boat in order to haul the seine, or that two days later, after some very heavy weather and a good deal more snow, both he and Solander should have gone ashore to collect shells and plants and to visit an Indian settlement, inquiring as closely as they could into the Fuegian way of life; but such is the case.

On 21 January the *Endeavour* sailed, having completed her water at Good Success Bay, and four days later she was probably off the Horn in moderate weather, but too foggy for them to be certain of the Cape. Cook made sure that he was clear of the land by keeping to his south-westerly course day after day, until by the end of the month they reached sixty degrees of south latitude: and here, in seventy-five degrees of longitude west of Greenwich, with plenty of sea-room all round him, Cook shaped his general north-west course for Tahiti.

Something in the nature of four thousand miles lay between this point and the island on which he was to observe the transit of Venus: four thousand miles that is to say in a straight line, which no ship dependent upon wind could possibly hope to follow. These were largely unknown waters, for although by this time about a dozen sailors had taken their ships round the world and although Cook and Banks between them possessed either these captains' own accounts or Charles de Brosses' or Harris's or Alexander Dalrymple's versions of them (Dalrymple, in spite of his feeling of ill-usage, had handsomely given Banks his printed but as yet unpublished octavo *Account of the Discoveries made in the South Pacifick Ocean previous to 1764* with its valuable chart), vast areas were wholly unknown, the comparatively few reports of winds and currents could not be relied upon as giving a general rule, and since the earlier voyagers had travelled without chronometers or accurate tables of lunar distance, they could not lay down the longitude of the various islands and reefs they had seen with any accuracy. Obviously the *Endeavour* had to proceed with caution; though on the other hand she must not be late for the transit, and if at all possible she should be there a month or so before to prepare the observatory. The bark was slow; she might meet with calms or with headwinds; clearly there was not a moment to be lost. Yet it was equally clear that there was no room for excessive zeal, for in this part of the world there were no marine stores to be had, no sailcloth, no cordage, no spars to replace those broken or worn out.

These problems were Cook's own particular province. Banks had no part in them whatsoever: he was mildly concerned to show that the theoretical southern continent, Brosses' Australasia, did in fact exist, but he was very much more interested, passionately interested, in the various forms of animal and vegetable life that were to be seen on the way to Tahiti and then south and west, perhaps to the Terra Australis Incognita.

In the early days of this voyage in the Pacific, when the *Endeavour* was still in the rich waters of the far south or in the broad Humboldt current, so cold that it carries seals and penguins right up the coast of Peru and as far as the Galapagos, there were still a great many birds, above all petrels and albatrosses; and whenever the weather allowed Banks went out in his boat and shot them. To those who find the number of birds he killed distressing, it may be some little comfort to know that having been measured, weighed, scientifically described and sometimes drawn they were at least eaten: the entry for 5 February 1769 reads:

> All but calm today: myself a little better than yesterday [he had been bilious], well enough to eat part of the Albatrosses shot on the third, which were so good that every body commended them and Eat heartily of them tho there was fresh pork upon the table. The way of dressing them is thus: Skin them over night and soak their carcases in Salt water till morn, then parboil them and throw away the water, then stew them well with very little water and when sufficiently tender serve them up with a Savoury sauce.

It was quite clear, by the way, that nobody aboard had the least notion of any ill-luck connected with the shooting of an albatross; indeed, over a hundred years later, and well after the *Rime of the Ancient Mariner*, sailors in the high southern latitudes were still catching them, because their "webbed feet make capital tobacco pouches by drawing out all the bone and leaving the claws as ornaments. The wing-bones make excellent pipe stems. The breast, if carefully cured, a warm though somewhat conspicuous muff. The beak, in the hands of a skilled artificer, a handsome paper-clip."[7]

February wore by with mixed weather and this kind of entry: they are given in full:

> 8 Fair wind, blew fresh.
>
> 9 Blew fresh all last night which has given us a good deal of westing. This morn some sea weed floated past the ship and my servant declares that he saw a large beetle fly over her: I do not beleive he would deceive me and he certainly knows what a beetle is, as he has these 3 years been often employd in taking them for me.
>
> 10 During all last night the ship has pitchd very much so that there was no sleeping for land men. Today misty with little wind.
>
> 11 Fair wind, stand to the westward.
>
> 12 Foul wind, but prodigious fine weather and smooth water makes amends to us at least.
>
> 13 Wind still foul and blew fresh, at night a little mended.

14 Wind South, water soon became smooth, at night little wind.
15 Calm this morn: went in the boat and killd *Procellaria velox, Nectris munda* and *fuliginosa*, which two last are a genus between Procellaria and Diomedea: this we reckon a great acquisition to our bird collection. My stay out today was much shortened by a breeze of wind which brought me aboard by 11 o'clock and before night blew very fresh.

So February carried them westwards, week after week, with runs of 48, 59, 36 and 103 miles a day and little to report except on the twenty-fourth when "At 12 last night the wind settled at NE; this morn found studding sails set and the ship going at the rate of 7 knotts, no very usual thing with Mrs Endeavour", while on the twenty-sixth, when they were in latitude 41°8′S and far, far to the west of the Peruvian current, "albatrosses began to be much less plentiful than they had been", and on the last day of the month a large school of killer whales came round the ship.

Banks began March 1769 by pulling off an underwaistcoat, the weather being so fine, and on the third he had a field-day among the birds, killing no fewer than sixty-nine, nearly all of them petrels of one kind or another which, when one considers the relative inefficiency and slowness of the muzzle-loading flintlock fowling-piece of his time, gives some notion of the great numbers that must have been present. He also found "a large *Sepia* cuttle fish laying on the water just dead but so pulled to peices by the birds that his Species could not be determind; only this I know that of him was made one of the best soups I ever eat. He was very large, differd from the Europaeans in that his arms instead of being (like them) furnished with suckers were armd with a double row of very sharp talons, resembling in shape those of a cat and like them retractable into a sheath of skin from whence they might be thrust at pleasure."

Throughout the month the *Endeavour* carried steadily on, nearly always managing to keep her course north-west; the weather grew warmer; tropic birds were reported, and on the thirteenth Banks "saw one for the first time hovering over the ship but flying very high; if my eyes did not deceive me it differd from that describd by Linnaeus, *Phaeton aethereus*, in having the long feathers of his tail red and his crissum black." Tropic birds and sometimes tropical rain; flying-fish; satisfaction with the Tierra del Fuego water, "which now drinks as brisk and pleasant as when first taken on board, or better, for the red colour it had at first is subsided and it is now as clear as any English spring water". So the days passed, a long, long series; and it is reasonable to suppose that Banks and Solander spent much of their time describing and determining their earlier and their present specimens, while the draughtsmen worked away, particularly young Mr Parkinson – there is the physical evidence of these activities. And it is reasonable to suppose from what is implied here and there that at least sometimes they dined cheerfully together. Nowhere does Banks directly say so, however, nor does he mention any of his shipmates except on one occasion. The bark carried a small detachment of marines under a sergeant; one of them, a young fellow, was on sentry duty at the cabin door; inside the cabin one of the captain's servants was about to cut up a sealskin to make tobacco pouches; the sentry asked for one, but was refused; the servant was called away and the marine took a piece of skin. There was a quarrel when the servant returned; but having recovered the piece he said he would not report the theft. Unhappily it came to the sergeant's ears, and he saw fit to be moral about the whole thing – the honour of the corps was concerned and it was the sergeant's duty to inform the officers. At dusk the young man went forward as though to the head, the seamen's lavatory, and dropped into the water: he was not missed until too late.

On 24 March they crossed the tropic of Capricorn again, and a few days later they hooked their first Pacific shark; but he broke their line, and although he soon came back with the hook and chain dangling from his mouth they could not induce him to take the bait.

By the end of the month Banks was feeling poorly; as he thought his symptoms not unlike those of scurvy he took some of Dr Hulme's lemon juice. Cook had hitherto kept his people free of the disease – the horribly prevalent sailors' disease that had so diminished Anson's and Byron's crews in these same waters – by inducing them to eat sauerkraut and drink a decoction of malt. But in any case, by 2 April land was no great way off. "Many birds about noon passd by the ship making a noise something like gulls, they were black upon the back and white under the belly probably of the sterna kind; in company with them were 20 or 30 Men of war birds soaring over the flock, probably the whole were in pursuit of a shoal of fish." The same shore-based birds were seen the next day, together with the terns seamen call egg-birds; and on 4 April in 18°47′S and 139°28′W, they saw their first South Sea island, an atoll some two miles across. They stood in to within about a mile and with their telescopes they counted twenty-four of its inhabitants, eleven of whom "walkd along the beach abreast of the ship with each a pole or pike as long again as himself in his hand and every one of them stark naked and appearing of a brown copper colour; as soon however as the ship had fairly pass'd the Island they retird higher up on the beach and seemd to put on some cloaths or at least cover themselves with something which made them appear of a light colour. The Island was coverd with trees of many very different verdures; the Palms or Cocoa nut trees we could distinguish particularly two that were amazingly taller than their fellows and at a distance bore a great resemblance to a flag. The land seemd all very low tho at a distance several parts of it appeard high yet when we came near them they proved to be clumps of Palms. Under the shade of these were the houses of the natives in places cleard of all underwood so that pleasanter groves can not be imagind, at least so they appeard to us whose eyes had so long been unus'd to any other objects than water and sky." It was seventy-two days since they had sailed from Tierra del Fuego.

This delectable island was followed by others, for the *Endeavour* was now sailing almost due west through the Tuamotu archipelago. Banks stayed at the masthead the whole evening admiring one of them: "in shape it appeard to be like a bow the wood and string of which was land and the parts within occupied by a large lake of water, which bore about the same proportion to the land as the void space within the bow does to the string and wood. The string of the bow was a flat beach without any signs of vegetation on it but heaps of sea weed laying there in ridges as higher or lower tides had left them; this was 3 or 4 Leagues long and appeard not more than 200 yards wide . . . the Horns or angles of the bow were two large tufts of Cocoa nut trees." By sunset they were halfway along the bow; they sounded, but finding no ground with 130 fathoms they sailed on through the sudden tropical night, steering by the sound of the breakers. More islands appeared in the following days, but they landed on none: "The people on the shore made many signals but whether they meant to frighten us away or invite us ashore is difficult to tell: they waved with their hands and seemd to beckon us to them but they were assembld together with clubs and staves as they would have done had they meant to oppose us." And as Banks observed, it would have been improper to run the risk of having to hurt them: in any case all these coral islands were low and small, whereas Tahiti, volcanic in origin, had mountains rising seven thousand feet and it was about thirty miles long, as all those who had been there with Wallis knew very well. There were several former Dolphins aboard apart from Gore the second lieutenant and Molineux the master; and although they had not stayed long enough to learn much about the country – just over a month – they were perfectly acquainted with its appearance from the sea and with the reef upon which their ship had grounded.

Very high land in the west was what they and the whole bark's company were looking for, high green land covered with trees almost to the mountaintops and laced white with cascading streams, and on 10 April, after a dirty night with the wind in every direction and heavy rain, some people thought they saw it through the haze, twenty-five leagues away. The next day brought "little wind and variable with Squalls from all points of the Compass bringing heavy rain. Georges Island in sight appearing very high in the same direction as the land was seen last night, so I found the fault was in our eyes yesterday tho the non-seers were much more numerous in the ship than the seers." By evening the wind died and "Georges Land appeared plain tho we had not neard it much." Then the journal for 12 April 1769 reads:

12 Very nearly calm all last night, Georges Land was now but a little nearer to us than last night, the tops of the hills were wrap'd in clouds. About 7 a small breeze sprung up and we saw some Canoes coming off to us, by ten or eleven they were up with us. I forbear to say any thing about either people or canoes as I shall have so many better opportunities of observing them: we however bought their cargoes consisting of fruits and cocoa nuts which were very acceptable to us after our long passage.

13 This morn early came to anchor in Port Royal bay King George the third's Island. Before the anchor was down we were surrounded by a large number of Canoes who traded very quietly and civily, for beads cheifly, in exchange for which they gave Cocoa nuts Bread fruit both roasted and raw some small fish and apples . . . As soon as the anchors were well down the boats were hoisted out and we all went ashore where we were met by some hundreds of the inhabitants whose faces at least gave evident signs that we were not unwelcome guests, tho they at first hardly dare approach us, after a little time they became very familiar. The first who approached us came creeping almost on his hands and knees and gave us a green bough the token of peace, this we receivd and immediately each gatherd a green bough and carried it in our hands. They march'd with us about ½ a mile and then made a general stop and scraping the ground clean from the plants that grew upon it every one of the principals threw his bough down upon the bare place and made signs that we should do the same: the marines were drawn up and marching in order dropd each a bough upon those that the Indians had laid down, we all followed their example and thus peace was concluded.

Chapter 4

TAHITI AND THE TRANSIT OF VENUS

IT WOULD NEED a great deal of space and a great deal of specialized learning to give an adequate account of the *Endeavour*'s three-month stay in Tahiti and to describe the disruptive effect of the contact between the very highly organized hierarchical Polynesian society, already much shaken by war, and the far better armed and materially far richer Europeans.

What is proposed here is much less ambitious: a brief account of Tahiti as Banks saw it, and of Banks and his shipmates on that island. His view of this complex society was limited by a total ignorance of the language for the first period and by some misinterpretations and mistaken notions later. (On 14 May 1769, for example, when he had been there for a month, he could still write "We have not yet seen the least traces of religion among these people, maybe they are intirely without it", although as the specialists all agree religion, a sense of the holy, was as present as the air – one has but to consider the innumerable examples of taboo to see how important that aspect of piety was in Polynesia: though to be sure the purely ethical side of religion was less evident.) Then again much of his time was devoted to the flora and fauna. Yet although his account may be wanting in some respects it has the great advantage of being first-hand and unaffected by any preconceptions: the idea of the Noble Savage had of course been current ever since Rousseau's foolish *Discours*, but it does not seem to have had much effect upon Banks. He was a capital observer, cheerful, good-humoured and kind; he liked the Polynesians and he got along remarkably well with them; he had superabundant energy and he seems never to have been troubled by fear at any time.

Some while after he had left the islands he wrote "I found them to be a people so free from deceit that I trusted myself among them almost as freely as I could do in my own countrey, sleeping continualy in their houses in the woods with not so much as a single companion." From their candour he went on to their physical appearance:

> They are of the larger size of Europaeans, all excellently made, and some handsome both men and women, the only bad feature they have is their

noses which are in general flat, but to balance this their teeth are almost without exception even and white to perfection, and the eyes of the women especially are full of expression and fire. In Colour they differ very much: those of inferior rank who are obligd in the excersise of their professions, fishing especialy, to be much exposd to the sun and air are of a dark brown; the superiors again who spend most of their time in their houses under shelter are seldom browner (the women especialy) than that kind of Brunette which many in Europe preferr to the finest red and white. Complezion indeed they seldom have tho some I have seen shew a Blush very manifestly; this is perhaps owing to the thickness of their skins, but that fault is in my opinion well compensated by their infinite smoothness much superior to any thing I have met with in Europe. The men as I have said before are rather large, I have measurd one 6 feet 3; the superior women are also as large as Europaeans but the inferior sort generally small, some very small owing possibly to their early amours which they are much more addicted to than their superiors.

From the earliest days there has been a great deal of talk about the amorous propensities of the Tahitians: indeed Bougainville who was there in 1768, shortly after Wallis, called their island La Nouvelle Cythère; and it has retained its popularity among sailors to the present. Yet the idea of its being a free and general bawdy house was no doubt exaggerated, for although as Banks said in his *Thoughts on the manners of Otaheite*, written later in the voyage, "In the Island of Otaheite where Love is the Chief Occupation, the favourite, nay almost the Sole Luxury of the inhabitants; both the bodies and souls of the women are modeld into the utmost perfection for that soft science idleness the father of Love reigns here in almost unmolested ease, while we Inhabitants of a changeable climate are obligd to Plow, Sow, Harrow, reap, Thrash, Grind Knead and bake our daily bread and Each revolving year again to Plough, sow &c &c" the Tahitian had but to climb the breadfruit tree, "and this Leisure is given up to Love". He nevertheless went on

> Chastity in this Land of Liberty is Esteemed as a virtue, those who possess it are respected on that account; they say, we esteem that woman because she is chaste, as we say, we esteem her because she is charitable, yet the want of Chastity does not preclude a woman from the esteem of those who have it, no more than the want of Charity in this countrey: the consequence of this is, that the proportion of Chaste women there is much smaller than here, where the punishments bestow'd on a breach of it are so severe; yet there are women there as inviolable in their attachments as here a virtue which is probably the necessary consequence of mutual and sincere love.

It was not the want of a kind welcome that caused the trouble between the *Endeavour*'s people and the Tahitians, nor was it any repulsive reserve on the part of the young women or illiberal jealousy on the part of the men, but theft.

By the standard of the islanders the three ships that had come to Tahiti, Wallis's *Dolphin*, Bougainville's *La Boudeuse* and the *Endeavour*, were floating treasure-houses, inconceivably wealthy. The Tierra del Fuegians, on being shown the *Endeavour*, expressed no particular surprise and showed little interest in what they saw: they lived almost naked in a bitterly cold, wet and blowing climate (Darwin saw one who possessed only a single piece of fur, which he shifted according to the wind and the rain or snow) and their imaginations were stunted, limited to what food was available, coarse shellfish, dead seals, damp fungi. The Tahitians on the other hand, well fed and used to the finest weather in the world, were filled with astonishment: they admired, they coveted, they stole.

They stole with quite remarkable skill, and straightaway – the very first time Bougainville came ashore and dined with a chief one of his officers had his pocket picked – which is curious, since theft did not seem at all usual among them. Their houses were quite open and nothing was shut away; and it was not that there was nothing to take, for some forms of cloth and the red feathers of the tropic bird were highly valued. But nothing the island produced could remotely compare with the wealth of the ships. It is impossible to exaggerate the value of iron and steel to a highly ingenious seafaring people, great canoe-makers, fond of carving and shaping wood, who had hitherto been obliged to rely upon stone adzes, shells and sharks' teeth. To them even a common tumbler would be as splendid as hollowed rock-crystal, and a blue glass bead would give as much delight as a sapphire or more, while a plain piece of paper was always sure to please; but it was metal that attracted them most, not only and perhaps not mainly for its use in daily life but also because it was so very much more deadly than their own slings and spears and hardwood skull-splitters – they were much given to warfare.

They knew that theft, particularly the theft of weapons, was much resented, and that the Europeans were dangerous. Wallis had turned the *Dolphin*'s great guns upon them with terrifying effect, yet the first thing they stole when Bougainville arrived was a pistol, and the first real trouble during the *Endeavour*'s visit was caused by an islander snatching a sentry's musket at the watering-place and running off with it. The marines fired into the flying crowd, then pursued the man and killed him.

This was on 15 April and up until then all had been going well. Cook, Banks and Solander had been received in the friendliest way, one chief giving them presents of cloth and poultry (Banks responded with "a large lacd silk neckcloth I had on and a linnen pocket handkerchief") and another chief a mile along the strand gave them dinner in a large and crowded house.

> The adventures of this entertainment I much wish to record particularly, but am so much hurried by attending the Indians ashore almost all day long that I fear I shall scarce understand my own language when I read it again.
>
> Our cheifs own wife (ugly enough in conscience) did me the honour with very little invitation to squat down on the mats close by me: no sooner had she done so than I espied among the common croud a very pretty girl with a fire in her eyes that I had not before seen in the countrey. Unconscious of the dignity of my companion I beckend to the other who after some intreatys came and sat on the other side of me: I was then desirous of getting rid of my former companion so I ceas'd to attend to her and loaded my pretty girl with beads and every present I could think pleasing to her: the other shewd much disgust but did not quit her place and continued to supply me with fish and cocoa nut milk. How this would have ended is hard to say, it was interupted by an accident which gave us an opportunity of seeing much of the peoples manners. Dr Solander and another gentleman who had not been in as good company as myself found that their pockets had been pickd, one had lost a snuff box the other an opera glass.

The things were recovered after a while, a woman "bringing the glass in her hand with a vast expression of joy on her countenance, for few faces have I seen which have more expression in them than those of these people", and all ended happily; but the taking of the musket the next day and its consequences was an infinitely graver matter, and in an entry typical of Banks he says "we retird to the ship not well pleased with the days expedition, guilty no doubt in some measure of the death of a man who the most severe laws of equity would not have condemned to so severe a punishment."

The next day poor Buchan, the figure and landscape painter, had another fit; this one killed him, and at Banks's suggestion (the temper and the customs of the island being unknown) he was buried at sea – a wise precaution, particularly at this present juncture. The formerly crowded shore was now almost deserted, which argued ill for the attitude of the Tahitians as a whole; and those few the *Endeavour*'s people saw when they landed "were rather shy of us".

The future was uncertain; the prospect of carrying out the observation of Venus and of victualling the bark in the face of universal hostility cannot have been at all agreeable; and when, against all likelihood, the two chiefs from westward along the strand came to pay a visit, each bringing a present of breadfruit and a pig, they were most heartily welcome. (Banks had not yet been able to make out the chiefs' names: he called the first Lycurgus, the name having some dim association in his mind with the execution of justice, and the other Hercules, for obvious reasons.)

There seemed to be a general agreement that the man who took the musket had brought his fate upon his own head, and from now onwards relations with the islanders returned to their former easy, friendly state. The captain and his people went ashore to trace the lines of an encampment, and Cook spent the night there in a tent, he and Green the astronomer observing the eclipse of one of Jupiter's moons.

The encampment was to be fortified and the next day all hands set to. The islanders helped them carry the wood they cut to support their rampart, and also brought so much food that buying had to stop: the rate was four or six breadfruit or coconuts for one pea-sized bead.

The settlement was soon in being, and it was a sociable life that Banks and the others led there in their tents; friends often came to see them, generally bringing presents; and since the Tahitians were acutely aware of differences of rank, most of those who visited Banks and the officers were arii, people of chiefly families. It was a singularly interesting life too, with innumerable new things to see, a fresh and very agreeable language, with no declensions, to learn, and an abundance of female company, so rare at sea. Yet it was not quite ideal. There was a little much rain for an earthly paradise, and the flies were so troublesome that poor Parkinson had to be confined in mosquito-netting that also covered his chair and table: ". . . but even that was not sufficient, a fly trap was necessary to set within this to attract the vermin from eating the colours. For that purpose yesterday tarr and molasses was mixt together but it did not succeed." Then again there was the islanders' perpetual acquisitiveness.

> April 25 I do not know by what accident I have so long omitted to mention how much these people are given to theiving. I will make up for my neglect however today by saying that great and small cheifs and common men all are firmly of opinion that if they can once get possession of any thing it immediately becomes their own. This we were convinced of the very second day we were here, the cheifs were employd in stealing what they could in the Cabbin while their dependants took every thing that was loose about the ship, even the glass ports not escaping them of which they got off with 2. Lycurgus and Hercules were the only two who had not yet been found

> guilty, but they stood in our opinion but upon ticklish ground as we could not well suppose them intirely free from a vice their countrey men were so much given up to.

Here however Banks was mistaken. He could not find his knife: he accused Lycurgus: Lycurgus denied it, went to Banks's tent, and there one of Banks's servants, seeing him search for the knife, produced it – it was the servant who had happened to put it out of the way.

> Lycurgus then burst into tears making signs with my knife that if he was ever guilty of such an action he would submit to have his throat cut. He returned immediately to me with a countenance sufficiently upbraiding me for my suspicions; the scene was immediately changd, I became the guilty and he the innocent person, his looks affected me much.

In any case the thefts were not all on one side: not only had Wallis taken possession of the entire island and its dependencies, which brings to mind the remark about the relative guilt of the man who steals a goose from off a common and the other who steals the common from under the goose, but the *Endeavour*'s butcher, having failed to buy a stone axe from Tomio,* Lycurgus' wife, for a nail, took it by force and offered to cut her throat with a reaping-hook that he happened to have in his hand. Cook had the man flogged, and Banks brought Tubourai (he had learnt Lycurgus' Tahitian name by now) and Tomio aboard to witness the punishment.

> . . . they stood quietly and saw him stripd and fastned to the rigging but as soon as the first blow was given interferd with many tears, begging the punishment might cease a request which the Captn would not comply with.

It was at this period that Oberea and her chief counsellor Tupia first appeared upon the scene. The *Dolphin*'s people had taken her for the queen of Tahiti, and this was how they described her in England; they were mistaken, and in any case she and her semi-detached husband Oamo had recently been defeated by their enemies from the south-eastern part of the island; but she was still a person of great consequence. She and Oamo had held an office not unlike that of high king in Ireland, only in Tahiti there were three of them, three regions in which a great chief ruled more or less over a number of smaller chiefs: the office passed, at least nominally, to their son very early in his life,

* All the Tahitian personal names and most of the words are given in Banks's version; it rarely agrees with the spelling adopted by modern scholars, and sometimes it is mistaken, but Banks had a good ear and the experts say that he reproduces what he heard with tolerable accuracy. The geographical names however follow the modern usage, so that they can be found on a map.

although obviously at first the authority remained with the regent parents. To begin with Cook and his companions had not appreciated her standing, any more than they now realized the importance of Dootahah, the former Hercules; they could tell the difference between the ordinary people and the chiefs, but the finer distinctions, so important in Tahiti, were unperceived. Oberea was sitting with a number of other visitors in Banks's tent one morning, comparatively unnoticed, when Mr Molineux, the master of the *Endeavour*, walked in: Molineux was of course a former Dolphin and they recognized one another directly.

> Our attention was now intirely diverted from every other object to the examination of a personage we had heard so much spoken of in Europe: she appeard to be about 40, tall and very lusty, her skin white and her eyes full of meaning, she might have been hansome when young but now few or no traces of it were left.
>
> As soon as her majesties quality was known to us she was invited to go on board the ship, where no presents were spard that were thought to be agreeable to her in consideration of the service she had been of to the Dolphin.

The next day Banks was aboard the *Endeavour* to see the butcher flogged.

> On my return ashore I proceeded to pay a visit to her majesty Oberea* as I shall for the future call her. She I was told was still asleep in her Canoe-awning, where I went intending to call up her majesty but was surprizd to find her in bed with a hansome lusty young man of about 25 whose name was Obadee. I however soon understood that he was her gallant a circumstance which she made not the least secret of. Upon my arrival Her majesty proceeded to put on her breeches which done she clothd me in fine cloth and proceeded with me to the tents.

But before the acquaintance could ripen the prime object of the voyage seemed to be compromised: the unique astronomical quadrant, which had been brought ashore on 1 May, was stolen by 2 May, and without it there could be no accurate observation of the transit. It was hoped that the thief would soon throw such an object away, it being so useless to him; but not at all – it was nowhere round the camp.

> I now went into the woods to get intelligence no longer doubting but that it was in the hands of the Indians. Tubourai met me crossing the river and immediately made with 3 straws in his hand the figure of a triangle; the

*At the first mention of Tahitian names Banks usually adds marks to show stress or pronunciation: here they are omitted.

> Indians had opened the cases. No time was now to be lost; I made signs to him that he must instantly go with me to the place where it was, he agreed and out we set accompanied by a midshipman and Mr Green, we went to the Eastward. At every house we went past Tubourai enquird after the theif by name, the people readily told him by which way he had gone and how long ago it was since he pass'd by, a circumstance which gave great hopes of coming up with him. The weather was excessive hot, the Thermometer before we left the tents up at 91 made our journey very tiresome. Sometimes we walk'd sometimes we ran when we imagind (which we sometimes did) that the chase was just before us till we arrivd at the top of a hill about 4 miles from the tents: from this place Tubourai shew'd us a point about 3 miles off and made us understand that we were not to expect the instrument till we got there. We now considerd our situation, no arms among us but a pair of pocket pistols which I always carried, going at least 7 miles from our fort where the Indians might not be quite so submissive as at home, going also to take from them a prize for which they had venturd their lives.

The result of the consideration was that they sent the midshipman back "to desire Captn Cooke to send a party of men after us, telling him at the same time that it was impossible we could return till dark night". Banks, Green and Tubourai went on, recovered the quadrant almost entire, together with a horse-pistol belonging to Banks – this in the presence of some hundreds of islanders, who might easily have knocked Banks and Green on the head – and so "pack'd all up in grass as well as we could and proceeded homewards. After walking about 2 miles we met Captn Cooke with a party of marines coming after us, all were as you may imagine not a little pleased at the event of our excursion."

Perhaps it was as well that Cook had not come earlier. His colder, more authoritarian, severer approach might not have answered as well as Banks's youthful confident spontaneity: in this emergency he had already taken the unfortunate step of giving orders that no canoes were to be allowed to leave the bay. Gore, the second lieutenant, went beyond these orders and sent the bosun to bring back some that were moving along the shore. Dootahah was in one; he was probably handled without much ceremony by the bosun and he was certainly confined, "to the infinite dissatisfaction of all the Indians". Banks, arriving before the main party, could do nothing – he had no sort of authority in the naval line – and although Cook released the chief as soon as he came the mischief was done and Dootahah was never cordially friendly again.

The next day Banks and Solander, who were in charge of the trading, waited in vain for provisions to be brought to the encampment; and although Dootahah did invite them and Cook to watch a wrestling match a few days after this, the general resentment continued, and even a week later and twenty miles away hogs were not to be had for love or iron nails "because they belonged to Dootahah". Yet coconuts and breadfruit reappeared fairly soon, and Banks spent his time pleasantly enough, sometimes looking for plants, sometimes in the company of Oberea, her pretty young companion Otheathea (his particular favourite), and Tupia, an interesting, intelligent middle-aged priest who belonged to a chiefly family in the island of Raiatea, from which he had been driven by invaders from Borabora.

It is true that the stealing continued: indeed on one occasion when they had gone to see Dootahah at some distance and when Banks spent the night in Oberea's canoe (these canoes were often big, double-hulled craft with a platform across and a little house upon it) he lost his coat, waistcoat, pistols and powder-horn, though they had been put in Oberea's charge, while Cook lost his stockings and two midshipmen their jackets. However by now they were more or less inured to it, and their loss did not spoil their pleasure in a sight they beheld later that morning.

> In our return to the boat we saw the Indians amuse or exercise themselves in a manner truly surprizing. It was in a place where the shore was not guarded by a reef as is usualy the case, consequently a high surf fell upon the shore, a more dreadful one I have not often seen: no European boat could have landed in it and I think no European who had by any means got into it could possibly have saved his life, as the shore was coverd with pebbles and large stones. In the midst of these breakers 10 or 12 Indians were swimming who whenever a surf broke near them divd under it with infinite ease, rising up on the other side; but their cheif amusement was carried on by the stern of an old canoe, with this before them they swam out as far as the outermost breach, then one or two would get into it and opposing the blunt end to the breaking wave were hurried in with incredible swiftness. Sometimes they were carried almost ashore but generally the wave broke over them before they were half way, in which case they divd and quickly rose on the other side with the canoe in their hands, which was towd out again and the same method repeated. We stood admiring this very wonderful scene for full half an hour, in which time no one of the actors attempted to come ashore but all seemd most highly entertaind with their strange diversion.

But now the day upon which Venus should pass across the sun was coming near. Cook, bearing in mind Lord Morton's advice, decided to have the transit observed from two places so far apart that if the sky were clouded over the one it might be clear over the other, and he fixed upon Gore and Monkhouse as the observers and the island now called Moorea as the second place. The longboat, with Banks, Tubourai, Tomio and the observers aboard, pulled eastwards most of the night of 1 June, lying off Moorea till dawn, when a canoe showed them the way through a gap in the reef. Here in the lagoon they found an islet, a "very proper situation for our Observatory", and while Gore and the seamen were setting up their tents and their instruments Banks went to the main island to trade for provisions, which he did with great success. The chief came along the coast to see him, and after an exchange of presents (the chief produced an edible dog), Banks brought him and his party to see the planet moving across the sun. The weather was perfect for the observation; and Banks, returning to Moorea, found some plants he had not seen in Tahiti; while in the evening "3 hansome girls came off in a canoe to see us, they had been at the tent in the morning with Tarroa [the chief], they chatted with us very freely and with very little perswasion agreed to send away their carriage and sleep in the tent, a proof of confidence which I have not before met with upon so short an acquaintance."

In Tahiti itself the observation had been equally successful; but on the other hand all the officers were ashore during the transit and in their absence the more enterprising sailors had stolen almost all the ship's remaining nails, the chief form of currency. One was detected, but he only had seven left out of a hundredweight; and in any case flogging did not induce him to inform upon his companions.

The publicly acknowledged purpose of Cook's voyage had now been carried out, but his secret orders also required him to prosecute the design of making discoveries in the South Pacific Ocean by proceeding to the south as far as the latitude of 40°; then if he found no land, to proceed to the west between 40° and 35° till he fell in with New Zealand, which he was to explore and thence to return to England by such route as he should think proper. There only remained the preparation and victualling of the bark and the surveying of the coast.

In any case it was quite time for him to go, since the *Endeavour*'s requirements were exhausting the island's supplies of food just at a period when the main breadfruit season was coming to an end, while the islanders' continual and even increasing thefts, combined with the *Endeavour*'s often tactless treatment of them and ignorance of taboo, threatened to spoil a relation that had, upon the whole, been reasonably happy.

What is more, a longer stay might have resulted in a mutiny. The men of the *Endeavour* appreciated the charms of Tahiti as much as did those of the *Bounty* ten years later, and according to James Magra, who was then one of Cook's midshipmen, there were some who were determined to stay. Neither Cook nor Banks had any notion of it at the time and it was not until 1790, when Matra (he changed his name) was British Consul in Tangier, a post that he owed to Banks's kindness, that he wrote this account in a long, rambling letter[1] to his patron:

> The escape of poor Bligh & his companions is a miracle that has not been equalled these 1700 years – Inglefield may now burn his old Blanket. As the poor men are safe, one only feels for the loss of the Trees, but that is a serious point, as what has happened may deter from a fresh trial. It is a pity that in all such distant plans, they dont employ two vessels – something like what Bligh's People did, was designed by most of the People of the Endeavour headed by Anderson & Grey, I think – they were for remaining – which in truth, prevented 2 or 3 gent[n] from doing so – When the scheme was discovered, the only successful Argument against it was the Pox – the disease being there, their getting it certain & dying rotten most probable, was what I insisted on, & it turned the scale, otherwise Cook with the two superior messes, must have found his way home, had the Ship been spared – Had the Men, not formed such a Scheme, I was a ringleader among a few who had prepared for remaining.

It may be doubted whether the scheme was very serious. Anderson and Gray, both of them Scots, were obviously valuable men – the one sailed as gunner and the other as bosun in the *Resolution* some time later – and Cook certainly had enough confidence in them and the other hands to leave them while he charted the whole island, whereas speaking of Magra in his journal he described him as "one of those gentlemen, frequently found on board Kings Ships, that can very well be spared, or to speak more planer good for nothing".

Shortly before Cook and Banks set out in the pinnace for their circumnavigation of Tahiti, Banks learnt that two ships in company had been there since the *Dolphin*, Spanish ships, he thought, judging from the ensign that Tubourai picked out; but in fact they were the French king's frigate *La Boudeuse*, commanded by Louis-Antoine de Bougainville, a fellow-member of the Royal Society, and *l'Etoile*, a store-ship, in which there sailed the well-known botanist Philibert de Commerçon. Banks also took part in a mourning ceremony, blackened and wearing only a loincloth, as one of the attendants upon Tubourai, strangely masked and robed for the occasion. But at this point some islander succeeded in stealing a coal-rake, and Cook, pushed perhaps a little too far, seized twenty-five big sailing canoes that had just come in loaded with fish. The rake was given up, but Cook now said that the canoes should not be released until everything else that had been stolen was also restored. Banks thought this unsound, as the canoes did not belong to the people concerned and so it proved, since nothing was returned, nothing was brought to the market, and the fish went bad. Friends such as Tubourai, Oberea and Tupia brought them food as presents, including a particularly fat vegetable-fed dog, which Tupia cooked and which made an excellent dish "for us who were not much prejudiced against any species of food", but the regular supply of provisions had not started again by the time Cook and Banks set off to travel round the island, and this caused a certain amount of tension, which may perhaps account for the "very high words" which passed between Banks and the surgeon Monkhouse after an obscure incident concerning Otheathea and some other girls in Banks's tent and of which Parkinson said "I expected they would have decided it by a duel, which, however, they prudently avoided."[2]

The journey took them just under a week, sometimes walking, sometimes in the pinnace, always sleeping ashore, often with people they knew. They saw many interesting things, including an English goose and a turkey cock left by the *Dolphin* "both of them immensely fat and as tame as possible, following the Indians every where who seemd immensely fond of them", a more than life-size wickerwork figure of a man covered with white feathers for skin and black for hair and tattooing, and a certain number of jawbones and skulls preserved as trophies of war, while at one point Cook and Banks ran as hard as ever they could through the night after a chief who had stolen a cloak. But by far the most impressive sight was Oberea's marae, a place for sacrifice, religious ceremony and burial; they had seen several others on their way, some decorated with carvings, but this eclipsed them all entirely:

> We no sooner arrivd there than we were struck with the sight of a most enormous pile, certainly the masterpeice of Indian architecture in this Island so all the inhabitants allowd. Its size and workmanship almost exceeds beleif, I shall set it down exactly. Its form was like that of *Marais* in general, resembling the roof of a house, not smooth at the sides but formed into 11 steps, each of these 4 feet in hight making in all 44 feet, its lengh 267 its breadth 71. Every one of these steps were formd of one course of white coral stones most neatly squard and polishd, the rest were round pebbles, but these seemd to have been workd from their uniformity of size and roundness. Some of the coral stones were very large, one I measurd was 3½ by 2½ feet. The foundation was of Rock stones likewise squard, one of these corner stones measurd 4 ft 7 in by 2 ft 4 in. The whole made part of one side of a spatious area which was walld in with stone, the size of this which seemd

> to be intended for a square was 118 by 110 paces, which was intirely pavd with flat paving stones. It is almost beyond beleif that Indians could raise so large a structure without the assistance of Iron tools to shape their stones or mortar to join them, which last appears almost essential as most of them are round; it is done tho, and almost as firmly as a European workman would have done it . . .

On the shore not far from the marae they found countless human bones and they learnt that this was the battlefield where the men of the south-east had defeated Oberea's forces, taking away with them not only skulls and jawbones but also the *Dolphin*'s turkey and goose.

Back at Matavai Bay, where the *Endeavour* lay at anchor, they were charmingly welcomed by their friends, but they found the situation unchanged: the stolen objects had not been given back and the canoes were still detained. Cook released them, running into more trouble as he did so, since people claimed canoes that did not belong to them. After this, while the captain concentrated on getting his ship ready for a very long voyage indeed, Banks explored the nearer mountains, sowed watermelon, orange, lemon and lime pips in a variety of soils, watched the slow and painful operation of tattooing a girl's bottom, and, when someone managed to steal the staple and hook on the great gate of the now half-dismantled camp

> I (as usual) set out on my ordinary occupation of theif catching. The Indians most readily joind me and away we set full cry much like a pack of fox hounds, we ran and walkd and walkd and ran for I beleive 6 miles with as little delay as possible, when we learnt that we had very early in the chase passd our game who was washing in a brook, saw us a coming and hid himself in the rushes. We returnd to the place and by some intelligence which some of our people had got found a scraper which had been stole from the ship and was hid in those very rushes; with this we returnd and soon after our return Tubourai brought the staple.

There seemed to be little malice in all this, however; it was more like a rather dangerous game, and it did not affect relations with the islanders as a whole, those cheerful, likeable people. But then, when the ship was ready for sea, two marines deserted. A midshipman and a corporal were sent after them, but as the islanders thought it most unlikely that they would be brought back Cook took the very decided step of seizing nine arii, including Oberea, and sending a boat that captured Dootahah. Some of the hostages were kept in the ship, some in the fort with Banks. About eight o'clock one deserter was brought back, but the other and the men sent after him were to be kept, said the islanders, until Dootahah was released.

> The night was spent tolerably well, the women cryd a little at first but were soon quieted by assurances that at all events they would not be hurt. At day break a large number of people gatherd about the fort many of them with weapons; we were entirely without defences so I made the best I could of it by going out among them. They were very civil and shewd much fear as they have done of me upon all occasions, probably because I never shewd the least of them but have upon all our quarrels gone immediately into the thickest of them. They told me that our people would soon return.

So they did, and the hostages were set free; they all seemed thoroughly dissatisfied, offended and cross, with the exception of Tupia, who had long wished to stay in the *Endeavour* for the rest of the voyage and who was now decided upon it, "a circumstance which gives me much satisfaction. He is certainly a most proper man, well born, cheif *Tahowa* or preist of this island, consequently skilld in the mysteries of their religion; but what makes him more than any thing else desireable is his experience in the navigation of these people and knowledge of the Islands in these seas; he has told us the names of above 70, the most of which he has himself been at. The Captn refuses to take him on his own account, in my opinion sensibly enough, the government will never in all human probability take any notice of him; I therefore have resolved to take him. Thank Heaven I have a sufficiency and I do not know why I may not keep him as a curiosity, as well as some of my neighbours do lions and tygers at a larger expence than he will probably ever put me to; the amusement I shall have in his future conversation and the benefit he will be to this ship, as well as what he may be if another should be sent into these seas, will I think fully repay me." (When Banks was young – and in 1769 he was only 26 – he sometimes wrote remarks as chilling as this "curiosity" piece; but seeing that neither then nor subsequently did his conduct match them, they may fairly be put down to youthful cynicism.)

The hostages' resentment did not last: the next afternoon there was a reconciliation with Oberea and Dootahah, and on the morning of 13 July, when the *Endeavour* was to sail, Oberea, Otheathea and five others stayed aboard until the anchor was weighed and then took their leave with tears, while many canoes all round the bark called out in formal lamentation.

> Tupia who after all his struggles stood firm at last in his resolution of accompanying us parted with a few heartfelt tears, so I judge them to have been by the Efforts I saw him make use of to hide them. He sent by Otheathea his last present, a shirt to Potomai, Dootahah's favourite mistress. He and I went to the topmast head where we stood a long time waving to the Canoes as they went off . . .

Chapter 5

NEW ZEALAND, BOTANY BAY AND THE GREAT BARRIER REEF

THE *Endeavour* sailed north-westward through the Society Islands with a fair wind and the next day, far and high, they saw two islands, which Tupia told them were called Huahine and Raiatea. In spite of calms they landed on Huahine two days later; with Tupia to introduce them they were hospitably received, and they found the people just like those of Tahiti except that the women, though fairer, were not quite so handsome. Another difference was the islanders' habit of making a kind of hasty pudding from coconuts and yams: this, when fried, was relished by the seamen. The island yielded twelve new plants and a hitherto unknown scorpion, as well as several pigs.

On 20 August they sailed on to Raiatea and Tahaa, two islands encircled by the same coral reef. No one could have shown them Raiatea better than Tupia, who had been an important chief here before the island was conquered by the warriors of Borabora. He explained the peculiar excellence of the Raiatean canoes, which were indeed the finest in those parts: Banks measured a pahi, a double canoe, and although it was by no means the largest, he found that the main hull, not counting the tall curved stem and stern pieces, was fifty-one feet long with a beam of thirty-five inches and a depth of three feet four inches; the whole was built up of several members exactly shaped with stone adzes and sewn together, the holes for the sewing being made by the bone of a man's upper arm, ground very sharp. Tupia said that these craft would make voyages of twenty days, which seems to have left Banks sceptical although it was in fact an understatement; but at least there was no doubting that they were kept in prodigious boathouses, measuring as much as sixty yards by eleven. Another thing they saw on Raiatea was a heiva, a performance in which dancing, music and mime were combined, the performers being arioi, members of that singular Polynesian society of what might be called strolling players if they had not been of high social status and possessed of religious as well as aesthetic attributes – a society not celibate (very far from it indeed) but childless, infanticide or disgrace being the result of pregnancy. Banks had seen heivas in Tahiti, but this was the performance of ceremony raised to the highest degree: it "detained us 2 hours and during all that time entertained us highly indeed".

At one point during their stay Cook, hoisting a flag, took possession of Raiatea and the other islands in sight, including Borabora, "for the use of his Britannick majesty", and at another Banks and Solander, guided by some of the islanders, walked up the steep paths to the lofty middle point (like Tahiti it was volcanic in origin) so that they could see the other side; but they found only two new plants.

Then, on 9 September, having laid in a fine stock of provisions, especially plantains,

> we again Launched out into the Ocean in search of what chance and Tupia might direct us to.
>
> 10 Myself sick all day.

Chance and Tupia brought them to Rurutu on the thirteenth and the next day they tried to land; but for once they met with a hostile reception. A canoe came out to meet the boat, and although its people received nails "seemingly with great satisfaction", a moment later they tried boarding in force – one snatched Banks's powder-horn – and they had to be deterred with musket-fire. There was another attempt at coming to terms and even a little trading on a shoal some way from the strand, but it did not really answer, and "after leaving these inhospitable people we Stood to the Southward as usual and had in the evening a great dew which wetted everything."

Now began a voyage through unknown seas, steering steadily south-west, seven weeks and more with never a sight of land nor any greater certainty of it in the end than Tasman's word and his possibly erroneous, possibly misleading longitude and latitude, estimated more than a hundred years ago. In the early days of this voyage – they had crossed the tropic of Capricorn on 15 August – there were not a great many birds or sea creatures to observe, and Banks, no doubt influenced by Linnaeus's rule that the naturalist should report upon every aspect of a foreign people, spent much of his time reflecting on his recent experience, discussing many aspects of it with Tupia, and setting his ordered thoughts down on paper.

In one of the many prefaces he wrote for other authors' books, Johnson observed that the size of a man's mind was in direct proportion to the extent of his curiosity; and judged by this criterion Banks comes out very well indeed. The range of his interests and the amount of information that he managed to gather in his three months' stay is really most surprising, particularly when one recalls that at the same time he was making and preserving large natural history collections, acting as market-man for the encampment, and learning the language in which much of this knowledge was conveyed.

The results of his reflection cannot be given here – they would occupy the space of two chapters – but the heads of his discourse will at least give a notion of the scope and nature of his enquiry. He speaks of tattooing – universal, painful, and wonderfully accomplished – and of the people's scrupulous cleanliness. He goes on to describe their dress at some length, their few ornaments, and their habit of anointing themselves with scented but sometimes also rancid coconut-oil (a smell that he soon came to like). He praised their wall-less houses, "admirably calculated for the continual warmth", open to the breeze and built not in villages but standing separately among their own trees, most being about twenty-four feet by eleven, though some were very much larger. Then comes a long and quite earnest account of food, including "Bananas of 13 sorts the best I have ever eat" and dog – "few were there of the nicest of us but allowed that a S'Sea dog was next to English lamb". After this there is a description of their games, music and dancing, which runs on naturally enough to love-making and thence to the arioi and their practices. Returning to cloth he deals with their raw material (the inner bark of various trees), the various beating and washing processes in the making of the different kinds, and then the dyeing, all very carefully observed, particularly the mixing of two vegetable juices to produce a beautiful red. He moves on to matting, basketwork, fishing nets, lines, harpoons and mother-of-pearl hooks; then to tools, the building of the canoes, great and small, the sailing of them and the "clever ones'" navigation by the stars, above all by the rising and setting of the constellations throughout the year.

Then leaving material things he comes to the calendar, with the typical proviso "For their method of dividing time I was not able to get a compleat idea of it. I shall however set down what little I know", and so to counting and then to the language, with some interesting remarks on its relation to others and a vocabulary of about a hundred words, in a spelling which, says the expert Professor Beaglehole, gives a very fair equivalent of the Tahitian terms he had collected. Then he speaks of illness (comparatively rare), death and mourning. This brings him to religion and cosmogony, where he was on exceptionally difficult ground, for not only was "religion . . . cloak'd in mysteries inexplicable to human understanding" in all countries and periods, but the Polynesians had an esoteric language for such matters, so that although Tupia was a priest and a learned man, full of good will, it is not surprising that

Banks should say "I knew less of the religion of these people than of any other part of their policy."

He does however give an account which to judge by the expert's commentary is rather more often right than wrong: it is rather a disapproving account, and when he was told, or thought he was told, that the chiefs and rich men went to heaven when they died whereas the common people went to hell (a modest hell, with no torments: only less of the luxuries of life) he says "This is one of the strongest instances that shew that their religion is totaly independent of morality." He also makes a few of his usual flings against the priesthood. Although he was perfectly liberal and devoid of national prejudices in everything to do with natural philosophy, the John Bull in him was sure to be roused by foreign priests, Popish or pagan.

From religion he went on to the social system, and here, curiously enough, he seems to have made more mistakes than he did with the much more difficult subject of the gods, being misled about the political divisions and about the high chief, as well as the nature of the relations between the three main classes.

But in any event these were not subjects very dear to him. He does not seem to have had any strong religious sense nor any taste for politics or abstract theory. He was happier giving a scientifically exact description of a plant or working on some hitherto unknown bird: and the farther south they went, the colder the sea, the more birds he saw and noted in his journal. Here are a few of the many entries:

> 30 [of August 1769] More sea today than yesterday heaving in from WSW. Several birds, Pintados, Albatross's of both kinds, the little silver backd bird which we saw off Faulkland Isles and Cape Horn, *Pr. velox* and grey shearwater. Peter saw a green bird about the size of a dove, the colour makes us hope that it is a land bird, it took however not the least notice of the ship. Some sea weed was also seen to pass by the ship but as it was a very small peice our hopes are not very sanguine on that head. The thermometer today 52 which pinches us much who are so lately come from a countrey where it was seldom less than 80. A swell from SW.
>
> 10 [of September] This morn a fog bank was seen upon our quarter which much resembled land, we bore after it but were soon convinced of our mistake. More birds than yesterday: Pintado birds, both the albatrosses, the small grey backd bird like a dove (Mother Carey's dove), the grey backd shearwater of the 31st, and a small kind of Mother Carey's chicken black above and white underneath.
>
> 23 Dr Solander has been unwell for some days so today I opend Dr Hulme's Essence of Lemon Juice, Mr Monkhouse having prescribed it for him, which provd perfectly good, little if at all inferior in taste to fresh lemon

juice. We also today made a pye of the North American apples which Dr Fothergill gave me, which provd very good, if not quite equal to the apple pyes which our freinds in England are now eating, good enough to please us who have been so long deprivd of the fruits of our native Country. In the main however we are very well off for refreshments and provisions of most species: our ships *beef* and *Pork* are excellent as are the *peas*; the *flour* and *oatmeal* which have at some times faild us are at present and have in general been very good. Our *water* is as sweet and has rather more spirit than it had when drank out of the river at Otahite. Our *bread* indeed is but indifferent, occasioned by the quantity of Vermin that are in it, I have seen hundreds nay thousands shaken out of a single bisket. We in the Cabbin have however an easy remedy for this by baking it in an oven, not too hot, which makes them all walk off, but this cannot be allowd to the private people who must find the taste of these animals very disagreeable, as they every one taste as strong as mustard or rather spirits of hartshorn. They are of 5 kinds, 3 *Tenebrios*, 1 *Ptinus* and the *Phalangium cancroides*; this last is however scarce in the common bread but was vastly plentiful in white Deal bisket as long as we had any left.

Cook had so far kept his men extraordinarily free from scurvy, serving out sauerkraut and malt; he now gave them a kind of wheat porridge, and Banks's entry goes on:

this has I beleive been a very useful refreshment to them as well as an agreeable food, which myself and most of the officers in the ship have constantly breakfasted upon in the cold weather

1 [of October] Very little wind and yet vast quantities of small birds are about the ship which has been to us a very uncommon sight in such fine weather; a Seal seen from the ship. Several peices of sea weed are taken and among them a peice of wood quite overgrown with *sertularias*; it must have been a long time at Sea yet more hopes are drawn from this than the sea weed, as we now have in our possession a part of the produce of our Land of Promise. Among the weed are many sea insects which are put into spirits weed wood and all, so we shall at least have this to shew. Several whales have been seen today

3 Calm almost this morn. About 5 a sudden squall came on with such violence that the officer of the watch was obligd to settle the topsails, it did not however last above 5 minutes; this we look upon as a sure sign of land as such squalls are rarely (if ever) met with at any considerable distance from it. I go in the boat and kill *Procellaria capensis*, *longipes* and *latirostris*. In the course of the day several peices of sea weed are taken up of species very new and one peice of wood coverd with Striated Barnacles *Lepas Anserina*?

Now do I wish that our freinds in England could by the assistance of some magical spying glass take a peep at our situation: Dr Solander setts at the

Cabbin table describing, myself at my Bureau Journalizing, between us hangs a large bunch of sea weed, upon the table lays the wood and barnacles; they would see that notwithstanding our different occupations our lips move very often, and without being conjurors might guess that we were talking about what we should see upon the land which there is now no doubt we shall see very soon.

5 Our old enemy Cape fly away entertaind us for three hours this morn all which time there were many opinions in the ship, some said it was land and others Clouds which at last however plainly appeard. 2 seals passd the ship asleep and 3 of the birds which Mr Gore calls Port Egmont hens, *Larus Catarrhactes*, and says are a sure sign of our being near land.

6 This morn a Port Egmont hen and a seal were seen pretty early. At ½ past one a small boy who was at the mast head Calld out Land. I was luckyly upon deck and well was I entertaind, within a few minutes the cry circulated and up came all hands, this land could not be seen even from the tops yet few were there who did not plainly see it from the deck till it appeard that they had lookd at least 5 points wrong. Weather most moderate. We came up with it very slowly; at sun set myself was at the masthead, land appeard much like an Island or Islands but seemed to be large.

The next day they had little wind until the evening and by sunset the land was still over twenty miles away, though many hills could be seen and a mountain-range beyond them: "Much difference of opinion and many conjectures about Islands, rivers, inlets &c, but all hands seem to agree that this is certainly the Continent we are in search of."

It was in fact New Zealand, the north island of New Zealand. The Maoris, who lived there, having come from Polynesia in the fourteenth century retaining their language and many of their customs, were exceedingly fierce and warlike. Their very first contact with Europeans had been disastrous for the strangers; it took place in 1642, when Tasman brought his two ships to Murderers' Bay on the north coast of the south island. They lay there at anchor, and a boat was passing between them when canoes from the shore attacked it without any hesitation, killing four of the crew. Tasman passed on, never landing at all. Then just after Cook's visit, Marion du Fresne, in a voyage undertaken, at least in part, to carry Bougainville's Tahitian Aotourou back to his own country, did land: the Maoris knocked him on the head, together with two of his officers and thirteen of his men, and probably ate them all. This was how they behaved to people they did not know, and this was how they behaved to Cook. The "inhabitants are a Robust, lively and very ingenious People," said Banks in a letter[1] two years later. "They always strenuously oppos'd us, so that we sometimes were laid under the disagreeable necessity of effecting our Landing by

Force; they were however when subdued, unalterably our friends and carried that sentiment to lengths which in Europe we are unacquainted with."

Banks however knew nothing of their more agreeable side on 8 October 1769 when, having described the ship's approach to the land and the sight of canoes, houses, a stockade that was thought to be a deer-park or an enclosure for cattle but which was in fact a Maori fortification, and of people on the strand, he wrote:

> In the evening went ashore with the marines &c. March from the boats in hopes of finding water &c. Saw a few of the natives who ran away immediately on seeing us; while we were absent 4 of them attackd our small boat in which were only 4 boys, they got off from the shore in a river, the people followd them and threatned with long lances; the pinnace soon came to their assistance, fird upon them and killd the cheif. The other three dragged the body about 100 yards and left it. At the report of the musquets we drew together and went to the place where the body was left; he was shot through the heart. He was a middle sized man tattowed in the face on one cheek only in spiral lines very regularly formd; he was coverd with a fine cloth of a manufacture totaly new to us, it was tied on exactly as represented in Mr Dalrymple's book p.63; his hair was also tied in a knot on the top of his head but no feather stuck in it; his complexion brown but not very dark.
>
> Soon after we came on board we heard the people ashore very distinctly talking very loud no doubt, as they were not less than two miles distant from us, consulting probably what is to be done tomorrow.
>
> 9 We could see with our glasses but few people on the beach; they walked with a quick pace towards the river where we landed yesterday, most of these without arms, 3 or 4 with long Pikes in their hands. The captn ordered three boats to be manned with seamen and marines intending to land and try to establish a communication with them. A high surf ran on the shore. The Indians about 50 remaind on the farther side of the river; we lookd upon that as a sign of fear, so landing with the little boat only the Captn Dr Solander, Tupia and myself went to the river side to speak to them. As soon almost as we appeard they rose up and every man produced either a long pike or a small weapon of well polished stone about a foot long and thick enough to weigh 4 or 5 pounds, with these they threatned us and signed us to depart. A musquet was then fird wide of them the ball of which struck the water, they saw the effect and immediately ceasd their threats. We thought that it was prudent to retreat till the marines were landed and drawn up to intimidate them and support us in case of necessity. They landed and marched with a Jack carried before them to a little bank about 50 yards from the river, which might be about 40 broad; here they were drawn up in order and we again advanced to the river side with Tupia, who now found that the language of the people was so like his own that he could tolerably well

> understand them and they him. He immediately began to tell them that we wanted provisions and water for which we would give them Iron in exchange: they agreed to the proposal but would by no means lay by their arms which he desird them to do . . .

After a great deal of talk about who should come to whom, an unarmed Maori swam across "and landed upon a rock surrounded by the tide, and now invited us to come to him. Cook finding him resolved to advance no farther, gave his musket to an attendant, and went towards him . . . they saluted by touching noses . . ."[2]

> he was followed by two more and soon after by most of the rest who brought with them their arms. He gave them Iron and beads, they seemd to set little value upon either but especially the iron the use of which they certainly were ignorant of. They caught at whatever was offerd them but would part with nothing but a few feathers: their arms indeed they offerd to exchange for ours which they made several attempts to snatch from us; we were upon our guard so much that their attempts faild and they were made to understand that we must kill them if they snatched anything from us. After some time Mr Green in turning himself about exposd his hanger, one of them immediately snatchd it, set up a cry of exultation and waving it round his head retreated gently. It now appeard nescessary for our safeties that so daring an act should be instantly punished, this I pronounced aloud as my opinion, the Captn and the rest Joind me on which I fird my musquet which was loaded with small shot, leveling it between his shoulders who was not 15 yards from me. On the shot striking him he ceasd his cry but instead of quitting his prize continued to wave it over his head retreating as gently as before; the surgeon who was nearer him, seeing this fird a ball at him at which he dropd. Two more who were near him returned instantly, one seized his weapon of Green talk, the other attempted to recover the hanger which the surgeon had scarce time to prevent. The main body of them were now upon a rock a little way in the river. They took the water returning towards us, on which the other three, for we were only 5 in number, fird on them. They then retird and swam again across the river.

The two sides now parted, the Maoris carrying off their wounded and the Endeavours returning to their boats, meaning to pull round the bay in the hope of a sheltered anchorage on the other side. They had almost reached the farther shore when they saw two canoes coming in: intercepting them would establish communication with the people on shore.

> The boats were drawn up in such a manner that they could not well escape us: the paddling canoe first saw us and made immediately for the nearest land, the other saild on till she was in the midst of us before she saw us, as

> soon as she did she struck her sail and began to paddle so briskly that she outran our boat; on a musquet being fird over her she however immediately ceasd padling and the people in her, 7 in all, made all possible haste to strip as we thought to leap into the water, but no sooner did our boat come up with her than they began with stones, paddles &c to make so brisk a resistance that we were obliged to fire into her by which 4 were killd.[3] The other 3 who were boys leapd overboard, one of them swam with great agility and when taken made every effort in his power to prevent being taken into the boat, the other two were more easily prevaild upon. As soon as they were in they squatted down expecting no doubt instant death, but on finding themselves well used and that Cloaths were given them they recovered their spirits in a very short time and before we got to the ship appeared almost insensible of the loss of their fellows.

The boys were cheerful enough on board at first, encouraged no doubt by the presence of Tupia and his young follower Tayeto; they ate enormously and asked questions "with a great deal of curiosity"; but later on Tupia was obliged to comfort them, and they sang a song of their own "like a Psalm tune".

> After dark loud voices were heard ashore as last night. Thus ended the most disagreeable day My life has ever seen, black be the mark for it and heaven send that such may never return to embitter future reflection.

Indeed things never were so bad again, though nearly all first encounters were both difficult and dangerous. They put the boys ashore the next day and walked along, guarded by five Marines on a rise, to a duck-filled marsh; but Maoris were seen, apparently encircling them, and they retreated to the boats, for "we now despaired of making peace with men who were not to be frightened with our small arms". Some confused conversation followed, perhaps of a promising nature, since a green bough was produced and yesterday's bodies were carried off, but Cook decided not to stay: apart from anything else, the place seemed to be on the boundary between two hostile tribes, for the boys had at one time said that they would be eaten unless they were taken to another part of the bay.

> 11 This morn We took our leave of Poverty bay [Cook's name for the place, it having yielded nothing] with not above 40 species of Plants in our boxes, which is not to be wonderd at as we were so little ashore and always upon the same spot; the only time we wanderd about a mile from the boats was upon a swamp where not more than 3 species of Plants were found.

Yet as the *Endeavour* was going some canoes put off, and Tupia, shouting loud, tried to persuade them to come closer. Eventually one was seen coming from Poverty Bay or near it with four men aboard: they came alongside directly and very soon they were aboard the ship. They were followed by fifty more, all unarmed but two, one of whom sold his patoo-patoo, a polished green talc skull-splitter like that which Banks had seen during the first encounter.

> We were very anxious to know what was become of our poor boys, therefore as soon as the people began to lose their first impressions of fear that we saw at first disturbd them a good deal we askd after them. The man who first came aboard immediately answerd that they were at home and unhurt and that the reason of his coming on board the ship with so little fear was the account they had given him of the usage they had met with among us.

Banks went on to describe their colour (dark brown), their tattoo (often in spirals and deeply incised, rather than pricked in the way he had seen hitherto), their clothes – something very like hemp for the poor, while the richer

> had garments probably of a finer sort of stuff, most beautifully made in exactly the same manner as the S. American Indians at this day, as fine or finer than one of them which I have by me that I bought at Rio de Janeiro for 36 shillings and was esteemed uncommonly cheap at that price. Their boats were not large but well made, something in the form of our whale boats but longer; their bottom was the trunk of a tree hollowed and very thin, this was raised by a board on each side sewd on, with a strip of wood sewd over the seam to make it tight; on the head of every one was carvd the head of a man with an enormous tongue reaching out of his mouth. These grotesque figures were some at least very well executed, some had eyes inlaid of something that shone very much; the whole servd to give us an Idea of their taste as well as ingenuity in execution, much superior to any thing we have yet seen.
>
> Their behaviour while on board shewd every sign of freindship, they invited us very cordialy to come back to our old bay or to a small cove which they shewd us nearer to it. I could not help wishing that we had done so, but the captn chose rather to stand on in search of a better harbour than any we have yet seen. God send that we may not there have the same tragedy to act over again as we so lately perpetrated: the countrey is certainly divided into many small principalities so we cannot hope that an account of our weapons and management of them can be conveyed as far as we in all probability must go and this I am well convincd of, that till these warlike people have severly felt our superiority in the art of war they will never behave to us in a freindly manner.

Alas, the prediction was true in the main. As the *Endeavour* sailed south along the coast war-canoes put off and threatened her, sometimes in such numbers that it was necessary to fire a gun a little ahead of them. It might happen that having sung their war-song and shaken their spears for a while, they would listen to Tupia, change their minds, come alongside and trade; but this too might end in death. On one occasion Tayeto was standing in the chains, some way down the ship's side, passing things to and fro: the men in one canoe dragged him off and they all paddled away. The Marines were ordered to fire, and when one man dropped the others loosed their hold on the boy, who dived straight into the water; at this an armed war-canoe turned, but musket- and canon-fire sent it off again. The boy was picked up unhurt: and Cook named the nearby headland Cape Kidnappers.

> As soon as Tayeto was a little recovered from his fright he brought a fish to Tupia and told him he intended it as an offering to his Etua or god in gratitude for his escape. Tupia approvd it and ordered him to throw it into the sea which he did.

The day after this, on 16 October and by the ship's reckoning in latitude 40°34′S, longitude 182°56′W, Cook decided that because of the nature of the coast, carrying on towards the south would not be useful either from the point of view of a good harbour or of valuable discovery, so calling the promontory to starboard Cape Turnagain he tacked the ship and stood to the northwards with a fresh breeze at west. As they were once more passing the island they had called Portland on the way south, a canoe with five men in it, two of them chiefs, came aboard in the friendliest way and stayed the night although they were told that the ship would travel far in the darkness. "The countenance of one of these men was the most open I have ever seen, I was prejudiced much in their favour and surely such confidence could not be found in the breasts of designing people," said Banks, who was fond of the Maoris in spite of their shortcomings; and some time later, after the ship had passed Poverty Bay, he found that his prepossession was justified. Two more chiefs came off, elderly men, one wearing "a Jacket ornamented after their manner with dogs skin, the other in one coverd almost entirely with small tufts of red feathers", who invited them to come ashore to a bay where there was plenty of fresh water. This they did and now for the first time Banks could see ordinary life in New Zealand and he and Solander could botanize in a less precarious way.

> We were receivd with great freindship by the natives in general who seemd carefull of giving us umbrage by collecting in too great bodies: each family or the inhabitants of 2 or 3 houses which generally stood together were collected in a body, 15 or 20 men women and children, these sat on the

ground never walking towards us but inviting us to them by beckoning with one hand movd towards the breast. We made them small presents, walked round the bay, and found a place for watering where the people are to land tomorrow and fill some at least of our empty cask.

21 This morn at daybreak the waterers went ashore and soon after Dr Solander and myself; there was a good deal of Surf upon the beach but we landed without much difficulty. The natives sat by our people but did not intermix with them; they traded however for cloth cheifly, giving whatever they had tho they seemd pleasd with observing our people as well as with the gain they got by trading with them. Yet they did not neglect their ordinary occupations: in the morn several boats went out fishing, at dinner time every one went to their respective homes and after a certain time returnd. Such fair appearances made Dr Solander and myself almost trust them. We rangd all about the bay and were well repaid by finding many plants and shooting some most beautiful birds; in doing this we visited several houses and saw a little of their customs, for they were not at all shy of shewing us any thing we desird to see, nor did they on our account interrupt their meals the only employment we saw them engaged in.

Their food at this time of the year consisted of Fish with which instead of bread they eat the roots of a kind of Fern *Pteris crenulata*, very like that which grows upon our commons in England. These were a little roasted on the fire and then beat with a stick which took off the bark and dry outside, what remaind had a sweetish clammyness in it not disagreeable to the taste; it might be esteemd a tolerable food was it not for the quantity of strings and fibres in it which in quantity 3 or 4 times exceeded the soft part; these were swallowed by some but the greater number of people spit them out for which purpose they have a basket standing under them to receive their chewd morsels, in shape and colour not unlike Chaws of Tobacco.

Banks saw no sign of any tame animals apart from dogs, very small and ugly, but it was clear that at other times of the year the Maoris had plenty of vegetables: their remarkably well cultivated fields or gardens, running sometimes to ten acres, were planted with sweet potatoes, yams and taro, "some in rows other in quincunx all laid by a line most regularly" and each was "fencd in generaly with reeds placd close one by another so that scarce a mouse could creep through".

When we went to their houses Men women and children receivd us, no one shewd the least signs of fear. The women were plain and made themselves more so by painting their faces with red ocre and oil which generaly was fresh and wet upon their cheeks and foreheads, easily transferrable to the noses of any one who should attempt to kiss them; not that they seemed to have any objection to such familiarities as the noses of several of our people evidently shewd, but they were as great coquetts as any Europeans could be

> and the young ones as skittish as unbroken fillies. One part of their dress I cannot omit to mention: besides their cloth which was very decently rolld round them each wore round the lower part of her waist a string made of the leaves of a highly perfumed grass, to this was fastend a small bunch of the leaves of some fragrant plant which servd as the innermost veil of their modesty.

Having noted the privies or necessary houses and the consequent cleanliness of the ground (by no means always the case in Tahiti) Banks went on:

> In the evening all the boats being employd in carrying on board water we were likely to be left ashore till after dark; the loss of so much time in sorting and putting into order our specimens was what we did not like so we applied to our freinds the Indians for a passage in one of their Canoes. They readily launchd one for us, but we in number 8 not being usd to so ticklish a convenience overset her in the surf and were very well sousd; 4 then were obligd to remain and Dr Solander, Tupia, Tayeto and myself embarkd again and came without accident to the ship well pleased with the behaviour of our Indian freinds who would the second time undertake to carry off such Clumsy fellows.

Unhappily this did not last and after three days' sailing Banks wrote "Breeze continued fair: Countrey very pleasant to appearance. Several canoes came off and threatned us at a distance which gave us much uneasiness, as we hop'd that an account of us and what we could do and had done had spread farther than this; we had now our work to begin over again and heartily joind in wishing that it might be attended with less bloodshed than our late unfortunate encounters."

Threats, insults, stone-throwing, and cheating in trade accompanied them as they sailed up the coast, sometimes admiring its rich and wooded appearance; but eventually, when Cook went ashore to find a suitable place for observing the transit of Mercury that was to take place on 9 November he found another good-natured elderly chief by the name of Torava, whose people seemed to be in this rather barren spot for the mackerel fishing. But they were not the only Maoris to be attracted by the fish: other canoes filled with men of a different temper appeared, and in the trading Gore, the senior officer left aboard, was openly cheated and defied: he shot the man dead and frightened the canoes off with a cannonball over their heads. This alarmed Torava's people, but when the case was explained they agreed that the shot was fair enough and showed the Endeavours not only two pa's, those remarkably powerful fortifications called for in such a warlike country, but also an oyster-bed:

> here the long boat was sent and soon returnd deep loaded with I sincerly beleive as good oysters as ever came from Colchester and about the same size. They were laid down under the booms and employd the ships company very well who I verily think did nothing but Eat from the time they came on board till night, by which time a large part were expended, but that gave us no kind of uneasiness as we well knew that not only the boat but the ship might be easily loaded in one tide almost, as they are dry at half Ebb.

Torava's name protected them from hostility more or less, as they travelled up the coast, coming to Hauraki Bay. This they decided to explore and at the bottom of it they found a fine broad river which pleased Cook so much that he called it the Thames. A grandson of Torava's lived in these parts, and when the Endeavours landed the people "were most perfectly civil, as indeed they have always been where we were known, but never where we were not". And it was here, on the Thames, that they saw "the finest timber my Eyes ever beheld, of a tree we had before seen but only at a distance in Poverty bay and Hawks bay; thick woods of it were every where upon the Banks, every tree as streight as a pine and of immense size: still the higher we came the more numerous they were."

Northwards far beyond Torava's influence to the Bay of Islands, where a little later poor Marion du Fresne was to meet his fate and where "Several canoes came off and traded for fish but were most abominably saucy, continualy threatning us, at last they began to heave stones with more courage than any boats we had seen. This made it necessary to punish them: the Captn went upon the Poop where they immediately threw at him, he levelled a gun loaded with small shot at the man who held a stone in his hand in the very action of throwing and struck him. He sunk down so immediately into the Canoe that we suspected he was materialy hurt; this however did not prevent another Canoe from coming up with stones in their hands who met another load of small shot at about 50 yards distant which struck several of them and at once stopt their speed."

That evening the wind came foul, and as it continued foul the next day Cook bore away for a nearby bay to leeward, where he anchored in the shelter of the many islands. Canoes came off; there was a certain amount of trading and a certain amount of trouble that seemed to have been thoroughly dealt with by the firing of a round-shot; and the boats went ashore. They had barely landed in an almost deserted sandy cove about three-quarters of a mile from the ship when every canoe put off and armed men came running over the headlands that formed the cove while others appeared on the high land behind it – the ship reckoned five or six hundred of them: Banks did not see so many, but then he was hemmed in.

> We now every man expected to be attacked but did not chuse to begin hostilities so the Captn and myself marched up to meet them. They crouded a good deal but did not offer to meddle with us, tho every man had his arms almost lifted up to strike. [Cook drew a line in the sand, as he had often done before, meaning that they were not to pass it.] They now began to sing the war song but committed no hostility till 3 steppd to each of our boats and attempted to draw them ashore. It was now time to fire, we whose Guns were loaded with small shot did so which drove them back. One man attempted to Rally them; he who was not 20 yards from us came down towards us waving his *Patoo patoo* and calling to his companions; Dr Solander whose gun was not dischargd fird at him on which he too ran. They now got upon rising ground about us from whence we dislodged them by firing musquet balls, none of which took effect farther than frightening them. In this way we were about of an hour, resolving to maintain our ground, when the ship had brought her broadside to bear and fird at the Indians who were on the tops of the hills. The balls went quite over them notwithstanding which they went off and at last left us our cove quite to ourselves, so that the musquets were laid down upon the ground and all hands employd in gathering Cellery which was here very plentiful.

The next day however they went ashore and were kindly received: "One general observation I have set down, that they Always after one nights consideration have acknowledgd our superiority but hardly before", and this continued for the rest of their week's stay, during which Banks botanized on the Continent (a name Banks often used for New Zealand, being a supporter of the theory of a vast land-mass counterbalancing that of the northern hemisphere) and on the island:

> I do not know what tempted Dr Solander and myself to go where we almost knew nothing was to be got but wet skins, which we had very sufficiently for it rained all the time we were ashore as hard as I ever saw it.

Some days after they had left the anchorage, but before they had outsailed the reputation of their guns, they met some timid canoes who told them "that at a distance of three days rowing in their canoes, at a place called *Moorewhennua*, the land would take a short turn to the south ward and from thence extend no more to the West". This Cook rightly concluded to be Tasman's Cape Maria van Diemen, but contrary winds and foul weather prevented him from reaching it for a long while. On Christmas Eve the *Endeavour* was far out at sea to the west of the islands called the Three Kings, and when the breeze dropped to a calm Banks went out in his boat shooting birds,

in which I had good success, killing cheifly several Gannets or Solan Geese so like the Europaean ones that they are hardly distinguishable from them. As it was the humour of the ship to keep Christmas in the old fashioned way it was resolvd of them to make a Goose pye for tomorrows dinner.
25 Christmas day: Our goose pye was eat with great approbation and in the Evening all hands were as Drunk as our forefathers usd to be upon the like occasion.
26 This morn all heads achd with yesterdays debauch. Wind has been Easterly these 3 or 4 days so we have not got at all nearer the Island than we were.

1769 ended with heavy weather – "all our sea people said that they never before were in so hard a summers Gale" – but although the first days of 1770 were less turbulent the winds were still unkind: the bark did see Cape Maria, but there was a great deal of toing and froing before she could start her steady run down the west side of the North Island.

During this run, and indeed during the rest of the circumnavigation of New Zealand, both Banks's and Cook's journals grow rather meagre, as though they had been storm-tossed too long. On 12 and 13 January they saw Mount Egmont, thick in snow, "certainly the noblest hill I have ever seen", and on 14 January, having run down five or six hundred miles of coast without landing they came to what Banks took to be Murderers' Bay. It was not in fact Murderers' Bay, but it was in the South Island (the channel between the two great islands had been passed unseen) and the inhabitants did behave in a somewhat murderous fashion to begin with, threatening them and throwing stones; but then a most unusual thing occurred: a very old man showed an inclination to come aboard, and although the other people in his canoe were against it, the Endeavours helped him up the side and treated him kindly.

After this they retird to their town and we went ashore abreast of the ship where we found good wood and water and caught more fish in the Seine than all our people could possibly destroy, besides shooting a multitude of Shaggs. The Country however did not answer so well to Dr Solander and myself as to the ship, we finding only 2 new plants in the whole even.

The next day, 15 January, about a hundred Maoris came to the ship "bringing their women with them, a sign tho not a sure one of peaceable inclinations". One man indeed tried snatching the price of his fish without giving them up, but a few small-shot striking his knee dealt with that, "on which they all left off to trade but paddled peaceably enough round the ship and at last came under the stern to Tupia and discoursed with him about their antiquity and Legends of their ancestors."

After dinner Cook, Banks, Solander, Tupia and some hands took the boat towards a cove about a mile from the ship; on the way they saw the floating body of a Maori woman, and when they came to the cove, where a small party of Maoris were preparing a meal, they found that the dead woman was a relative of theirs: it was their custom to bury their friends at sea and presumably the stone meant to carry her down had come off.

The family were employed when we came ashore in dressing their provisions, which were a dog who was at that time buried in their oven and near it were many provision baskets. Looking carelessly upon one of these we by accident observed 2 bones, pretty clean picked, which as apeard upon examination were undoubtedly human bones. Tho we had from the first of our arrival upon the coast constantly heard the Indians acknowledge the custom of eating their enemies we had never before had a proof of it, but this amounted almost to demonstration: the bones were clearly human, upon them were evident marks of their having been dressed on the fire, the meat was not intirely picked off from them and on the grisly ends which were gnawd were evident marks of teeth, and these were accidentaly found in a provision basket. On asking the people what bones are these? they answered, The bones of a man. – And have you eat the flesh? – Yes. – Have you none of it left? – No. – Why did you not eat the woman who we saw today in the water? – She was our relation. – And who then is it that you do eat? – Those who are killd in war. – And who was the man whose bones these are? – 5 days ago a boat of our enemies came into this bay and of them we killed 7, of whom the owner of these bones was one. – The horrour that appeard in the countenances of the seamen on hearing this discourse which was immediately translated for the good of the company is better conceivd than describd.

17 This morn I was awakd by the singing of the birds ashore from whence we are distant not a quarter of a mile, the numbers of them were certainly very great who seemd to strain their throats with emulation perhaps; their voices were certainly the most melodious wild musick I have ever heard, almost imitating small bells but with the most tuneable silver sound imaginable to which maybe the distance was no small addition.

A small canoe came this morn from the Indian town: as soon as they came along side Tupia began to enquire into the truth of what we had heard yesterday and was told over again the same story. But where are the sculls, sayd Tupia, do you eat them? Bring them and we shall then be convinced that these are men whose bones we have seen. – We do not eat the heads, answerd the old man who had first come on board the ship, but we do the brains and tomorrow I will bring you one and shew you. – Much of this kind of conversation passed after which the old man went home.

18 In the course of this days excursion we shot many shaggs from their nests in the trees and on the rocks. These birds we roast or stew and think not bad provisions, so between shaggs and fish this is the place of the greatest plenty of any we have seen.

20 Our old man came this morn according to his promise, with the heads of 4 people which were preserved with the flesh and hair on and kept I suppose as trophies, as possibly scalps were by the North Americans before the Europaeans came among them; the brains were however taken out as we had been told, maybe they are a delicacy here.

We made another excursion today. The bay every where where we have yet been is very hilly, we have hardly seen a flat large enough for a potatoe garden. Our friends here do not seem to feel the want of such places as we have not yet seen the least appearance of cultivation, I suppose they live intirely upon fish dogs and Enemies.

22 Made an excursion today in the pinnace in order to see more of the Bay. While Dr Solander and Myself were botanizing the captn went to the top of a hill and in about an hour returnd in high spirits, having seen the Eastern sea and satisfied himself of the existence of a streight communicating with it, the Idea which had occurd to us all from Tasman as well as our own observations.

The Captain had discovered what is now known as the Cook Strait, and he was eager to carry his ship through to the other end; but foul weather and foul winds prevented him from doing so for two weeks. During this period the *Endeavour*'s people spent much of their spare time trading for souvenirs of cannibalism: the practice of course filled them with horror, but they did not dislike having their flesh made to creep, and gnawed human bones "are now become a kind of article of trade among our people who constantly ask for and purchase them for whatever trifles they have". Upon the whole trading was fair here in the South Island, but on 3 February, when the ship was getting ready to sail,

> One of our gentlemen came home to day abusing the natives most heartily whoom he said he had found to be given to the detestable Vice of Sodomy. He, he said, had been with a family of Indians and paid a price for leave to make his addresses to any one young woman they should pitch upon for him; one was chose as he thought who willingly retird with him but on examination provd to be a boy; that on his returning and complaining of this another was sent who turned out to be a boy likewise; that on his second complaint he could get no redress but was laughed at by the Indians.

On 7 February 1770 the *Endeavour* got under way: her passage of the strait was by no means easy, with foul winds followed by a calm and a tide that ran like a millstream, hurrying her towards rocks although she had an anchor down in seventy-five fathom water and one hundred and fifty fathoms of cable out ahead, but by the next day they were at its southern entrance, formed by Cape Campbell (named after Hawke's flag-captain at Quiberon Bay, the scientific sailor who introduced Cook to the Royal Society) on the one hand and Cape Palliser (Cook's and Banks's friend in Newfoundland) on the other.

For a short while the bark carried on down the coast, but then to deal with the hypothesis of an isthmus connecting the two islands, Cook changed course and sailed northward with a favourable breeze until Cape Turnagain appeared, bearing N by E ¼E seven leagues away, and making it clear that the *Endeavour* had sailed right round the North Island.

With this established Cook set about circumnavigating the South Island. At first calms, in which Banks shot albatrosses and petrels from his boat, made it rather a slow process; and then, just after they had passed what Cook named Banks's Island (it turned out to be a peninsula) Mr Gore was persuaded that he saw land in the south-east, which had to be disproved by a long detour; but then as they ran south and south past apparently uninhabited country the wind became more lively, and on 25 February, when they were off Cape Saunders, it started to blow hard from the south-west. The next day, after a pause, it settled at west-south-west, split the foresail to ribbons and reduced the bark to two courses. On 27 February it was still blowing so hard that the ship had to lie to: "Weather a little more moderate," wrote Banks, "but no standing upon legs without the assistance of hands: hope however that the heart of this long-winded gale is broke according to the sea phraze."

Broke it was, but the great swell from the south-west not only "made the ship very troublesome" but also encouraged the "no Continent" party, which by now included almost everybody aboard except for Banks and "one poor midshipman", since if there had been a vast body of land to the south the *Endeavour* would have been under its lee.

By now they were no great way from sub-Antarctic waters and on 4 March one or two penguins appeared, "making a noise something like the shrieking of a goose". The ship was also nearing the southernmost point of New Zealand.

6 Very moderate and exceedingly clear. Land seen as far as South so our unbelievers are almost inclined to think that Continental measures will at last prevail.

But this land, like so many others, turned out to be cloud, and

> 10 Blew fresh all day but carried us round the Point to the total demolition of our aerial fabrick calld continent.

Now that this point was dealt with Cook ran as straight up the west coast of the South Island as the winds would let him. He did name one small bare island after Solander, but otherwise he made no concessions to the naturalists. At one time Banks was very earnest with him to put into a comfortable-looking harbour, but Banks was not a seaman and he did not perceive that (as Cook put it) "no winds could blow there but what was either right in or right out", which might not happen above once a month. So there was no stopping, no stopping at all, and the botanists were hurried right up the whole length of the west coast with never a pause for a plant. On 24 March they reached the northern extremity of the west coast and turned east for their starting-place to complete their circumnavigation; and they were at once met with an easterly wind: "The sea is certainly an excellent school for patience," wrote Banks. However they did drop anchor at last, and while Cook was getting in water and wood, Banks and Solander botanized, creeping about in the wet, although Banks was feeling ill – creeping with no success.

> 30 Myself quite recovered except a little soreness at my stomach occasioned I suppose by reaching yesterday. The weather being fair I resolvd to climb some hill in hopes of meeting some plants in the upper regions as none had been found in the lower. I did with great difficulty, walking for more than a mile in fern higher than my head; success however answerd my wishes and I got 3 plants which we had not seen before.

At the end of the month Cook consulted with his officers and presumably with Banks upon how best to proceed for the advantage of the service: Cook would have liked to go home eastward by the high latitudes and round Cape Horn, thus finding the southern continent if it existed, but it was agreed that the ship was not in a state to make such a voyage in the depths of the austral winter. Returning by the way of the Cape of Good Hope, however, though easy enough (the *Endeavour* still had six months' provisions at two-thirds allowance, and she was tolerably well found) would lead to no discoveries. So it was unanimously agreed "to return by way of the East Indies by the following rout: upon leaving this coast to steer to the westward untill we fall in with the East Coast of New Holland and then to follow the direction of that Coast to the northward or what other direction it may take untill we arrive at its northern extremity, and if this should be found impractical then to endeavour to fall in with the lands or Islands discover'd by Quiros."

This they began the next day, sailing with a fair wind and taking their departure from Cape Farewell.

For the next eighteen days they sailed west-north-west: after a week or so the wind, though generally fair, dropped sometimes to a calm, sometimes to light airs, and the weather became strangely hot and damp, so that things went as mouldy as though the ship were between the tropics; indeed, the red-tailed tropic bird appeared, as well as flying fish and other creatures of the warmer seas. Banks was often out in his boat, shooting birds, catching fish, dipping for marine organisms, and investigating the stinging mechanism of the Portuguese man-of-war. He regretted his southern continent and he was a little resentful of the ship's company's obvious longing for home and roast beef: "That a Southern Continent really exists, I firmly beleive; but if ask'd why I beleive so, I confess my reasons are weak; yet I have a prepossession in favour of the fact which I find it difficult to account for." But the renunciation did not sour him at all; there were the riches of the air and sea, there was the writing of his long, considered essay on New Zealand and the Maoris; there were his collections to attend to; and at dawn on 19 April 1770 there was the cry of land. "At 10 it was pretty plainly to be observd; it made in sloping hills, coverd in Part with trees or bushes, but interspersed with large tracts of sand. At Noon the land much the same."

He was interrupted at this point by three water spouts but his next entries show it to have been a promising land.

> 20 The country this morn rose in gentle sloping hills which had the appearance of the highest fertility, every hill seemd to be cloth'd with Trees of no mean size; at noon a smoke was seen a little way inland, and in the Evening several more.
>
> 21 In the morn the land appeard much as it did yesterday but rather more hilly; in the even again it became flatter. Several smoaks were seen from whence we concluded it to be rather more populous; at night five fires.

They coasted along it, heading northwards, for a little more than a week, sometimes at a distance of twenty miles, sometimes close enough "to discern 5 people who appeared through our glasses to be enormously black: so far did the prejudices which we had built on Dampiers account influence us that we fancied we could see the Colour when we could scarce distinguish or not they were men"[4] and to see the smoke of fires. On this totally unknown shore, sometimes with calms and sometimes with contrary winds, Cook was obliged to proceed with great caution: for not only was there the horrible possibility of being caught on a lee shore, but although the *Endeavour* was reasonably well supplied with provisions, her bosun's and carpenter's stores, after nearly two years at sea, were running very low: only a little before this he had had to condemn sixty fathoms of the best bower anchor's cable as being only good for junk, and a few days later he wrote "The Spritsail topsail being wore to rags it was condemn'd as no longer fit for its proper use and taken to repair the two topgallant sails they being of themselves so bad as not to be worth the expence of new Canvas but with the help of this sail may be made to last some time longer." They coasted along, finding no good anchorage but taking great notice of the shore. On 25 April Banks wrote "The countrey tho in general well enough clothd appeard in some place bare; it resembled in my imagination the back of a lean Cow, coverd in general with long hair, but nevertheless where her scraggy hip bones have stuck out farther than they ought accidentle rubbs and knocks have intirely bard them of their share of covering."

However, after dinner on 27 April "the Captn proposd to hoist out boats and attempt to land, which gave me no small satisfaction." Yet it was no more than a moderate satisfaction for the pinnace leaked too much to be used that day and the yawl, which could only just contain Cook, Banks, Solander, Tupia and four rowers, was too small and too deep-laden to attempt landing through the heavy surf. This was particularly vexing, because just at this time four men were seen walking briskly along the shore, two of them carrying a small canoe. It was hoped that the canoe would put off to meet them; but not at all: the aborigines sat on the rocks until the yawl was within a quarter of a mile and then ran hastily into the country – "they appeard to us as well as we could judge at that distance exceedingly black." The surf was indeed impassable, "so we were obligd to content ourselves with gazing from the boat at the productions of nature which we so much wishd to enjoy a nearer acquaintance with. The trees were not very large and stood seperate from each other without the least underwood; among them we could discern many cabbage trees but nothing else which we could call by name. In the course of the night many fires were seen."

This was on a frustrating Saturday, but on Sunday a bay appeared at last, with people on the shore, and although the wind was blowing right out of it Cook sent the master in the pinnace to sound the entrance. In the afternoon the wind backed southerly and the ship stood in, sailing between the two arms of the bay, Point Solander and Cape Banks.

28 . . . During this time a few of the Indians who had not followed the boat remaind on the rocks opposite the ship, threatning and menacing with their pikes and swords – two in particular who were painted with white, their faces seemingly only dusted over with it, their bodies painted with broad strokes drawn over their breasts and back resembling much a soldiers cross belts, and their legs and thighs also with such like broad strokes drawn round them which imitated broad garters or bracelets. Each of these held in his hand a wooden weapon about 2 feet long, in shape much resembling a scymeter; the blades of these lookd whitish and some thought shining insomuch that they were almost of opinion that they were made of some kind of metal, but myself thought they were no more than wood smeard over with the same white pigment with which they paint their bodies. These two seemd to talk earnestly together, at times brandishing their crooked weapons at us in token of defiance. By noon we were well within the mouth of the inlet which appeard to be very good. Under the South head of it were four small canoes; in each of these was one man who held in his hand a long pole with which he struck fish, venturing with his little imbarkation almost into the surf. These people seemd to be totaly engag'd in what they were about: the ship passed within a quarter of a mile of them and yet they scarce lifted their eyes from their employment; I was almost inclind to think that attentive to their business and deafnd by the noise of the surf they neither saw nor heard her go past them. At 1 we came to an anchor abreast of a small village consisting of about 6 or 8 houses. Soon after this an old woman followed by three children came out of the wood; she carried several peices of stick and the children also had their little burthens; when she came to the houses 3 more younger children came out of one of them to meet her. She often lookd at the ship but expressd neither surprise nor concern. Soon after this she lighted a fire and the four Canoes came in from fishing; the people landed, hauld up their boats and began to dress their dinner to all appearance totaly unmovd at us, tho we were within a little more than ½ a mile of them. Of all these people we had seen so distinctly through our glasses we had not been able to observe the least signs of Cloathing: myself to the best of my judgment plainly discerned that the woman did not copy our mother Eve even to the fig leaf.

After dinner the boats were mann'd and we set out from the ship intending to land at the place where we saw these people, hoping that as they regarded the ships coming in to the bay so little they would as little regard our landing. We were in this however mistaken, for as soon as we approachd the rocks two of the men came down upon them, each armd with a lance of about 10 feet long and a short stick which he seemd to handle as if it was a machine to throw the lance. They calld to us very loud in a harsh sounding Language of which neither us or Tupia understood a word, shaking their lances and menacing, in all appearance resolvd to dispute our landing to the utmost tho they were but two and we 30 or 40 at least. In this manner we parleyd with them for about a quarter of an hour, they waving us to be gone, we again signing that we wanted water and that we meant them no harm. They remaind resolute so a musquet was fird over them, the Effect of which was that the Youngest of the two dropd a bundle of lances on the rock at the instant in which he heard the report; he however snatchd them up again and both renewd their threats and opposition. A Musquet loaded with small shot was now fird at the Eldest of the two who was about 40 yards from the boat; it struck him on the legs but he minded it very little so another was immediately fird at him; on this he ran up to the house about 100 yards distant and soon returnd with a sheild. In the mean time we had landed upon the rock. He immediately threw a lance at us and the young man another which fell among the thickest of us but hurt nobody; 2 more musquets with small shot were then fird at them on which the Eldest threw one more lance and then ran away as did the other. We went up to the houses, in one of which we found the children hid behind the sheild and a peice of bark in one of the houses. We were conscious from the distance the people had been from us when we fird that the shot could have done them no material harm; we therefore resolvd to leave the children on the spot without even opening their shelter. We therefore threw in to the house to them some beads, ribbands, cloths &c. as presents and went away. We however thought it no improper measure to take away with us all the lances which we could find about the houses, amounting in number to forty or fifty. They were of various lenghs, from 15 to 6 feet in lengh; both those which were thrown at us and all we found except one had 4 prongs headed with very sharp fish bones, which were besmeared with a greenish colourd gum that at first gave me some suspicions of Poison. The people were blacker than any we have seen in the Voyage tho by no means negroes; their beards were thick and bushy and they seemd to have a redundancy of hair upon those parts of the body where it generally grows; the hair of their heads was bushy and thick but by no means wooley like that of a Negro; they were of a common size, lean and seemd active and nimble; their voices were coarse and strong.

This was really all that Banks could say about the aborigines at that time, for although they were often seen, particularly by the waterers and grass-cutters, and although they sometimes came within shouting distance, acting in a generally menacing fashion and sometimes throwing an ineffectual spear at those who ran away for fun, they declined all closer contact throughout the *Endeavour*'s nine-day stay, though it is true that one midshipman, out shooting, suddenly came upon a very old man and woman and some children sitting under a tree, who refused the parrots he offered, withdrawing from his hand "in token either of extreme fear or disgust".

But in the early days it was possible that they might be dangerous, so when Cook, Banks and Solander went some way into the country the party numbered twelve muskets.

1 [May 1770] we saw many Indian houses and places where they had slept upon the grass without the least shelter; in these we left beads ribbands &c. We saw one quadruped about the size of a Rabbit. My Greyhound got sight of him and instantly lamed himself against a stump which lay concealed in the long grass; we also saw the dung of a large animal clawd like a dog or wolf and as large as the latter; and of a small animal whose feet were like that of a polecat or weesel. The trees over our heads abounded very much with Loryquets and Cocatoos of which we shot several; both these sorts flew in flocks of several scores together.

Yet though the birds were plentiful, they could not possibly compete with the plants, which were present in extraordinary abundance.

2 The morn was rainy and we who had got already so many plants were well contented to find an excuse for staying on board to examine them a little at least. In the afternoon however it cleared up and we returned to our old occupation of collecting, in which we had our usual success.

3 Our collection of Plants was now grown so immensely large that it was necessary that some extraordinary care should be taken of them least they should spoil in the books. I therefore devoted this day to that business and carried all the drying paper, near 200 quires of which the larger part was full, ashore and spreading them upon a sail in the sun kept them in this manner exposd the whole day, often turning them and sometimes turning the quires in which were plants inside out. By this means they came on board at night in very good condition. During the time this was doing 11 Canoes, in each of which was one Indian, came towards us. We soon saw that the people in them were employd in striking fish; they came within about ½ a mile of us intent on their own employments and not at all regarding us. When the damp of the Even made it necessary to send my Plants and books on board I made a small excursion in order to shoot any thing I could meet with and found a large quantity of Quails, much resembling our English ones, of which I might have killd as many almost as I pleasd had I given my time up to it, but my business was to kill variety and not too many individuals of the same species.

4 Myself in the woods botanizing as usual, now quite void of fear as our neighbours have turned out such rank cowards.

5 As tomorrow was fixd for our sailing Dr Solander and myself were employd the whole day in collecting specimens of as many things as we possibly could to be examind at sea. The day was calm and the Mosquetos of which we have always had some more than usualy troublesome.

Banks and the men who cut grass for the hardy livestock still surviving on board brought back very rich harvests; so did the fishermen, for on this same day Gore beat his previous record of a 239 lb stingray with another of 336 lb, both of them without their guts. Indeed so many and such excellent stingrays were speared in shallow water as they followed the making tide that the place was very nearly called Sting-Rays Harbour; but in the end Cook wrote, "Sunday 6th. In the evening the yawl return'd from fishing having caught two Sting rays weighing near 600 pounds. The great quantity of New Plants &ca Mr Banks and Dr Solander collected in this place occasioned my giveing it the name of *Botany Bay*." Banks did not seem particularly sensible of the compliment at the time, often calling the anchorage Stingrays Bay in his journal, which continues:

> 6 Went to sea this morn with a fair breeze of wind. The land we saild past during the whole forenoon appeard broken and likely for harbours; in the afternoon again woody and very pleasant. We dind today upon the sting-ray and his tripe: the fish itself was not quite so good as a scate nor was it much inferior, the tripe every body thought excellent. We had with it a dish of the leaves of *tetragonia cornuta* boild,[5] which eat as well as spinach or very near it.

Now began a slow, careful, exactly documented voyage up the coast, with Cook continually making draughts, taking bearings, fixing his position by observations, and giving names to what he saw, many of them naval – Cape Hawke, Cape Byron, Hervey Bay, Keppel Bay – while Banks, Solander, Spöring and above all Parkinson were busy with the immense collections of new plants – Parkinson indeed "in 14 days just . . . made 94 sketch drawings, so quick a hand has he acquired by use": drawings, that is to say, of the Botany Bay plants, "which had been kept fresh till this time by means of tin chests and wet cloths".

Northwards, usually with fair winds, towards the tropic of Capricorn again, the steady south-east trades and the entirely unsuspected danger of the Great Barrier Reef. Entirely unsuspected, for although this prodigious formation stretches over 1250 miles, from Torres Strait right down to below the tropic line, no European had seen it. Only Bougainville had some notion of its existence: coming from the eastwards along the fifteenth parallel in June 1768 he heard the tremendous roar of the surf upon it, the breakers having the fetch of the whole South Pacific with the trade wind to urge them on. "This was the voice of God," he said, hauling his wind for the Louisiade Archipelago, thus missing Australia altogether, "and we obeyed it."

The *Endeavour* moved gently towards these perils, rarely travelling a degree of latitude a day, though occasionally she spread her studding-sails and ran over a hundred miles between noon and noon. After more than a fortnight of this they were in 24°4′S., and there being a convenient bay at hand they anchored in five fathom water with a sandy bottom and went ashore. They had already seen with their telescopes that there were quantities of a pandanus that they had found only in the South Sea islands, and when they landed they found "a great variety of Plants, several however the same as those we ourselves had before seen in the Islands between the tropics and others known to be natives of the east Indies, a sure mark that we were upon the point of leaving the Southern temperate Zone." They were bitten by green ants in the mangroves and stung by green caterpillars and they were almost intolerably hot, but they also found many birds, including pelicans and bustards, one of which Banks shot: it provided an excellent dinner, and the place is still called Bustard Bay. It was at this time, or rather in the night before the landing, that Orton, the captain's clerk, had his clothes and ears cut off by some member or members of the midshipmen's berth while he was dead drunk. Perhaps Orton or Magra (the supposed culprit) did not interest Banks; perhaps the pelicans and the bustards overlaid them; in any event he never mentioned the incident at all, though in a long and detailed entry he did speak of the oysters, some being of the kind that produces pearls.

Banks was in some ways a curiously impersonal man. Parkinson for example who worked so hard on the Botany Bay drawings is only called "one draughtsman", and even Solander returns to a shadowy existence only at very long intervals. Yet Banks was kind and well liked aboard; many of the officers corresponded with him afterwards, and in later years no fewer than six of the foremast hands and two of the Marines applied to him for help. But impersonal or not he was by no means insensitive to beauty: on 26 May he was fishing out of the cabin window and crabs seized the bait, holding on so hard that they could be brought aboard. "They were of 2 sorts, *Cancer pelagicus* Linn. and another much like the former but not so beautiful. The first was ornamented with the finest ultramarine blew conceivable with which all his claws and every Joint was deeply tingd; the under part of him was a lovely white, shining as if glazd and perfectly resembling the white of old China; the other had a little of the ultramarine on his Joints and toes and on his back 3 very remarkable brown spots."

By the end of May the navigation had already become more difficult, with islands and shoal water, and the boats were often out sounding ahead, while Cook sometimes anchored for the night; but on the twenty-ninth, finding a convenient bay, he put in for water. There was no fresh water in Thirsty Sound, but Banks did find termites, millions – literally millions – of butterflies, and a little fish, a goby, that could and voluntarily did skip about on dry land; he also traversed a mangrove-swamp, knee-deep in mud, bent double under the arching roots, persecuted by clouds of mosquitoes, taking an hour to go a quarter of a mile.

There were two more short and not very fruitful landings and then, having passed a headland in about 18°20'S that Cook, perhaps at Banks's request, named Cape Sandwich, they spent the night of 9/10 June lying north of Cape Grafton.

> 10 Without us as we lay at an anchor was a small sandy Island laying upon a large Coral shoal, much resembling the low Islands to the eastward of us but the first of the kind we had met with in this part of the South Sea. Early in the morn we weighd and saild as usual with a fine breeze along shore, the Countrey hilly and stoney. At night fall rocks and sholes were seen ahead, on which the ship was put upon a wind off shore. While we were at supper she went over a bank of 7 or 8 fathom water which she came upon very suddenly, this we concluded to be the tail of the Sholes we had seen at sunset and therefore went to bed in perfect security, but scarce were we warm in our beds when we were call'd up with the alarming news of the ship being fast ashore upon a rock, which she in a few moments convinced us of by beating very violently against the rocks. Our situation became now greatly alarming: we had stood off shore 3 hours and a half with a pleasant breeze so we knew we could not be very near it: we were little less than certain that we were upon sunken coral rocks, the most dreadful of all others on account of their sharp points and grinding quality which cut through a ships bottom almost immediately. The officers however behavd with inimitable coolness void of all hurry and confusion; a boat was got out in which the master went and after sounding round the ship found that she had run over a rock and consequently had Shole water all round her. All this time she continued to beat very much so that we could hardly keep our legs upon the Quarter deck; by the light of the moon we could see her sheathing boards &c. floating thick about her; about 12 her false keel came away.
> 11 In the mean time all kind of Preparations were making for carrying out anchors, but by reason of the time it took to hoist out boats &c. the tide ebbd so much that we found it impossible to attempt to get her off till next high water, if she would hold together so long; and we now found to add to our misfortune that we had got ashore nearly at the top of high water and as night tides generaly rise higher than day ones we had little hopes of getting off even then. For our Comfort however the ship as the tide ebbd settled to the rocks and did not beat near so much as she had done; a rock however under her starboard bow kept grating her bottom making a noise very plainly to be heard in the fore store rooms; this we doubted not would make

a hole in her bottom, we only hopd that it might not let in more water than we could clear with our pumps.

In this situation day broke upon us and showd us the land about 8 Leagues off as we judgd; nearer than that was no Island or place on which we could set foot. It however brought with it a decrease of wind and soon after that a flat calm, the most fortunate circumstance that could Possibly attend people in our circumstances. The tide we found had falln 2 feet and still continued to fall; Anchors were however got out and laid ready for heaving as soon as the tide should rise but to our great surprise we could not observe it to rise in the least.

Orders were now given for lightning the ship which was begun by starting our water and pumping it up; the ballast was then got up and thrown over board, as well as 6 guns (all that we had upon deck). All this time the Seamen workd with surprizing chearfulness and alacrity; no grumbling or growling was to be heard throughout the ship; no not even an oath (tho the ship in general was as well furnishd with them as most in his majesties service). About one the water was faln so low that the Pinnace touchd ground as she lay under the ships bow ready to take in an anchor, after this the tide began to rise and as it rose the ship workd violently upon the rocks so that by 2 she began to make water and increased very fast. At night the tide almost floated her but she made water so fast that three pumps hard workd could but just keep her clear and the 4th absolutely refusd to deliver a drop of water. Now in my opinion I intirely gave up the ship and packing up what I thought I might save prepard myself for the worst.

The most critical part of our distress now approached: the ship was almost afloat and every thing was ready to get her into deep water but she leakd so fast that with all our pumps we could just keep her free: if (as was probable) she should make more water when hauld off she must sink and we well knew that our boats were not capable of carrying us all ashore, so that some, probably the most of us, must be drownd: a better fate maybe than those would have who should get ashore without arms to defend themselves from the Indians or provide themselves with food, on a countrey where we had not the least reason to hope of subsistance had they even every convenience to take it as netts &c. so barren had we always found it; and had they even met with good usage from the natives and food to support them, debarrd from a hope of ever seeing their native countrey or conversing with any but the most uncivilizd savages perhaps in the world.

The dreadfull time now aprochd and the anxiety in every bodys countenance was visible enough: the Capstan and Windlace were mannd and they began to heave: fear of Death now stared us in the face; hopes we had none but of being able to keep the ship afloat until we could run her ashore on some part of the main where out of her materials we might build a vessel large enough to carry us to the East Indies. At 10 O'Clock she floated and was in a few minutes hawled into deep water where to our great satisfaction she made no more water than she had done, which was indeed full as much as we could manage tho no one there was in the ship but who willingly exerted his utmost strength.

12 The people who had been 24 hours at exceeding hard work now began to flag; myself unusd to labour was much fatigued and had lain down to take a little rest, was awakd about 12 with the alarming news of the ships having gaind so much upon the Pumps that she had four feet water in her hold: add to this that the wind blew off the land a regular land breeze so that all hopes of running her ashore were totaly cut off. This however acted upon every body like a charm: rest was no more thought of but the pumps went with unwearied vigour till the water was all out which was done in a much shorter time than was expected, and upon examination it was found that she never had half so much water in her as was thought, the Carpenter having made a mistake in sounding the pumps.

We now began again to have some hopes and to talk of getting the ship into some harbour as we could spare hands from the pumps and get up our anchors; one Bower however we cut away but got the other and three small anchors far more valuable to us than the Bowers, as we were obligd immediately to warp her to windward that we might take advantage of the sea breeze to run in shore.

This they did by carrying anchors in the boats with the cables trailing behind, dropping the anchor, heaving with the capstan until the ship was over it, weighing the anchor and beginning again, a very toilsome process indeed. The ship had struck at about 23.00 hours on Monday 11 June; at 11.00 hours on Tuesday she was still fast at high water; at 17.00, with the tide rising again, the leak was very bad; at 22.30 hours, lightened by 40 tons, she floated was heaved off and warped to the south-east. At 11.00 on Wednesday, having sent up the foretopmast and the foreyard, they got under sail with a light breeze at east-south-east, and, as Cook says, "some hands employ'd sowing ockam wool &ca into a lower studding sail to fother the Ship, others employ'd at the Pumps which still gain'd upon the leak." (This time-table is taken from Cook, because Banks's account is not always easy to follow, but it is given in landsman's days and hours rather than Cook's naval time, in which the days run from noon to noon, so that Tuesday morning is still considered part of Monday.)

On Wednesday afternoon they got up the maintopmast and yard and then put the fothering sail over under the starboard forechains: the idea was that the wool and oakum fixed to the inside of the sail would stop the leak, and this it did to admiration, for the ship was pumped dry and thereafter she made no more than a single pump could easily deal with. All this was carried out, says Cook, by "Mr Munkhouse one of my

Midshipmen [the surgeon's younger brother who] was once in a Merchant ship which sprung a leak and made 48 inches water per hour but by this means was brought home from Virginia to London with only her proper crew, to him I gave the direction of this who exicuted it very much to my satisfaction."

They anchored in seventeen fathom water three miles from the shoal, the weather being blessedly calm, with everybody mortally tired but very cheerful.

> During the whole time of this distress [wrote Banks] I must say for the credit of our people that I beleive every man exerted his utmost for the preservation of the ship, contrary to what I have universaly heard to be the behavior of sea men who have commonly as soon as a ship is in a desperate situation begun to plunder and refuse all command. This was no doubt owing intirely to the cool and steady conduct of the officers, who during the whole time never gave an order which did not shew them to be perfectly composd and unmovd by the circumstances howsoever dreadfull they might appear.
>
> 13 One Pump and that not half workd kept the ship clear all night. In the morn we weighd with a fine breeze of wind and steerd along ashore among innumerable shoals, the boats keeping ahead and examining every appearance of a harbour which presented itself; nothing however was met with which could possibly suit our situation, bad as it was, so at night we came to an anchor. The Pinnace however which had gone far ahead was not returnd, nor did she till nine O'Clock, when she reported that she had found just the place we wanted, in which the tide rose sufficiently and there was every natural convenience that could be wishd for either laying the ship ashore or heaving her down. This was too much to be beleivd by our most sanguine wishes: we however hopd that the place might do for us if not so much as we had been told yet something to better our situation, as yet but precarious, having nothing but a lock of Wool between us and destruction.

Yet the refuge was all it was said to be: "The Captn and myself went ashore to view the Harbour and found it indeed beyond our most sanguine wishes: it was the mouth of a river the entrance of which was to be sure narrow enough and shallow, but once in the ship might be moord afloat so near the shore than by a stage from her to it all her Cargo might be got out and in again in a very short time; in this same place she might be hove down with all ease, but the beach gave signs of the tides rising in the springs 6 or 7 feet which was more than enough to do our business without that trouble." In the same entry Banks remarked that the finding of such a harbour so near was "almost providential", particularly as it had now come on to blow so hard in the offing that the ship must have perished had she stayed out a day longer:

these words and others on the next page are almost his only references to a higher power. Getting into this haven of peace on 17 June however was by no means easy: the *Endeavour*, having behaved beautifully so far, now missed stays twice, and twice she grounded in the narrow entrance. "The second time she remaind till the tide lifted her off. In the meantime Dr Solander and myself began our Plant gathering. In the Evening the ship was moord within 20 feet of the shore." It was high time, because quite apart from the perishability of the lock of Wool, scurvy had at last broken out on board: both Tupia and Green the astronomer were very ill, while eight or nine hands suffered less gravely "from various disorders".

By 22 June Tupia at least had cured himself by catching and eating fish, and the ship had been lightened so that her fore-part could be hauled ashore.

> 22 In the morn I saw her leak which was very large: in the middle was a hole large enough to have sunk a ship with twice our pumps but here providence had most visibly workd in our favour, for it was in great measure plugged up by a stone which was as big as a mans fist: round the Edges of this stone had all the water come in which had so near overcome us, and here we found the wool and oakum or fothering which had releivd us in so unexpected a manner.

He went on to describe the shocking great smooth gashes that the coral had made in the ship's bottom; he then observed that "the People who were sent to the other side of the water in order to shoot Pigeons saw an animal as large as a grey hound, of a mouse coulour and very swift", but it was not until three days later that he could write:

> 25 In gathering plants today I myself had the good fortune to see the beast so much talkd of, tho but imperfectly; he was not only like a grey hound in size and running but had a long tail, as long as any grey hounds; what to liken him to I could not tell, nothing certainly that I have seen at all resembles him.

But the pleasure of this entry was quite done away with by the next.

> 26 Since the ship has been hauld ashore the water that has come into her has of course all gone backwards and my plants which were for safety stowd in the bread room were this day found under water; nobody had warnd me of this danger which had never once enterd into my head; the mischeif was however now done so I set to work to remedy it to the best of my power. The day was scarce long enough to get them all shifted &c: many were savd but some intirely lost and spoild.

During the following weeks, while Cook and his men were busy on the ship, Banks did his utmost to repair his losses; he also came to know much more about Australia, or at least the northern tropical part of what is now Queensland, and its flora and fauna.

The ship was ready on Sunday 1 July and she was to be hauled off on Monday, the day of the highest spring tide; but when they climbed a hill at low water to see how they should sail out "the Prospect was indeed melancholy: the sea every where full of innumerable shoals, some above and some under water, and no prospect of any streight passage out."

The boats were sent to discover a passage and on July 3 the pinnace brought news of a way through most of the shoals but not all, and in any case it was directly to windward, right into the steady south-east trade. A land breeze was needed to take them out that way and so far they had known only one in all this time. On the other hand the boat did bring a full load of shellfish gathered at low water, including "a large kind of Cockles (*Chamas Gigas*) One of which was more than 2 men could eat" – small specimens of the famous giant clam of the Barrier Reef.

Yet even if the passage had been to leeward, the ship could not have taken it right away: she had been strained by being hauled up. She leaked, and more work had to be done on her. While this was being carried out the boats continued their exploration and presently they discovered turtles, "so many that three were taken only with the Boat hook. [Together they weighed 791 lb.] The promise of such plenty of good provisions made our situation appear much less dreadfull; were we obligd to Wait here for another season of the year when the winds might alter we could do it without fear of wanting Provisions: this thought alone put every body in vast spirits."

They now had turtles of two kinds, greenstuff comparable to spinach, a certain amount of fruit (indifferent plantains and what they called a plum), the great clams and so many fish that one day the seine brought in enough to give each man 2½ lb, and presently they were so familiar with the kangaroo that Banks could write:

> 27 This day was dedicated to hunting the wild animal. We saw several and had the good fortune to kill a very large one which weighd 84 lb.
>
> 28 Botanizing with no kind of success. The Plants were now intirely compleated and nothing new to be found, so that sailing is all we wish for if the wind would but allow us. Dind today upon the animal, who eat but ill, he was I suppose too old. His fault however was an uncommon one, the total want of flavour, for he was certainly the most insipid meat I eat.

Insipid or not (and an earlier kangaroo had "proved excellent meat"), for the hands this life ashore was not unlike Fiddler's Green, particularly the feasting upon enormous quantities of the best green turtle; and their work on the second repair lacked the furious drive of the first.

It was turtles however that caused the trouble with the aborigines. The black men first appeared on 10 July, four of them on the far bank of the river with an outrigger canoe; two of them were tempted across to the ship and they were given cloth, paper and the usual presents, "all which they took and put into the canoe without shewing the least signs of satisfaction: at last a small fish was by chance thrown to them on which they expressed the greatest joy imaginable, and putting off from the ship made signs that they would bring over their comrades." This they did, and once contact was established they came day after day, perfectly naked but painted with white lines and red patches, with bones across their noses. They in their turn presented a ritual fish, and they were quite polite, though somewhat later when "we attempted to follow them hoping they would lead us to their fellows where we might have an opportunity of seeing their Women; they by signs made us understand that they did not desire our company." Nor did they desire the *Endeavour*'s gifts, most of which were found later by the botanists "left all in a heap together as lumber not worth carriage", but they did desire the *Endeavour*'s turtles and one day ten of them came aboard and made their wishes known; on being refused they tried taking one; when this did not answer after two or three attempts they "all in an instant leapd into their Canoe and went ashore where I had got before them Just ready to set out plant gathering; they seized their arms in an instant, and taking fire from under a pitch kettle which was boiling they began to set fire to the grass to windward of the few things we had left ashore with surprising dexterity and quickness; the grass which was 4 or 5 feet high and as dry as stubble burnt with vast fury." Fortunately no great harm was done (one piglet scorched, one aboriginal peppered with small-shot) and peace was made the same day, but the old confident relations could hardly be restored, and in any event it was time for the *Endeavour* to go.

But, as Banks wrote in his journal, "where to go? – to windward was impossible, to leeward was a Labyrinth of Shoals, so that how soon we might have the ship to repair again or lose her quite no one could tell." It was a disagreeable outlook to be sure, yet on 4 August Cook had the ship warped across the bar and stood out to sea, east by north, with the pinnace ahead sounding.

Now followed a week of intensely anxious navigation as the *Endeavour* threaded the labyrinth, sometimes in fair weather, more often in foul with winds so strong that one dreadful night she dragged her anchor more than three miles, and when at dawn they saw that they were driving on to a reef and dropped another she dragged that too, never stopping even with a whole cable out on the one and two on the other until they struck both yards and topmasts down on deck. At last, on the eleventh, when there was a hope that they were clear of the shoals, they came within reach of a high island, Lizard Island, about fifteen miles from the mainland; Cook and Banks landed upon it and climbed to the top. "To my mortification," wrote Cook, "I discoverd a Reef of Rocks laying about 2 or 3 Leagues without the Island, extending in a line NW and SE farther than I could see on which the Sea broke very high." But a moment's reflection told him that the huge breakers almost certainly meant that he was looking at the outermost reef and that the gaps he saw were passages through to the unencumbered ocean. Early the next morning he sent the pinnace to sound one of the channels, and while they were waiting for the boat's return Banks found a few plants new to him and a small tract of woodland "which abounded very much with large Lizzards some of which I took". Back to the ship and Banks's journal runs

> 13 Ship stood out for the opening we had seen in the reef and about 2 O'Clock passed it. It was about ½ a mile wide. As soon as the ship was well without it we had no ground with 100 fathm of Line so became in an instant quite easy, being once more in the main Ocean and consequently freed from all our fears of shoals &c.

(Cook uses much the same expression – each saw the other's journal at times – but after shoals &c he adds "after having been intangled among them more or less ever since the 26th of May, in which time we have saild 360 Leagues without ever having a Man out of the cheans heaving the Lead when the Ship was under way, a circumstance that I dare say never happened to any ship before and yet here it was absolutely necessary.")

But it was a short-lived relief. All 14 August they sailed along happily out of sight of land with a steady south-east trade and a fine following sea: then the journal goes on

> 15 Fine weather and moderate trade. The Captn fearful of going too far from the Land, least he should miss an opportunity of examining whether or not the passage which is layd down in some charts between New Holland and New Guinea realy existed or not, steerd the ship west right in for the land; about 12 O'Clock it was seen from the Mast head and about one the Reef laying without it in just the same manner as when we left it. He stood

> on however resolving to stand off at night after having taken a nearer view, but just at night fall found himself in a manner embayd in the reef so that it was a moot Point whether or not he could weather it on either tack; we stood however to the Northward and at dark it was concluded she would go clear of every thing we could see. The night however was not the most agreeable: all the dangers we had escaped were little in comparison of being thrown upon this reef if that should be our lot. A Reef such a one as I now speak of is a thing scarcely known in Europe or indeed any where but in these seas: it is a wall of Coral rock rising almost perpendicularly out of the unfathomable ocean, always overflown at high water commonly 7 or 8 feet, and generaly bare at low water; the large waves of the vast ocean meeting with so sudden a resistance make here a most terrible surf Breaking mountains high, especially when as in our case the general trade wind blows directly upon it.

This is perfectly sound as far as it goes, but Banks was a landsman and he missed one essential point: as soon as Cook was sure that the Barrier Reef stretched north and south as far as eye could reach "we hauld close upon a wind which was now at ESE. We had hardly trimed our sails before the wind came to EBN which was right upon the Reef and of Course made our clearing of it doubtfull." Cook therefore clawed off the lee-shore as much as ever he could, steering first north and north by east and then south-south-east. Banks goes on:

> 16 At three O'Clock this morn it dropd calm on a sudden which did not at all better our situation; we judged ourselves not more than 4 or 5 l'gs from the reef, maybe much less, and the swell of the sea which drove right in upon it carried the ship towards it fast. We tried the lead often in hopes to find ground that we might anchor but in vain; before 5 the roaring of the Surf was plainly heard and as day broke the vast foaming billows were plainly enough to be seen scarce a mile from us and towards which we found the ship carried by the waves surprizingly fast, so that by 6 o'Clock we were within a Cables length of them, driving on as fast as ever and still no ground with 100 fathom of line. Every method had been taken since we first saw our danger to get the boats out in hopes that they might tow us off but it was not yet accomplishd; the Pinnace had had a plank stripped off her for repair and the longboat under the Booms was lashd and fastned so well from our supposd security that she was not yet got out. Two large Oars or sweeps were got out at the stern ports to pull the ships head round the other way in hopes that might delay till the boats were out. All this while we were approaching and came I believe before this could be effected within 40 yards of the breaker; the same sea that washd the side rose in a breaker enormously high the very next time it did rise, so between us it was only a dismal valley the breadth of one wave; even now the lead was hove 3 or 4 lines fastned together but no ground could be felt with above 150 fathm. Now was our case truly desperate, no man I believe but who gave himself

intirely over, a speedy death was all we had to hope for and that from the vastness of the Breakers which must quickly dash the ship all to pieces was scarce to be doubted. Other hopes we had none: the boats were in the ship and must be dashed in peices with her and the nearest dry land was 8 or 10 Leagues distant. We did not however cease our endeavours to get out the long boat which was by this time almost accomplished. At this critical juncture, at this I must say terrible moment, when all assistance seemd too little to save even our miserable lives, a small air of wind sprang up, so small that at any other time in a calm we should not have observd it. We however plainly saw that it instantly checkd our progress; every sail was therefore put in a proper position to catch it and we just observd the ship to move in a slaunting direction off from the breakers. This at least gave us time and redoubling our efforts we at last got out the long boat and manning her sent her ahead. The ship still moved a little off but in less than 10 minutes our little Breeze died away into as flat a calm as ever. Now was our anziety again renewd: innumerable small peices of paper &c were thrown over the ships side to find whether the boats realy moved her ahead or not and so little did she move that it remaind almost every other time a matter of dispute. Our little freindly Breeze now visited us again and lasted about as long as before, thrusting us possibly 100 yards farther from the breakers: we were still however in the very jaws of destruction. A small opening had been seen in the reef about a furlong from us, its breadth was scarce the lengh of the ship, into this however it was resolvd to push her if possible. Within was no surf, therefore we might save our lives: the doubt was only whether we could get the ship so far: our little breeze however a third time visited us and pushd us almost there. The fear of Death is Bitter: the prospect we now had before us of saving our lives tho at the expence of every thing we had made my heart set much lighter on its throne, and I suppose there were none but what felt the same sensations. At length we arrivd off the mouth of the wishd for opening and found to our surprize what had with the little breeze been the real cause of our Escape, a thing that we had not before dreamt of. The tide of flood it was that had hurried us so unacountably fast towards the reef, in the near neighbourhood of which we arrivd just at high water, consequently its ceasing to drive us any farther gave us the opportunity we had of getting off. Now however the tide of Ebb made strong and gushd out of our little opening like a mill stream, so that it was impossible to get in; of this stream however we took advantage as much as possible and it Carried us out near a quarter of a mile from the reef. We well knew that we were to take all the advantage possible of the Ebb so continued towing with all our might and with all our boats, the Pinnace being now repaird, till we had got an offing of 1½ or 2 miles. By this time the tide began to turn and our suspence began again: as we had gaind so little while the ebb was in our favour we had some reason to imagine that the flood would hurry us back upon the reef in spite of our utmost endeavours. It was still as calm as ever so no likely hood of any wind today; indeed had wind sprung up we could only have searched for another opening, for we were so embayd by the reef that with the general trade wind it was impossible to get out. Another opening was however seen ahead and the 1st Lieutenant went away in the small boat to examine it. In the mean time we strugled hard with the flood, sometimes gaining a little then holding only our own and at others loosing a little, so that our situation was almost as bad as ever, as the flood had not yet come to its strength. At 2 however the Lieutenant arrivd with news that the opening was very narrow: in it was good anchorage and a passage quite in free from shoals. The ships head was immediately put towards it and with the tide she towd fast so that by three we enterd and were hurried in by a stream almost like a mill race, which kept us from even a fear of the sides tho it was not above ¼ of a mile in breadth. By 4 we came to an anchor happy once more to encounter those shoals which but two days before we thought ourselves supreamly happy to have escap'd from. How little do men know what is for their real advantage: two days ago our utmost wishes were crownd by getting without the reef and today we were made happy again by getting within it.

Chapter 6

HOME AGAIN: *RESOLUTION*: ICELAND

ALTHOUGH the *Endeavour* still had the whole breadth of the world to travel, meeting with a great many dangers by land and sea, nothing else in the voyage equalled this racing passage through Providential Channel and the extraordinarily sudden transition from the full Pacific swell heaving them towards that mortal thundering surf to the quiet water where they lay safely at anchor inside the reef.

For the next few days they coasted along, and Cook could return to his charting of the main; the weather was remarkably agreeable, the breeze kind, and although the shoals were sometimes troublesome the Endeavours had by now become expert in distinguishing a white sand bottom from coral rock. The ship was in twelve and eleven degrees of southern latitude, and as Banks says "we began to look out for the Passage we expected to find between New Holland and New Guinea" – a somewhat hypothetical passage, it may be said. Torres had in fact sailed along the south coast of New Guinea in 1606, but in 1770 the existence of what is now called Torres Strait was by no means certain. The Président de Brosses showed it on his chart and Dalrymple, though with less confidence, on his; but Bougainville's knows nothing of it, though he was a friend of Brosses, while the map prepared by M. Bellin of the French navy (and also of the Royal Society) for the Abbé Prévost's *Histoire Générale des Voyages* in 1753 also shows New Guinea and Australia firmly joined and so do many, many, others.

However, on 21 August a narrow opening appeared, trending away to the west. Although it might well have been no more than an inlet, in the event it proved to be a channel between a group of islands and the main. Presently it broadened, with the continent bearing away south-west, and Cook "in great hopes that we had at last found a Passage into the Indian Seas", landed on an island, climbed its modest hill and saw that to the westward there was indeed nothing but island-studded ocean. He had sailed right up the east coast of Australia and now he had just passed its northern extremity, a cape that he named after the Duke of York, giving the strait the name of the ship. Once again he hoisted English colours and in the King's name took possession of everything between latitude thirty-eight south and this place, calling the whole

New Wales, the South being added a little later. Some natives had seen him land, but on his approach they retreated, and apparently they made no comment of any kind. The party fired three volleys, answered from the ship, and then they re-embarked.

A couple of days later, when they were off Booby Island, just beyond Endeavour Strait, where Banks found some new plants, they had trouble with the best bower's cable, which parted on weighing; but with typical perseverance they swept for the anchor, recovered it, and so on 27 August set sail for New Guinea: as Banks wrote, "In the morn fresh trade and fine clear weather made us hope that our difficulties were drawing to a period: it was now resolved to hawl up to the Northward in order to make the coast of New Guinea in order to assure ourselves that we had got clear of the South Sea which was accordingly done."

Two days later they fell in with the land, a low thickly-wooded shore guarded by mudbanks that stretched far out into the shallow sea: "Distant as the land was a very Fragrant smell came off from it realy in the morn with the little breeze which blew right off shore, it resembled much the smell of gum Benjamin; as the sun gathered power it dyed away and was no longer smelt. All the latter part of the day we had calms and light winds all round the compass, the weather at the same time being most intolerably hot."

They sailed on in the warm, turbid water, sometimes quite out of sight of land because of the shoals; it was not until 3 September that they could go ashore, and even then the party had to wade the last 200 yards. They found men's footprints on the strand and walked cautiously along (though Banks and Solander kept to the edge of the jungle for plants) until they came to a hut in a palm grove. They looked wishfully up at the coconuts but as there was no one even among the seamen who could climb those limbless trunks they passed on. A few minutes later three natives "rushed out of the wood with a hideous shout". The black men threw spears at them and something that flashed and smoked – the men watching from the boat took it for musket-fire but apparently it was tinder carried in a bamboo. There seemed little point in staying, so after a few harmless warning shots the Endeavours returned to the boat; and none too soon, for a hundred more naked Papuans appeared round the farther headland.

This was all Banks ever saw of Papua, but in his short stay he gathered or noted twenty-three plants, a poor total for such rich soil however and one that gave him a low opinion of the country's powers of vegetable variety.

> As soon as ever the boat was hoisted in we made sail and steerd away from this land to the No small satisfaction of I beleive three fourths of our company, the sick became well and the melancholy looked gay. The greatest part of them were now pretty far gone with the longing for home which the Physicians have gone so far as to esteem a disease under the name of Nostalgia; indeed I can find hardly any body in the ship clear of its effects but the Captn Dr Solander and myself, indeed we three have pretty constant employment for our minds which I beleive to be the best if not the only remedy for it.

The people might well be cheerful. These were known waters – the Dutch had been pushing eastwards along the southern shore of Papua for a long time – and with the ship's head turned west for Java they were virtually homeward-bound. They had but to refresh and refit at Batavia, the main Dutch settlement, and let the steady trade wind waft them across the Indian Ocean to the Cape: then they would be on the familiar path of the East Indiamen and they might expect to reach England in three or four months.

Of course there was a great deal of sailing still to be done, but for the most part it was ordinary routine blue-water sailing – no exploring, no men perpetually in the chains heaving the lead, no cry of All hands at any moment of the day or night, and once they had reached the Dutch settlements no more short allowance either: for by now their provisions were very low indeed.

Day after day they steered a little south of west, and as he had done for Tahiti and New Zealand Banks wrote a considered account of Australia, including a short vocabulary of the aboriginal words that he had gathered among the people of the Endeavour River, but also including some remarks that read strangely in the light of his subsequent zeal for the colony. "Barren it may justly be called and in a very high degree, that at least that we saw . . . upon the Whole the fertile soil Bears no kind of Proportion to that which seems by nature doomd to everlasting Barrenness."

The *Endeavour* passed south of Timor and on 18 September 1770 she reached the island of Savu, where the Dutch colours were to be seen, and people walking about in European clothes. The German agent of the Dutch East India Company and the local rajah were very fond of bribes and presents, but they did at least allow the people to supply the ship with buffaloes, sheep, hogs, rice, vegetables, fruit, palm wine and palm sugar, so that it was with even greater spirits that the *Endeavour* steered for Java Head, the Sunda Strait and then Batavia, that notoriously fever-ridden town, which she reached on 9 October 1770.

> A boat came immediately on board us from a ship which had a broad Pendant flying, the officer on board her enquird who we were &c and immediately returnd. Both himself and his people were almost as Spectres, no good omen of the healthyness of the countrey we were arrivd at; our people however who truly might be calld rosy and plump, for we had not a sick man among us, Jeerd and flouted much at their brother sea mens white faces.

Never was laughter more ill-timed: before the month was out the tents ashore were filled with the *Endeavour*'s sick and Banks himself had been seized with a tertian fever, "the fits of which were so violent as to deprive me intirely of my senses and leave me so weak as scarcely to be able to crawl downstairs".

On 5 November Monkhouse the surgeon died; he was followed by Tayeto and Tupia, three seamen and Green's servant Reynolds. By 9 November there were not above twenty men fit for duty and between the 17th and 25th, which the harassed Cook condensed into one entry, rarely more than twelve or fourteen could be mustered, although this was now the busiest time. The excellent Dutch shipwrights had heaved the ship down and had repaired her very badly damaged bottom (an eighth of an inch between them and eternity in places) and now she was to be re-rigged, her sails were to be mended, and water and stores were to be brought aboard and stowed below. With so few hands, and Cook himself ill part of the time, while his first lieutenant was sinking in a consumption, all this took until Christmas; and for much of this period Banks and Solander were extremely ill with fevers, first in the filthy, steaming town and then in a house some way out of it, a place with fresh air, "a thing of the utmost consequence in a countrey perfectly resembling the low parts of my native Lincolnshire". Their servants were all ill too, apart from some casual Malay slaves belonging to the house and a couple of women they had bought themselves, and at one time Solander's physician gave little hope of his living till morning; however, Banks, though very weak, sat up with him all night and brought him through. Before he became too ill himself, Banks was also extremely kind to poor Tupia.

Yet although almost everybody belonging to the *Endeavour* was ill at one time or another, only seven of them died in Batavia, and it was not until they were some way out in the Indian Ocean, working slowly against the western monsoon, that a sudden violent dysentery, a bloody flux, began to kill them in much greater numbers. On 24 January 1771 Corporal Truslove died, "a man much esteem'd by every one on board" said Cook. On 25th Spöring. On 26th Sydney Parkinson, that gifted, amiable young man. 29th Green the astronomer. 30th Moody and Haite, carpenter's crew. 31st Thompson, the ship's cook, Jordan, carpenter's mate, Nicholson and Wolfe, seamen, and by now so many were ill that the watches numbered only four. In February twelve more died, including the carpenter "Mr John Satterley, a man much esteem'd by me and every Gentleman on board", two midshipmen (one the capable young Monkhouse) and the bosun. But now they came to the brisk south-east trades at last, and with the ship running as much as one hundred and fifty miles between noon and noon the disease seemed to check; yet even so three of those who were already sick died on 27 February. Banks himself had had the flux in January and he suffered extremely for a week before recovering as suddenly as he had fallen ill: he says "I got out of bed in good spirits and free from pain." Relatively good spirits, no doubt, since for days he had been doubled up and unable to sleep, but there is a change in his journal: it is not so much the heart that is gone out of it as the gaiety and a good deal of the youth.

He is conscientious still, his curiosity ranges wide, and it is quite surprising, when one considers how little time he was on his feet in Batavia, to see his list of tropical fruit (rather disappointing, he thought), the length of his informed essay on Javan economy, Dutch rule and the spice trade, and his acute remarks about the relation between the Polynesian, Malay and Madagascan languages. But all these deaths had come suddenly: to be sure there had been Tierra del Fuego, and a bosun's mate had died of drinking the bosun's kindly present of a pint and a half of rum all at one go, and Cook had buried a consumptive seaman at Botany Bay; but the captain's care of his people had meant that the usual horrors of a long voyage had just not been seen at all. It would be strange if a good-hearted man had not been deeply saddened by the comparatively sudden and unexpected death of about a third of the shipmates he had been sailing with for two and a half years, many of them most respectable men. Banks was never a particularly witty writer, but he was a cheerful one and he could speak of the hands keeping to their "old trade of Booby Eating" and of the Savu women being "remarkably short and generaly squat built" and having "a kind of sameness of features among them which may well account for the chastity of the men for which virtue this Island is said to be remarkable": this is now laid quite aside, nor does it return.

They reached Cape Town on 14 March 1771, where still another seaman died and Solander was seriously ill. Here they heard of Bougainville again – the first time had been in Batavia – and it was thought that England and Spain were now on the brink of war. Before his voyage to Tahiti Bougainville, who had colonized the Falklands at his own expense, poor gentleman, had been obliged to give them up to Spain, the Spaniards having made a great noise in Paris. Now the English, the first discoverers, whose recently installed garrison had been removed somewhat later by the Spaniards of Buenos Aires, were making a great noise in Madrid, and arming the Royal Navy too.

Banks wrote a careful piece on the Dutch and the Hottentots – he saw little of the country – and in the middle of April they sailed for St Helena exercising their guns as they went, in case of war. They had a fairly easy passage, accompanied by albatrosses, and one May morning they saw the island right ahead, together with a dozen East Indiamen, HMS *Portland*, sent to protect them against the Spaniards, and HMS *Swallow*, just arrived with the news that the Spaniards had given way.

Banks and Solander had only part of two days to botanize and explore, which they did on horseback. Banks did not think much of the place or the people: he disliked the absence of wheelbarrows and the consequent loads on the labourers' heads, and he loathed the presence of slaves, even more their cruel treatment. Many years later Brougham called him a high Tory and so perhaps he was in the more amiable interpretation, as far as he was a political animal at all: but broadly speaking at that time the Tories were in favour of the slave trade, whereas Banks was as strongly opposed to it as was Darwin a generation or so later.

They sailed in company with the fleet on 4 May, keeping up as well as ever they could, and presently they saw Ascension: but by now the journal is no more than a brief record of losing the trade wind, seeing some gulfweed, losing the fleet, striking the odd fish, and picking up the north-east trades. It is a dull record, and perhaps Banks was still haunted by death. Molineux, the master, had died just after the Cape, and now in latitude 10°47′N the first lieutenant, Zachary Hicks, at last succumbed to his tuberculosis and was buried at sea. Then on the last sparse page come the entries

> 30 [June] Both yesterday and today a few Shearwaters were seen; in the night many were about the ship crying very much.
> 4 [July] My Bitch Lady was found dead in my Cabbin laying upon a stool on which she generaly slept. She had been remarkably well for some days; in the night she shreikd out very loud so that we who slept in the great Cabbin heard her, but becoming quiet immediately no one regarded it. Whatever disease was the cause of her death it was the most sudden that ever came under my Observation. Many Shearwaters were seen about the ship.

8 Calm; went in boat and shot Fulmar and Manks Puffin of Pennants *British Zoology*. Much sea weed but no more Lepades.
10 This Morning the land was discovered by Young Nick the same boy who first saw New Zeland: it provd to be the Lizzard.
12 At 3 O'Clock landed at Deal.

Banks went ashore at once and travelled up to London, a change more violent than any landing on far foreign shores – a different element and pace and mood of life, and above all sudden intense, varied sociability and varied business – a change from one world to another. Banks did not ordinarily keep a journal on land, only for particular expeditions, but if he had done so, and if he had had the leisure to make detailed entries, his diary would have shown an extraordinary burst of activity. The *Endeavour*'s return had been heralded by newspaper extracts of letters from Batavia, St Helena and various ships that had spoken her on the way home, and she was welcomed with the greatest enthusiasm. She may not have discovered any great southern continent full of diamonds and gold, but she had observed the transit of Venus and quite apart from that the voyage was an immense success compared with those of poor Byron or even Wallis, to say nothing of the unfortunate Bougainville. Banks and Solander were the talk of London – they were invited everywhere – and of the learned world: admittedly, Cook was presented to the King and promoted master and commander, but it was Banks who was received first, at a court held a week earlier; it was Banks and Solander who were summoned to Windsor, Banks and Solander who had, as the *Westminster Journal* put it, "the honour of frequently waiting on his Majesty at Richmond", Banks and Solander who travelled up to Oxford to receive the university's great compliment, the honorary doctorate of civil law, and it was to "the immortal Banks" that Linnaeus himself addressed a letter which is hard to read in places but whose tenor was that the entire cohort of botanists, vehemently and with a single voice called out Banks's praises – no one since the earth began had dared so much, no one had been so generous, no one had exposed himself to so many dangers – the botanists all thanked God for having brought him safely through such perils. Banks, who had surely seen more than any botanist who had lived before him, was the glory not only of England but of the whole world – he should be the botanists' oracle, and they should raise a monument to him more lasting than all the pyramids of Egypt, a monument that would endure as long as there were living men who recognized the Creator in His works. Linnaeus regretted that his age would probably prevent him seeing the publication of Banks's treasures, his last and greatest wish;

and he took leave with the words *Vale vir sine pare*, Farewell O unequalled man.[1]

Indeed the impression of Banks's pre-eminence was so general that a newspaper could refer to "Lieutenant Cook, of the Royal Navy, who sailed round the Globe with Messrs Solander, Banks etc." This literally preposterous notion may at least in part have originated in the King's attitude and his rapidly increasing friendship for Banks. George III's subjects might on occasion stone his carriage and mob his less popular ministers, but the crown had a political influence and a range of patronage inconceivable today, and quite apart from that, reverence or regard or respect for "his sacred Majesty" was still very great: so great in fact that it survived the unfortunate end of his reign and his still more unfortunate sons. And in his youth the King had been chiefly formed by his mother, now the Dowager Princess of Wales, and by her particular friend Lord Bute (it will be remembered that Frederick, Prince of Wales and George III's father, died in 1751, that is to say before George II): as political philosophers, with the highest of high-Tory opinions, they may not have been the most valuable tutors, but they were both devoted gardeners – the Princess of Wales might almost be considered the founder of Kew – and Lord Bute was a far more than ordinarily competent botanist; his *Botanical Tables containing the Different Families of British Plants* is a splendid production; his gardens at Luton Hoo were famous; and to his own herbarium he added that of Gronovius. He was also a great landowner, closely concerned with agriculture and forestry, and those interests too he handed on to his pupil.

It is little wonder then that George III, the farmer King, who knew nothing of the sea (in Byam Martin's memoirs there is a pleasant picture of him and his queen aboard a man-of-war at Weymouth wondering whether to go down a ladder backwards or forwards) should have more to say to Banks than to Cook. Besides, although Banks was not a landowner on the King's scale, his Lincolnshire estate alone had some 200 farms on it, which gave them still another point in common; and lastly they belonged to the same young generation, the King being a youngish thirty-three and Banks no more than twenty-eight, whereas Cook was now a hard-bitten and formidable forty-three.

The view of Banks as the leading figure, quite overshadowing Cook, made it seem natural for the *Gazeteer and New Daily Advertiser* of 26 August 1771[2] to say "Mr Banks is to have two ships from government to pursue his discoveries in the South Seas, and will sail upon his second voyage next March", while a week later the *Westminster Journal* improved upon it with "The celebrated Mr Banks will shortly make another voyage to St George's Island, in the South Seas, and it is said, that Government will allow him three ships, with men, arms and provisions, in order to plant and settle a colony there."

Cook does not appear to have been offended by all this: perhaps, in that age of such very strong social distinction, he thought it was in the ordinary course of things, and in any event he knew perfectly well how he was regarded in the service, the Admiralty (where Sandwich was First Lord again) and the Royal Society – by those whose opinion he valued most. Besides, he had a very real liking for Banks, and Banks had done the handsome thing by him: here is the letter that Cook wrote him on this occasion:

Wills Coffee House, Charing Cross
Sunday morng.[3]

Dear Sir,

Your very obliging letter was the first messenger that conveyed to me Lord Sandwich's intentions. Promotion unsolicited to a man in my situation in life must convey a satisfaction to the mind that is better conceived than described – I had this morning the honour to wait upon his Lordship who renewed his promises, and in so obliging a manner as convinced me he approved of the Voyage. The reputation I may have acquired on this account by which I shall receive promotion calls to my mind the very great assistance I received therein from you which will ever be remembered with most grateful acknowledgements by

Dear Sir Your most obliged Humble
servt
Jam[s] Cook

Lord Sandwich was a politician, but in this case he kept his promises: not only was Cook promoted (even in peacetime the Admiralty could scarcely have done less) but in November of that same year he was appointed to command the *Resolution*, a vessel of the same nature and provenance as the *Endeavour* but gauging 462 tons as opposed to 370, which with her consort the *Adventurer* of 336 tons, also a collier, was intended for an even more heroic voyage into the southern oceans, there either to discover the vast hypothetical continent or to disprove its existence.

Early in proceedings Sandwich asked Banks whether he would go too: though perhaps that is not quite the right expression, for some fifty years later Banks, making a deliberate statement to his librarian, that eminent botanist Robert Brown, put it in this way:

Soon after my return from my voyage round the world I was solicited by Lord Sandwich, the First Lord of the Admiralty, to undertake another

> voyage of the same nature. His solicitation was couched in the following words, "If you will go, we will send other ships." So strong a solicitation, agreeing exactly with my own desires was not to be neglected. I accordingly answered that I was ready and willing.

Whatever the form of the solicitation, suggestion or offer, it was certainly agreed that Banks should sail in the *Resolution*; and in principle the ships were to leave in March 1772. This meant of course that he would not have time to publish the results of his first voyage, for although Solander had already written a great many of the descriptions, a great many more still remained to be done, and then most of Parkinson's hundreds of drawings had to be completed: at times when the specimens were coming aboard at a great pace his practice had been to draw a very exact outline and give mere indications of the colours. Yet even if Banks had had all the time in the world, he would still have had to overcome his curious aversion to print; he had no notion of himself as a writer, and although his collections were open to all natural philosophers, no published account of his Newfoundland journey had yet been given to the learned world.

But before March Banks had an enormous number of things to do apart from that. In the very first place he had to remove the vast collections of plants, mammals, reptiles, birds, insects, marine creatures and ethnological objects, many of which, particularly the dried plants, required immediate and skilful care. And then his estates had to be set in order, for although he had been away so long and in no position to spend any money at all, it does not appear that his rents had accumulated to the extent he could have wished, since he had to borrow for the coming expedition. Then, or perhaps at the same time, there was the unfortunate matter of Miss Blosset to be cleared up. Perhaps this too was a costly process. Barrington, in the ill-natured gossiping letter quoted on page 66 says "Should he not . . . have immediately plac'd in the Stocks & in Miss Blosset's name a most noble satisfaction (as far as money could repair it) for this injury?", and it is not at all improbable that Banks saw things in the same light. He may have been a sinful creature (next year he took a Miss B—n into keeping and got her with child) but he was always a generous one. A little after this he had another unpleasant experience, though of a completely different nature: during the *Endeavour*'s voyage Sydney Parkinson had kept if not a formal journal then at least notes and even large drafts of a narrative, and before his death he asked Solander to see that James Lee the nurseryman (to whose gifted young daughter Ann he left his painting equipment and some pictures) should have a sight of these papers. He also left a copy of his will with Banks, who, upon reaching England, saw Sydney's brother Stanfield, an upholsterer in London, and told him of all this, adding that he would settle for Sydney's outstanding wages, which amounted to £151 8*s* 1*d*. He also handed over Sydney's collection of curiosities and his papers with the exception of "some loose sheets of a journal" which he understood to be for Mr Lee. As well as this he gave the upholsterer some work to do in his New Burlington Street house. Stanfield Parkinson however was an intensely suspicious man, already on the verge of the madness that soon brought about his confinement, and he was persuaded that Banks was defrauding him. Certainly he might reasonably complain that there was some delay, for at this time Banks was exceedingly busy; and it is possible that he may have found communication with Lee, Miss Blosset's guardian, distasteful. All this reinforced the upholsterer's suspicions; he voiced them, and the position soon became impossible. Fortunately a benevolent physician, Dr Fothergill, intervened; like Banks he was a Fellow of the Royal Society, and like Parkinson a Quaker; and in a letter to him Banks said "Now as S Parkinson certainly behaved to me, during the whole of our long voyage, uncommonly well, and with unbounded industry made for me a much larger number of drawings than I ever expected, I always did and still do intend to show to his relations the same gratitude for his good services as I should have done to himself."

In the end Banks gave the Parkinsons £500, at the same time lending Stanfield the MS to read, Dr Fothergill guaranteeing that it should not be misused: this was of some importance since an official account of the voyage, largely based on Cook's and Banks's journals, was to be compiled by Dr Hawkesworth, and before landing Cook had required all other journals to be handed in.

Of course the MS was misused. Stanfield Parkinson had it copied by one Kenrick, a hack of whom the *DNB* says that he "libelled almost every successful author and actor" and who put it into the form of a book. It appeared in Stanfield's name, together with a preface in which both Banks and Fothergill were grossly insulted.

But these were only two incidents in Banks's immensely active life, which had innumerable other aspects: his family meant a great deal to him and they were all to be visited, his mother, aunts, cousins, and above all his sister Sophia: not that he had far to go to see her, since they shared the house in New Burlington Street, being unusually devoted friends. There was the Royal Society and the Club of the Royal Philosophers, a group of Fellows who dined together every week before going on to the meeting, and to whose dinner at the Mitre he invited Cook in November; there was also the Society of Antiquaries, of which Banks was quite an active member, contributing papers from time to time. There were also many, many visitors who came to see the collections, and many, many dinners and evening parties. Before he set off for the South Seas Banks had been acquainted with a great number of people; now he met everybody else worth knowing and many more besides – he is to be found in the pages of Horace Walpole, Fanny Burney, Mrs Thrale, Mrs Delany, Lady Mary Coke and the rest, including Boswell of course, who records this letter from the Doctor:

To Sir Joshua Reynolds

Dear Sir,

Be pleased to send to Mr Banks, whose place of residence I do not know, this note, which I have sent open, that, if you please, you may read it. When you send it, do not use your own seal.

I am, Sir,
Your most humble servant,

Feb 27, 1772 Sam. Johnson

To Joseph Banks, Esq.

Perpetua ambitâ bis terrâ praemia lactis
Haec habet altrici Capra secunda Jovis

Sir,

I return thanks to you and to Dr. Solander for the pleasure which I received in yesterday's conversation. I could not recollect a motto for your Goat, but have given her one. You, Sir, may perhaps have an epick poem from some happier pen than, sir,

Your most humble servant,

Johnson's Court, Sam. Johnson
Fleet Street, Feb. 27, 1772

The goat in question, whose name I am sorry I cannot celebrate, was a truly remarkable animal. An obviously genuine though anonymous letter in the *Middlesex Chronicle* of 29 July 1772 contains this passage: "I must not omit how highly we have been indebted to a milch goat: she was three years in the West Indies, and was once round the world before in the Dolphin, and never went dry the whole time; we mean to reward her services in a good English pasture for life."

Boswell himself did not meet Banks until 22 March 1772, when he called upon Sir John Pringle, Lord Morton's successor as President of the Royal Society, "who had with him Lord Lyttelton and several other Gentlemen, in particular the famous Mr Banks and Dr Solander, whom

I had great curiosity to see. Mr Banks was a genteel young man, very black, and of an agreeable countenance, easy and communicative, without any affectation or appearance of assuming."

Johnson liked him too, in spite of the fact that in a cross-grained mood he uttered his well-known flings against the voyage – "Sir, there is very little of intellectual, in the course," and "Why, Sir, it was properly for Botany that they went out. I believe they thought only of the culling of simples" – and some time later, writing to Boswell, he said "The Club is to meet with the Parliament; we talk of electing Banks, the traveller; he will be a reputable member." Banks was in fact chosen as one of that illustrious body, being proposed by Sir Joshua Reynolds and seconded by Johnson; and among his fellow members he found Burke, Fox, Gibbon, Sheridan and Garrick, together with several others who need no Christian name. And long after, in 1784, Banks was one of the pallbearers at Johnson's funeral.

It was Reynolds too who painted the capital portrait mentioned in Chapter 2; and it seems probable that he painted it quite early in the preparations for Cook's second voyage, for Sir Joshua was a preternaturally gifted physiognomist, and the Banks of the portrait is the Banks of Boswell's description, without any appearance of assuming whatsoever. The same applies to West's comparatively dull picture in which Banks, wearing a Maori cloak over an English suit, is surrounded by objects from the South Seas; only here he looks understandably sheepish as well as genteel. The events that lay between Banks's first sight of the *Resolution* and June 1772 were still at some distance, together with the changes that caused them or that they brought about.

In the meanwhile Banks had all his personal preparations to make, and this time, although he was short of ready money, he made them on a magnificent scale. In the statement dictated to Robert Brown Banks listed three draughtsmen, two secretaries, and nine servants "all practised and taught by myself to collect such objects of Natural History as might occur", fourteen souls apart from Solander and himself. But that was not all. He had also persuaded Zoffany to go with him – Zoffany of all people – promising him £1000;[4] perhaps the royal influence may be seen in this surprising appointment and in its acceptance, for George III was fond of both of them. Then as a Fellow of the Royal Society and a not infrequent guest of the Lunar Society, that interesting and ultimately most influential group of men including Erasmus Darwin, Boulton, Wall, Wedgwood, Edgeworth and Priestley who met in Birmingham on the Monday after the full moon, Banks was well acquainted with Priestley, the most outstanding experimental scientist of his time with the possible exception of Henry Cavendish, and he proposed that he should join the expedition as a nominee of the Board of Longitude. Priestley agreed. To the Board, however, whose university members were necessarily clergymen, the fact that Priestley's religious opinions were unorthodox disqualified him from making accurate astronomical observations, and the scheme fell to the ground. Banks was more successful in parliament, where his friends induced the Commons to vote £4000 for the engagement of Dr James Lind, a physician and natural philosopher; and in the end his influence with the Board was great enough to bring about the appointment of the astronomers Bailey and Wales, sound Anglicans.

Throughout this period he was very much sought after, being not only the chief lion of the season but amusing and good company too; he often saw the King, which gave him an additional lustre in most eyes, including perhaps his own; he was much written about in the newspapers and magazines, and in the most flattering terms; and he was very frequently solicited, always with the utmost deference, by people who wished to join the expedition and who, like the journalists, took it as a matter of course that he was in command – that the whole undertaking had been set on foot primarily for him.

By the winter he had begun to believe them, and the belief grew on him during the months that followed. In 1771 Banks was still a young man, indeed an unusually young man for his age; he had spent three of his twenty-eight years shut up in a small bark with little in the way of ordinary social intercourse; and much of his time between fourteen and twenty-five had been devoted to botany. When Dr Johnson, some while after this, said to Mrs Thrale "You may remember, I thought Banks had not gained much by circumnavigating the world" he may very well have meant "not gained much skill in dealing with people, particularly his equals and superiors – not much notion of how other people saw him – not much perception of what was and what was not possible in a complex society". It is after all a matter of common observation that going through a war does not necessarily fit men for ordinary life; nor, however horrible their experiences, does it necessarily cause them to grow up; and the *Endeavour*'s voyage, with its discomfort, short commons, long stretches of doing nothing and moments of extreme danger, was not at all unlike a war.

Certainly Banks behaved in a somewhat juvenile, self-important way in the spring of 1772; and although accusation and counter-accusation make the detailed progress of the dispute difficult to follow the main lines seem to be these. The two colliers were chosen by Cook, and he thought the *Resolution*, in her original state, "the most proper ship for the service I ever saw"; but she did not suit Banks, since she could not accommodate all the people he meant to take, or at least could not accommodate them with anything resembling comfort; a forty-four-gun two-decker warship or an East-Indiaman would have been more to his mind. He told Lord Sandwich that he would not go unless the *Resolution* were improved, and in spite of the great reluctance of the Navy Board, then headed by Captain Palliser, Cook's friend and former patron, Lord Sandwich gave orders to increase her capacity. This was done by raising her upper works about a foot, adding a spardeck over her deep waist from quarterdeck to forecastle, and, since Banks and his people were to have the whole of the great cabin, building a roundhouse (that is to say a square cabin) on the after-part of the quarterdeck for the captain, its roof being the poop.

A collier with a poop seemed something of a monstrosity, but the Navy Board obeyed orders, and in May 1772 Banks gave a party aboard the nearly completed vessel. A few days later she was ordered down the river from the Deptford yard to the Long Reach and then to the Downs, the famous anchorage off the east coast of Kent. She had taken in her ballast, she had taken in her guns, yet even so all this raised work, all this top-hamper, was too much for her; Palliser had been quite right and the ship proved to be so crank, so hopelessly crank, so liable to be overset by the breeze if she carried even ordinary sail, that the pilot refused to take her beyond the Nore.

She had to be cut down and restored to something like her original state and Banks was deprived of some of his accommodation. His suggestions of a forty-four-gun ship or an old East-Indiaman were not attended to and in the end he refused to go. His example was followed by all his people, and another naturalist, the learned but unscrupulous and disagreeable Reinhold Forster of Nassenhuben near Danzig, was appointed, with his only slightly less disagreeable son Georg as his assistant. At the end of May, Banks sent to have his and his party's enormous amount of baggage put on shore again.

Cook replied

Sheerness, 2nd June, 1772[5]

Sir,

I received your letter by one of your people, acquainting me that you had ordered everything belonging to you removed out of the ship, and desiring my assistance therein.

I hope, Sir, you will find this done to your satisfaction, and with the care the present hurry and confused state of the ship required. . . .

If it should not be convenient to send down for what may be still remaining in the ship of yours, they shall be sent to you by

Sir,

Your most obedient and very humble servant,

James Cook

My best respects to the Doctor, and since I am not to have your company in the Resolution, I most sincerely wish you success in all your exploring undertakings.

Although there is no "dear" in front of the sir this cannot possibly be described as an unfriendly letter; and one of the most remarkable things about the unhappy affair is the way in which Cook, despite an unimportant and temporary coolness, managed to remain on good terms with Banks. Another is the degree of passion that it aroused in Banks, who, together with some of his friends, was convinced that he was the victim of a plot on the part of the Navy Board. Lord Brougham, for example, felt that Captain Palliser, the Comptroller, might properly be likened to one who *Hated learning worse than toad or asp*. The passion or at least the extreme acerbity on all three sides, Admiralty, Navy Board, and above all Banks would best be shown by quoting their letters in full; but passion does tend to grow intolerably wordy, and the general tone though perhaps not quite the full quivering sense of righteous indignation can be gathered from these extracts.

Banks to Sandwich, 30 May 1772[6]

My Lord,

The present situation of Things regarding the proposed Expedition to the South Seas which it was my intention and inclination to have taken an active share in will I trust render any other Apology to your Lordship for this intrusion unnecessary.

To avoid the appearance of inconsistency and to justify my Conduct in the Eyes of the Public and your Lordship I feel it incumbant upon me to state the reasons by which I am influenced to decline the Expedition. . . .

The Navy Board was . . . ordered to purchase two Ships, to fit them up in a proper manner for our reception that we might be enabled to exert our utmost Endeavours to serve the Public wheresoever the course of our Discoveries might induce us to proceed.

Two ships were accordingly purchased: but when I went down to see the principal Ship, I immediately gave it as my opinion that she was improper for the voyage and went so far as to declare that if the alterations which I proposed would not be made I would not go in her. . . .

When these alterations and those which were judg'd necessary also for the Accomodation of the Captain and the People were made, the ship in falling down the River was found absolutely incapable of pursuing her intended Voyage.

The Navy Board have attributed this incapacity to the alterations that had been made and are of opinion that when the ship is reduced to her original Situation, that in which I before refused her, she will be the fittest that can be had for answering the Nautical Purposes of the Expedition. Without suffering myself to controvert this Opinion of the Navy Board that the Ship will be very fit for Sea although many able Seamen concur with me in doubting it I must be allowed to say that the ship will thus be if not absolutely incapable at least exceedingly unfit for the intended Voyage.

We have pledg'd ourselves, my Lord, to your Lordship and this Nation to undertake what no Navigator before us has ever suggested to be practicable; we are to attempt at least to pass round the Globe through Seas of which we know no Circumstance but that of their being tempestuous in those very Latitudes in passing through which in Order to get round one Cape the whole Squadron commanded by Lord Anson narrowly escaped being destroyed. We have done more we have undertaken to approach as near the Southern Pole as we possibly can, and how near that may be no Man living can give the least guess. [There follow reflections upon health – essential in such expeditions – improbable in the ship's present condition.]

Shall I then my Lord who have engaged to leave all that can make Life agreeable in my own Country and throw on one side all the Pleasures to be reaped from three years of the best of my Life merely to compass this undertaking pregnant enough with Dangers and difficulties in its own Nature, after having been promised every security and convenience that the art of man could contrive without which promise no man in my situation would ever have undertaken the Voyage be sent off at last in a doubtful Ship with Accomodations rather worse than those which I at first absolutely refused and after spending above £5000 of my own Fortune in the Equipment upon the Credit of those Accomodations which I saw actually built for me? . . .

To explore is my Wish but the Place to which I may be sent almost indifferent to me whether the Sources of the Nile or the South Pole are to be visited I am equally ready to embark in the undertaking whenever the Public will furnish me with the means of doing it properly but to undertake so expensive a pursuit without any prospect but Distress and disappointment is neither consistent with Prudence or Public Spirit.

As to the position of no other Ship being fit for the Voyage because no other could take the Ground I cannot omit putting your Lordship in mind that within these few weeks the *Emerald*, one of our sharpest Frigates lay on shore in the Gunfleet a much longer time then the *Endeavour* did upon the coast of New Holland after which she was got off. Sir John Lindsay also hawled up the *Stag* another of our Frigates at Trincomaly and shifted her Rudder-Irons during the course of his last Voyage. What more, my Lord, did the *Endeavour* do or what more could any Ship have done in that particular point on which the opinion of the Navy Board so materially rests?

[He goes on to say that the *Launceston* (the forty-four-gun ship for which he had petitioned) could do even better and that he knows many commanders who would gladly take her on this expedition.]

I do not doubt that was not your Lordship prevented by forms of Office I should still continue to receive the same countenance and assistance and that if it should be thought proper to alter or enlarge the present equipment your Lordship would still continue your Protection; as I am not conscious that by any part of my Conduct I have forfieted that claim to it which your Lordship's great condescension and goodness originally confer'd upon me.

I am with the utmost respect
Your Lordship's
Most obliged and most obedient humble servant
Jos. Banks

Sandwich wrote a short and moderate reply, regretting Banks's decision but telling him that it was most improper to accuse the Board of sending men to sea in an unhealthy ship and to make her people uneasy in their minds by such an allegation. He then called for the Navy Board's comments on Banks's letter: these were sent on 3 June.[7]

Mr Banks's first objections to the Ship respected only the Conveniences for himself and was no more than this, that the forepart of the Cabin was "an inch or two too low". As to the proper kind of Ship and her fitness and sufficiency for the Voyage, his opinion was never asked nor could have been asked with propriety, he being in no degree qualified to form a right Judgement in such a matter [Banks had complained that the Navy Board did not consult him when they bought the colliers]; and for the same reason his opinion now thereon is not to be attended to. As to what concerned himself as he increased his Suite, and his Demands, every thing was done to satisfy him by which it happened that the Properties of the Ship were so much altered that it has been necessary to take away the additional works that had been done at his request; in doing which it was so contrived that the difference occasioned thereby to him was simply this – the great Cabin (6ft 6in high between Plank and Plank) was shortened from 22 to 16 feet long; and there was one small Cabin for his Attendants taken away. After this small reduction there remained on the whole much better Accomodation than he had in the former Voyage in the *Endeavour* and the great Cabin remained in Length and Height, though not in Breadth, equal to those in a 74 gun ship (*Bellona Superbe Arrogant* etc) for an Admiral who frequently embarks in such Ships to command His Majesty's Fleet at Sea, whose Cabins are only 16ft 2in long and 6ft 6in high. Mr Banks seems throughout to consider the Ships as fitted out wholly for his use; the whole undertaking to depend on him and his People; and himself as the Director and Conductor of the whole; for which he is not qualified and if granted to him would have been the greatest Disgrace that could be put on His Majesty's Naval Officers. [His statement about the ship's unhealthiness was mischievous and mistaken.]

The application of the Cases of the *Emerald* and *Stag* and the Conclusion he draws therefrom discovers him to have less knowledge of matters relating to ships than might be expected in one who has associated and conversed so much with His Majesty's Sea Officers. The First was on shore in a smooth-water Channel at home, not in a distant, strange, desolate or savage Coast at the Antipodes. Six ships instantly anchored by her, hauled alongside her, took out her Guns Provisions etc. [*Stag* in Trincomalee in much the same favourable position.] Had either of these ships been in the *Endeavour*'s place on the coast of New Holland, they would never have been heard of again. Even if they had got off the Rocks, they could not have been hauled up to repair Damage, as was done by the *Endeavour*.

Sandwich knew that Banks, following the custom of the time, was likely to make his grievance public in an anonymous letter to the newspapers; and a well-written letter from a man as popular as Banks – a man who was also a friend of the King's – might very well embarrass the ministry. He therefore took the precaution of preparing an equally anonymous reply that could appear at once. He was quite right: Banks had indeed drafted a letter signed Antarcticus and intended for the *Gazetteer*. In this he developed the theme of extreme ill will on the part of the Navy Board, and deliberate sabotage:

in order to secure their intention of rendering her unfit for the sea, [they] built these upper works so much stronger than was necessary, that the top of this same round house, was literally thicker than the deck on which the guns stood. . . . When by all these alterations the ship was rendered unfit for the sea these very people who had so dirtily undermined Mr Banks, orderd the ship to be reducd to her former state declaring that the alterations were *all* made at Mr Banks's desire: that they had cost government the monstrous sum of £14000: that the ship was still good enough for him, tho in the state in which he at first refusd her and that nothing but his whimsical and fickle disposition, prevented him from sailing in her.

Banks's letter was not sent and Sandwich's reply was not used, except to be submitted to the King in order to justify the Navy's conduct; but they show the strength of the feelings that had been aroused. Although Sandwich was a busy man he took great pains with his reply; he wrote it himself on the left-hand side of twenty folio pages, leaving the right-hand for the many changes and additions. It was in the archives of Lord Sandwich's family until this year, but as these words are written it is being offered for sale at Sotheby's. It is a much more urbane letter than Banks's, but it is also much more deadly; apart from all the Navy Board's points it makes several more:

> The first demand you made was in a written paper delivered to the first Lord of the Admiralty; it consisted of several articles, the principal tendency of which was, that Captain Cook should be ordered to follow your directions as to the time of sailing from the several places you should touch at in the course of the Voyage; which was in other words giving you the absolute command of the expedition, and a power of controuling two commanders in his Majesty's service; a thing that was never done and I believe never attempted before; but this demand was also to be a condition of your proceeding or not proceeding on the expedition. . . . The next request you pressed upon the first Lord of the Admiralty in the strongest manner was that the officers in the two ships should recieve promotion thro' your means, and this you urged by suggesting that if they were not to look up to you for preferment you should be considered as nobody . . . and this was another attempt on your part to get possession of the command.

The letter then refers to Banks's request for a larger ship, better suited for the tempestuous seas that nearly destroyed Lord Anson's squadron, and observes that although Anson did indeed have a hard time of it and although Pizarro's squadron sent in pursuit of him was obliged to put back,

> the Anna Pink, a Victualler belonging to that squadron [Anson's] a ship of the same construction as the Resolution did escape those same difficulties, tho' she had only her complement of men as a merchantman.

The writer, acknowledging Banks's public spirit and extensive knowledge as a naturalist, laments

> that you are no longer one of the crew of the Resolution, but it may not be improper to set you right in one particular which you possibly may have misunderstood, and that is that you suppose the ships to have been wholly fitted out for your use, which I own I by no means apprehend to be the case.

And he ends,

> Upon the whole I hope that for the advantage of the curious part of Mankind, your zeal for distant voyages will not yet cease, I heartily wish you success in all your undertakings, but I would advise you in order to insure that success to fit out a ship yourself; that and only that can give you the absolute command of the whole Expedition; and as I have a sincere regard for your wellfare and consequently for your preservation, I earnestly entreat that that ship may not be an old man of war or an old Indiaman but a New Collier.
>
> I am &c.

Sandwich could write a stinging letter, but neither he nor Banks was devoid of magnanimity; they were quite soon reconciled, and presently they went back to their old custom of fishing together.

Yet long before their reconciliation Banks took Sandwich's ironical advice almost to the letter: he chartered the *Sir Lawrence*, a 190-ton brig, and on 12 July 1772 he sailed away to Iceland with all his people except Zoffany, who had gone to Florence with a letter of recommendation to the Grand Duke from King George. He took not only Solander and Lind, his draughtsmen, secretaries and servants but also John Gore, formerly of the *Endeavour*, who happened to be without a ship, this being peacetime, Uno von Troil, that learned Swede, a gardener, a French cook, and a young gentleman recommended by a friend.

His reasons for going were, in the first place, his sense of obligation to his followers for their loyalty to him: Lind, who was not a man of private means, had given up a very fine appointment and they were all out of pocket in one way or another. Then he had some hope that the East India Company might provide a ship for an important voyage of discovery, and he wished to keep his team together. And as for Iceland, it was the nearest comparatively unknown place, easy to reach and easy to come back from, and he and Solander may well have had it in mind before their final renunciation of the *Resolution* voyage – Cook had wished Banks success in all his exploring undertakings, as though some at least had been mentioned. Besides, Iceland had volcanoes, and Banks's particular friend Sir William Hamilton, a Fellow of the Royal Society as well as HM envoy to Naples, was an expert on the subject, particularly upon Vesuvius and Etna; and then again J. G. König, a botanist who had studied under Linnaeus at the same time as Solander, had spent a year on the island, collecting plants, some time before.

It is true that in his journal of the Iceland voyage Banks makes no mention of König; indeed he says that the country "has been visited but seldom and never at all by any good naturalist to my knowledge"; but at this period he was neither wholly candid nor settled in his mind – the first part of the journal is once more taken up with his passionate grievances against Palliser and those who had "so dirtily undermined him".

Another possible reason for Banks's disturbed spirit and his sudden departure is an entanglement with a young woman. A letter from Cook, written when the *Resolution* was at Madeira on 1 August 1772 and probably but not certainly addressed to the Secretary of the Admiralty (a letter that strangely ended up among the Georgian Papers at Windsor) says among other things:

> Three days before we arrived a person left the Island who went by the name of Burnett he had been waiting for Mr Banks arrival about three months, at first he said he came here for the recovery of his health, but afterwards said his intention was to go with Mr Banks, to some he said he was unknown to this Gentleman, to others he said it was by his appointment he came here as he could not be receiv'd on board in England, at last when he heard that Mr Banks did not go, he took the very first opportunity to get of the Island, he was about 30 Years of age and rather ordinary than otherwise and employ'd his time in Botanizing &c[a] – Every part of Mr Burnetts behaviour and every action tended to prove that he was a Woman, I have not met with a person that entertains a doubt of a contrary nature, he brought letters of recommendation to an English House where he was accomodated during his stay, It must be observed that Mrs Burnett must have left England about the time we were first ready to sail.

All these things, the sense of ill-usage, the humiliation of finding that his consequence was less than he had supposed, his disappointment at the loss of the South Sea voyage and the possible emotional distress about Mrs Burnett might be expected to lead to a dismal journey. But that would be to underestimate Banks's resilience and his prodigious energy.

The *Sir Lawrence* left Gravesend, carrying a seasick Banks to the Downs, thence by way of Cowes to Plymouth and so in spite of contrary winds and still more seasickness round Land's End and up the Irish sea (missing the runic inscriptions on the Isle of Man because of bad weather) to the Hebrides.

Fortunately Banks was exceptionally robust, indifferent to the weather by land, and accustomed to hard lying, for his Western Isles were wetter and more primitive than Dr Johnson's; furthermore Banks was fond of Ossian, which the Doctor quite certainly was not, and the thought of Fingal roused his spirits amazingly as the brig sailed through the Sound of Mull – raised them indeed to a pitch of "Enthusiasm sweet affection of the mind which can gather pleasures from the Empty Elements" which little or nothing in his earlier or his later writing prepares one for. Conceivably it was encouraged by the presence of Uno von Troil, who knew Macpherson personally and delighted in his productions: he delighted in runes too, and sagas. The *Sir Lawrence* was on her way north, having visited some of the Inner Hebrides, when the tide forced her to anchor over against the dwelling of Maclean of Drumnin in the Isle of Mull. "We were immediately invited to land, and breakfasted there, with that hospitality which characterises the inhabitants of the Highlands of Scotland," says Troil;[8] and it was here that they first heard of Staffa, mentioned by no writer except Buchanan, and that but imperfectly. When he was told that its basalt columns resembled those of the Giant's Causeway, which he had always longed to see, and that the island was within reach, Banks determined to go at once, leaving the brig in the port of Tobermory.

It was an eight hours' pull in the longboat over a dead calm sea, guided by young Maclean, and when they got there four of them had to sleep in a primitive booth with the resident lice; but it was worth it. Not only was there the magnificent series of regular basalt colonnades, but, and above all, there was the truly prodigious Fingal's Cave, a grotto 227 feet long, 42 feet wide and 66 feet high, with at least four fathoms of sea-green water below; on the one side the columns (usually five or six sided) rose 18 feet, on the other no less than 36; and white, ochre, and sometimes crimson stalactites hung from the roof. Banks saw it in perfect weather, perfect light, and it would have been a duller soul than his that was not deeply moved. Yet he was also a natural philosopher, eager for measurable fact as well as aesthetic pleasure, and presently the whole party was busy with yardstick and plumbline, pencil and brush. His careful description of the island is one of his few pieces to be found in print: not that he published it – he published very little – but he gave it to Pennant for use in his *Tour in Scotland*, a work dedicated to Banks.

After this Iona in the rain was something of an anticlimax; and some days later they were unable to land on St Kilda, because of foul weather. The foul weather lasted, and perhaps continued seasickness gave them a jaundiced view of Iceland, for Troil, reporting their arrival on 28 August says, "We seemed here to be in another world; instead of the fine prospects that had fed our eyes, we now only saw the horrid remains of many devastations. Imagine to yourself a country, which from one end to the other presents to your view only barren mountains, whose summits are covered with eternal snow, and between them fields divided by vitrified cliffs, whose high and sharp points seem to vie with one another, to deprive you of the sight of a little grass which scantily springs up among them." But then again Banks recalled that "no Icelander was seen to laugh," an observation confirmed by Troil with his "so serious that I hardly remember to have seen any one of them laugh". It is true that the Icelanders had very little to laugh about. The island belonged to Denmark; a Danish company had the monopoly of trade – no foreigners, no competition allowed, no contact with other countries – and with the short-sighted grasping attitude so typical of monopolists it had reduced the Icelanders to something not far from beggary. And not only the government but also the climate had changed since the heroic age of the sagas: it was so cold in 1753 and 1754, says the accurate Troil (he, like his father, became Archbishop of Uppsala), that sheep and horses dropped down dead; and on 26 June 1756 three feet of snow fell, continuing to fall throughout July and August: this caused a famine of course, since there was no hay that year; and no corn, not even rye, could be grown at any time – the lichen called Iceland moss was almost their only vegetable food. Indeed the eighteenth century was marked by famines, and by smallpox and sheep disease, while in 1765 a mountain, never looked upon as a volcano, suddenly erupted, destroying "a tract of country about as large as an English county," as Banks put it.

There was not much merriment, but after an inauspicious beginning (the brig might have been an illegal trader, a smuggler, or even an Algerine corsair) the Icelanders gave them a hearty welcome. Both the governor-general and the local governor, Ólafur Stephensen, were particularly kind and helpful, the latter remaining on very friendly terms with Banks for the rest of his life. And for the rest of his life Banks remained much attached to the Icelanders, serious and humourless though they were; in the Napoleonic wars he was able to give his attachment practical expression, making their life less wretched than it might have been, with all supplies from the outer world cut off.

It was too late in the year for any serious collecting, although they did what they could and Solander's slim *Flora Islandica* may still be consulted in the Natural History Museum, while the draughtsmen made fourteen coloured drawings of Icelandic plants. But there were the famous hot springs – Geysir himself, throwing his great column 92 feet into the air, while close around his fellows bubbled away, sending up their jets with a gratifying roar – and above all there was Hekla, literally above all, since they had to climb some 5000 feet to reach the top.

They had a twelve days' journey before their climb, over "an uninterrupted track of lava" from the earlier eruptions of the countless other volcanoes, but unfortunately Banks's journal breaks off – the pages are lost – before this point and although we have Dr von Troil's remarks they have none of Banks's lively interest in the flora and fauna however sparse – and Iceland is after all the home of both the gerfalcon and the harlequin duck. In fact almost the only bird Troil mentions apart from the eider is the ptarmigan which took just six minutes to cook in one of the boiling springs. Yet a passage from the lost part of Banks's journal is preserved in his young friend Hooker's *Tour in Iceland*

(1809) and I will begin with it, going on with Dr von Troil. "We arrived at a green spot under Graufel-Hraun where we pitched our tents and proceeded to a crater which was an opening half a mile in circumference, but its western side is destroyed by the eruption . . . The lower part and the remaining walls are composed of nothing but ashes, cinders, and pieces of lava in various states . . . The scene of desolation all around is almost inconceivable.'

Dr von Troil:

> . . . we pursued our journey to the foot of the mountain. We had a tent pitched here, where we proposed to pass the night, to enable us to ascend the mountain with greater spirits in the morning. The weather was extremely favourable, and we had the satisfaction of seeing whatever we wished, the eruption only being excepted. . . . We made use of our horses, but were obliged to quit them at the first opening from which the fire had burst. This was a place surrounded with lofty glazed walls, and filled with high glazed cliffs, which I cannot compare with any thing I ever saw before.
>
> A little higher up we found a great quantity of grit and stones, and still farther on another opening . . . Not far from thence the mountain began to be covered with snow, some small spots excepted, which were bare . . . As we ascended higher, these spots became larger; and about two hundred yards from the summit we found a hole of about one yard and a half in diameter, from which so hot a steam exhaled, that it prevented us from ascertaining the degree of heat with the thermometer.
>
> The cold now began to be very intense, as Fahrenheit's thermometer, which was at 54° at the foot of the mountain, fell to 24°. The wind also became so violent, that we were sometimes obliged to lie down to avoid being thrown into the most dreadful precipices by its fury.
>
> We were now arrived at one of the highest summits, when our conductor, who did not take great pleasure in the walk [in another place Troil says that the walk took thirteen hours], endeavoured to persuade us that this was the highest part of the mountain. We had just finished our observations, and found by them that Ramsden's barometer stood at 24.238, and the thermometer, fixed to it, at 27°, when happily the clouds divided, and we discovered a still higher summit. We lost no time in deliberation, but immediately ascended it, and when at the top discovered a space of ground, about eight yards in breadth, and twenty in length, entirely free from snow; the sand was however quite wet, from its having lately melted away, for in the air Fahrenheit's thermometer was constantly at 24°, and when we set it down on the ground, it rose to 153.

Banks, still in Hooker's account, says that it was so cold that "we were covered with ice in such a manner that our clothes resembled buckram." He also observes that "Dr Solander remained with an

Icelander in the intermediate valley; the rest of us continued our route to the summit of the peak, which we found intensely cold, but on the highest point was a spot of three yards in breadth whence there proceeded so much heat and steam that we could not bear to sit down upon it."

This was on 24 September 1772, and although they did not leave Iceland until about 18 October they do not seem to have seen anything else nearly as gratifying as Hekla or the geysers. Indeed it is likely that they spent a good deal of the time resting, since the twelve days out over lava-beds on an Iceland pony, the thirteen hours' climb – hard going, for as Troil says only a small part of the mountain was lava, the rest being ashes with some stones from the craters – and the descent, and then the journey back must have worn even Banks's iron frame, to say nothing of the portly short-legged Solander. But worn or not, Banks followed his usual custom and gathered a remarkable quantity of facts about the country's history, geography, resources and potentialities, and the Icelanders' manners, laws and customs. He also collected minerals, of course – the *Sir Lawrence* took home a great deal of lava and tuff as ballast, some of which is still to be seen at Kew and in the Chelsea Physic Garden – and what was less usual about one hundred and twenty books, most of them printed in Iceland, and perhaps thirty manuscripts. These, with the addition of some others that Ólafur Stephensen acquired for him later, he gave to the British Museum; and this was probably the most important collection the voyage produced. As a botanizing expedition it did not amount to much, nor can Banks have expected it to do so; yet even for a circumnavigator it was a considerable experience; it set a great space between him and the events of May and June, and it helped to restore his self-esteem, indeed his happiness.

Chapter 7

THE GREAT *FLORILEGIUM*: OMAI: SOHO SQUARE

JOSEPH BANKS's first duty as a natural philosopher was to publish his results. The results of the Iceland voyage scarcely warranted anything more elaborate than the description of Staffa that he gave to Pennant and the little map of the island, with Hekla clearly marked and the Arctic Circle underlining his name, that he had engraved for use as a visiting-card, possibly out of compliment to his sister, who was very fond of such things and whose collection is now in the British Museum. And the results of the Newfoundland journey, though important, were comparatively sparse; in any case his herbarium and his animal specimens had long been available for all fellow naturalists to examine at their leisure – Pennant, for example, made the freest use of them in his *Arctic Zoology* and elsewhere, sometimes with due acknowledgement. But the results of the great *Endeavour* voyage, with its hundreds and hundreds of totally unknown plants, insects, fishes, reptiles, birds and mammals, required an equally great publication for the benefit of the learned world. The unlearned world was to be dealt with by Dr Hawkesworth, a miscellaneous writer and a friend (some said an imitator) of Dr Johnson, who had been commissioned to produce an account of the recent Pacific voyages for the general reader.

Banks was splendidly equipped for this formidable task. In the first place he not only had the collections but he also had room for them, and by now they were at last fully unpacked, prepared and arranged. No catalogue appears to have survived, but here is a description, taken from a letter written on 2 December 1772 by the Rev. W. Sheffield, Keeper of the Ashmolean Museum, to Gilbert White and printed in Bell's edition of White's *Natural History of Selborne*:

> My next scene of entertainment was in New Burlington Street at Mr Banks's. Indeed it was an invitation from this gentleman that carried me there; it would be absurd to attempt a particular description of what I saw there; it would be attempting to describe within the compass of a letter what can only be done in several folio volumes. His house is a perfect museum; every room contains an inestimable treasure. I passed almost a whole day there in the utmost astonishment, could scarce credit my senses. Had I not been an eye-witness of this immense magazine of curiosities, I could not have

thought it possible for him to have made a twentieth part of the collection. I have excited your curiosity; I wish to gratify it; but the field is so vast and my knowledge so superficial that I dare not attempt particulars. I will endeavour to give you a general catalogue of three large rooms. First the Armoury; this room contains all the warlike instruments, mechanical instruments and utensils of every kind, made use of by the Indians in the South Seas from Terra del Fuego to the Indian Ocean . . . It may be observed here that the Indians in the South Seas were entire strangers to the use of iron before our countrymen and Monsieur Bougainville arrived amongst them; of course these instruments of all sorts are made of wood, stone, and some few of bone. They are equally strangers to the other metals; nor did our adventurers find the natives of this part of the globe possessed of any species of wealth which would tempt the polite Europeans to cut their throats and rob them. The second room contains the different habits and ornaments of the several Indian nations they discovered, together with the raw materials of which they are manufactured. All the garments of the Otaheite Indians and the adjacent islands are made of the inner bark of the *Morus pyrifera* and of the bread tree *Chitodon altile*; this cloth, if it may be so called, is very light and elegant and has much the appearance of writing paper, but is more soft and pliant; it seems excellently adapted to these climates. Indeed most of these tropical islands, if we can credit our friend's description of them, are terrestrial paradises. The New Zealanders, who live in a much higher southern latitude, are clad in a very different manner. In the winter they wear a kind of mats made of a particular species of *Cyperus* grass. In the summer they generally go naked, except a broad belt about their loins made of the outer fibres of the cocoa nut, very neatly plaited; of these materials they make their fishing lines, both here and in the tropical isles. When they go upon an expedition or pay or receive visits of compliment, the chieftains appear in handsome cloaks ornamented with tufts of white dog's hair; the materials of which these cloaks are made are produced from a species of *Hexandria* plant very common in New Zealand, somewhat resembling our hemp but of a finer harl and much stronger, and when wrought into garments is as soft as silk: if the seeds of this plant thrive with us, as probably they will, this will perhaps be the most useful discovery they made in the whole voyage. But to return to our second room. Here is likewise a large collection of insects, several fine specimens of the bread and other fruits preserved in spirits; together with a compleat *hortus siccus* of all the plants collected in the course of the voyage. The number of plants is about 3000, 110 of which are new genera, and 1300 new species which were never seen or heard of before in Europe. What raptures must they have felt to land upon countries where every thing was new to them! whole forests of nondescript trees clothed with the most beautiful flowers and foliage, and these too inhabited by several curious species of birds equally strangers to them. I could be extravagant upon this topic; but it is time to pay our

> compliments to the third apartment. This room contains an almost numberless collection of animals; quadrupeds, birds, fish, amphibia, reptiles, insects and vermes, preserved in spirits, most of them new and nondescript. Here I was most in amazement and cannot attempt any particular description. Add to these the choicest collection of drawings in Natural History that perhaps ever enriched any cabinet, public or private: – 987 plants drawn and coloured by Parkinson; and 1300 or 1400 more drawn with each of them a flower, a leaf, and a portion of the stalk, coloured by the same hand; besides a number of other drawings of animals, birds, fish, etc. and what is more extraordinary still, all the new genera and species contained in this vast collection are accurately described, the descriptions fairly transcribed and fit to be put to the press. Thus I have endeavoured to give you an imperfect sketch of what I saw in New Burlington Street; and a very imperfect one it is.

Then again Banks had the young Edward Jenner (later famous as Vaccination Jenner) to arrange the specimens, he having been recommended by John Hunter, no less, as being most exceptionally gifted for fine work in dissection and anatomical presentation. Still more important he had Solander, learned, immensely industrious and perfectly familiar with scientific method, for the descriptions. And his devoted sister was just at hand: she had copied his Newfoundland journal and she was now writing out the one he kept aboard the *Endeavour*, sometimes removing or obscuring coarse words such as buttocks, sometimes slightly improving the moral tone but always having a sad time of it with the Latin names.

Yet even though Banks had all these advantages there was still a very great deal of work to be done before the work as a whole could go to the press. What he had in mind was a truly heroic publication with no fewer than 743 plates based on Parkinson's finished drawings or his sketches, each plate being about eighteen inches by one foot, accompanied by a large amount of text. It is possible to form a clear idea of his project by looking at one of the most remarkable feats of modern publication, the *Banks's Florilegium*, which the Alecto Historical Editions, using the 738 undamaged plates that Banks left to the British Museum, is now bringing out, so that one may see the botanical treasures of the *Endeavour* voyage in a series of noble portfolios: the set costs something in the neighbourhood of sixty thousand pounds.

A great deal of work was called for; a great deal of work was done; and in 1782 Banks told Edward Hasted, a fellow member of the Royal Society, that he hoped soon to publish "as I have now near 700 folio plates prepar'd: it [the book] is to give an account of all the new plants discovered in my voyage round the world, somewhat above 800."[1] And in 1784, writing to Johan Alströmer, he said "All that is left is so little that it can be completed in two months, if only the engravers can come to put the finishing touches on it."[2]

In fact Banks's energy was such that if he had been a simple uncomplicated natural philosopher he would have driven the work through to an end long before this. But he was not a simple uncomplicated natural philosopher and some strange turn or quirk in his mind made him exceedingly reluctant to come to the final point and publish, so reluctant that this great work, virtually completed, never saw the light of day. Banks's turn of mind has been variously explained: an alleged fear of criticism has been put forward, so has Solander's death in 1782, and so has Banks's answer to H. F. Greville's invitation of June 1807 to join his Belles Lettres Society, "I am scarce able to write my own Language with Correctness, and never presumed to attempt Elegant Composition, Either in Verse or in Prose in that or in any other tongue." But in 1782 the book, which at no time called for elegant composition, was almost entirely in being; and as for correctness, Banks had no hesitation in writing an enormous number of letters, all of them clear enough and some of them remarkably fine, or in writing long, closely reasoned reports on a variety of subjects for the administration and the East India Company. The explanations that have been advanced have their force, but they are not sufficient: the effect of his strange turn of mind is clear – Banks's published writings amount to little more than a few pamphlets on the export of wool and on blight in corn, together with some papers in the Annals of Agriculture and the proceedings of the Horticultural and Antiquaries' societies – but its cause, at least to the present writer, is impenetrably obscure.

It is not enough to say that Banks was not wholly a natural philosopher, not wholly given over to science like his friend the even wealthier Henry Cavendish; for although it is true that he had many other activities, and that he was a considerable landowner, much taken up with the improvement of Revesby and the draining of the Fens like his father before him, as well as a highly sociable being, the book was virtually ready a few years after its inception, Solander's twenty manuscript volumes of description were fair-copied (they still lie, unprinted, in the British Museum), the immense price both in effort and in money had been paid. And yet he did not publish.

Among these other activities was advising poor Dr Hawkesworth on his three-volume account of Byron's, Wallis's, Carteret's, and Cook's voyages. Poor Dr Hawkesworth, for although Lord Sandwich had commissioned him (as a favour to Garrick, it is said) to write this account and had persuaded Banks to lend him his journal, when the harmless, rather dull book came out it was fallen upon and torn to pieces. Many of the reviewers were penurious hacks and Hawkesworth's remarkable fee may have sharpened their rage. He was a tender-minded, scrupulous man, and he died before the year was out. "Poor Dr Hawkesworth," wrote Mrs Thrale, "hunted out of his life for that unlucky six thousand pounds which at last he never received, this unfortunate Man had not Strength of Mind to despise his Persecutors, but broke his heart & died – no imitation of Johnson in that at least – *He* would not easily be teized to Death, his enemies may let alone trying."

Another far more important activity had to do with Kew. The Princess Dowager died in 1772; Lord Bute had long since faded from the political scene; now he faded from that of botany and George III took over Kew House and its gardens, to which the princess had added those of Richmond Lodge. He soon began to ask Banks for his views on the development of the whole and although Banks's position as scientific adviser was not clearly established until the next year or so, as early as 1772 he and Sir John Pringle, the then President of the Royal Society, recommended that the King should send one of the under-gardeners, Francis Masson, to the Cape. This was done, and Masson became the first of the long line of Kew plant-collectors.

Then there were many other interests, the social life of London, the Royal Society, the Society of Antiquaries, a little later the Society of Dilettanti, and naturally enough in a young man of a lively, sanguine complexion, the company of young women.

Since the return of the *Endeavour* Banks had been something of a public figure and presently caricatures, more or less comic verses, and scandalous tales about him began to appear. At the time of his sudden rush of pomp to the head he may have made himself rather unpopular, for most of these productions are ill-natured: though indeed such things are rarely intended to give the subject pleasure. All his serious biographers have seen the tales, and all except Averil Lysaght have dismissed them as customary exercises of the time, without real significance. But she, going through Banks's correspondence, found a letter from Fabricius that others must have dismissed as being wholly concerned with botany but which in fact ended in a much more personal manner – a manner that gave substance to an article in that vulgar publication *The Town and Country Magazine* for September 1773.

According to this article Banks had taken a Miss B—n into keeping: he had known her as a schoolgirl, and on returning from the South Seas had found her fatherless and penniless, Mr B—n having gambled away his fortune and died. She was living as companion to an old lady, an unenviable position from which Banks removed her, placing her first with a respectable family and then taking a house for her in Orchard Street.

Fabricius's letter ends "My best compliments and wishes in Orchard Street, what has she brought you? Well, it is all the same, if a Boy, he will be clever and strong like his father, if a girl, she will be pretty and genteel like her mother."[3]

The letter was written from Copenhagen in November 1773, but from the article it appears that in fact the child had already been born by September; and as far as any credit can be given to such a publication, Miss B—n was indeed "remarkably genteel, and her countenance particularly engaging" while "all the elegant accomplishments were united in her, and were only surpassed by her mental improvements". The feeling that this was true is strengthened by Fabricius's message. He was a man of considerable standing, being not only a remarkable polymath and one of the foremost entomologists of his day but also, at the time of this letter, professor of economy at Kiel, to which natural history and finance were added somewhat later – a man Banks would scarcely have introduced to anyone remotely resembling an ordinary woman of the town. It seems that Banks and his Miss were deeply attached, and the magazine, for what it is worth, says that they were pleased with their baby. But what happened to their attachment or to the little Banks does not appear. No scandal-sheet, no diarist, mentions them any more; nor is any other trace of them to be found in Banks's correspondence.

In the spring of 1773, well before the arrival of this baby, Banks went off to Holland with his friend Charles Greville. It was not a voyage to be compared with that to Iceland, still less to that of the *Endeavour*. But he enjoyed it in a quiet way, travelling along the canals of a flat country very like his native Fens and admiring the splendid drainage system, particularly one section of it, "a fine work ten times larger and more magnificent than our Grand Sluice in Lincolnshire and yet the Dutch think little of it."

But this was more than a sight-seeing tour: Banks wanted to learn about the waters of the far north, and the Dutch, whose whalers had been fishing beyond Spitsbergen and even beyond Novaya Zemlya for more than a hundred years and who had the most numerous and experienced fleet in those parts, were the people to tell him. In March, he says in his journal of the trip, when he was at the Hague, he "had a

Levee of Groenland* Captains, who had been sent for from Rotterdam, in order to give me such information as they might be able, which might forward Captn Phipps' plan of sailing towards the Pole."

This voyage had long been agitated in the Royal Society, above all by Daines Barrington, and as a result of the society's letter to Sandwich and Sandwich's interview with the King two bomb-vessels belonging to the Royal Navy were selected. These were very strongly built to withstand the shock of heavy mortars during the bombardment of a citadel or town and it was thought that with even stronger reinforcement they would also withstand the pressure of the northern ice: the one was the *Racehorse*, the other the *Carcass*, and the command of the expedition was given to Captain Phipps.

At one time Banks had thought of going with him, but in the end – conceivably because of this coming baby – he stayed at home and Phipps took Dr Irving for natural philosophy and general medicine and Banks's old friend Israel Lyons as astronomer. Banks's participation was limited to the information he had gathered in the Netherlands and a document headed *Instructions sent out with Captain Phipps on his Northern Voyage*, which he presumably wrote on behalf of the Royal Society, since Phipps would scarcely have relished personal directions from his old schoolfellow.

The paper begins formally enough with remarks on the preservation of insects and the gradual drying of plants; a young white bear, brought home alive, would be desirable (it might differ even generically from the brown or black bears); seals required; information on the areas from which the great annual shoals of herring, mackerel, pilchard and so on come; a desideratum, whale foetuses, if they are to be had from the whalers; birds, if large, to be skinned, their heads and feet put into spirits; blubbers by no means to be neglected; mosses and lichens desirable: how best preserved; but formality entirely vanishes in the last lines and the letter ends in a perfectly natural tone of voice:

> God bless you and send you to the Herring Hall or the source of the migration of macerel and thence home to your ever affect but never emulating
>
> J Banks

That *never emulating* is surely most significant. Ordinarily competition plays such an important part in the relations between men, and is the cause of so much decay in friendship, that a "never emulating" companion, one who does not feel (as Johnson felt) that all encounters

* Greenland, in whalers' language, included Spitsbergen.

are contests, with evident superiority on one side or the other, must be wonderfully restful. Banks had a great many friends; he kept almost all, even the self-seeking Blagden; and this unstriving quality may well have been the most important reason.

During the voyage Phipps sent a letter back by the *Rockingham*, an English whaler:

> My dear Banks July 4th, 1773
>
> I am in 79°30′ & have not seen a single bit of ice & have been these three days without any fire and have no one day had a fire all day – I have got you two small Blubbers – a Seal's Bill of Fare out of his belly containing sundry non-descript: Crabs & other things several Birds stuffed amongst them non descripts particularly a *Larus Rissa* with only 8 Remiges Primores tho' Linnaeus attributes 10 you know to all Birds – a *Larus Niveus* undescribed a Beautiful Bird etc. etc. Remember me to Solander & believe me most sincerely
>
> Yours C J Phipps
>
> Irvine is well – would probably have said something had he been up it is now 4 O'Clock in the Morning & the wind fair
> God bless you
> Racehorse off Spitsbergen
> Lat. 79°30′ July 4th

It is a pity that Banks did not go on the voyage. For one thing it might have arrested the process of settling down that was already perceptible in him: he might have carried on with exploration – the sources of the Nile that he had mentioned before, another circumnavigation with Cook, inland Australia – and with his enormous energy, his capital health and his handsome fortune he was wonderfully well suited for the task; he was an ardent collector rather than an armchair botanist in spite of his herbaria, and in any case he did not possess the intellectual equipment of a Jussieu or a Brown, the very rare equipment that might have allowed him to strike out a new theory of classification superseding that of Linnaeus, which had already served its time. And he might have been happier as an outdoor man rather than as a largely sedentary philosopher deep in paperwork, growing heavier and heavier, goutier and goutier, more and more authoritative. For another, although the expedition did not accomplish a great deal, going no farther than 80°48′ north (Phipps never claimed to be going *to* but only *towards* the North Pole) it was surprisingly eventful and adventurous. The day after Phipps' letter the ships met a solid wall of ice; they ran eastwards along it for more than ten degrees, all the apparent openings proving worthless. They returned to Spitsbergen for surveying and scientific observations and then pushed on again. By the end of July they were among the Seven Islands, where the reindeer, intensely curious, came within hand's reach and breathed upon them; and the breeze falling to a flat calm, the ships' people played leapfrog on the ice. But soon it became apparent that there was imminent danger of the ships being frozen in until next year. Heroic measures were called for; heroic measures were taken. First they tried cutting a passage through the ice with axes and ice-saws, but a day's work gained only three hundred yards; they then tried dragging the boats over it towards the open sea and Spitsbergen and they managed two miles in the day. The next day, with improved harness, they achieved three miles but now the ice around the ship was opening, and after a very anxious spell of snowy weather with the west wind right in their teeth they broke free on 10 August. Having lain in the harbour of Smeerenburg until the nineteenth to recover and refit the ships they tried sailing north again, but now the wall of ice was even more impenetrable, and with the season so advanced and dirty weather coming they were obliged to turn for home.

Had Banks been with them he would have shared in all these delights: he would have seen some remarkable arctic jellyfish, glaciers dropping huge "lively light green" icebergs into the sea, the far northern birds, and the polar bear, and all this in very pleasant company.[4] The friendship between Phipps and Banks is illuminating and at this point it may be useful to see something of how others saw them. They had both developed much since their days together in Newfoundland – literally developed, for Banks now weighed close on fourteen stone and Phipps no less than sixteen, though one would scarcely think so from the Gainsborough portrait that shows him at full length against the inevitable draped curtain, a post-captain leaning on a dim sideboard with his sword and cocked hat upon it and his book on the northern voyage propped up on a chair – and in both the middle-aged man was clearly visible. A little later than this, in 1777, Mrs Thrale wrote

> Lord Mulgrave [Phipps had inherited his father's title in 1775] is a Man of high Birth, high Courage, an inquisitive Disposition and a cultivated Mind: he studies diligently, and always seems to have learned something new since the last Time one saw him: there is however too much of the Boatswain mixed with the Nobleman; such boisterous Merriment and a Laugh so like a *Post horn* as Bodens says; that his Mirth puts an end to that of many People instead of exciting theirs: for my Part I am not so much afraid of any Man

living as of Lord Mulgrave: one knows he will stop at nothing for a Joke, and one is never invited by his Behaviour to that security which in a mixed Company can alone promote Conversation: he sometimes will swear too I believe though I never heard him; and that seems to be bringing the Quarter-Deck to dinner rather too completely.

And somewhat later still, when Banks had put on yet more weight in every sense, Farington's diary had this to say,

Malone observed how difficult it would be to establish a plan for collecting select Society in the way Sir Joshua Reynolds carried his on. Malone only knows three persons who could undertake it; and each is unfit in many respects. Sir Joseph Banks, as President of the Royal Society, and possessing a large fortune, might undertake it; but his knowledge and attention is very much confined to one study, Botany; and his manners are rather coarse and heavy. [The other two were Burke and Windham.][5]

But to return to 1773, when Banks was still reasonably slim and perfectly capable of climbing Snowdon: he spent part of the summer in a botanical excursion to Wales, accompanied by his old friend the Rev. John Lightfoot, a new friend Dr Charles Blagden (a young Scots physician), and perhaps by Solander and Paul Sandby the artist. Lightfoot was the Duchess of Portland's chaplain, and like Solander he worked regularly on her famous natural history collections. He had the happiest memories of the journey and after it wrote to Banks

My Gratitude will be for ever indebted to you for the numberless Pleasures you have treated me with, & the many Advantages I receiv'd in your Company during our Welch Tour: and yet you still continue to encrease the Debt by your Politeness in saying I was useful to you. If I was in any Degree, it gives me a very sensible pleasure, as I can truly say I never became a Party in any Scheme which afforded me more Satisfaction or sincere delight. It was a Journey above all others I wish'd to take: & I had every circumstance accompanying it that could render it most agreeable. We certainly were most remarkably successful, tho' we did not find *every individual* Plant we wish'd; for I believe it may without vanity be said, that few, if any, Botanical Excursions in Great Britain have exceeded our Collection, either in Number or Rarity of Plants or Places.[6]

(In a somewhat later reply to Banks in the same year he says "*Thirteen Hundred Specimens* of Plants from the Cape cannot fail to abound with many Monsters, & your kind Invitation to me to come & see them is too provoking for me to refuse.")

It was also in this year, 1773, that Banks's position as botanical adviser to the King became so fully and permanently established.

Banks was an excellent choice for many reasons, and one of them was that his appointment caused no heart-burning in the men whose work he was to direct. William Aiton, the superintendent at Kew, was an old acquaintance, having been trained in the Chelsea Physic Garden by Philip Miller, a still older acquaintance, or rather indeed friend and mentor, the famous botanist whose vast herbarium Banks purchased in 1774 – its removal took a fortnight.

The Chelsea garden was in its first conception utilitarian; Miller turned it into a place known all over the learned world not only for the excellence of its medicinal plants but also for the extent of its purely botanical research and its horticultural range, with specimens sent as seeds, bulbs, roots, cuttings or growing plants by correspondents and fellow botanists from Africa, Asia and America. His ideal was a true botanic garden, a *Delightful scientifick Shade! For Knowledge, as for Pleasure made*, and he came closer than most of his contemporaries to realizing it; but the ground at his disposal amounted to only a little over three acres; his means were severely limited; and he did not get on well with his employers the Apothecaries, whose professional interest lay in the maintenance of a *physic* garden, not in the very much wider scope of disinterested botany.

The King's gardens at Kew were in their first conception pleasure grounds. Banks and Aiton, who might almost be called Miller's disciples, formed the idea of turning them – but without in the least taking away from the Delightful part of the Shade – into a full botanic garden with a strong economic emphasis; and in this they were supported by the King. Kew, although it was nothing like the size it is now, was still very much larger than Chelsea; and the funds that those in charge could draw upon were very much greater too. Initiative, enlightened energy, and a wide range of scientific contacts were required to make the plan a success, and all these Banks possessed in abundance. Banks could also send out collectors instead of having to rely on exchange or chance benevolence; and as time went on the royal patronage – an intelligent, closely concerned patronage – the extraordinary extent of Banks's botanical acquaintance and the increasing authority of his name made Kew an outstanding example of what a botanic garden might be, with connections and offshoots all over the world, particularly in the East India Company's territories (which included St Helena) and the West Indies. But all this was a matter of years and years: a great collection such as that described in Aiton's *Hortus Kewensis* (a work in which he had a great deal of help from Banks and Solander) could not be brought together overnight. Indeed,

Banks's concern with Kew, like his even more intimate concern with Revesby, was part of his being; and although since the history of both was in the main uneventful neither call for comment, so that they may easily be overlooked, both were of very great importance to him as long as he lived.

The Royal Society was to become even more important. He was already an active member, an assiduous attendant at the meetings whenever his travels made it possible, and in 1774 he was invited to join the Council, the body of twenty-one Fellows who saw to the running of the whole.

Yet a more immediately striking event in 1774 was the return of the *Adventure*: this was the ship that accompanied Cook's *Resolution* when he set out for his second voyage in July 1772, leaving the disgruntled Banks behind; and she was commanded by Captain Tobias Furneaux, who had been second lieutenant in the *Dolphin* under Wallis. The two ships, having traversed a very great expanse of ocean in the high southern latitudes, going even beyond the Antarctic Circle and seeing countless great icebergs but no hint of a continent, having separated for three months and having rejoined in New Zealand, stood on with the intention of reaching 49°S, although this was the middle of the austral winter. After three weeks of this however the *Adventure*'s people, unlike those aboard the *Resolution*, began to come down with scurvy and Cook bore away for Tahiti to refresh. After a fortnight among their old friends (poor Oberea was now aged, much reduced, and of little account), they touched at Huahine. Here they found a young man they called Omai, a native, like the ill-fated Tupia, of Raiatea, who had also taken refuge in Tahiti when the men of Borabora conquered his island. In Tahiti he had known the people of the *Dolphin* and then of the *Endeavour* and now he asked to be taken aboard the *Adventure*. Captain Furneaux agreed, rating him able seaman to comply with the regulations, and he appears in the muster-book as *Tetuby Homey Huahine, Society Islands, 22, A.B.*

The two ships then steered for New Zealand again, their rendezvous in case of separation being once more Ship Cove in Queen Charlotte's Sound. Very heavy weather did indeed separate them, and when at last the much-battered *Adventure* reached the cove Captain Furneaux found a message from Cook, dated six days earlier and stating that having waited from 2 November to the twenty-fourth he was now pursuing his voyage. Apparently the message said that Cook would look for the *Adventure* in the straits between the north and south islands for a few days, and apparently it gave a general notion of his intended course, but without fixing any distinct rendezvous.

Furneaux, having repaired his ship by 23 December 1773 bore away eastwards, though with a sadly diminished crew, for just before sailing he had sent the large cutter with a master's mate, a midshipman and eight hands to gather fresh greenstuff for the voyage, and they had all been eaten by the New Zealanders. The *Adventure* sailed on for a little over a month, the strong westerlies carrying her over a hundred and twenty-one degrees of longitude; but when she reached the height of the Horn Captain Furneaux inspected her stores, and "upon opening some Casks of Pease and Flour that had been stowed on the Coals, found them much damaged and not eatable so thought it more prudent to stand for the Cape of Good Hope" – more prudent than carrying on with the exploration.

She reached the Cape on 19 January 1774 and sailed for England on 16 April. All this while Omai, though nominally a foremast hand, had been "indulged in the Captain's cabin", so although the language tended to escape him* it is scarcely surprising that by the time the *Adventure* dropped anchor at Spithead on 14 July 1774 he had a fair understanding of English manners and conventions. Besides, although he was of somewhat humbler origins than the elegant and learned Tupia, he was of chiefly or at least of land-owning rank, and he carried a ceremonial stool† (almost his only baggage) to prove it; furthermore he had natural good manners, tact, and quickness of apprehension. "Omai," said Captain Cook, "has certainly a very good understanding, quick parts, and honest principles; he is of good natural behaviour, which rendered him acceptable to the best company."

This was just as well, because it was the very best company to which he was introduced: Banks and Solander travelled down to Portsmouth at once, and as Solander told a friend,

> When he saw Mr Banks who happen'd to have no powdre in his hair he knew him instantly; The first intercourse with me was droll enough; I came into Capt Furneaux room and began to converse with him, which Omai heard who was in the next room, and came running in calling out – I hear Tolano's voice (obs. Tolano = Solander) but coming into the room he recollected not my figure, so he walked quite round me, constantly looking at me, but at last thought himself mistaken. He then desired Capt Furneaux to make me speak, which I had no sooner done than he cried out, he was sure I was Tolano, but much encreased in bulk. We soon made ourselves known

*As it escaped other even more intelligent Polynesians, whose own tongue lacked many European sounds, so that "Toot" was the nearest they could get to Cook and "Opano" to Banks.

† He gave this stool to Captain Furneaux, in whose family it remained until 1986, when it came up for sale at Christie's. The Tahiti Museum, with the help of two collectors, Lord McAlpine and Mr Ortiz, bought it for £80,000.

by conversing pretty freely with one another in his Language. It has been very pleasing to us, to him and many others, that both Mr Banks, myself, & Mr Banks's servant James have not forgot our South Sea Language, – So we all can well keep up a Conversation with him.[7]

The next visitor was the First Lord of the Admiralty. Lord Sandwich and Banks had long since been reconciled, and they carried Omai up to London, where Banks entertained him in New Burlington Street and Sandwich, after due preparation, presented him to the King at Kew.

Omai was dressed in the European manner, in a brown velvet coat, white waistcoat and grey satin breeches, and he had been taught the appropriate motions and replies. It was widely reported that he grasped the King's hand, crying "How do, King Tosh!"; and that he was afraid he might be eaten. The second report was mere nonsense and the first absurdly exaggerated, though Sophia Banks did record that "he droppd upon one knee & said How do you do King George, I hope you are very well", a greeting that may possibly have been concocted as being suitable for a Polynesian.

At present George III is probably remembered chiefly from the gross caricatures of later years, from tales of "Farmer George" and his simplicity, from the results of his American policy, and from his mental illness; yet at this period he was the man of whom Johnson could say "Sir, they may talk of the King as they will, but he is the finest gentleman I have ever seen" and "Sir, his manners are those of as fine a gentleman as we may suppose Lewis the Fourteenth or Charles the Second"; and the interview passed off very well indeed. The King gave Omai a handsome sword, granted him an allowance during his stay, promised that he should eventually be taken home, and recommended inoculation against smallpox.

He was probably thinking of a most unhappy incident the year before. In January 1773 Banks at last saw the Eskimos that had eluded him in Labrador and Newfoundland. His friend and correspondent Major George Cartwright, who had been living for some time in Labrador as a trapper and fur trader, brought a small party to London, where large numbers of people came to look at them. The Eskimos seem to have enjoyed their visit upon the whole, but it ended wretchedly. When they reached Plymouth on their homeward journey they fell ill. It proved to be the smallpox, a disease unknown in the far north, and they all died but one young woman. She recovered, but she carried the infection back to Labrador and her whole tribe was wiped out.

It was Banks who attended to the inoculation, taking Omai to the eminent Dr Dimsdale's Institute at Hertford, and it answered quite well. Omai was somewhat affected, but he was carefully looked after – Banks and Solander were there most of the time and Banks's servant James all the time, together with the *Adventure*'s surgeon, Mr Andrews – and writing to Blagden in August Banks could say that he was over the worst, while in October he was completely recovered.

He spent much of the autumn and winter with Banks and Sandwich in the country, particularly at Hinchingbrooke, Sandwich's vast Elizabethan house in Huntingdon, in whose park he quite often cooked meat in the Polynesian manner, that is to say covered with leaves and laid on hot stones in a dug-out earth oven. Banks wrote to his sister "Omai dressed three dishes for dinner yesterday, & so well was his cookery liked that he is desired to cook again today not out of curiosity but for the real desire of Eating meat so dress'd: he succeeds most prodigiously: so much natural politeness I never saw in any Man: wherever he goes he makes friends & has not I believe as yet a Foe."[8]

Certainly he had thoroughly pleased Lord Sandwich, and when he returned from Huntingdon to London he brought Banks a letter that ran in part "Omai is the bearer of this. I am grown so used to him and have so sincere a friendship for him, from his very good temper, sense and general good behaviour that I am quite depressed at his leaving me." It went on to ask Banks to look after him: "we were highly blameable if we did not make use of all the sagacity and knowledge of the world which our experience has given us to do everything we can to prove ourselves his real friends."

There was no need to ask Banks to be kind: he too was much attached to Omai and he did very handsomely by him, making sure that he met a great many people who would be interesting or amusing or both and who in their turn would introduce him to others. In this way Omai dined with Dr Johnson at the Thrales' house in Streatham: Lord Mulgrave was there too. "They sat with their backs to the light fronting me," said Johnson to Boswell some time later, "so that I could not see distinctly; and there was so little of the savage in Omai, that I was afraid to speak to either, lest I should mistake the one for the other." This the Doctor attributed to Omai's having passed his time only in the best company; and certainly he met with some very grand people indeed – so much so that he became something of a snob: he enjoyed the performance at Sadler's Wells, which was then rather like a music hall, with a variety of turns; but when he asked whether noblemen went there and learnt that they did not do so often, he said that he should go no more. "Very well, said my Brother," wrote Miss Banks, "I will carry you tomorrow to the Play where Great People frequently amuse themselves." And at another time, when the Duchess of Gloucester gave him her handkerchief, he was observed to kiss the coronet.

Something of a snob, but not very much nor very offensively; and indeed it may only have been a recollection of the very strong Polynesian awareness of rank. In any case he was perfectly amiable when James Burney, who had been second lieutenant of the *Adventure*, came over to Banks's box at the theatre and invited Omai to dinner.

The Burneys were not Great People (Fanny had not yet published *Evelina* nor Dr Burney his *History of Music*) and they would have seemed even less so that afternoon, as Omai came straight from the House of Lords, where he had been taken to hear the King make his speech from the throne. In her diary Fanny Burney recorded that

> As he had been at Court, he was very fine; he had on a suit of Manchester velvet, lined with white satten, a *bag*, lace ruffles, and a very handsome sword the King had given to him. . . . He makes *remarkable* good bows – not for *him*, but for *anybody*, however long under a Dancing Master's care. Indeed he seems to shame Education, for his manners are so extremely graceful, and he is so polite, attentive, and easy, that you would have thought he came from some foreign court.
>
> At dinner I had the pleasure of sitting next to him, as my cold kept me near the fire. The moment he was helped, he presented his plate to me, which, when I declined, he had not the *over-shot* politeness to offer *all round*, as I have seen some people do, but took it quietly again. He eat heartily and committed not the slightest blunder at table, neither did he do anything *awkwardly* and *ungainly*. He found by the turn of the conversation, and some wry faces, that a joint of beef was not roasted enough, and therefore when he was helped, he took great pains to assure mama that he liked it, and said two or three times "very *dood* – very *dood*".

It was not only the Burneys and the Thrales that Omai met apart from the Great People: he dined no fewer than ten times with the Royal Philosophers' Club, where there were some particularly interesting Fellows, including the Rev. Sir John Cullum, an antiquary (like so many of the members of the Royal Society at that time) and botanist, whose memorandum for 3 December 1774, first published by Mr Smith in 1911, included this passage:

> When I dined with him . . . a small magnifying glass had been newly put into his hands; he was perpetually pulling it out of his pocket, and looking at the Candles etc. with excessive delight and admiration. We all laughed at his simplicity, and yet probably the wisest person present would have wondered as much, if that knick-knack had then for the first time been presented to him. He had seen Hail before he came to England, and

> therefore was not much surprized at the first fall of Snow, which he called, naturally enough, white Rain. But he was prodigiously struck, when he first saw and handled a piece of Ice; and when he was told that it was sometimes thick and strong enough to bear men, and other great weights, he could scarcely be made to believe it.

He was portrayed by Sir Joshua Reynolds, William Parry (who showed Banks at his side, pointing out the tattoo marks on his hand while Solander, portly and seated, takes notes), and Nathaniel Dance, who, commissioned by Banks, also painted the famous portrait of Captain Cook. He does not however seem to have attracted the attention of the caricaturists, though they did pay some attention to Banks, for by now poor Hawkesworth's version of the Pacific voyages was in wide circulation, and this, together with the return of the *Adventure*, not only revived interest in the South Seas but also provided more information about Tahiti, thus enabling the pamphleteers who had been so witty about Banks in earlier days to be wittier still, making him Oberea's lover and the father of her child or indeed children.

At one time or another (for the caricatures and rhymes went on into the next century) Banks was accused of a good many vices, though catching butterflies on the far side of the world and collecting inedible plants seemed to anger these authors far more than any moral turpitude, yet not one of them appears to have made use of the fact that he left Omai an illiterate heathen, although properly handled this could have been made to appear worse than gathering simples.

Omai had quick parts. He learnt to play chess and backgammon and at Streatham he beat Baretti, Mrs Thrale observing "everybody admired at the savage's good breeding and at the European's impatient spirit". And Sir John Cullum remarked upon his not being taught to read, saying that Banks seemed "to keep him as an object of curiosity, to observe the workings of an untutored, unenlightened mind". But this really does not seem to square with Banks's character as it is seen from actions, letters and records stretching over a long and very busy lifetime, a character strongly marked by benevolence; a somewhat rough, heavy benevolence at times, but constantly there and quite opposed to the cold objectivity suggested by Sir John's remark. Banks knew Omai infinitely better than Cullum and he could place him in the context of his native civilization. He may very well have supposed that for Omai literacy in a language of which he had so imperfect a grasp was scarcely attainable and since he was to go back to a bookless Tahiti of little relevance even if by great labour it were attained.

Much the same applies to conversion. Apart from anything else

Omai would have made but an indifferent Christian: what little time he could spare from having fun he devoted to planning revenge upon the men of Borabora – revenge and the recovery of his family's land. And yet it was strange that neither Miss Banks nor her mother, both deeply religious women, ever seem to have raised the point; nor did any of Banks's many botanical friends who were also parsons, even bishops. The only person who does appear to have concerned himself with Omai in this respect was Granville Sharp, the founder of the British and Foreign Bible Society and that for the conversion of Jews, who presented him with an illustrated Bible when he went back to Tahiti. In Banks's case comparative indifference combined with a respect for the Polynesian's own piety and religious sense may be a large part of the answer. It was certainly not lack of kindness. His wish to be a friend to Omai was no passing enthusiasm: in the summer of 1775 he took him to Yorkshire as one of a party that included Constantine Phipps (Mulgrave Hall, near Whitby, was their destination), his young brother Augustus, George Colman the playwright, said by his friends to be the wittiest man of the age, and Colman's son, also called George, who left an account of the journey in his *Random Records*. It has often been quoted, but these extracts are too valuable to be left out:

> The coach in which we rumbled from York was the ponderous property of Sir Joseph, and as huge and heavy as a broad-wheeled waggon; but however ill-constructed for a quick conveyance over the rough roads and steep acclivities which we had to encounter, its size was by no means too large for its contents . . . [For in addition to six inside passengers and Phipps' stores for a long stay] Sir Joseph's stowage was still more formidable; unwearied in botanical research, he travell'd with trunks containing voluminous specimens of his *hortus siccus* in whitey-brown paper; and large receptacles for further vegetable materials, which he might accumulate, in his locomotions. . . . We never saw a tree with an unusual branch, or a strange weed, or anything singular in the vegetable world, but a halt was immediately order'd; out jump'd Sir Joseph; out jump'd the two boys (Augustus and myself) after him; and out jump'd Omai, after us all. Many articles, "all a growing, and a growing", which seem'd to me no better than thistles, and which would not have sold for a farthing in Covent Garden Market, were pull'd up by the roots, and stow'd carefully in the coach, as rarities.

Eventually they reached Scarborough and young George Colman's first sight of the sea: the next day

> I was upon the point of making my maiden plunge, from a bathing-machine, into the briny flood, when Omai appear'd wading before me. The coast of Scarborough having an eastern aspect, the early sunbeams shot

> their lustre upon the tawny Priest, and heighten'd the cutaneous gloss which he had recently received from the water; he look'd like a specimen of pale moving mahogany, highly varnish'd; not only varnish'd, indeed, but curiously veneer'd; for, from his hips, and the small of his back, downwards, he was tattow'd with striped arches, broad and black, by means of a sharp shell, or a fish's tooth, imbued with an indelible die, according to the fashion of his country. He hail'd me with the salutation of *Tosh*, which was his pronunciation of *George*, and utter'd certain sounds approaching to the articulation of – "back" – "swim" – "I" – "me" – "carry" – "you" [in the event Omai carried the boy far out to sea on his back], and he constantly cried, "*Tosh not fraid*"; but Tosh *was* fraid – and plaguily frighten'd indeed; that's the plain truth.

In time they reached Mulgrave, and there Banks started to teach the boys something of botany, sending them out in the morning to gather plants in the woods.

> We could not easily have met with an abler master. Although it was somewhat early for us to turn natural philosophers, the novelty of the thing, and rambling through wild sylvan tracts of peculiarly romantic beauty, counteracted all notions of studious drudgery, and turned science into a sport. We were prepared over-night for these morning excursions by Sir Joseph. He explained to us the rudiments of the Linnean System, in a series of nightly Lectures, which were very short, clear, and familiar; the first of which he illustrated by cutting up a cauliflower.[9]

Colman's account appeared fifty-five years after the journey, and a confusion of two separate visits or an imperfect memory will account for certain inconsistencies (he has grouse being shot, for example, which could scarcely have happened in June or July, and he speaks of their being in Yorkshire in August or September, when Banks can be shown to have been elsewhere). But there were no inconsistencies whatsoever about the return of the *Resolution.* Captain Cook brought her into Spithead on 30 July 1775 and at once set out for London with a full report of his triumphant voyage. It was a triumphant voyage – and the fact was instantly recognized – not so much because it had, by the most arduous traversing and retraversing of the far southern Pacific and Atlantic oceans, disproved the existence of the Terra Australis as it was universally understood, but because it had proved the possibility of keeping men alive and healthy for very long stretches far and far from land. Cook had sailed more than twenty thousand miles, taking more than a thousand days – three years and eighteen days, to be exact – and he had lost only one man out of 118. He had also discovered several new islands, while the naturalists, according to Forster's letter to

Barrington from the Cape, had found 260 new plants and 200 new animals; and all this had been done without Banks, in a vessel that he had called unhealthy and "exceedingly unfit for the intended voyage", a voyage which could have "no prospect but Distress & disappointment".

The news came when Banks, Phipps and Omai were guests aboard the Admiralty yacht in which Lord Sandwich, accompanied by Miss Ray, was inspecting the royal dockyards. It was not entirely unexpected, since there had been letters from the Cape, but even so its effect was very great indeed. Sandwich's delight was whole-hearted, without the least reserve (unless perhaps he felt a little compassion for his friend) and he and Miss Ray posted up to London at once. But Banks had behaved like a fool in 1772; the extent of his folly was now strikingly apparent; and by this time he was too sensible a man for his pleasure at Cook's return not to be mingled with feelings of regret, shame, and embarrassment.

He did not return to London for some weeks, and in the mean time Solander kept him informed by post: here is the first of his letters, written on 1 August 1775.

> Two oClock Monday – This Moment Capt Cook is arrived. I have not yet had an opertunity of conversing with him, as he is still in the board-room – giving an account of himself & Co. He looks as well as ever. By and by, I shall be able to say a little more – Give my Compl^{ts} to Miss Ray and tell her I have made a Visitation to her Birds and found them all well.
>
> Captn Cook desires his best Compl^{ts} to You, he expressed himself in the most friendly manner towards you, that could be; he said: nothing could have added to the satisfaction he has had, in making this tour but having had your company. He has some Birds, in Sp.V. for you &c &c that he would have wrote to you himself about, if he had not been kept too long at the Admiralty and at the same time wishing to see his wife. He rather looks better than when he left England. Mr Hodges came up in his chaise, I saw him and his Drawings. He has great many portraits – some very good – . . . Foster Senr and Junr are also come up, but I have not seen them, they did not call at the Admiralty. . . . Inclosed You will find a Letter from Ch' Clark. . . .[10]

It will be remembered that Charles Clerke was Banks's shipmate in the *Endeavour*, a master's mate with little interest who had already reached the dangerously advanced age of twenty-seven; but he ended the voyage an acting-lieutenant, and he was confirmed in that rank and appointed to the *Resolution*, probably because of Banks's influence. They were much of an age, and Clerke, like Banks, was firmly rooted in the land, being a farmer's son: theirs was a strong, uncomplicated friendship, and at the time of the unpleasantness over the *Resolution* in 1772 Clerke had written to say that he would "go to sea in a Grog Tub" with Banks if he desired it. The letter that Solander enclosed was written aboard the *Resolution* and it was dated Sunday Morn: 5 o'clock.

> We're now past Portland, with a fine fresh NW Gale and a young flood tide, so that in a very few Hours we shall anchor at Spithead from our Continent hunting expedition. I will not now set about relating any of the particulars of our Voyage, as I hope very soon to have the Honour and happiness of paying my personal respects, when I can give you a much clearer idea of any matters you think worth inquiring after, than it is possible to do at this distance.
>
> I hope I need not assure you that it is utterly out of the power of length of time, or distance of space, to eradicate or in the least alleviate the gratitude your friendly offices to me has created. I assure you I've devoted some days to your service in very distant parts of the Globe; the result of which I hope will give you some satisfaction; at least it will convince you of my intentions and endeavours in that particular. I shall send this away by one of our civil Gentry, who will fly to Town with all the sail they can possibly make. God bless you and send me one Line just to tell me you're alive and well, if that is the case, for I'm as great a stranger to all matters in England as tho' I had been these 3 Years underground – so if I recieve no intelligence from you I shall draw bad conclusions and clap on my suit of black; but you know I never despair, but always look for the best, therefore hope and flatter myself this will find you alive and happy, which that it may, is the sincerest Hope and Wish of, Dear Sir, Your Gratefully Oblig'd & most H'ble Servt Chas Cler^{ke}.
>
> Excuse the Paper, its gilt I assure you, but the Cockroaches have piss'd upon it. – We're terribly busy – you know a Man of War. My respects and every social wish to the good Doctor. I'll write to him as soon as possible – here's too much damning of Eyes and Limbs to do anything now.

Solander's next letter, dated 14 August 1775, five days after Cook had been promoted post-captain, ran thus:

> Our Expedition down to the Resolution, made yesterday quite a feast to all who were concerned. We set out early from the Tower, review'd some of the Transports; Visited Deptford yard; went on board the Experiment, afterwards to Wolwich, where we took on board Miss Ray & Co, and then proceeded to the Galleon's where we were welcomed on board of the Resolution – and Lord Sandwich made many of them quite happy.
>
> Providentially old Captn Clements died 2 or 3 days ago, by which a Captain's place of Greenwich was made Vacant. This was given to Capt Cook, and a promise of Employ whenever he should ask for it. Mr Cooper was made Master and Commander. Mr Clerke was promised the command of the Resolution to carry Mr Omai home. . . .

All our friends look as well as if they had been all the while in clover. All inquired after You. In fact we had a glorious day and long'd for nothing but You & Mr Omai. Mr Edgcomb and his Marines made a fine appearance. – Ld Sandwich asked the Officers afterwards to dine with us at Woolwich.

Most of our time, yesterday, was taken up in ceremonies, so I had not much time to see their curious collections. Mr Clerke show'd me some drawings of Birds, made by a Midshipman, not bad, which I believe he intends for you. I was told that Mr Anderson one of the Surgeons Mates, has made a good Botanical Collection, but I did not see him. There were on board 3 live Otaheite Dogs, the ugliest & most stupid of all the Canine tribe. Forster had on board the following Live Stock: a Springe Bock from the Cape, a Surikate, two Eagles, & several small Birds, all from the Cape. I believe he intends these for the Queen. If I except Cooper & 2 of the new made Lieutenants I believe the whole Ship's Company will go out again. Pickersgill made the Ladies sick by shewing them the New Zealand head of which 2 or 3 slices were broiled and eat on board of the Ship.* It is preserved in Spirit and I propose to get it for Hunter, who goes down with me to morrow on purpose, when we expect the Ship will be at Deptford.

Still another letter, dated 22 August, said:

Several of the Resolutions Men have called at Your House, to offer you their curiosities:– Tyrrell was here this morning. Poor Clarke, as I hear, has been in a sad scrape. Upon going out, he gave a joint Bond with his Brother, for paying Sir John Clarke's debts. I've wondered much why I had not seen Mr Clarke since the Ship came up to Deptford, but I this day learnt, that he had been obliged to live among Lawyers &c 'till he could quiet the Creditors, which I hope he has now done, at least I was told so. Sir John Clarke has sent some Money home from India but not enough – and now I have been told Ch Clark is to pay them 100£ immediately and part of his pay quarterly. However I don't know if it is so.

Capt Cook has sent all his curiosities to my apartments at the Museum. All his shells is to go to Lord Bristol – 4 Casks have your name on them and I understand they contain Birds & fish, &c the Box D° with Plants from the Cape . . .

In time however Banks overcame his reluctance and putting what face he could upon it went back to New Burlington Street and renewed his friendship with Cook. They dined together several times at the Royal Philosophers' Club and presently Banks had the pleasure of seeing Cook unanimously elected a Fellow of the Society. In passing it may be observed that Cook thereby became an associate of Benjamin Franklin, who had belonged to the Society for many years but who was very soon to become one of King George's most vigorous opponents; for what was

* This happened in New Zealand, and it was Maoris who did the eating.

to become the American War of Independence had already begun at Lexington in April 1775, and the transports that Lord Sandwich inspected were probably those hired to carry the wonderfully injudicious reinforcements of Hessian and Brunswick troops across the Atlantic. Yet on the other hand Franklin gave orders that the newly-formed United States Navy was on no account to interfere with Cook on his voyage of discovery. And as for Banks, so unpolitical a creature was he that his friendship with Franklin was quite unaffected by the war.

Hawkesworth's version of the first voyage had caused Cook some embarrassment and now in spite of strong misgivings about his literary powers he decided to write his own account of the second: this angered the remarkably disagreeable, dishonest and grasping Forster, who swore that Sandwich had promised him the honour, the glory and above all the profit of doing so and who went into a prolonged Teutonic frenzy against the First Lord, "who endeavoured to ruin me by the weight of His power and opulence", Cook, who had "forfeited the Appelations and the Characters of a Gentleman", and even Banks himself at last; but it also meant that we have a fine, straightforward book, though Cook still thought it necessary to say "I shall therefore conclude this introductory discourse with desiring the Reader to excuse the inaccuracies of Style . . . and that when such occur he will recollect that it is the production of a man who has been constantly at sea from his youth and though, with the assistance of a few good friends, he has passed through all the stations belonging to a seaman from an Apprentice Boy in the Coal trade to a Post-Captain in the Royal Navy, he has had no opportunity of cultivating Letters."

Banks helped him with botanical drawings, notes and descriptions, and Dr John Douglas, later a Fellow of the Royal Society and Bishop of Salisbury, agreed to look over the text. In fact the Doctor found almost nothing to change, but he and Banks did see the book through the press, a task that Cook could not undertake, since while it was still in the printers' hands he left for his third great voyage.

This third voyage was concerned primarily with the North-West Passage, but it also called for an immense journey through the Pacific, passing by many known and almost certainly by many unknown lands with who knows what botanical and zoological wealth. Cook was going in the *Resolution*, with Gore as his first lieutenant, William Bligh as the master and Omai as a passenger; his consort was the *Discovery*, with Charles Clerke in command (once he could get free of his debtors' prison), James Burney as first lieutenant and William Anderson, an able naturalist, as surgeon; and in both ships there were many of

Banks's old shipmates among the warrant officers and foremast hands. Yet at no time does he seem to have thought of going too. Banks contributed great good will and sensible advice, and he successfully urged the taking of David Nelson, a gardener from Kew; but he took no further part in the voyage, and in the last letter Cook wrote him from England – it was dated from *Resolution* in Plymouth Sound, 10 July 1776, the day before the wind allowed him to sail – this situation is taken for granted. Cook speaks of certain botanical illustrations in his book, that Banks will deal with as he thinks best; of Omai, "much carressed here by every person of note" but upon the whole rejoicing at the prospect of going home; gives the splendid news that "Sr J^{no} Pringle writes me that the Council of the Royal Society have decreed me the Prize Medal of this year. I am obliged to you and my other good friends for this unmerited honour." (He is referring to the Copley medal, the Society's great distinction, awarded for Cook's paper on the prevention of scurvy.) And the letter ends "Omai Joins his best respects to you and Dr Solander with, Dear Sir, your Most Old and very humble servt. Jam^{s} Cook".

At this time Banks was only thirty-three; he had not yet grown bulky – in the fine Wedgwood cameo made a few years later he looks tolerably slim and youthful – and the gout that tormented the later part of his life had not made its first appearance. Yet hindsight shows that he was approaching a possible metamorphosis. There are many marine creatures, including the barnacle and the oyster, the very types of sedentary unstirring life, that have an active free-swimming youth; then when they are still quite young something comes over them – they find a convenient place, settle there, change shape, and never move again.

Much the same appeared to be happening to Banks. His convenient place was a corner house in Soho Square, number thirty-two, a fine great house with an Adam drawing room and plenty of space for the now prodigious herbarium, space too for his business papers and his correspondence, already important and soon to become enormous, requiring and receiving systematic treatment: it is from this period that the record becomes much more nearly continuous, in spite of later disruptions.

He moved in with his sister, obviously a most companionable being: she was devoted enough to copy his journals to the most surprising extent and to include prayers for him in her memoranda; and when, somewhat later, he was deeply concerned with sheep, her devotion went as far as the wearing of three dresses made from his wool, dresses called Hightum (for grand occasions), Titum (for occasions not so grand), and Scrub (for ordinary wear); but she was perfectly capable of leading her own life as well. Like her brother she was generously built and in 1794 she weighed fourteen stone three pounds (Banks had a pair of scales at Soho Square and he recorded the weights of his friends: sometimes of their dogs too) but in earlier life, to judge by Angelica Kauffmann's portrait, she was quite pretty in a broad-shouldered, dark-haired, round-headed way, and she was rather dashing in her dress: she drove a four-in-hand with style, she was fascinated by ballooning, and she collected not only visiting cards but also coins, tokens, objects of natural history, books, broadsides, caricatures, and newspaper cuttings – the British Museum has them still.

A philosophical oyster or barnacle could hardly have chosen a more agreeable settling-place than Soho Square, with the herbarium, the rapidly growing library, Solander at hand, and the Royal Society and the Antiquaries conveniently near. Yet the figure can easily be pushed too far, since whereas the barnacle is truly and permanently fixed, Joseph Banks and his sister could spend much of the late summer and early autumn at their beloved Revesby, and in addition to Norfolk there was always the King's garden at Kew. And there were strong signs that Banks was by no means resigned to a regular sedentary existence – that the approaching metamorphosis was no more than an illusion.

In this same year of 1776 for example, at the little town of Newbury on that famous trout-stream the Kennet, Lord Denbigh said that he, "Lord Sandwich, Lord Mulgrave, Mr Banks, and two or three Ladies of Pleasure had pass'd five or six days there, and intended to pass all this Week and the next in the same Place; that their chief object was to enjoy the trouting Season; that they had been very successful; that Lord Sandwich had caught Trouts near twenty inches long, which gave him incredible Satisfaction . . ."[11] And then in Stig Rydén's *The Banks Collection* we find a letter from Johan Alströmer, written in October 1777, that runs in part "Sunday, dinner at Banks's and *Soupé* at his *Maitress*' Mistress walls, with only Banks and Solander" while a little later he writes "I now spend every day with Banks and Solander, and this I am writing at Mme Walls's, Mr Banks's *maitress*, where we have dined, and Solander asks me now as always to convey his respects."

Banks may have moved house, but he had not wholly committed himself; nor had he entered upon a regular marriage, which he looked upon as incompatible with natural philosophy, with a life of scientific research, and there was still the possibility that he might become a free-swimming organism once more, travelling to remote countries filled with nondescripts.

Chapter 8

PRESIDENT OF THE ROYAL SOCIETY: MARRIAGE: THE KING AND KEW: BOTANY BAY

IN 1778 Banks was again asked to serve on the Council of the Royal Society, whose President was then Sir John Pringle. Sir John was a distinguished medical man of good lowland Scottish family, and he had been joint professor of pneumatics and moral philosophy at Edinburgh before becoming physician-general to the forces in Flanders and then in 1774 physician to King George III. But he was now past seventy; he was on bad terms with the King; and although he had been President for only six years he decided not to ask for re-election.

The quarrel or rather the disagreement with the King arose out of the wholly unnecessary American war, now alas being fought in deadly earnest. Benjamin Franklin, a Fellow of the Royal Society since 1756, but now one of the leading rebels, probably knew more about electricity than anyone else of his generation, and among other things he had invented lightning conductors (they were long known as Franklin's rods) for which he had been awarded the Copley medal in 1753. In 1769 the Dean of St Paul's, alarmed by the striking of St Bride's, asked the Royal Society how best to preserve his cathedral; the Society appointed a committee, which of course included Franklin and which told the Dean what should be done. In 1772 the Government, alarmed by the striking (and destruction) of some powder-magazines in Italy, asked the Society how to protect the English magazines at Purfleet; again the Society appointed a committee, and the report, drawn up by Franklin, particularly recommended pointed conductors. There was one dissentient however, Benjamin Wilson, who felt passionately that conductors should end in a knob; he wrote a long paper for the *Philosophical Transactions* to this effect and when the Purfleet magazines were in fact struck (though not destroyed) in spite of their spiked conductors he and his friends appeared to triumph. Wilson was an extraordinarily versatile man, a successful portraitist, manager of the Duke of York's theatre, Hogarth's successor as serjeant-painter to the King, and a Copley medallist in 1760 for electrical experiments; he had many friends, some of whom the King must have respected, for when they told him that Franklin was as bad an electrician as he was a subject he believed them. The Americans had declared their independence; the King now declared his support for the knob and desired Sir John and the Society to do the same. Sir John being so familiar with the royal person was probably less awed than other men might have been and he said "Sire, I cannot reverse the laws and operations of nature."

At any other time the reply would have been harmless enough, but now, among those who were politically inclined, feelings for or against the Americans had risen to a very high pitch indeed, far out of the reach of mere reason. The division in the country followed the strangest lines. Johnson, for example, having remarked as early as 1769 that the Americans were a race of convicts and "ought to be thankful for any thing we allow them short of hanging", went on to write his extremely violent pamphlet *Taxation no Tyranny*, and by 1778 they had become "Rascals – Robbers – Pirates" fit to be burnt and destroyed; yet Boswell, so right-wing and usually so full of respect for the Doctor's opinions, took the other side entirely. The King, however, with his education and his conception of the royal office, could have only one view of the matter; and in this view, which was shared by his more vehement supporters, the contest between the Knobs and the Spikes took on a ludicrous symbolic importance. The natural philosophers could not be expected to take much notice of it, nor could they be expected to renounce their commitment to Franklin, particularly as some of them, like Priestley, thought that Franklin was not only physically but also politically and morally right.

Yet the Society needed the King's good will, just as it needed the political and social influence of its many noble and wealthy but not always very clever members; for although there were wealthy Fellows – Henry Cavendish was immensely rich – the Society itself was poor; its budget at this time was less than £1500 a year, and without the King's grant it could never have sent people out to observe either of the recent transits of Venus.

Once it was known that Sir John Pringle meant to resign the more active and concerned members, particularly those sitting on the Council, saw that at this juncture they would have to look about for an unusually suitable President. As for the great men with a certain interest in science who adorned the list of Fellows none seemed to answer. Henry Cavendish, for example, was grand enough, and indcpendently of that his scientific attainments would have done the Society honour; but he was too much of a recluse to consider standing for office.

And for political, social, or scientific reasons none of the Society's forty-seven peers aroused much enthusiasm.

Leaving grandeur aside therefore two likely candidates appeared, Alexander Aubert and Joseph Banks. Aubert was a very wealthy City man (he was at the head of the London Assurance Company), but his great love was astronomy and although he had published little he had made some remarkable observations. He was of course used to business methods; he also knew French and Italian; and some Fellows thought these valuable qualities in a President. The election of an astronomer would also please the many mathematicians, and what is more Sir John himself favoured Aubert. But Banks's friends were of a different opinion, and on 11 August 1778 Solander wrote to him:

> My dear Sir, – This morning Mr Planta told me that Sir John Pringle has certainly declared that he intends to resign; and Mr Cavendish says that Sir John has mentioned it at the *Mitre*. It is true that he has given hints about Mr Aubert, but all look to you. Dr Pitcairne and others have desired me to tell you that.[1]

and then on 17 August, "If you cannot find out a man of high rank who will accept of the Chair, you must listen to the Voice of the People. All talk of you."[2]

Banks did listen to the Voice of the People and discreetly began to canvass for votes, relying particularly on his fellow Antiquaries for support in the election at the end of the year – many Fellows of the Royal Society were also Fellows of the Antiquaries' Society, FRS and FSA. During the intervening months there was of course a great deal of informal talk among the members and other names were suggested, but at the Council's last meeting in November their choice fell on Banks. The choice was not self-evident: Banks's reputation as a botanist was not based on any publication: his family, though respectable, was not at all grand; his wealth, though considerable, was not to be compared with that of Cavendish or even Aubert; and then at thirty-five he was unusually young for the post. It is almost certain that his friendship with the King had great weight with the Council, together with the fact that he was a man whom people liked and respected, and a man who had nothing to do with politics, so that he got along perfectly well with Whigs and Tories and even, when they made their appearance, with Radicals.

The Council's recommendation, which came before the Anniversary Meeting of the Society on St Andrew's Day, was decisive, and when Banks wrote to Sir William Hamilton four days later it was to tell him, in a rather elaborately off-hand way,* of his triumph, observing that he was now tied by the leg to an armchair, alluding no doubt to the splendid carved affair in which the President of the Royal Society took (and still takes) his seat rather than to imprisonment by gout, for he was not attacked until 1787, and his nimbleness in 1778 is attested by this extract from a letter written by the Rev. Sir John Cullum to the Rev. Michael Tyson, quoted by Smith:

> December 7, 1778
>
> Mr Banks was elected President, unanimously to appearance by 220 votes. There were 127 of us at dinner, among whom were several of the Nobility. The dinner was late, owing to the new President, who waited for the declaration of the new Secretary, which was Mr Maty, by a majority of two to one . . . The President came in a great hurry, quite out of breath, and sitting down (I was opposite to him) said with good humour, but with rather too little dignity: "I believe never did a President of the Royal Society run so fast before." However, his behaviour throughout was very proper . . .

This was the last time that Banks could ever be accused of behaving with too little dignity as President of the Royal Society. In the course of his life he had many honours: he was given a baronetcy and the Order of the Bath, he became a Privy Councillor, he had honorary degrees, and he was made a member of many, many learned societies, including the *Institut National*, the most learned of them all; but he valued none as much as this presidency. He had a very high notion of the office and he filled it with the utmost conscientiousness and gravity; and indeed a man might well be deeply, permanently impressed by finding himself chosen as Newton's successor at the head of a society whose 570 members included almost all the outstanding mathematicians, astronomers, chemists, physicists, engineers, medical men, botanists and naturalists of the western world.

The election made Banks happy; it also made his metamorphosis inevitable. A conscientious President, attending 417 Council meetings out of a possible 450 in the course of forty-one years and some months, cannot also climb volcanoes or explore the South Seas. Within a few days of the first, another election brought him still more happiness: on 11 December Sir Joshua Reynolds, PRA, informed Joseph Banks, Esq., PRS, that he was now a member of the Club.

Happiness is often found to open men's hearts, and this was the case with Banks. Within a few months – on 23 March 1779 to be exact – he married a young lady from Kent, Dorothea Hugessen, the daughter and co-heiress of William Western Hugessen of Provender.

*The letter itself is printed on pages 307–8.

If being tied to a presidential chair had not completed Banks's metamorphosis, then being tied in a matrimonial knot must have finished the process. Yet although a President of the Royal Society and a married one at that was necessarily in the position of an oyster that has found its permanent bed, the marriage seems to have been thoroughly suitable and, unencumbered by children, thoroughly happy.

The Hugessens were of rather better family than the Bankses, long settled in their county and Miss Hugessen, though by no means as wealthy as her husband, had plenty of money of her own. Sir John Cullum, writing to another parson on 12 May 1779,[3] said "... Yesterday morning I took a breakfast with Mr Banks, who told me he was always glad to see his friend at that meal. And when can one see him so well? For after breakfast he retires into his study with those that please to attend him; where those who are likely to visit him will meet with ample entertainment. His wife is a comely and modest Young Lady."

Comely is not very high praise, yet the portrait by Russell does not seem to warrant anything more extravagant; but she had a pleasant young face (she was twenty-one) and she was unusually sweet-natured. She got along very well not only with her husband but also with his sister, and with his mother, who had her own room at Soho Square and who came there to be nursed in her last illness. Sophia Banks and Dorothea Banks shared the house just as they shared many of their interests; they both wore the woollen dresses from Banks's own shearing; they travelled down to Norfolk together every year; and he always referred to them as "my ladies". (They also put on weight together. Sophia Banks increased from 11 stone 8 lb in 1778 to 14 stone 3 lb in 1794, while between 1781 and 1794 Dorothea Banks rose from 9 stone 6 lb to 13 stone 12 lb.) Then again although the scanty remains of her accounts show her to have been kind and charitable, contributing to hospitals and to the education of various children, she was not markedly holier than thou, as may be seen from this postscript to one of her husband's letters to Sir William Hamilton in 1791: "Lady Banks desires to join with me in Best wishes to Lady Hamilton for whose Friendship she means hereafter to propose herself a candidate."

Dorothea Banks's younger sister Mary married Sir Edward Knatchbull of Mersham Hatch in Kent, the eighth baronet, and in time this marriage provided a tenuous link between Joseph Banks and Jane Austen, for Mary Knatchbull's son Edward, the ninth baronet, married Fanny Knight, Jane Austen's favourite niece. It was this Sir Edward Knatchbull and his son Lord Brabourne who were ultimately responsible for Banks's papers, once so neatly kept and now so cruelly destroyed, lost, or scattered over the face of the earth: not that Lord Brabourne was nearly so much to blame as some people have said – the British Museum refused a very moderate offer in 1884, so the papers were sold at auction, several lots fetching a shilling a piece.

But papers have a way of surviving, and Averil Lysaght, delving in the Kent County Archives, found not only Lady Banks's account book mentioned above but also a fine letter (it escaped Warren Dawson) which tells a good deal about Banks, his ladies, and the rigours of eighteenth-century life: it is printed on page 308.

If Banks had known the enormous amount of work that the Presidency of the Royal Society as he conceived it would entail he might have desired the honour less. It is true that he possessed an enormous amount of energy, a very great capacity for work, but he also had many other calls on his time: botany, of course, even if it became more and more elbow-chair herbarium botany, "tumbling over dried plants"; Revesby, which he always felt to be his true home, with its gardens, its fine deer-park,[4] the estate, the reclamation of the Fens, the shooting and fishing and archery (he and his sister had always been very fond of the longbow); the social life of London and the country; the King's gardens at Kew and somewhat later the King's sheep, a subject of perhaps almost equal importance for many years.

The Society over which he was called to preside was made up, for the most part, of unusually intelligent men; yet from the point of view of administration and corporate efficiency, the whole was very much less than the sum of its parts; although many of the Fellows were thoroughly conversant with scientific method few had much notion of business and they left the running of the Society to the active members of the Council and even more to the Secretaries. This did not answer very well and a typical instance of muddle-headedness arose in Banks's first year as President. Since Newton's time the Society had had its being in Crane Court, off Fleet Street, where it possessed two houses. The place had been bought in 1710 for £1450 by the then President, at the head of a committee that included Sir Christopher Wren, a judge of houses; it was described as "being in the middle of the town and out of noise", and it was conveniently near the Mitre tavern, where the Royal Philosophers used to dine. After some fifty or sixty years however the Society took to asking the Government, which after all it frequently advised, to provide bigger and better accommodation, and in 1776 the Government said they might have rooms in the huge new Somerset House that Sir William Chambers was building on the site of the old one, between the Strand and the river. The Government also said that Chambers would show the Society his plans and discuss them with the Council. It appeared to the Council that there would not be enough room for their offices, meetings, books and collections: Chambers told them that a greater area was impossible, but that a different disposition of the available space would make it quite suitable. After some deliberation the Council accepted the offer: this happened at the end of Sir John Pringle's presidency and the move took place in that of Banks's, the 1780 Anniversary Meeting being held in the new quarters. But in the event there was not room for the collections, which had to be given to the British Museum; and then during the move quantities of records appear to have been lost, while a great many that were preserved were spoilt by damp in the new building; and the meeting room itself impressed Faujas de Saint-Fond,[5] a visiting Frenchman, as unworthy of the Royal Society: "Much too small, like a Concert Hall; the seats only benches ranged in parallel rows." He also condemned the President's chair (which though no doubt perfectly at home in Crane Court would have looked a little strange in the cold severity of Chambers' building) as Gothic: the President "is seated in an elevated chair, of a colossal form. It is made of mahogany, and surmounted with an escutcheon, on which are painted the insignia of the Society. Nothing could be more gothic or worse taste than this ornament." The Council then rounded off this singularly unprofitable transaction by selling Crane Court for £1000, which, taking the seventy years of inflation into account, was a very serious loss for such a poorly endowed Society.

But even if astronomical or mathematical ability had also meant business ability there was the fact that the members of the Council were often drawn not from the scientists but from the many antiquaries, archaeologists, bibliophiles, literary men (such as Horace Walpole) and even painters (Sir Joshua was an FRS) who were Fellows, while the Secretaries and the Treasurer tended to be librarians or historians or something of that kind; and all these gentlemen had other occupations as well, a clerk, a housekeeper and a manservant or two being almost the only full-time staff. To one accustomed to the severely scientific Royal Society of the last hundred years it seems strange that in a body expressly founded "for the improving of Natural Knowledge by experiments" the greater number should from the beginning not have been scientific men at all; yet such was the case, and Sir Henry Lyons, himself a Fellow and for a long while the Treasurer, shows in his deeply informed and well-documented account that the ratio of scientific to unscientific Fellows rose steadily in the eighteenth century to reach

1 : 2.4 in 1770; and it had reached a slightly higher figure by the time of Banks's election.

This was of no great importance under such strong and eminently scientific Presidents as Sir Isaac Newton and Sir Hans Sloane, that is to say from 1703 to 1741; but Sloane was followed by an antiquary, and although Lord Macclesfield and Lord Morton, the gifted astronomers who came next, did their best for natural science, still another antiquary was elected in 1768. The tone of the Society gradually changed, and although it still had almost all the best natural philosophers, the fact that the Councils and sometimes the committees consisted largely of men ignorant of science while many of the councillors did not attend regularly meant that inferior papers appeared in the *Philosophical Transactions* – indeed, the word "puerile" was used of some of them – and inferior candidates were admitted to the fellowship; and at the same time accounts, correspondence, and records were in a sadly deficient state.

Sir John Pringle had been aware of these shortcomings and he had made attempts, largely ineffectual, at reform. They were even more evident to Joseph Banks, who was above all things a classifier. An herbarium – and his was already one of the most important in the country – is meaningless without classification, a mere collection of isolated curiosities. Much the same applies to a voluminous correspondence, and once Banks was President of the Royal Society he wrote and received letters on a heroic scale. These were preserved with as much care and method as the dried plants, and after they had spent their due season in the files they were bound in book form. There were at least 124 of these handsome great volumes, and it is worth repeating that Warren Dawson put the figure of the Soho Square correspondence alone, quite apart from the letters at Revesby and elsewhere, at 50,000 or even as high as 100,000. Then again a considerable landowner, with some hundreds of farms and a very lively interest in agriculture, stockbreeding and fen-reclamation, would be in a wretched condition unless his papers were rationally ordered, above all if he lived most of the year in London. Banks's papers were in extraordinarily good order. Arthur Young, speaking of Revesby, said:

> His office of two rooms is contained in the space of 80 feet by 16. There is a bricked partition between with an iron grated door so that a room in which a fire is always burning might be burnt out without affecting the inner one.
>
> There is a catalogue of names and subjects in every drawer so that whether the enquiry concerned a man or drainage, or an enclosure, or a farm, or a wood, the request was scarce named before a mass of information

> was before me. Such an apartment and such apparatus must be of incomparable use in the management of every great estate or indeed in any circumstances.[6]

Banks was pre-eminently a man of order (in parenthesis it may be observed that although there are few easier ways of losing money than farming, as even a man as intelligent and well-informed as Arthur Young found to his cost, Banks made a resounding success of it, increasing his income from six to thirty thousand a year, partly no doubt because of his system), and as an orderly man he saw the want of method in the Royal Society with distress. But as an Englishman he also knew something of the dogged resistance to change that was to be encountered in an old, comfortably established body, thoroughly set in its ways, however faulty; he knew that sudden radical reform was quite out of the question and that the modest changes he wished to bring about, particularly in the administration and in the selection of new Fellows, must be introduced gradually – no zealous new broom would sweep to any purpose.

And in any event at this point he was much taken up with finding a country house or villa within dining distance of London, for he and his ladies cruelly missed a garden of their own. Soho Square was very well; it looked out on to trees, and it was to remain their principal dwelling; but a real garden was essential to complete happiness. The house they pitched on was called Spring Grove and it stood a little off the Hounslow road in Isleworth, two or three miles beyond Kew and not far from the river. The locality was also called Heston, that being the parish, and sometimes Smallberry Green. Spring Grove was an agreeable fair-sized square building; it stood in tolerably rural though already villa-studded country – as early as 1747 Horace Walpole at nearby Strawberry Hill had said that "dowagers were as plenty as flounders" – and it had a fine spreading garden with a pond in it, and pasture enough for Mrs Banks to have a dairy. Very properly this was the first private garden in which a Banksian rose was grown, it having been sent from China by William Kerr, and a Kew collector; but in 1779 the Banksian rose was still in the future, together with the American cranberries on their island in the pond. For the time being Banks was obliged to pay attention to his new responsibilities, and not only to the presidency itself but also to the ex officio duties that came with it. He was now for example a trustee of the British Museum, an institution he knew very well because he read in its library and because Solander worked there as keeper of the natural history collections, while both the Royal Society's secretaries, Dr M. Maty and Mr J. Planta, were librarians. He also had a seat on the Board of Longitude, and as soon as the Board of Agriculture was set up, with his friend Young as secretary, he was a member of that too. And as the head of the most learned society in the kingdom he was the person to whom the authorities turned for answers to difficult questions; sometimes, indeed very often, the questions lay outside his personal range and he had to refer to other Fellows, but this was not always the case and when he was called upon to give evidence before a House of Commons committee that was considering prisons and prisoners he gave it as his opinion that Botany Bay might prove a suitable place for those sentenced to a long term. He spoke emphatically and in considerable detail.

Not long after these words, which can be seen as by far the most important statement he ever made in his life, Botany Bay, the great *Endeavour* voyage and his shipmates during those three years were brought to his mind with present, living clarity. There had been reports of Cook from time to time, and then some uneasy rumours coming by way of Dutch East Indiamen; but now in the late summer of 1780 Lieutenant James King arrived at the Admiralty having travelled post from Stromness, where the *Resolution* and the *Discovery* had been driven by southerly gales, with first-hand news of the expedition. Both ships were safe – they reached the Nore on 4 October 1780 – having lost only five men from sickness in well over four years and having made important discoveries; but Cook had been killed in Hawaii, and Clerke had died off the coast of Kamschatka. A few days before his death he wrote this letter to Banks:

Resolution: at Sea 18. Aug. 1779

My ever honoured Friend,

The disorder I was attacked with in the King's bench prison has proved consumptive with which I have battled with various success, although without one single day's health since I took leave of you in Burlington Street: it has now so far got the better of me, that I am not able to turn myself in my bed, so that my stay in this world must be of very short duration: however, I hope my friends will have no occasion to blush in owning themselves such, for I have most perfectly and justly done my duty to my country, as far as my abilities would enable me; for, where that has been concerned, the attention to my health which I was very sensible was in the most imminent danger, has never swerved me a single half mile out of the road of my duty; so that I flatter myself I shall leave behind me that character it has ever been my utmost ambition to attain, which is that of an honest & faithful servant to the Public whom I had undertaken to serve.

I have made you the best collection of all kinds of matter I could that have fallen in our way in the course of the voyage; but they are by no means so compleat as they would have been, had my health enabled me to pay more attention to them – I hope, however, you will find many things among them worthy your attention and acceptance: in my will I have bequeathed you the whole of every kind: there are great abundance so that you will have ample choice.

I must beg you to present my warmest & most affectionate compliments to Dr Solander and assure him I leave the world replete with the most social Ideas of his much esteemed & ever respected Friendship.

I must beg leave to recommend to your notice Mr Will. Ellis, one of the Surgeon's mates, who will furnish you with some drawings & accounts of the various birds which will come to your possession: he has been very useful to me in your service in that particular, & is, I believe, a very worthy young man, and I hope will prove worthy of any services that may be in your way to confer upon him.

The two Clerkes of the two ships, Mr W. Dewar & Mr Greg. Bentham, have, I believe, been very honest servants in their stations, & having by Capt Cook's and now very soon by my death lost those, to whom they looked up to for protection are, I fear, destitute of friends: if it should be in your power to render them any services, I flatter myself they will be worthy of such attention.

If I should recollect any thing more to say to you, I will trouble my friend, Mr King, with it, who is so kind to be my amanuensis on the occasion; & I will make no apology in recommending him to a share in your friendship, as I am perfectly assured of his being deserving of it, as in that also of the worthy Doctor's.

Now, my dear & honoured friend, I must bid you a final adieu: may you enjoy many happy years in this world, and in the end attain that fame your indefatigable industry so richly deserves. These are most sincerely the warmest and sincerest wishes of your devoted affectionate departing Servant

Chas Clarke*

I quote this letter in full partly because I find Captain Clerke such a very likeable man and partly because it shows Banks by reflection. He had indeed what might be called a genius for friendship if it were not for the fact that on occasion his amiability outweighed his judgement, so that self-seeking people sometimes attached themselves to him for long periods. In general he kept his friends; and a little after this time Dr Kippis, FRS, wrote of him "He appears to be manly, liberal and open in his behaviour to his acquaintance and very persevering in his

*Clarke for Clerke is of course a copyist's error, but the whole is given exactly as it stands in DTC I 266/7.

friendship. The man who, for a course of years, and without diminution, preserves the affection of those friends who know him best, is not likely to have unpardonable faults of temper."[7]

His range of friendships was very wide, and at the top stood the King. Obviously it is very difficult for a king to have any friends at all in the ordinary sense, but in this case, two men of much the same age and with many of the same interests could come reasonably close to it, particularly as it was quite impossible for anyone to call Banks interested. In spite of the American war, which had spread to war with France, Spain and Holland, the King still managed to find time to attend to his gardens at Kew, now in full expansion; he and Banks saw one another often, and their liking increased.

In the spring of 1781 the King made Banks a baronet, so that it was as Sir Joseph that he finished the 1780/81 sessions of the Royal Society, the first at Somerset House. He then turned to Kew, and together with Carl Linnaeus, the great man's son, Solander and Dryander, yet another learned Swede who had studied botany under the same master, he worked right through the summer, from ten in the morning until four in the afternoon, four days a week, on the great *Flora Kewensis* that appeared in 1789 under Aiton's name. And so, leaving both Kew and the nascent gardens at Spring Grove, he travelled down with his Ladies to the others, far more mature, at Revesby.

This was perhaps Banks's happiest time. It is true that he had now fixed himself as firmly as any barnacle and that his roving days were over; but the presidential chair made no bad resting place for an extremely energetic, social man, delighting in the society of natural philosophers; and if at times he regretted coconut palms bowing to the trade wind he could console himself with the gardens at Kew and Spring Grove, whose rising hothouses promised wonderful results, while the palms themselves could be enjoyed by proxy – by the botanical collectors he and Aiton sent out. He could also reflect that he was healthy (though he already weighed fifteen stone), young, and rich, that he enjoyed the particular good will of his sovereign, the company of a young, amiable and well-bred wife, and a commanding position in the learned world, soon to be strengthened by the publication of his immense work on the Pacific voyage, the plates for which were almost ready.

He was surrounded by friends and his house in Soho Square was rapidly becoming the chief meeting place for scientific men in the capital. He was a hospitable creature and he took great pleasure in inviting people to breakfast as well as other meals; and quite apart from receptions and set entertainment his vast and rapidly growing herbarium, library and natural history collections were open to all properly introduced naturalists, the properness of the introduction having to do only with their scientific zeal and attainments; nationality, age, rank and wealth being of no consequence at all.

There were times when his house was filled with guests almost as various as those in his glass cases, and one might find a tongue-tied botanical young surgeon's mate from an East-Indiaman next to Herschel, who had just discovered Uranus, together with Cavendish, Priestley, a philosophical bishop or two, Marsden the historian of Sumatra, and a group of visiting Danes.

And unpolitical though he was, Banks must have rejoiced at the near approach of peace. The British capitulation at Yorktown mean the end of the war in America, while Rodney's victory over Admiral de Grasse and the defeat of the French and Spanish at Gibraltar meant that it did not end ignominiously as far as Europe was concerned. Lord North and the other ministers, including Sandwich, resigned after Yorktown. The Whigs, the Rockingham Whigs, were in power and peace was in sight. The provisional articles were signed in Paris in November 1782, and long before the definitive treaty declared that it had "pleased the Divine Providence to dispose the hearts of the most serene and most potent Prince, George the Third, by the Grace of God, King of Great Britain, France and Ireland, Defender of the Faith, Duke of Brunswick and Lunenburgh, Arch-Treasurer and Prince Elector of the Holy Roman Empire, &c. and of the United States of America, to forget all past misunderstandings and differences", travellers and above all natural philosophers from "enemy" countries joined the visitors at Soho Square. Antoine-Laurent de Jussieu, the most famous of a family of eminent botanists, was among them; so was young Broussonet, to whom Banks was such a good friend when Broussonet had to escape from the Terror that his own zeal for reform had helped to bring about; so, though somewhat later, was Cuvier, the palaeontologist who as Perpetual Secretary was eventually to sum up Banks's career in a noble funeral oration delivered before the *Académie des Sciences*.

Since Banks spoke not a word of French or any other modern European language, the polyglot Solander was particularly useful at these gatherings; and quite apart from that he was very much esteemed, not only as a naturalist but also as a cheerful, obliging, highly social being. He was a short, bulky man, thick-necked and Teutonic in appearance, not at all good-looking; he was fond of bright-coloured waistcoats but otherwise he did not care how he dressed. He never married. It is said that he was ungrateful to Linnaeus and it is certain that he was bitterly unkind to his widowed mother, almost never writing and leaving her letters unopened. But Banks loved Solander and his sudden death from apoplexy in May 1782 grieved him extremely. Indeed it is not impossible that his grief may explain Banks's failure to publish; for although, writing to Alströmer after a long interval (the letter[8] is dated 16 November 1784) he said "The botanical work with which I am presently involved is nearing its conclusion. Because everything was produced by our common effort, Solander's name will appear on the title page next to mine. While he was alive there was hardly a passage composed in which he was not represented . . . All that is left is so little that it can be completed in two months; if only the engravers can come to put the finishing touches on it," in the same letter he also said "Through his death, I have suffered a loss which will be impossible for me to fill even if I should find another person as learned and as noble. At my present age it is not possible for my heart to replace the impression which twenty years ago it took as easily as wax and which now will not be effaced until the heart itself dies."

It is typical of Banks that his surviving correspondence should contain at least one letter from Solander's mother thanking him for the money he had sent her and telling him of her position and her debts, while some time later there are half a dozen between Banks and a Swedish savant, Banks asking what capital would be required to meet the needs of Solander's sister. The answer was that £250 would yield £15 a year, which would enable her to live comfortably for the rest of her life. Banks was probably less surprised than most, since he knew something about the extraordinary cheapness of living in Sweden, but surprised or not he sent the money, enjoining strict secrecy and asking that eventually the income should be added to the stipend of the professor of botany at Stockholm, who was at that time his friend Olof Swartz.

Physically Solander's place as Banks's librarian was taken by Jonas Dryander, but although Dryander was able and conscientious the relation could not be the same: the great expanse of shared experience was irreplaceable and even apart from that Banks's saving of Solander's life in Tierra del Fuego had created a very special bond.

It was in this same unhappy year and the next that two things happened to endanger the reputation of the Royal Society and therefore of its President. The first concerned James Price, an Oxford man and a chemist who had recently been elected a Fellow. In May 1782 he stated that he knew how to change quicksilver into gold. It was not exactly the philosopher's stone that he had discovered but rather two powders, a white one that would change fifty times its own weight into silver and a red one that would turn it into an even larger quantity of gold. Statements of this nature have been made time out of mind, but never by a Fellow of the Royal Society, and it was to an uncommonly distinguished audience, including the Lord Lieutenant and a number of peers, that he first exhibited these powders and their capabilities in his laboratory near Guildford in Surrey. The gold and silver were assayed, found to be pure, and shown to the King. Oxford then gave Price a degree in recognition of "his chemical labours". The post hoc is certain: the propter hoc has been faintly denied.

This affair began when Banks had just lost Solander and he was hardly over the first shock before he and all his family were struck down with influenza, so although letters passed between him and Blagden it is difficult to follow the first stages of the wretched business, though it is clear that neither thought the problem very serious to begin with.

Presently however the full discredit that a Fellow's well-publicized antics must bring on the Royal Society became apparent. The obvious course was to require Price to repeat the experiments before the Society's chemists or expel him; and some were in favour of plain expulsion. It appears that Price's answers to letters were evasive and unsatisfactory, and eventually a senior Fellow, William Godschall, who lived quite near, called upon him at Banks's request and "told him one or two things were expected, either to repeat the experiment at a foreign laboratory or disclose the composition of the powder. He said he would wait on you previous to the next meeting and learn, ex Cathedra, all that was required of him. This shut up my mouth."[9]

After further delay Price did see Banks; he maintained his assertions but took refuge in secrecy – the discovery about silver was not his own – yet eventually he did agree to receive a delegation from the Society. For some time before the arrival of the Fellows he employed a boy to collect and distil laurel leaves; he also made his will. Having welcomed his visitors he drank the laurel-water and died.

The second unhappiness of this period arose from Banks's wish to deal with the more obvious shortcomings in the Royal Society and it was of course very much more complex. He had always said, from the very beginning of his presidency, that admittance to the Society was too easy, that the secretaries should no longer propose candidates on their own initiative; and he had already done something in this direction, inviting aspirants to breakfast and if he thought them suitable recommending them to the Council and to influential Fellows, or saying so quite clearly if he did not. But until 1782 he had not touched the administration: in that year, in an evil hour and without the support of his best, most diplomatic adviser, he set about it in the wrong way.

At that time the Royal Society had two secretaries, Dr Maty and Mr Planta: the post of Foreign Secretary did not exist, yet as correspondence with foreigners was obviously called for a Fellow was appointed to deal with it and to translate foreign papers and make extracts from foreign books; he was called the Assistant to the Secretaries and he was given £20 a year. In 1782 these duties were being performed by Dr Charles Hutton, the professor of mathematics at Woolwich Academy. He was an exceedingly hard-working man – a Newcastle coalminer's son who could write FRS and LLD after his name could hardly be anything else. Yet in January it was reported to the Council that the foreign correspondence was not dealt with promptly. It was also said that the pay was not enough. The President then suggested that the translation and extraction should cease and that a committee should redefine the remaining duties. Hutton accepted their redefinition, which confined him to the letter-writing side alone, and he carried on for about a year, when it was decided (Dr Maskelyne and Dr Maty dissenting) that for the good of the Society the business should be attended to by a person residing in London. Upon this Hutton resigned.

On the face of it he had been shabbily treated and many Fellows were so indignant that at the meeting of 11 December 1783 there was a motion that the Society's thanks should be given to Dr Hutton in recognition of his services. Banks, opposing this, said "Only the President and Council know whether the duties have been efficiently performed or not and I, who do know, am of opinion that they have not." The motion was nevertheless carried by 30 to 25 and Banks, putting what face he could upon it, then thanked Dr Hutton in the name of the Royal Society.

At the next meeting Hutton put in a written defence of his conduct; on hearing it read 45 of the 60 Fellows present voted that "if he had been censured, he had fully justified himself"; and to be sure he showed that he had dealt with the foreign letters as and when they were given to him. But he did not mention what Lord Brougham calls "a much more serious charge, that he held no communication with the President; and certainly this was mainly imputable to his residing at a distance".[10]

Perhaps he had not time to do so, for at this point the Rev. Dr Horsley, another mathematician, burst out with a remarkably violent attack upon Banks, obviously matured for some time in an angry bosom that seized upon the Hutton incident as a pretext. Horsley had the support, though much more moderately expressed, of Dr Maskelyne, the Astronomer Royal, of Baron Masseres, a cursitor baron of the Exchequer who was also an able mathematician, and of several others; it was therefore decided that the matter should be brought before a later meeting.

It may have surprised Banks to find quite how many enemies he had, or at least how many people were ready to vote against him; but he had long been aware, if only from Blagden's letters, that he had offended both secretaries and their particular friends by his firmness over the election of Fellows, and that the mathematicians and astronomers, looking upon themselves as much more worthy successors of Newton than zoologists or botanists, tended to see the Society as divided between "the macaronis and the men of science". He therefore sent out a memorandum informing the Fellows that important matters would be discussed at the next ordinary meeting.

Some 170 Fellows attended, and Banks's friends, following Lord Mulgrave's characteristic advice "that the present situation should be settled finally and that there should be no temporizing" moved "that this Society do approve of Mr J. Banks as their President, and mean to support him in that office". The motion was seconded by Cavendish and in spite of violent opposition it was carried by 119 to 42.

This might have been thought to be decisive, but for once numbers seemed to have lost their meaning for the mathematicians and they returned to the charge again and again. It would be tedious to go into details, but the main charges urged at the repeated meetings against Banks by Horsley and his friends were that he gave natural history a wrongful pre-eminence over mathematics, astronomy and chemistry; that he interfered improperly in the election of Fellows; that he packed the Council; and that he was overbearing and despotic. The tone of the debates was most uncommonly acrimonious: a President who tried "to amuse the Fellows with frogs, fleas and grasshoppers" was not worthy of his illustrious predecessors; he stood at the head only of the ignorant and non-scientific Fellows; and unless the scientific Fellows prevailed, secession would be the result.

This last threat is variously reported. Lord Brougham, basing himself on the official record, has Dr Horsley exclaiming "The President will then be left with his train of feeble amateurs and that toy [pointing to the mace] upon the table; – the ghost of the Society in which Philosophy once reigned, and Newton presided as her minister."

Banks himself recalled it in these words: "'If we cannot do this' say'd he, 'we will secede and leave that bauble (the mace) upon the table, the empty shadow of what the Royal Society was.'" To which Dr Maskelyne immediately answered "Yes, sir, for where learning is, there will be the Royal Society."

It was rough going, and though in the course of it Banks wrote "At 8 we met, a full meeting . . . I felt at that moment like a bull going to be baited but I felt like a game bull, who having been frequently brought out likes sport as well as the dogs and has more than an equal chance of success"[11] – although he wrote this, it is probable that he was not sorry when it was all over and he could return to Kew, Spring Grove, his Thursday morning breakfasts and his herbarium.

Horsley's excessive vehemence and his evident yearning to be President disgusted more and more of his followers: his respectable minorities dwindled steadily and ignominiously and in March 1784, when he put forward his last proposal, only Hutton and one other Fellow voted with him.

This was the end. Horsley withdrew; Maty resigned as secretary and was replaced by Dr Blagden, who had campaigned for the President with the utmost zeal and who was elected in preference to Hutton by a majority of 139 to 39. Banks was re-elected President at the Anniversary Meeting that year, the next year, and every subsequent year until his death: he had triumphed, yet although he did not alter his attitude towards the fellowship, he never touched the administration of the Society again, leaving it in its age-old muddle, with vast heaps of Miscellaneous Manuscripts unfiled, unsorted, uncatalogued, and its finances in deep obscurity.

But Banks wore his triumph with a most conciliating modesty, as a man conscious of shortcomings in himself as well as in his opponents. Brougham represents *them*, and particularly their leader, as being contemptible; but Horsley did become Bishop of St Asaph and Robert Brown, the most distinguished botanist who was Banks's librarian in his later years, said that Brougham "rates Dr Horsley as a mathematician surely much too low" and "overrides the scientific talent array'd against him [Banks], namely Maskelyn Masseres Horsley Hutton Shuckborough . . . [and several other less legible names]".[12]

At this distance of time who can tell how much truth there was in some of the charges? By a very careful study of the lists Sir Henry Lyons has disproved the packing of the Council and bias in the selection of papers and the awarding of medals. On the other hand Brougham, though saying that Banks prevented the admission of several unsuitable applicants, does admit that he kept out one valuable mathematical candidate, Major Desbarres; while Dr Kippis does say "It is possible that Sir Joseph Banks may have assumed a firm tone in the execution of his duty as President of the Society, and have been free in his rebukes, where he apprehended that there was any occasion for them," and it is probable that he could be rather authoritarian; but it is even more probable that the Society which voted so massively in his favour and which went on voting in his favour for another thirty-six years, thought that with all his faults he suited them tolerably well.

His faults were obvious enough in the bull-like clumsiness with which he began this affair, but so were his virtues in the equally bull-like strength and courage with which he repelled attack after attack, and in his magnanimity afterwards – he pursued no mean revenge of any kind, and it is worth observing that in March 1784, only a few weeks after the conclusive votes, one of his mathematical opponents, Sir George Shuckburgh-Evelyn, wrote asking him to support a candidate.

With this battle over, Banks could retire for the rest of the session to the quiet of his gardens and library, and to the easy sociability of Soho Square. Here he was always sure of seeing a good many friends walk in without ceremony, either to read in his books or study in his herbarium or merely to talk over a cup of coffee: one of the last kind was William Herschel, who knew more about stars than simples but who was particularly dear to Banks, primarily because Herschel had both a brilliant mind and a particularly sympathetic nature, but perhaps to some degree because Banks had been able to do him a kindness. It will be remembered that Herschel was the son of a Hanoverian bandsman and that at fourteen he too blew on a military oboe; when he was about nineteen he came to England and made a thin living as a musician, eventually becoming an organist at Bath, when he sent for his beloved sister Caroline to come and share his scanty means. Music, mathematics and astronomy fascinated him; he did manage to buy some excellent books, but a real telescope was far beyond his purse: he and his sister therefore made their own, grinding away at scores or even hundreds of mirrors with infinite patience and growing success until by 1781 they possessed a seven-foot reflector with a six and a half inch aperture. With this Herschel discovered the planet that he so politely named Georgium Sidus but that is commonly known as Uranus. The Royal Society made him a Fellow and awarded him the Copley medal.

But the Copley medal, though solid gold, could not nourish its man for long, and Herschel was wretchedly poor – forced to play the organ and give music lessons to feed himself and his sister during the day for their nightly study of the sky: with no regular education and no university degree he could not hope for employment by any learned body. So Banks for once made use of his influence with the King, observing that although there was of course an Astronomer Royal, his Majesty had no *private* astronomer of his own. The King took the point, sent for Herschel to Windsor and offered him the post, together with a house, £200 a year for himself, and a little later £50 a year for his sister. Now they could both devote themselves entirely to astronomy, and this they did, Herschel continuing his career with the sublime discovery of true double stars while his sister detected no fewer than eight comets, besides several nebulae. (There is a very pleasant letter from Herschel in January 1784, thanking Banks for a particularly large pair of shoes, for he had to wear seven pairs of stockings star-gazing by night in twenty-seven degrees of frost: he was afraid his great speculum might crack, but, however, he continued his observations and all was well.)

Now they could pass part of their waking day in seeing their friends, and Herschel often came to Spring Grove or to Soho Square, where among many others he met the Monsieur Faujas de Saint-Fond who has been mentioned before. Faujas, though a well-informed man, was something of a coxcomb and on occasion he irritated Banks extremely: a letter of October 1784 to Blagden says "How Faujas is ever to show his face again I do not easily guess, or rather how he is to be received. Effrontery which that good man possesses in an eminent degree may make him feel little but those who see him will not easily forget his conduct on his Scotch tour." Yet brazen though he may have been he must also have had some good qualities, for Banks put up with him for another twenty-four years, and in 1810 he also went to a great deal of trouble to have Faujas' son, a prisoner of war, sent back to France. Banks was indeed kind to Faujas from the beginning – polite and affable, as Faujas says in his *Travels in England, Scotland, and the Hebrides*: "The house of this celebrated traveller who is President of the Royal Society is the rendez-vous of those who cultivate the sciences; and foreigners are always received there with politeness and affability. They assemble every morning in one of the apartments of an extensive library, which consists entirely of books on Natural History and is the completest of its kind in the World." On the day of his introduction Banks gave Faujas some Chinese hemp seed that he had just received from Canton; Faujas took it back to France and shared it with eleven of his botanical and scientific friends, who grew it with great success. Banks also introduced him to many of his friends and he was invited to dine at the club and then to go on to the Royal Society's meeting; and in his *Annals of the Royal Society Club* Sir Archibald Geikie FRS says that Faujas' description of this dinner is the only guest's view of the Royal Philosophers that we possess.

About forty members of the Royal Society have been for more than twenty-five years, in the habit of dining together socially in one of the taverns of London. Each member has the right of bringing two guests, whom he chooses, among foreigners or friends of his own acquaintance in the Royal Society. The President may bring a greater number and may select whoever he pleases for guests.

We sat down to dinner about five o'clock. Sir Joseph Banks presided and filled the place of honour. No napkins were laid before us; indeed none were used; the dinner was truly in the English style.

A member of the club who is a clergyman (I believe it was the astronomer Maskelyne) made a short prayer and blessed the company and the food. The dishes were of the solid kind, such as roast beef, boiled beef and mutton prepared in various ways, with abundance of potatoes and other vegetables, which each person seasoned as he pleased with the different sauces which were placed on the table in bottles of different shapes.

The beefsteaks and the roast beef were at first drenched with copious bumpers of strong beer, called porter, drunk out of cylindrical pewter pots, which are much preferred to glasses because one can swallow a whole pint at a draught.

This prelude being finished, the cloth was removed and a handsome and well-polished table was covered, as if it were by magic, with a number of fine crystal decanters filled with the best port, madeira and claret; this last is the wine of Bordeaux. Several glasses, as brilliant in lustre as fine in shape, were distributed to each person and the libations began on a grand scale, in the midst of different kinds of cheese, which, rolling in mahogany boxes from one end of the table to the other, provoked the thirst of the drinkers.

To give more liveliness to the scene, the President proposed the health of the Prince of Wales; this was his birthday; we then drank to the Elector Palatine, who was this day to be admitted into the Royal Society. The same compliment was next paid to us foreigners of whom there were five present. [Broussonet was one of them.]

The members of the Club afterwards saluted each other, one by one, with a glass of wine. According to their custom, one must drink as many times as there are guests, for it would be thought a want of politeness in England to drink to the health of more persons than one at a time.

A few bottles of champagne completed the enlivenment of every one. Tea came next, together with bread and butter and all the usual accompanyments: coffee followed, humbly yielding the preference to the tea, though it be the better of the two. In France we commonly drink only one cup of good

> coffee after dinner; in England they drink five or six of the most detestable kind.
>
> Brandy, rum and some other strong liqueurs closed this philosophic banquet, which terminated at half past seven, as we had to be at a meeting of the Royal Society summoned for eight o'clock. Before we left, however, the names of all the guests were written on a large sheet of paper and each of us paid seven livres, four sols French money; this was not too dear. [It was about six shillings.]
>
> I repaired to the Society along with Messrs Banks, Cavendish, Maskelyne, Aubert, and Sir Henry Englefield. We were all pretty much enlivened but our gaiety was decorous.

Faujas may have been a little taken aback by being asked to pay, but he was rich enough for it not to spoil his appetite for further sightseeing: he peered through Herschel's telescope, dined at Spring Grove, where there were quantities of pineapples on the table, presumably from one of Sir Joseph's hothouses, and admired the botanical gardens at Kew, where he saw among many, many other things the recently introduced *Magnolia grandiflora* and some of the lava that Banks had brought back from Iceland, now growing a splendid collection of mosses.

Banks however did not always spend two and a half hours over his dinner, drinking porter, port, champagne and brandy, though the fact that he did so pretty often must account for his increasing bulk – he had passed fifteen stone by now and he was to reach seventeen stone two – and may account for the gout that set in two or three years later. He had more intellectual occupations, and two, both very important and both eventually related, were presently to come to the forefront of his mind and to shape the future of Australia.

In his first year as President of the Royal Society Banks had told a parliamentary committee that New South Wales might serve as a place for the transportation of criminals; and he had spoken at some length upon its suitability as a colony – good climate, variety of soil, few wild beasts or inhabitants, plenty of fish, grass and water. Four years later, on 28 July 1783, James Matra, the somewhat ambiguous figure of American Loyalist origins who had sailed with Banks in the *Endeavour* and who regarded him as his patron, wrote to say that he had heard of projected settlements in the South Seas and New South Wales – would Banks please tell him more? At this time Matra was living as "a solitary fugitive", though not long before he had been secretary to the embassy in Constantinople.

Banks's reply has not survived, but during August Matra sent the ministry a plan for the colonization of New South Wales which he said

Sir Joseph strongly approved: the plan spoke of Cook's favourable opinion of the country and stressed the fact that it might provide "An asylum to those unfortunate American Loyalists, whom Great Britain is bound by every tie of honour and gratitude to protect and support, where they may repair their broken fortunes and again enjoy their domestic felicity."[13]

Three years later, under the somewhat more energetic ministry of William Pitt, the authorities took the matter up again, probably because of Banks's earlier evidence but possibly because of Matra's plan, though the American Loyalists were quite ignored. With no transportation to the now independent America, conditions in the overcrowded prisons and the fearful prison-hulks – dismantled ships that were introduced in 1776 as "a means of devising a severe mode of punishment short of death" – were becoming intolerable. They consulted Banks and they received a paper entitled *Heads of the Plan for Botany Bay* that appears to sum up and confirm previous conversations: it is not signed but it was almost certainly written or at least drafted by him.

> Heads of a plan for effectually disposing of convicts and rendering their transportation reciprocally beneficial, both to themselves and to the State, by the establishment of a colony in New South Wales, a country which by the fertility and the salubrity of the climate, connected with the remoteness of its situation (from whence it was hardly possible for persons to return without permission) seems peculiarly adapted to answer the views of the Government with respect to providing the remedy for the evils likely to result from the late alarming and numerous increase of felons in this country, and more particularly in the Metropolis.
>
> It is proposed that a ship of war of a proper class, with a part of her guns manned and a sufficient number of men aboard for her navigation, and a tender of about 200 tons burthen, commanded by discreet officers, should be got ready as soon as possible to serve as an escort to the convict ships, and for other persons hereinafter mentioned.

Then followed various practical recommendations: two companies of Marines, as many of them as possible craftsmen, carpenters, sawyers and so on; a chaplain (to stay in the settlement), a surgeon and his mate; the ships to touch at the Cape or some other convenient place for livestock and seed; seven or eight hundred convicts, including one vessel for women; the ships to be victualled for two years, one year at full allowance and the other at half; the convicts being settled, the man-of-war and tender might fetch more livestock from the Cape or the Moluccas and perhaps "a further number of women from the Friendly

Islands, New Caledonia etc., which are contiguous thereto and from whence any number may be procured without difficulty"; the whole regulation and management to be committed to a discreet officer; and the paper ends:

> It may not be amiss to remark in favour of this plan that considerable advantage will arise from the cultivation of the New Zealand hemp or flax plant in the new intended settlement, the supply of which would be of great consequence to us as a naval power, as our own manufacturers are of the opinion that canvas made of it would be superior in strength and beauty to any canvas made of the European material, and that a cable of the circumference of ten inches would be superior in strength to one of eighteen inches made of the latter. The threads or filaments of the New Zealand plant are formed by nature with the most exquisite delicacy, and may be so minutely divided as to be manufactured into the finest linens.
>
> Most of the Asiatic products may also, without doubt, be cultivated in the new settlement, and in a few years may render our recourse to our European neighbours for these productions unnecessary.
>
> It may also be proper to attend to the possibility of procuring from New Zealand any quantity of masts and ship timber for the use of our fleets in India, as the distance between the two countries is not greater than between Great Britain and America. It grows close to the waters edge, and is of size and quality superior to any hitherto known and may be obtained without difficulty.

Upon this the ministry made its decision with surprising speed: in August 1786 the Admiralty was told to arrange for a fleet of convict ships to be sent to Botany Bay and to do so "with all possible expedition". This they did with such zeal that the fleet, under the command of Captain Arthur Phillip of the Royal Navy, was able to put to sea by May of the following year. But the zeal was headlong and excessive, and what with the Admiralty saving every minute of time and the Navy Board every penny of expense, Captain Phillip was obliged to sail in conditions that would have daunted any but an exceptionally able and resourceful man, the very type of the "discreet officer" that had been called for. His command consisted of HMS *Sirius*, 20 guns, the *Supply*, an armed tender, three storeships and six transports; they carried 564 male and 192 female convicts, 303 Marines including their officers, five medical men, a bull and four cows, a stallion and three mares, twelve swine, twenty-nine sheep and many fowls, as well as the seamen; and they were shockingly ill provided.

Captain Phillip had done his best before the time of sailing, but he had had three different sets of civil servants to deal with, those belonging to Lord Sydney, the relevant Secretary of State, those belonging to the Admiralty and those belonging to the Navy Board; there were also magistrates, legal people and prison authorities concerned, some of them extraordinarily callous and incompetent. Hitherto transportation had meant crossing the Atlantic to Virginia, a course known for centuries, two months' sailing at the most. Now it was to be a voyage that had only been made once before and that might take four or five times as long; furthermore all the preparations were to be made in great haste, partly because the Navy Board had arranged for some of the vessels to come home by way of China – if they hurried they would be in time to carry back the tea harvest, thus saving expense. The combination of haste and novelty made several of the officials lose their heads entirely; for example, after the fleet had been at sea for some time it was found that the Marines had no small-arms ammunition whatsoever. Fortunately the governor of Rio, where Phillip put in, was quite unlike his predecessor in Cook's day, and he provided ten thousand musket balls.

In spite of all the sometimes appalling shortages, Captain Phillip brought his ships into Botany Bay on 20 January 1788 and shortly after this he moored them safely in the splendid great harbour that he found a little way to the north and that he named after Lord Sydney. The settlement too was presently moved to Port Jackson, but for all that the name Botany Bay stuck fast. It was used all through the time of transportation and even today it describes a certain kind of fine wool from Australia. Yet curiously enough Banks usually referred to the place as New South Wales: he very often had occasion to refer to it, since he was to a very large degree responsible for its existence and he felt his responsibilities keenly. Because of the almost unbelievable want of official foresight or even common sense the colony very nearly perished in its painful, half-starved birth, but he did all he could to help it, worrying the successive ministers at home, encouraging the successive governors out there, Phillip, Hunter, King and Bligh, and sending the botanical and agricultural advice that he was so well qualified to give. The governors were all his personal friends and they – and indeed the world in general, both official and unofficial – looked upon him as the moral proprietor of New South Wales; and he certainly loved the country dearly.

Yet it is noteworthy that neither in his first praise of New South Wales nor in his scheme for its colonization is there any mention of sheep. In fact for years and years he had no notion of Botany Bay as a place for wool; it proved remarkably difficult to persuade him that he was mistaken, and as late as 1803 he could still write "I have no reason to believe from any facts that have come to my knowledge, either when I was in that country or since, that the climate and soil of NS Wales is at all better for the production of fine wools than that of other temperate climates and am confident that the natural growth of grass of the country is tall, coarse, reedy and very different from the short and sweet mountain grass of Europe upon which sheep thrive to the best advantage."[14]

This mistaken judgement stands out with all the greater contrast because the other new matter that came to preoccupy his already busy mind in 1787 was the King's sheep, about which his judgement has proved so entirely right.

Chapter 9

HM'S SHEEP: PLANT COLLECTORS: BLIGH AND *BOUNTY*: REVOLUTION IN FRANCE

THE LONG, peaceful, thriving part of Pitt's first administration, that is to say from 1784 to the end of 1792, was a time in which Sir Joseph Banks grew in weight: literally, of course, but even more so figuratively. The Royal Society increased in international prestige partly because of its intrinsic value and partly because of the wave of Anglomania that swept over France, and at home its standing was remarkably high: Banks was consulted as President and as a private gentleman keenly interested in agriculture, on a wide variety of subjects.

It was natural then that the King should turn to him in both these capacities, and in that of a personal friend, when the subject of sheep was raised in the New Year of 1787. As a Lincolnshire landowner Banks had been concerned with wool ever since he came into his inheritance, the sheep of his county being a famous long-wool breed, and in 1781, when, because of the American war and the closing of continental markets, the price of local wool dropped from about eightpence a pound to threepence halfpenny he joined the Lincolnshire Wool Committee, which wanted a change in the law to enable them to send wool abroad, where it was fetching three and four times as much.

He went deeply into the matter, sending a polyglot Swede to question merchants on the Continent, and in 1782 he wrote a particularly able though unsigned pamphlet *The Propriety of Allowing a Qualified Exportation of Wool, Discussed Historically. To which is added an Appendix, containing a Table, Which shows the Value of the woolen Goods of every kind that were entered for Exportation at the Custom-house, from 1697 to 1780 inclusive, as well as the Prices of Wool in England during all that period*, a pamphlet whose first page shows his detached attitude towards the American war and his passionate concern with agriculture in general and sheep-raising in particular: "What genuine Englishman did not feel a more poignant anxiety when he beheld the graziers of Lincolnshire assembling to inquire into the fallen state of their wool, than when he heard of the gallant Cornwallis's fate [it was Cornwallis who had been obliged to surrender at Yorktown]; since the last may be regarded as the wound of a sword, which by the efforts of nature is soon closed in a scar, while the former ought to be dreaded as a gangrene that generally ends in death." The pamphlet was of course written in support of the Committee's position that the absolute prohibition of sending raw wool abroad, in force since 1660, was in the present circumstances unsound, causing great hardship and encouraging the owlers, who smuggled it out of the country. The woollen and worsted manufacturers flew to the protection of their monopoly (for only they could purchase, and at prices fixed with no thought of foreign competition) and brought in a Wool Bill that would strengthen the present regulation and call for even stricter control of each man's clip.

Banks hated the political arena, but he hated the Wool Bill even more and, together with Arthur Young, he testified before the Commons and the Lords; but although he was heard with respect, the manufacturers were much better organized than the landowners and farmers and the bill was passed. All Banks could do was to induce the bill's supporters to agree to a few amendments of no great importance.

But it was clear that he was one of the leading men among the wool-growers. Not only did he know a great deal about the technical aspects and not only did he have a great many sheep on his various estates, but at Spring Grove he had started a little experimental station. His brilliant young friend Broussonet, whom he had helped so materially during his long stay in England, providing him with specimens and information for his *Ichthyologia Decas I*, was now assistant professor of rural economy at Alfort under the famous Daubenton. Daubenton knew a great deal about sheep and he was in charge of the Spanish flocks at Alfort and Montbard: they had been brought to France in 1766 and just how far they were pure-bred merinos of the best kind is not quite clear. But in any case they were very closely allied to that much coveted and jealously guarded race, and knowing Banks's concern with sheep, Broussonet begged a pair for him. He had to beg hard and long, but on 16 June 1785 he was able to send the news that a ram and a ewe, wearing iron collars with Banks's address stamped on them, were now starting their journey.

They were the first merinos or near-merinos ever to reach England and it was with them that Banks began his experimental crosses with Southdowns, Herefords from Robert Bakewell's farm, Norfolks from Mr Coke of Norfolk, and others, gathering a certain experience of the Spanish sheep as he did so.

It was in January of 1787 that the King turned to Banks, and he did so after a long discussion with his equerry Colonel Greville as they walked through Richmond Gardens looking at the royal flock of Wiltshires and talking about the way the Elector of Saxony (a Catholic prince) had improved the Saxon wool by the introduction of Spanish blood. The King made his approach through Greville, Greville being a Fellow of the Royal Society and a friend of the President's, and of course Banks said that he would do everything in his power to obtain some merinos for His Majesty. "Sir Joseph Banks is just the Man," said the King. "Tell Him from Me that I thank Him, and that his assistance will be most welcome."[1]

But Banks's position and the King's were by no means the same. The President of the Royal Society could ask another man of science for specimens quite naturally and in fact Daubenton had already asked Banks whether he had any duplicate zoophytes to spare just before the two sheep came over. The King could not risk a refusal and in any event he was not on such terms with the rulers of France or Spain that he could make the request; and there was no question of buying the animals without royal permission. Furthermore the King's aims went very much farther than Banks's; he looked upon the venture of improving the country's wool as "a most national object", and only a considerable flock would answer his purpose.

And indeed wool was a national object to an extent that is not readily conceivable at present: it had been described as "the flower and strength and revenue and blood of England" and at this period woollen manufactures accounted for about a quarter of the kingdom's exports in value – £3,500,000, or more than iron and cotton combined. The jenny had been invented but it was not suitable for fine work, and although Crompton's mule was an improvement a very great deal of spinning and weaving was still done by hand, giving employment to an immense number of people – a million, said Dr Campbell in his *Political Survey* of 1774 – many of them women. In his pamphlet Banks quoted Arthur Young's figures of 25,589,214 sheep in the country yielding an annual profit of £13,860,824.

Yet an important part of this great industry relied upon finer wool than British sheep could produce and for many generations the manufacturers, particularly those who made the famous West Country broadcloth, had been importing merino wool from Spain, so fine that a pound could be spun out into ninety-two miles of yarn as opposed to the forty-three-odd of a Lincoln – not, however, that the merino was used pure: rather less than a quarter mixed with English wool produced very fine cloth indeed. But the imports cost money (about £750,000 a year at this time) and they could always be cut off by war or political disagreement. Clearly it would be very much to the country's advantage to have natural-born British merinos, if only the breeding stock could be obtained and if only their descendants' wool did not grow coarse in a climate so unlike that of Spain. The general opinion was that the merinos' fineness was dependent on environment and on the seasonal migration of the flocks from one mountain pasture to another. Banks, basing himself on Daubenton's experience and on his own, believed that the general opinion was mistaken and that the fineness could be maintained; he joined in the King's project with the utmost good will and with sanguine enthusiasm.

This is a most uncommonly well-documented aspect of Banks's life, because although his carefully arranged papers were dispersed in a way that would make a modern historian weep, it so happens that the files dealing with the King's Spanish sheep remained more or less together and more or less intact. They were bought by an American collector, Mr Adolph Sutro of San Francisco; they survived the loss of half his library in the earthquake of 1906 and they are now housed in the Sutro Branch of the California State Library. They were quite unknown to Banks's earlier biographers but in the 1950s copies were made and these were studied by Mr H. B. Carter over a period of years: they form the basis, or a large part of the basis, of his closely detailed and percipient book *His Majesty's Spanish Flock* (Angus and Robertson 1964), a work of the most devoted scholarship running to some five hundred pages that I have often consulted, never without profit.

Banks turned first to Broussonet, and as the King's name could not be mentioned he was obliged to be a little devious. After a pause Broussonet (who had recently sent a box of edible frogs and some visiting cards for Miss Banks) replied that he had been promised some sheep and would send eight or ten when Banks was ready for them. His next letter, in May 1787, said that Daubenton had now promised fifteen or twenty and perhaps a hundred from Spain. In June Daubenton was reported as having changed his mind or at least as seeming reluctant. Then suddenly, after letters on entirely different subjects – the statues on Easter Island (recently seen by La Pérouse) – Banks's need for an umbrella, reported by Wedgwood, the umbrella commissioned by Broussonet – Coulomb's gratitude for Banks's kindness to him in England – came the news that the sheep were actually on the road, walking up from Provence. They came by way of Montbard and Alfort, where others joined them, so that at one time the little flock amounted to five rams and thirty-nine ewes. Two ewes died on the journey, but on the other hand six lambs were born, so that forty-eight sheep reached

Dover on 3 January the next year and Kew nearly a fortnight later. They were a mixed lot, fifteen of the ewes being acknowledged cross-breeds, while two of the four rams and twelve of the ewes came from M. de La Tour d'Aigue's more or less Spanish flock in the south of France – none from Spain itself. Still, it was a beginning, and after a while – ships did not often come from New South Wales – Banks sent Broussonet a kangaroo as an acknowledgement of his kindness, the first kangaroo ever seen in France. But this was the fatal year of 1789, and even earlier Broussonet had said that people were paying little attention to anything but politics: France was indeed in a most distracted state, and within a few days of the kangaroo's arrival the Bastille was taken by storm. Broussonet was all in favour of the revolution; he knew Banks well, and it is significant that he should have had no doubt that his account of the events would be anything but welcome in Soho Square.

Yet apart from Broussonet's preoccupation with politics there was obviously little future in the French "merinos", limited in quantity and uncertain in descent, and well before this Banks turned to another source entirely. The true merinos, the "travelling sheep of Spain", spent much of their lives moving from one place to another, always at stated intervals: in the late summer there would be great flocks in the mountains behind Bilbao, the port from which their wool was shipped to England, and in the autumn they would begin their journey to the winter pastures in Estremadura, on the borders of Portugal. There was therefore a possibility that smugglers might bring some sheep down to English merchants in Bilbao or Lisbon.

The Foreign Office made discreet enquiries and at first it seemed that Bilbao was the more promising, so promising indeed that Banks, on the point of sending a definite order, went down to Kew on 10 August 1787 in the hope of seeing the King: he preferred a chance meeting in the gardens to anything that might remotely resemble importunity or intrusion. But the chance meeting did not take place, so Banks wrote to say that with time pressing he had ordered two rams and four ewes; he was "not sure but that he should have ordered a larger number, but he can by this night's post either countermand those already ordered if his Majesties pleasure which he will be ever solicitous to obey with the most punctilious exactness is signified to him".

His Majesty at once replied:

> The King is much hurt that he was not apprised on Tuesday that Sir Joseph Banks was at Kew; (indeed he never heard of it till he received his note this day) or he would have found time to see him.

> The King is much pleased that two Rams and four Ewes are sent for and should wish the Commission could be extended to twenty Ewes and ten Rams; as from the judicious remark of Sir Joseph Banks that Spain may soon find the evil of granting such exportations, it may not be possible long to continue acquiring those useful Animals.
>
> The King trusts this number from Bilbao will not stop the attempts of getting some through France as well as others through Portugal . . .

But these hopes were disappointed or at least deferred. Bilbao yielded no sheep that year, and in the autumn Banks was attacked by gout, an enemy that was never to leave him. On 27 November 1787 His Majesty wrote "The King is sorry to find Sir Joseph is still confined; and though it is the common mode to congratulate persons on the first fit of the Gout, he cannot join in so cruel an etiquette. . . . The hopes that, through Portugal, Spanish Sheep will also be attained, seems now to bear a good appearance."

And it was in fact Portugal that produced the first undoubtedly genuine merinos. They were obtained by Mr Marsh, a merchant of Lisbon, and they were brought by Captain Firth of the *Betsy*, who wrote to Sir Joseph from off Dover on 4 March 1788, "I have got for you 2 Yews & one Ram of the Best Spanish Breed."

The best breed they were; Banks rated them excellent and it was from this day that he dated the true beginning of His Majesty's Spanish flock; while the King was so pleased when he saw them that he sent Captain Firth a present of twenty guineas.

Bilbao did produce a solitary ram in June, but the rest of the year was passed, as far as sheep were concerned, in fruitless correspondence. In November the King's mind became deranged: he was very seriously disturbed in December – he terrified Miss Burney by running after her in Kew gardens – but in January 1789 he was somewhat better and in February he said he would like to see Banks. The humane Dr Willis arranged a casual meeting at the nearby Marsh Gate farm; it was clear that Banks was a most suitable and soothing companion and from then onwards the King and he took their walk together almost every day until His Majesty's recovery in the spring. There was a thanksgiving service at St Paul's at the end of April, together with a great deal of sincere public rejoicing, for the King was very popular; and shortly after this he had the pleasure of seeing four more merinos, also from Bilbao.

So they came, sometimes from Lisbon and sometimes from Bilbao, but always in dribs and drabs – ten in 1789, twenty-seven in 1790 – and a sad time Banks had with them. The King's shepherds were idle and quite remarkably incompetent, and it does not appear that they liked these foreign sheep or took any pride or pleasure in their wool, which though fine was exceptionally greasy and difficult to shear. The merinos were ill-managed and kept on unsuitable pastures; they had foot rot, scabmite and ticks, lungworm and liver fluke, their horns were maggotty from want of cleanliness and they were flystruck. Their early sexual maturity was not observed and ram-lambs still running with their mothers tupped ewes of the earlier generation, playing Old Harry with the studbook. Banks had no official position and royal servants were much inclined to resent orders or recommendations given by anyone outside the household. A less dogged and conscientious man might well have given up, particularly if he had had as much to do as the President of the Royal Society, the owner of Revesby, and the scientific director of Kew.

But by 1791 he was fully committed: in August of that year he had a formal meeting with the King, and they reviewed the situation. The flock now amounted to over a hundred, almost in spite of their shepherds; the King clearly stated that he approved of Sir Joseph's measures; and they settled accounts. They also decided who should have the surplus rams, for now at last the true merino blood was to be mixed with that of the native sheep: Arthur Young had one, and the King added Banks's name to the list for another – eight were given away in all.

In the autumn of this same year the flock was suddenly increased in number and even more in quality. Although Banks had laid down from the beginning that His Majesty's name was never to be mentioned in this long and fundamentally illegal transaction, the chargé d'affaires in Madrid, Mr Merry, let it be known that the sheep he wished to obtain were for the King of England. On hearing this a former ambassador to the court of St James's, Count del Campo de Alange – or rather his wife, since it is always she who is represented as the moving spirit – at once produced some forty picked merinos from his famous Negretti flock and insisted that they were a present.

Banks was furious at first, partly because of the blunder, partly because the sending of the sheep was very badly mismanaged – when he first heard of them he was at Revesby and they were in the hands of the Customs officers at Southampton and everybody was put to a world of trouble – and partly because Mr Merry thought the present called for a set of eight English carriage horses in return. Like many rich men Banks very much disliked being overcharged. He was generous, exceptionally generous, but he knew the value of money and he did not like having it extorted from him: when he was in Batavia with Cook, for example, he carefully checked his bills for board and lodging, and now, looking back over his accounts, he saw that in the Spanish market the sheep were worth about £25 whereas the horses would cost perhaps £400, which rankled. However, he recovered his good humour in time, and all the more rapidly because what was now so emphatically His Majesty's merino flock, with many of its rams and breeding ewes far superior to anything that smugglers could pick up, was on its way to being a great success.

The next year, 1792, saw the arrival of forty-seven more sheep from Lisbon, and with them the importations ceased. The international scene was hardly encouraging for a rural economist: in France the revolution was reaching its paroxysm, and the country was already at war with Austria and Prussia, while Spain was almost certain to join in very shortly. In any case the King's flock had nearly reached its proper working strength of between two and three hundred, and from now on Sir Joseph supplied the King with more or less annual reports that soon began to show a gratifying dispersal of the merino blood, that most national object.

He still had to struggle with gross inefficiency, though perhaps not with ill will; the shepherds were now used to Sir Joseph and to the foreign sheep, and the fact that presently their wool fetched the extraordinary sum of four shillings and eightpence a pound was not without its effect in making them respectable. It also proved that Banks had been right: the merinos' wool did not lose its fineness with change of environment; nor indeed has it done so in the two hundred years since his first sheep reached Spring Grove. In 1795 however he gave up his own flock "to do away with all idea of Rivalship", sending it to Arthur Young at Bradfield Hall in Suffolk. And it was in this year that no fewer than twenty-three rams and sixty-one ewes were sent to various breeders throughout the kingdom. Rather later, after the shocking winter of 1796 to 1797, with its very heavy mortality, the flock was moved from Kew (the ewes) and Windsor (the rams) to the much more suitable pasture in the great park of Oatlands, a house belonging to the Duke of York. Now at last Sir Joseph was in thorough control; the people in charge of the sheep were answerable to him and the newly-appointed shepherd was required to send him a monthly report, while at about the same time a valuable assistant appeared in the person of Henry Lacocke, an expert wool-sorter and a man after Banks's own heart.

The stage was now set for the recovery of the flock and for its growing fame. At first the King had given breeding stock to those who were thought most suitable, though in time the surplus sheep were sold by private contract and later by public auction; but this is leaping too far ahead entirely, passing over a great many events of the first importance, and giving a strangely lop-sided picture of Sir Joseph Banks.

The Spanish sheep were important to him, very important, but the Royal Society, Kew and Revesby were even more so; and there were other subjects of almost equal weight. Kew was maturing and developing splendidly, and when the East India Company consulted Sir Joseph about their own botanic garden at Calcutta in 1788 he observed that the King's was now cultivating no fewer than fifty thousand trees and plants. And Faujas de Saint-Fond, going there in 1784, said:

> The gardens at Kew are so well laid out, the order and the taste which pervade them are so admirable, and art has here so studiously endeavoured to resemble all that is beautiful and striking in nature that I place this garden above every thing of the kind that I have ever seen. . . . Amidst a multitude of rare and singular plants, one of them attracted my particular attention: it was the *Dionea muscipula*. I had seen it once before in the Jardin des Plantes of Paris. Franklin had it sent over in its native state from the marshes of South Carolina as a present to Buffon. It arrived in good condition: but it was so delicate, that it lived only six months. In the garden of Kew, however, the plant was in the best possible state of vegetation.

The hothouses were successful in rearing some remarkably fine exotics such as the *Strelitzia regina* (pleasantly named after the Queen, who came from Mecklenburg-Strelitz) the pride and joy of many of the gardeners; but although Banks dearly loved a handsome flower his chief concern was economic botany. The New Zealand flax and New Zealand spinach were his first important steps in that direction, and presently, to take just one example, Kew was shipping the camphor tree and the mango to the botanic gardens of Jamaica, there to be acclimatized, while a little later Banks, at the cost of a great deal of disinterested trouble and research, was instrumental in causing the East India Company to plant tea in their dominions.

Yet the many collectors he sent out were quite certainly not bound down to any glum apparent utilitarianism: if they happened to chance upon some plant of great economic value, so much the better, but their essential function was to increase botanical knowledge. Many of them were truly remarkable men, immensely hardy, resourceful and devoted, and they were the finders of the greater part of the nearly seven thousand new exotics that came to England in this reign.

Two of them are often cited as exemplary collectors, Francis Masson and Archibald Menzies, both Scotsmen. Masson was first sent to the Cape in 1772, where he met and travelled with the Swedish physician Carl Thunberg, still another of Linnaeus's pupils and in Japan the happy discoverer of *Lilium speciosum*. Sometimes with Thunberg and sometimes alone he went far into the botanically unexplored Kaffir country, and Banks was so pleased with the hundreds of plants and bulbs he brought back that he persuaded the King – for all the men employed at the royal garden were paid out of the royal purse – to send him to the Canaries, the Azores, Madeira and the West Indies. Then he went to the Cape again, where the Dutch authorities allowed him to go to the Hottentots Holland mountains, but only for five days: yet in those five days he found some of the rarest species of *Erica* and *Protea* in seed, which he instantly gathered and sent to Kew together with a parcel of 117 valuable plants. Then came Canada, but this was not so successful; the climate did not suit him, his harvest was meagre, and presently he fell ill and died. Linnaeus named the genus Massonia after him.

Canada, and America in general, was kinder to Archibald Menzies. He had begun life by working in the Edinburgh botanic garden while at the same time he studied medicine at the university. Having qualified he joined the Navy as a surgeon and saw service on the Halifax station, botanizing whenever he was ashore. At the suggestion of John Hope, FRS, professor of botany at Edinburgh and an old friend of Banks's, he sent Sir Joseph some seeds from the United States (this was in 1784 and the war was over) and the West Indies. They corresponded for some time but did not meet until 1786, when Menzies brought a letter from Professor Hope: "Dear Sir, I presume to introduce to you the bearer of this, Mr Archibald Menzies; who was early acquainted with the culture of plants, and acquired the principles of Botany by attending my lectures . . ." Menzies' ship, the *Assistance*, had just been paid off, but he had heard of a merchant venturer who was fitting out a ship to sail round the world; he longed to be her surgeon – it would satisfy his utmost ambition and give him endless opportunities in natural history.

Banks already had a very wide acquaintance and he knew the merchant in question, Mr Etches, who had asked his advice on trade with Japan, and a few days after his visit Menzies had the appointment he so desired. The expedition in fact consisted of two vessels, the *Prince of Wales* and the *Princess Royal*: they were to go by way of the Horn to the Pacific coast of North America which Cook had explored and thence with furs to Japan and China, coming home by the Cape. All this they did, taking three years over it, with Menzies losing only one patient out of both crews, and that a man much given to drunkenness. He came back with a rich collection of dried plants, and a little later, in 1790, through Banks's direct influence with the King, he was appointed naturalist to HMS *Discovery*, a ship of much the same kind as the *Endeavour*, which, with her smaller consort the *Chatham* was to go to Nootka Sound in what is now British Columbia and take over the territory from the Spaniards, who, faced with a brisk rearmament of the Royal Navy, had relinquished their claim. Their task was also to survey as much of the Pacific coast of America as was feasible and to make further explorations far to the south and far to the west. The command was given to George Vancouver, who had sailed as a youngster with Cook in his second and third voyages. Perhaps this was an unfortunate choice, for although he was a most conscientious surveyor and a capable seaman, he appears to have been ill bred and tyrannical. Banks had his doubts from the beginning, and in a letter to Menzies he said, "How Captain Vancouver will behave to you is more than I can guess, unless I was to judge by his conduct towards me, – which was not such as I am used to receive from persons in his situation. . . . As it would be highly imprudent in him to throw any obstacle in the way of your duty, I trust he will have too much good sense to obstruct it."

These doubts were well founded, for after another heroic voyage out by way of the Cape, New Zealand, Tahiti and Hawaii to Nootka Sound, and then, after a great deal of surveying, back by way of California, the Galapagos Islands, Chile and the Horn once more, Menzies' first letter to Banks, written in September 1795, observed that he had been under arrest since July, so that the plants for Kew were either dead or spoiled. It seems that his servant, taken from him to act as a seaman, had failed to cover some seedlings in a storm; Vancouver took no notice of Menzies' complaint and when he protested flew into a rage, accusing him of insolence and contempt and confining him to his cabin, which in a vessel the size of the *Discovery* was little more than a cupboard. It was, as Banks had said, "highly imprudent" in Vancouver; but perhaps he was not quite right in the head. He repeatedly and severely flogged one of his midshipmen; that was not very unusual, though at seventeen the youth was rather old for such treatment, but what *was* very unusual was his turning this same midshipman out of the ship at Hawaii to find his way home as best he could. It might conceivably have been justified from the point of view of discipline; from that of common prudence it was insane, for the young man had started the voyage as the Hon. Thomas Pitt and he ended it as Lord Camelford, his father having died meanwhile; his cousin was prime minister, his brother-in-law was foreign secretary, while another cousin was First Lord of the Admiralty, no less; and at this time Vancouver, though by courtesy a captain, was in fact only a master and commander, utterly dependent upon official favour for promotion. Banks took this treatment of Menzies and Menzies' plants very ill; he prepared a statement, setting out Vancouver's violence to Camelford and others and his arrest of Menzies, and this might well have led to strong official action if Vancouver had not died first.

However, before this unpleasantness Menzies had made immense collections, some of which had been sent home by other ships; it was he who discovered the *Sequoia sempervirens*, and it is to him that we owe the monkey puzzle tree – he came by the seed in Chile, and one of the very first batch was planted at Spring Grove. And he was tough: he did not let Vancouver's eccentricities spoil his love for the Navy or for plant collecting and presently he was to be found actively botanizing in the West Indies.

Plant collectors had to be tough, but few were as tough as John Ledyard, though perhaps he should be considered more as a traveller and explorer than a collector. He was born at Groton in Connecticut in 1751; he attended the recently-founded Dartmouth College for a while, having some notion of being a missionary to the Indians; he lived among the tribes of the Six Nations and he then studied theology, but as he could find nobody who would make a clergyman of him he took to the sea, eventually enlisting in the Marines. He was posted as a corporal to the *Resolution* in time for Cook's third voyage, and although the journal he kept was like all others surrendered to the Admiralty on his return, he wrote an account from memory when he was back in America, a book whose chief merit is that it gives a first-hand account of Cook's death. After this he tried to interest various merchants in trading for fur on the north-west coast – he had of course been there with Cook – but this came to nothing either in the States or in Europe. However, he was determined to go to Nootka Sound and since the ship that was to take him there from London turned back before she left the river, he decided to go by land, travelling across Russia and the whole of Siberia until he reached the Pacific. Before this he had met Banks, who gave him some money, some encouragement, and, it is to be presumed, a commission to collect plants. Ledyard reached Stockholm in January 1787, meaning to cross the Baltic on the ice; but this happened to be an exceptionally mild winter; there was ice enough to stop shipping but not enough to carry him over, so he was obliged to walk round by way of Sweden, Lapland, Finland and so to St

Petersburg, about 1200 miles. He arrived in March, his shoes worn out entirely, his purse empty. He was fortunate enough to meet Banks's friend Pallas, who was kind to him; the Portuguese ambassador, who cashed him a perfectly unauthorized bill drawn on Banks for twenty guineas; and Dr Brown, a Scots physician in the Russian service, who took him some three thousand miles eastward, to Barnaul in Siberia. He pushed on by himself to Tomsk and even to Irkutsk and Lake Baikal; he then dropped down the Lena to Yakutsk. Here, in 130°E and 5691 miles from St Petersburg, he met Joseph Billings, who had sailed with Cook as an able seaman, who was known to Banks, and who was now in the Russian service, exploring the north-eastern parts of the empire. Ledyard had known Billings in the Navy and he went back to Irkutsk with him to wait for the spring, when Billings said he would take him to Okhotsk. But here Ledyard was arrested (he thought the jealousy of the Russian-American Fur Company was the cause of it) and hurried westward week after week until his guards reached the Polish frontier, where they told him that if ever he returned to Russia he should certainly be hanged. Here again he found someone who would accept a bill drawn on Sir Joseph Banks, and presently he reached Soho Square. This was in 1788, just at the time when the African Association was formed, and it occurred to Banks that Ledyard was the ideal man to explore the interior of that continent, and perhaps to discover the course of the Niger. Ledyard agreed: he was to go to Cairo, join a caravan travelling right up to the Blue Nile and then strike south-west. He reached Cairo happily enough, and he made his preparations; but just before his caravan set off for Sennar he fell ill with what was called a bilious complaint, and either this or the vitriol he took to cure it killed him.[2]

Yet professional collectors were not the only source of plants: far from it indeed, for not only was there the vast and continuously growing network of botanists, but travellers with at least some knowledge of plants would often send Banks specimens, sometimes of the greatest interest. An example is James Bruce, FRS, and his correspondence with Banks makes very agreeable reading: it runs from his return to Europe after having explored Abyssinia and discovered the source of the Blue Nile to shortly before his death. In a letter brought from Florence by Zoffany in 1774 Bruce speaks of seeds sent to Kew: then comes a present of petrifications from the Troglodyte country below Abyssinia. In 1777 Bruce is much honoured by seeing one of his Abyssinian plants, *Brucea*, named after him, and he offers Banks some of the seeds of Egyptian and Nubian plants he has recently received, together with a Syrian treecreeper shot near his house in Scotland. In 1789 a ship from Glasgow brings a box containing a papyrus plant and specimens of myrrh, balsam of Mecca, and other delights. In 1789 Bruce condoles with Banks over his accident (his carriage was overturned by a drunken coachman and Banks spent more than two months in bed) and wishes to name the cusso, a plant he discovered, *Banksia abyssinica*: it is a powerful vermifuge.

From all these sources and by purchase Banks and the Aitons, father and son, received extraordinary numbers of seeds, bulbs, trees and plants for Kew; they also distributed a great many, particularly to other botanic gardens and to enterprising planters, as may be seen throughout Banks's correspondence – one example among many is a letter from Mr Wallen of Cold Spring in Jamaica, dated 2 April 1779, thanking Banks for "the seeds, which have been planted and will greatly benefit the island": Mr Wallen has many plants for Shakespear, employed by Banks, and will get him a passage to the Bay of Honduras. But there was one very important side of economic botany that called for more than ordinary means and for the cooperation of the Royal Navy. Sir Joseph Banks was not the only person to have noticed the significance of the breadfruit or to have reflected upon the probability of its great value if it were transplanted to the not dissimilar climate of some of the West Indian colonies: as early as 1772 Governor Morris of St Vincent had asked him whether it could be done, while Mr East raised the subject again when he was in London in 1786, as other Jamaicans had done before him. But Banks alone had the authority and the experience and the influence to set the project going. When the President of the Royal Society and the scientific director of Kew said that the probability of a successful transplantation was very great, people believed him. And among these people there were important men, members of parliament, ministers and the like, who had sugar or indigo plantations or other interests in the West Indies. These plantations were worked by black slaves; feeding them was difficult, and this might prove a solution, a wonderfully cheap solution, to the problem. The plantation owners were eager to believe in the breadfruit and to hasten its bringing over; and in fact the scheme advanced with unusual speed.

Apart from the correspondence between Banks and people in the West Indies the earliest trace of the plan is a letter he wrote on 30 March 1787 to his particular friend Charles Jenkinson, Lord Hawkesbury, then President of the Board of Trade. (He subsequently became the first Earl of Liverpool and he is sometimes confused with his son, Robert Banks Jenkinson, the second Earl, Byron's *bête noire*, who headed the reactionary government from 1812 to 1827.) The letter is obviously the outcome of earlier discussions, for Banks says "It is full my opinion that the plan of sending out a vessel from England for the sole purpose of bringing the Bread-fruit to the West Indies is much more likely to be successful than that of despatching Transports from Botany Bay"[3] – the fitting-out could be done better at home, and in any case it is clear that Banks looked upon the matter as settled, since he had already engaged David Nelson, a gardener, to look after the plants at a salary of £50 a year and £25 for his outfit. Nelson was an ideal man for the task: he had worked at Kew and he had sailed with Cook on his third voyage as Banks's plant collector – he was used to the sea, used to Polynesians and their language, and he was a thoroughly reliable gardener. The letter also spoke of the best kind of vessel, the best season for her sailing, and the route she should take.

Other conferences followed, and as early as 5 May 1787 Lord Sydney, the Home Secretary, wrote to the Lords Commissioners of the Admiralty telling them that His Majesty had thought fit that measures should immediately be taken for the procuring of some breadfruit trees and for conveying them to the said West Indies islands, and that "I am in Consequence to signify to your Lordships His Majesty's command that you do cause a vessel of the proper Class to be stored and victualled for this Service, and to be fitted with proper Convenience for the Preservation of as many of the said Trees as from her Size can be taken on Board, giving the command of her to some able and discreet Officer, and when she shall be ready for sea, your Lordships are to direct the said Officer to proceed in her to the Society Islands, situated in the Southern Ocean . . ." The letter went on to paraphrase what Banks had said about the route and the kind of tree to be taken aboard in Java on the way home to replace any breadfruits that might have died: it also said that David Nelson and William Brown were to join the ship in order to choose the plants and look after them. She was to sail in September 1787.

The Admiralty at once sent orders to the Navy Board, which looked at a number of vessels, picking out two for the inspection of Sir Joseph and David Nelson. The *Bethia* of 215 tons was chosen; with Sir Joseph's approval her price was fixed at £1950 on 23 May and she was moved to the Deptford yard to be copper-bottomed and modified for her new functions. In June the Admiralty told the Navy Board that she was to be classed as an armed vessel, that her complement would be forty-five, and that she was now to be called the *Bounty*.

Just when or how it was decided that the able and discreet officer to command her should be Lieutenant William Bligh cannot be said; but he had sailed as master of the *Resolution* on Cook's third voyage, so he was obviously well known to Nelson, his shipmate for those four years, while his uncle by marriage Duncan Campbell, a shipowner with interests in Jamaica, was acquainted with Banks. Mr Campbell had a high opinion of Bligh, who had commanded some of his ships during these last four peacetime years of half-pay; and Banks had a high opinion of officers who had served with Cook.

In any event on 6 August 1787 Bligh wrote to Sir Joseph[4]

> Sir,
>
> I arrived yesterday from Jamaica and should have instantly paid my respects to you had not Mr Campbell told me you were not to return from the country until Thursday. I have heard the flattering news of your great goodness to me, intending to honour me with the command of the vessel which you propose to go to the South Seas, for which, after offering you my most grateful thanks, I can only assure you I shall endeavour, and I hope succeed, in deserving such a trust. I await your commands, and am, with the sincerest respect, Sir, your much obliged and very Hmble Servant,
>
> Wm Bligh

From this it might be thought that the appointment was in Banks's gift, which was not the case at all. Although his recommendation carried great weight the Admiralty would not have agreed if there had been a very black mark against Bligh's name. Not that those who made decisions there were really devoted to Bligh – they had refused him a commission (as master he was only a warrant officer) after the *Resolution*'s return when so many were promoted, and if he had not been present at the battle of the Dogger Bank in 1781 he might never have been a lieutenant. But they did know that at present most other officers with experience of the South Seas were either dead or too high in rank for the *Bounty*, which was not even a sloop but an unrated vessel of about the cutter's modest level, and they did know that he was an able surveyor and a competent navigator, so they gave him the command; yet even now they refused him the step to master and commander that he asked for – a foolish request, it may be added, since that very great man Cook had taken the *Endeavour* round the world as a mere lieutenant.

The next letter on the subject was from Lord Sydney; it was dated from Whitehall on 15 August 1787 and its contents can hardly have astonished Sir Joseph very much:[5]

> Dear Sir,
>
> The Admiralty have I understand purchased a vessel for the purpose of

> conveying the bread-fruit tree and other useful productions from the South Sea Islands to His Majesty's West India Possessions. She is to be commissioned in the course of a few days, to be called the *Bounty* and to be commanded by Lieutenant Bligh. As I am totally unacquainted with the nature of the instructions which are proper to be given to Nelson and Brown, the two gardeners who are to collect the trees and plants and to be entrusted with their care and management during their continuance on board the ship, I shall think myself particularly obliged to you if you will prepare such instructions as you may judge adequate for their guidance.
>
> I have the Honour to be, with great regard
>
> Your obedient humble servant
>
> Sydney

Banks set about it with great good will, turning the *Bounty* into a truly botanical ship, a gardener's floating paradise. "The master and crew of her must not think it a grievance to give up the best of her accommodation for that purpose [of carrying plants]." Casks sawn down, with their bottoms pierced, would be the best containers; but

> As these casks, which will be very heavy, must frequently be brought on deck for the benefit of the sun, the crew must assist in moving them; as indeed they must assist the gardener on all occasions in which he stands in need of their help. Besides there must be provided tubs so deep that the tops of the plants will not reach to their edges. These must be lashed all round the Quarter-deck, along the booms and in every place where room can possibly be found for them and for each a cover of canvas must be made to fit it, which covers, it will be the duty of the gardener to put on or take off as he judges fit, and no one else must interfere with him in so doing on any account whatever.

Then as the plants would often have the salt dampness from the sea air washed off, the ship

> must be supplied with as large a quantity [of water] as possible, so that the gardener may never be refused the quantity of water he may have occasion to demand.
>
> No Dogs, Cats, Monkeys, Parrots, Goats, or indeed any animals whatever must be allowed on board, except Hogs and Fowls for the Company's use; and they must be carefully confined to their coops. Every precaution must be taken to prevent or destroy the Rats, as often as convenient. A boat with green boughs should be laid alongside with a gangway of green boughs laid from the hold to her, and a drum kept going below in the vessel for one or more nights; and as poison will constantly be used to destroy them and cockroaches, the crew must not complain if some of them who may die in the ceiling make an unpleasant smell.[6]

It does not appear that the crew took strong exception to the smell of poisoned rats, but they did take very strong exception to Captain Bligh and it is common knowledge that they or many of them turned him out of the ship in the South Seas, so that he and those who followed him into the twenty-three-foot launch were obliged to undertake the desperate voyage westwards in the hope of reaching Timor some four thousand miles away, while the mutineers sailed the *Bounty* back to Tahiti.

Any man with a large acquaintance is bound to know some people who turn out to be less agreeable than they seemed at first, but it may be thought that Banks was either unluckier than most or that in this respect his judgement was not very acute, so that he kept on hoping that the good would predominate over the bad. It took him years and years to find out that Blagden was so interested, that Pennant was to say the least unscrupulous and that Sinclair was capable of very curious behaviour in the pursuit of money. And he never did find out that Bligh had an unpleasant character, although this soon became obvious to a great many people who came into contact with him. That is not to say that Bligh was not a courageous and eminently capable seaman – no one else could have accomplished that astonishing open-boat voyage – nor that he was not an efficient subordinate; but he was not fitted for command; he was not the "able and discreet Officer" who was required. He does not seem at all an interesting or attractive figure in himself, and he would never be heard of unless he had been turned out of the *Bounty*; but since he throws a certain light on Banks he is worth a page or two. It is true that the light thrown is not entirely creditable, but then this is not hagiography. William Bligh was born in 1754, the son of a minor customs official in Plymouth, and although his name was on the books of the *Monmouth* in 1762 he did not actually go to sea until 1770, when he joined the *Hunter*, a ten-gun sloop, with the nominal rating of able seaman. He was rated midshipman the next year, and he served in various other ships on the West Indies station. A midshipman who had served his six years could look forward to two lines of service: if he was lucky he would have a commission as a lieutenant and the possibility of further promotion; if he was not, the most he could expect was a master's warrant, which meant inferior status and no advancement in rank for the rest of his time. To what extent merit was concerned it is difficult to say: so many factors, such as family background, service connection, important patronage and the Navy's current needs, as well as the young man's worth as an officer, came into play with varying strength at different times. But at all events Bligh was passed over, and 1776 found him master of the *Resolution*, apparently bound for a subfusc career.

He responded well to the leadership of such a man as Cook and he carried out some excellent surveys, with accurate charts, during the earlier part of the voyage; but after Cook's death in Hawaii he fell out with most of the other officers. James King, second lieutenant of the *Resolution* until he succeeded to the command of the *Discovery*, completed Cook's account of the voyage, and in the margins of a copy in the Admiralty Bligh wrote "a most infamous lie"[7] against one of his statements, while the other comments are of much the same nature.

The same aggressiveness and use of gross language came with him into the *Bounty*, made all the worse by his having no superiors or even equals, and it is said that by the time she reached Tenerife, about a fortnight after sailing from Spithead, he was scarcely on speaking terms with his officers.[8] The mutiny itself is sometimes put down to the charms of Tahiti; but the charms were the same for Wallis's men, for Cook's and for Bougainville's and these commanders had no very grave problems. The trouble seems to be that Bligh lacked natural authority and tried to make up for it by railing and cursing. During that terrible voyage to Timor he quarrelled steadily with the master and the carpenter of the *Bounty* and when he reached home he had the carpenter brought before a court martial for disobedience and disrespect: it is difficult to imagine Cook behaving in such a manner.

There was another court martial some years later, when Bligh, in command of the *Warrior* 74, was accused of tyrannous, oppressive and unofficerlike behaviour to Lieutenant Frazier and other commissioned, warrant and petty officers. The evidence showed that Bligh was a foul-mouthed bully – his lower-deck nickname was the *Bounty* Bastard – and the court found the charges "in part proved". Bligh was reprimanded, told to be more correct in his language, and sent back to run the *Warrior* with a set of men who had testified against him.

An uncomfortable situation of this kind could be dealt with at home by exchanges and removals, but in New South Wales the case was altered. Shortly after the *Warrior* trial Bligh was appointed governor of the colony at Banks's instance. On the way out in 1806 he quarrelled furiously with Captain Short of HMS *Porpoise*, the officer in command of the transports; he assumed the governorship in January 1807 and presently he was on very bad terms with a large number of the free inhabitants, particularly the officers of the New South Wales Corps; in January 1808 the soldiers deposed him, taking him from under a bed in Government House and imprisoning him until 1809, when he agreed to go aboard the *Porpoise*, promising on his honour "as an officer and a gentleman" to take her to England. He did not do so, but kept her sailing to and fro between Sydney and Tasmania for the rest of the year, when a somewhat half-hearted Nemesis arrived in the form of Lachlan Macquarie, his replacement, accompanied by the 73rd Regiment.

When he came home the Admiralty gave Bligh his flag – he was at the top of the post-captains' list – but it is hardly surprising to learn that he was never employed again. Apart from anything else there was the feeling aroused by the cases of Short and Kent. Short seems to have been quarrelsome, irritating and touchy, and there is no sort of doubt that he was foolish to offend a governor under whose orders he would find himself on reaching New South Wales, and still more foolish to fire a shot across the bows of the transport in which the Governor was travelling to make her haul her wind, but even so Bligh's revenge was out of all proportion. Short had come out with his wife and children and a large quantity of farming material intending to settle on the 600 acres that he had been promised. Governor Bligh said he had no satisfactory evidence of the grant and could not proceed without instructions from London; he also took advantage of a disagreement between Short and his officers to send them back to England for a court martial. Short was obliged to take his family home with him: his pregnant wife and one of the children died on the way: and the court martial honourably acquitted him, with strong censure of his officers (for Bligh did not appear directly) and a recommendation that the Admiralty should give him some appointment by way of compensation. Kent was the officer in command of the *Porpoise* in New South Wales during that uneasy period of the soldiers' usurpation. He had not done anything against Bligh but he had not done anything against the military either: he had not bombarded Sydney. Bligh put him under close arrest for twenty-three months before bringing him before a court martial on charges of having sailed from Sydney without the Governor's permission and with having unlawfully removed Bligh's broad pennant. Kent too was acquitted. But acquitted or not both these officers' lives were shockingly damaged.

What does seem strange is that through all this, from the time of the *Bounty* onwards, Banks should have remained such a man's patron, supporter and indeed friend. It is true that Bligh's letters to him were as respectful and obliging as a not very highly literate man could make them, and it is true that in point of fact they did not see very much of one another; yet even so there does seem to be a certain want of discrimination.

Of course it is also true that Bligh's second attempt to transplant the breadfruit under Banks's direction in 1791 was successful. He had two vessels this time, the *Providence* and the *Assistant*; one of his officers was a nephew and another was an old friend; he was sick in bed and low-spirited much of the time and he made few scenes; his lieutenants were competent and the plan was carried out. Banks's gardeners (poor Nelson had died at Batavia after the launch journey) potted up 2126 plants and although some died in the heat of the Torres Strait there were plenty for St Helena, St Vincent and Jamaica. This was balm to an economic botanist's soul (a balm slightly soured some years later when it was found that although the trees did well the blacks would not eat their fruit) and it may account for at least some part of the improbable connection between Banks and Bligh.

Fortunately Banks had many, many other and far more suitable friends. No one was more regular than he at the cheerful meetings of the Royal Philosophers' Club except for that strange, timid, lonely, brilliant physicist Henry Cavendish; and many of those who dined with him there were strikingly agreeable and accomplished men – Broussonet, Cuvier and Jussieu, Boulton, Watt and Gibbon, to mention a very few. More friends again at the graver sessions of the Royal Society itself, where he presided with even greater regularity – neither sheep nor breadfruit could keep him away, though gout threatened to do so – and where the Fellows re-elected him year after year throughout the 1780s, so that he came to seem a settled, natural figure in that great chair, gathering authority with the years, as indeed did the Society itself.

More friends at the Board of Longitude, where he sat ex officio, and still more friends, very many more friends, in Lincolnshire, where he was among people he had known all his life – cousins, fellow land-owners, tenants and dependants by the hundred – and where he narrowly escaped being High Sheriff in 1788, it not being a matter of choice but of appointment, an appointment full of honour, trouble and cost: a friend writing to him about gibbets said "to put them up I know to be expensive, for alas it cost me £50 to hang Broughton the mail robber when I was Sheriff". He was also urged to be a member of parliament, but that was a matter of choice and he would have nothing to do with politics whatsoever, giving his very considerable interest in those parts to an established country gentleman whose local ideas he liked, whether he was Whig or Tory on the grander scale.

Back in London he and yet other friends founded the African Association to explore that continent, and in the same year, 1788, James Edward Smith, with Banks's full support, founded the Linnean Society. At the time of Linnaeus's death in 1778 Banks had offered to buy his herbarium: the younger Linnaeus preferred keeping it, but when he too died, in 1783, his heirs offered Sir Joseph not only the herbarium but the zoological and mineral collections and the botanical and zoological library, together with Linnaeus's manuscripts, correspondence, dried fishes, insects, shells and other things.

It is said[9] that when the proposal came from Sweden Banks was having breakfast in Soho Square; among the guests was a young man, James Edward Smith, the son of a well-to-do and cultivated Norwich merchant and one of Professor Hope's pupils in botany. Banks passed Smith the letter, advising him to ask his father to buy him the collections. Smith took him at his word and a thousand guineas procured him not only an astonishing mass of significant and sometimes very beautiful objects but also, since he was already an exceptionally intelligent young man, an outstanding and very much envied position in the learned world. He set off for a tour of Europe, bearing letters of introduction from Sir Joseph to a great many eminent men; and when he came back he founded the society, with Banks as one of the three honorary fellows.

Why did Banks hand the letter over? Certainly he was fond of the young man, who turned out to be a life-long friend, sending Norfolk turkeys far into the next century; but that scarcely seems a sufficient cause. Conceivably the thought of housing 19,000 sheets of pressed plants, 3200 insects, 1500 shells, 750 pieces of coral, 2500 mineral specimens, 2500 books and the whole of Linnaeus's vast correspondence, to say nothing of the birds and dried fish, made him hesitate; but Soho Square was a fine great building, sparsely inhabited, and he had an excellent librarian and curator in Jonas Dryander. Nor was a thousand guineas out of the way for him. May it not be that the very highest tide of botany was over in Banks's heart, and that the administrator was beginning to prevail over the naturalist?

The word administration brings to mind a small difficulty that occurred in the running of the Royal Society: it would not be worth mentioning, since Blagden was not much more interesting as a person than Bligh, but for the fact that it says a good dead about Banks's character and about the disadvantages of being rich. At the time of the dissensions Maty resigned as secretary and Dr Charles Blagden took his place, being elected with Banks's powerful support. They had known one another since at least as early as 1773; Banks was happy to have him there and all went well until January 1789, when Blagden suddenly began writing to Banks in the cold, inimical formality of the third person. Banks was startled and wounded: he could not understand it at all. For a long while his requests for an explanation produced nothing but such remarks as "That your general conduct has been for some time past that of a Friend I cannot think," but eventually Blagden came up with this: "No man has a right to engage the time and attention of another, unless he has good reason to believe that the other will find in his employment of them an adequate advantage. If Sir Joseph has acted upon this principle, nothing further can be required of him", and at last it became clear to Banks that Blagden had regarded him not as a friend all this time but as a patron, a source of tangible benefits.

Blagden was not the most estimable of characters – Brougham, in his article on Cavendish, says "Having formed a high opinion of Dr (afterwards Sir Charles) Blagden's capacity for science, he settled a considerable annuity on him, upon condition that he should give up his profession and devote himself to philosophy; with the former portion of which condition the Doctor complied, devoting himself to the hopeless pursuit of a larger income in the person of Lavoisier's widow, who preferred marrying Count Rumford." [Brougham's footnote: He left Sir Charles a legacy of £15,000; which was generally understood to have fallen much short of his ample expectations.] Yet when avarice was not upon him he was good company. "Blagden, Sir, is a delightful fellow," said Dr Johnson, from whom intellectual benefit alone could be expected. Banks was an exceptionally tolerant man; his liking for Blagden survived the loss of his illusions and they corresponded in the friendliest way until 1820, the year they both died. Banks's last letter to him brought the news that two Newfoundland puppies were on the way to Paris, where Blagden had been living for some years. Yet this experience and several others of the same nature lay behind a passage in the autobiography of Sir Benjamin Brodie, FRS: Charles Hatchett, the chemist, had inherited a great deal of money and Banks "used to say to him in his rough way that 'he would find being a gentleman of fortune was a confounded bad trade'".

Normally an account of Joseph Banks's life for the next few years would carry on with his steady, active round of Soho Square, Spring Grove and the Royal Society, the royal sheep and Kew during the winter, spring and early summer, with Revesby and its country contentments for the rest of the year, going by way of Overton Hall, on his Derbyshire estate, sometimes stopping on the road at his friend Matthew Boulton's house and prodigious manufactory at Soho near Birmingham; all this combined with new responsibilities, some to do with the Board of Longitude and the furious disagreements between rival chronometer-makers, and others with the many government departments that consulted him officially and unofficially, the whole culminating with the establishment of the Board of Agriculture in 1793.

This was the creation of Sir John Sinclair, FRS, the economist, scientific farmer and statistician, and of Arthur Young, FRS, to whose periodical *Annals of Agriculture* the King had contributed under the name of Ralph Robinson; Banks was a little reserved at first, perhaps feeling that he would like a little time to himself free from official duties, but presently he came round; and indeed it was an admirable centre from which a rational stock breeder and an economic botanist could radiate, communicating on a governmental level with his colleagues in Europe, particularly Broussonet and his fellow workers in France.

But before the Board was set up Broussonet was no more. That is to say there was no quiet, studious Perpetual Secretary of the Society of Agriculture in Paris but only an anxious fugitive, in Montpellier for the moment but soon to escape across the Pyrenees.

He had welcomed the Revolution, and as a Girondin he was pretty far to the Left; in 1791 he was chosen a member of the *Assemblée* and he told Banks that he meant "to press for the improvement of agriculture in the tranquility that we are at last to enjoy". At this time his illusions were shared by most people in England. During the first stages of the enormous change the general feeling on this side of the Channel was of mild approval; it seemed perfectly reasonable that the French should want parliamentary government, legal and fiscal equality, and even a constitutional monarchy; the English peers, that very small class which retained almost no particular advantage other than that of being hanged with a silken halter, applauded the renunciation of their great privileges, above all their freedom from taxes, by the thousands and thousands of French nobles; and although this warmth entirely vanished after the King's flight and his recapture and the events leading to the war with Austria and Prussia, Pitt could still, as late as the spring of 1792, congratulate the House on the prospect of a long, untroubled peace, while even until the end of the year, even after the September massacres and the French victories over the Prussians and Austrians, he hoped that England might remain neutral.

It was in this year that Broussonet withdrew to Montpellier, and it was early in the next, 1793, that the full nature of the Revolution became apparent. Louis XVI was beheaded on 21 January; the French envoy was ordered to leave London; and on 1 February the Republic declared war on England.

Chapter 10

WAR: NEW SOUTH WALES: THE PRIVY COUNCIL

BROADLY SPEAKING the country was much in favour of the war and there were many patriotic demonstrations and loyal addresses; but the war was conceived as an operation carried out by professionals, costly in lives and treasure no doubt, but having little direct impact on the lives of civilians. Banks had known the War of the Austrian Succession, the Seven Years War and the War of American Independence; and although islands in the West Indies changed hands, while far more important changes took place in Canada and India, these conflicts had not affected the relations between the natural philosophers on either side nor the lives of ordinary English people living in the country.

But now the case was altered, for this time the French were fighting something not unlike a holy war – preaching a new religion rather than carrying on with the old dynastic quarrel – and they fought extremely well. According to all the rules well equipped, well trained and highly disciplined troops should prevail over disorganized bands with few professional officers and little in the way of commissariat; yet the Austrian regiments and even the Prussian Guard recoiled before the French, and very soon revolutionary enthusiasm had conquered the Austrian Netherlands, Holland, the Rhenish states, Savoy and Nice, while an English army under the Duke of York was obliged to re-embark, and the powerful Dutch fleet, frozen in at the Texel, was most absurdly captured by a troop of French hussars galloping over the ice.

Yet English armies had never been very fortunate on the Continent since Marlborough's day, and military disaster could be put down to military incompetence, which was nothing new, while the impression that the familiar pattern was to be repeated was strengthened by the familiar conduct of the Royal Navy, for on the glorious first of June 1794 Lord Howe with twenty-five line-of-battle ships met Admiral Villaret de Joyeuse with twenty-six; of these he sank one, took six and mauled the rest to a shocking degree.

It was long before the rulers of the country came to realize that the French were fighting a new kind of war, a largely ideological war and one that made them exceptionally dangerous; but at least some part of this radical change became apparent to Banks early in the conflict. The triumph of the Jacobins in the Convention and the consequent reign of terror meant that there was not a man of any eminence who was safe from arbitrary arrest, a mock trial before the Revolutionary Tribunal and almost certain condemnation. Upon the whole men of science were more inclined to republican views than otherwise and in any case few were of any political consequence, but this did not prevent eight of the eleven with whom Faujas had shared the Chinese hemp seed given him by Banks from being guillotined, "dragged to the scaffold", as Faujas says, "without respect for names signalized by virtue and talents. Buffon was dead – they took his son – he was unrelentingly assassinated . . ." It is true that five of them had noble names, and under the Law of Suspects anyone of noble birth might be taken up and imprisoned, but neither Lavoisier nor Broussonet belonged to that class. Lavoisier, a member of the *Académie des Sciences*, a Fellow of the Royal Society and the most distinguished natural philosopher of France, was brought before the tribunal, and part of the evidence against him was the fact that English letters were found in his house – of course he corresponded with Priestley, Black, Cavendish, Banks and others – while he was also accused of having adulterated the citizens' tobacco. On 8 May 1794 he was put to death, together with 123 others, the president of the court observing "*La République n'a pas besoin de savants*".

Broussonet however had left Paris well before this and when the Terror reached its height he crossed the mountains into Spain. The whole eastern frontier, from the Mediterranean to the Cerdagne, was alive with Republican troops, repelling the Spaniards, so he went far inland, taking the remoter paths he knew from having botanized in the Pyrenees with Sibthorp, and climbed the very high, very cold, very dangerous track through snow and ice over the shoulder of the Maladetta and so down to Benasque in Aragon. From here, on 25 July 1794, he wrote to Banks, telling him of his flight and his plan to emigrate to America, and begging him to arrange a passage to England in a man-of-war. He wrote again from Saragossa, in great distress, asking Banks to send replies to Madrid and Cadiz. These early letters did not reach London until 6 September: Banks replied at once. But still urgent letters kept coming from Spain, dated August and September – in Madrid the savants Ortega and Canavilles were very kind, but in Cadiz, which Broussonet reached in September, most of his meagre baggage had been stolen. From Lisbon in November he wrote to say that he did not know whether Banks had received any of his letters: he had not been able to wait for replies as all Frenchmen had been ordered to move twenty leagues inland from the frontier. Broussonet had therefore come to Portugal, to wait until he heard from Banks; he had collected about forty tortoises for him and then, in hourly expectation of a permit to leave in a British man-of-war, he had put them, together with his remaining possessions, on board: but the permit came too late and the ship and tortoises and baggage had sailed without him. This letter reached London on 24 November and Banks answered the same day: and then at last one of his many earlier replies, written on 7 September, did reach Lisbon, being forwarded from Cadiz – Broussonet was overjoyed at its contents. Banks had evidently been exceedingly active, using his influence in every direction, for now letters came in as fast as the indifferent communications would allow, bringing the permit and papers that would obtain a passage in a man-of-war. From Gibraltar Broussonet sent him thanks: he was particularly grateful to Banks for having rescued his trunk and the tortoises, and he outlined a suitable diet for them; people were being very kind to him in Gibraltar and General Rainsford had made a collection of fossil bones for Banks. Broussonet was also sending off a parcel of bulbs and seeds. In June he was still on the Rock, but by now Banks had put him in touch with Matra, the consul in Tangier, and he was going there; as Banks had suggested, Broussonet was drawing upon him – the money he would in time be able to repay, the kindness never, he said. In Morocco he found a country almost unexplored from the point of view of natural history and among other charming things he discovered a new species of fox; but by this time the Terror was over, Robespierre had, quite literally, lost his head, and Broussonet could go back to France. His next letter was from his family house in Montpellier, and his first care on reaching home was to tell Banks of his gratitude once more. Their correspondence continued at intervals throughout the Revolutionary War and beyond, and at various times Broussonet, who travelled a good deal, sent Banks two gazelles, a whole dried Canary Islander, and of course large quantities of plants, while from Banks's side came the gingko now growing in the botanic garden at Montpellier, where Broussonet had been given the chair of botany – a gingko whose seed produced the sapling that can be seen from the present writer's window.

With the end of the Terror something like sanity returned to France, together with a far greater efficiency in administration, and although much of the revolutionary fervour remained, making Bonaparte's armies so very formidable, Pitt and his colleagues returned to the conduct of a traditional war (in so far as they had ever changed their attitude at all), most emphatically an islanders' war, perceived by many of its inhabitants as a conflict carried on by subsidies and by naval guns, a matter of ever-increasing taxation, glorious but distant fleets, and the presence of militia regiments all over the country – the kind of war familiar to Jane Austen and her characters.

But for the mass of the nation the Terror had utterly discredited reform. Pitt, who had been so much in favour of a more reasonable House of Commons, now treated those who wished to change that almost entirely unrepresentative body as seditious criminals; and what hopes Banks may have retained, what schemes for a Royal Society whose organization, management and finances should be more worthy of a body that plumed itself upon intelligence, withered away, never to revive, so that the illustrious assembly (as Charles II called it) blundered along in its old inefficient way until well after his presidency.

Intelligence: the word brings not only natural philosophers to mind but also secret agents; and of course a corporation like the Royal Society with connections reaching over the whole civilized world was well placed for gathering and transmitting political or strategic information, all the more so as several of its Fellows were eminent chemists or engineers. When Blagden, the Secretary of the Royal Society, was visiting Paris during the Peace of Amiens, for example, Napoleon was convinced that he was a spy. The role of secret agent hardly seems to suit Sir Joseph, and yet there is some correspondence in the early days of the Revolution which seems to show that he made some motions in that direction. The first letter,[1] addressed to Pitt, states that a set of numbers (presumably a coded accreditation) which the court of Berlin should have sent to the Prime Minister ought to induce him to see Banks's friend, particularly as the present situation should be known to the Cabinet. A note in an official hand attached to this and the following letters reads "I conceive these . . . to refer to the same subject as Mr Pitt's preceding MS draft of Feb 3rd 1790 – namely the presence in London of an accredited Agent from the Insurrectionary Congress of Belgium and the desire of the Agent to explain the circumstances to Mr Pitt." In the next letter Banks, assuming that, since his friend had not heard from Mr Pitt, the set of numbers had not arrived, vouches for his character and states that the Prime Minister ought to have this information, which might be of great importance in pending negotiations. It is clear that this letter had its effect and Pitt saw the man, since five days later Banks asks for a second hearing for his friend as soon as possible, as the suspense is preying on his health. In the next day's letter Banks's friend has had Pitt's letter read to him: Banks will see that he is ready at the appointed time; but as the friend fears he is being watched, Banks suggests meeting Pitt in front of St Anne's church in Soho and taking him to his house by a back door.

Perhaps some writer more learned in the fine points of European history could tell what it was all about, and it would be pleasant to have a clarification of the reference, in Banks's third letter of 30 March 1790, to the Emperor of Russia's death at a time when the formidable Catherine was still firmly on the throne; but the real point of this aside is to show that Banks had direct access to Pitt and that some foreign organization, presumably aware of this, saw him as a discreet and wholly reliable intermediary.

Yet it was early in the troubles that this singular interchange took place, and it appears that the mission was not altogether satisfactory, for in the last letter of the series Banks says that his friend, feeling that he may not have stated his case with perfect clarity by word of mouth, is putting it in writing for Mr Pitt's consideration. In any event, although opportunities were not lacking, this seems to have been an isolated incident; the record shows no sign whatsoever of any repetition, and Banks's actual war appears to have been an entirely conventional kind.

Like most country gentlemen he belonged to the country militia, and presently, in spite of gout and advancing years, he was in arms as Lieutenant-Colonel of the Lindsey Battalion; but for the most part his activities were of a peaceful nature. Or fairly peaceful: one of his most important commitments, after the Royal Society, the royal sheep and Kew, but probably before the Board of Agriculture or the Society of Antiquaries, was the Board of Longitude. This body was set up in 1713 to encourage methods of finding the longitude at sea more exactly than by dead-reckoning, which in a long voyage might be wrong by hundreds of miles. The most obvious way of doing so was to compare local time, easily established by observing the sun, with Greenwich time, since every hour of difference means 15° of longitude east or west: but this entailed carrying Greenwich time aboard the ship, and from the first very large rewards were offered for timekeepers – no less than £20,000 for one that would be accurate to within thirty sea miles, that is to say two minutes by the clock or half a degree of longitude at the equator, £15,000 within forty miles and £10,000 for sixty. These sums aroused vehement competition and vehement passions, and although the great prize was won by Harrison in 1762 and the last instalment grudgingly paid in 1773, the offers and the passions were renewed that same year. Indeed the passions were if anything increased, because there were now the lunarians, a rival school who maintained that the moon's motions were so well understood at present that longitude could be calculated from lunar distances with greater accuracy than from any chronometer. The foremost lunarian was the Rev. Dr Nevil Maskelyne FRS, the Astronomer Royal, who first published the Nautical Almanac in 1766, giving the distance between the moon and the sun or certain fixed stars for every three hours throughout the following year. The navigator had but to make his observation of local time (which he would do at noon in any case to find his latitude), measure his lunar angle, make the necessary adjustments for parallax and refraction, and so find Greenwich time by proportional logarithms. The chronometer-makers said that though all these calculations might be made without much error in clear weather by an able mathematician who had a good instrument, the result was in no way superior to that given by an excellent watch: there was a great likelihood of mistake and it was obviously far better to have Greenwich time there at hand, instantly readable without any calculation at all. This the lunarians denied, and since their chief, the Astronomer Royal, was both a most influential member of the Board of Longitude and in most cases the judge of the performance of the various timekeepers that were submitted for the great rewards, the watchmakers, particularly Thomas Mudge the King's watchmaker, often accused him of unfairness, apparently with some justice: his answer to Mudge's furious book is said to be unsatisfactory.

Dr Maskelyne was a capital astronomer and mathematician, a man of considerable private means about ten years older than Banks; he had been Astronomer Royal since 1765, he had had the Copley medal for his work on the attraction of mountains, and he made some 90,000 published astronomical observations. He was a masterful man, used to having his own way, and he had taken the side of the other mathematicians against Banks during the dissensions in the Royal Society. Banks was also a man of considerable private means and used to having his own way, and since the President of the Royal Society and the Astronomer Royal were the most regular attendants at the meetings of the Board, conflict seemed probable. Banks was no mathematician, nor was he anything of an astronomer, but he could tell what o'clock it was as well as any man, and he maintained that Arnold made better chronometers than Earnshaw, Maskelyne's protégé. They fell out over this fairly early in proceedings, and in time their disagreement grew really serious, with printed protests flying; but it is worth observing that neither let his feelings get out of hand – there was never an oath from beginning to end, no wigs on the green, no personalities; for although Banks was a big, formidable man and one who was not afraid of any antagonist whatsoever, he had a particularly courteous way of telling his opponent that he was mistaken or that his conduct left something to be desired. He could be testy on occasion, and as his fits of gout grew more frequent so did the occasions; but an almost invariable urbanity, contrasting a little with his heavy, dominant, somewhat bucolic presence, was often remarked upon.

He needed all his urbanity in the year 1794, when he was unable to avoid being chosen High Sheriff of Lincolnshire. This made him nominally responsible for many things such as the execution of those condemned to death and the safe custody of criminals which in fact he caused to be done by his under-sheriffs; but he was obliged to attend the judges of assize when they came round on their stately circuit, and custom required him to entertain them and many of the barristers too, as well as great numbers of the country gentlemen, justices of the peace and others, who came in to pay their respects. Far more significant however were his duties with regard to parliamentary elections and the summoning of the grand jury; and now, in wartime, his influence with the leading men of the county was of the first importance. Unpolitical though he was – he would never consider a seat in parliament – at this juncture he was wholly in agreement with Pitt's administration, and he induced the important Lincolnshire men there assembled not to limit themselves to expressions of loyalty and of determination to defend the county against any hostile attempt but to contribute liberally to a subscription that would give their words effect – a move that may or may not have been constitutional for a man in his position (the Opposition questioned it) but that was certainly made in the most perfect good faith.

He needed it again in April of the same year when Henry Dundas, the Home Secretary, wrote offering him the Bath. The order was then very highly prized, coming second in England only to the Garter; it had not yet been enlarged, and apart from the sovereign and the officials it consisted of no more than thirty-six knights, who wore their red ribbon with perhaps even more pleasure than the twenty-five knights of the Garter (twenty-five not counting the royals) wore their blue, because the Bath was much less often a reward for being a duke. Then again Banks was an antiquary as well as a botanist; he was sensitive to the charm of the past, and although the order had but a shaky existence before George I's coronation a good many people liked to trace it back to 1399. What is more, he had a high, somewhat romantic notion of these things: when a few years after this Sir John Sinclair had the ill-advised notion of starting a subscription for himself in acknowledgment of his own merits, Banks observed to a common friend who had also been solicited that it was "a disparagement for a Gentleman of Blood and Coat-Armour to ask for money on any terms but that of a loan". In any case, none of his rising family had ever had a remotely comparable honour; and the prospect had been familiar to him since 1789, for it was in that year that the King had told him he should have it (presumably when there was a vacancy). But Dundas had grievously mistimed the offer, so that it looked like a reward for political services; or he may of course have mistaken his man. The letter has disappeared, but a fair assumption is that in more or less explicit terms it also required further political support. However that may be, Banks felt obliged to refuse, and this he did in a very fine letter. The manuscript was once in the collection of Sir Gavin de Beer, who holds it up as a particularly good example of Banks, "one of the greatest letter-writers in the English language",[2] and with the very kind permission of Yale University, the present owners, it is now published for the first time on pages 310–12.

Urbane though his letter was, there is no sort of doubt that this was a severe disappointment to Banks; yet on almost the very same day we find him answering an uneducated young man from Manchester, George Caley, who had sent him a *Drosera* and a moss he could not identify though he had studied botany for eight years, and who had at the same time asked Sir Joseph to find him work as a botanist's assistant or the like. Banks's answer was long, careful and kind: he identified the plant as *Drosera longifolia* (Linn.) but could not be certain about the moss without seeing more; he told young Caley that botany was the most unprofitable trade he knew, but that the best way for him to learn about exotic plants and their cultivation was to work as a labourer in a botanic garden; this might lead to more, and if Caley wished he would recommend him for such a situation. Caley did so wish, and there now began an association which like several others originating in an act of kindness brought Banks little but annoyance, trouble and expense for the rest of his days. Caley may have been a tolerable botanist, but being persuaded that "there are more geniuses of the lower class in manufacturing towns than elsewhere" he tended to rate his own abilities too high; and this, or an unfortunate temperament, made him singularly querulous. He was dissatisfied with the low wages at the King's botanic garden (and indeed nine shillings a week was not much), but by going to work elsewhere he lost the opportunity of studying the Australian plants that were already being grown and he was therefore not qualified to be sent out to New South Wales as an official collector for Kew some years later. Eventually, having put up with a surprising amount of rudeness, Banks sent him on his own initiative, without a government appointment but with a recommendation to Governor Hunter, giving him his outfit and fifteen shillings a week and requiring only that he should send rare plants for the herbarium in Soho Square and seeds for Kew – no other conditions at all. Presently it appeared that Caley had been misused, slighted or oppressed by almost everyone in the colony, a place "miserable beyond description", though he did have a certain liking for the deposed Bligh. He was quite diligent; but of course he disagreed with that really eminent botanist Robert Brown and the Kew artist Bauer (one of Banks's happiest appointments) when they came out, and after many years Banks wrote to say that he no longer needed him as a collector. But the letter[3] went on to say that because of Caley's past services Banks would settle £50 a year on him for life, whether he stayed on his farm in Australia or came back to England. Yet this was not the end of Caley; he did return to England, and Banks obtained the post of superintendent of the botanic gardens of St Vincent for him. He went there by way of Barbados, taking a schooner for the rest of the way and drawing on Banks for its hire: the gardens, he said, were in a wretched state, ill-conceived, neglected and on poor soil; the superintendent's house was damp, full of vermin and in bad repair; the climate most unpleasant. From subsequent letters Banks learnt that St Vincent was inhabited by wicked, violent and litigious people; the judges and the juries were against Caley; he was sorry he had ever gone there; and although the very last admits that the cloves, nutmegs, cinnamon and mangoes were doing well, it also says he has proof that the blacks were being bribed to steal plants from the garden.

It must have been a relief to turn from Caley to Dryander, that good botanist and even better librarian: he was quiet, wholly reliable and wholly devoted to his books. Brodie,[4] who knew him well, says "Dryander was indeed a pattern as a librarian. The library over which he presided was to him *all in all*. Without being a man of science himself, he knew every book, and the contents of every book in it. If anyone enquired of him where he might look for information on any particular subject, he would go first to one shelf, then to another, and return with a bundle of books under his arm containing the information that was desired."

Banks's ladies might call him Old Dry, and indeed he was not such a sociable, amusing creature as Solander; but he was an invaluable assistant, dealing with foreigners, staying in London when Banks was in the country and sending him word of whatever was going on just as Solander had done, and in even more perfect English; and in this same year of 1795 he was ready to begin the printing of that remarkable work the *Catalogus bibliothecae historico-naturalis Josephi Banks, Baronetti*, which came out in five handsome volumes between 1796 and 1800. And then apart from choosing the type and paper for the great catalogue another very pleasant thing happened in 1795, and this was the investiture of Sir Joseph as a Knight of the Bath. Nothing in the surviving correspondence shows how the offer was renewed or rephrased, but there is a very strong likelihood that the King, on hearing of Sir Joseph's refusal, took the matter in hand himself – they were after all in frequent contact over the sheep and the botanic gardens* – and there is the certainty that on 29 June 1795 the Registrar of the Order wrote to Banks saying that His Majesty had signified his intention of investing him with the Insignia of the Order of the Bath and directed him to attend at St James's Palace to receive them on 1 July.

This was often done at St James's before the Drawing Room, and although it lacked the Gothic splendour of the subsequent installation at Westminster Abbey, with bells pealing and almost the whole Order present, each knight attended by three esquires and all of them in their mantles, with Bath king of arms, Scarlet Rod, and a variety of pursuivants, and their friends and families watching from on high, it was still a very fine occasion indeed. In an age when anyone who had an order wore its ribbon and star from breakfast-time onwards, in the country or in town, there was no shamefacedness about titles, ceremonies, formality and decorations, and Sir Joseph thoroughly enjoyed his investiture, as may be seen from his letter to his Hawley cousins on page 312. He fully appreciated the King's kindness, and the distinction itself, but it did not make him feel overwhelmingly important. In his book on the King's merinos Mr Carter has a pleasant quotation to this effect: it is from J. H. Adeane's *The Girlhood of Maria Josepha Holroyd* (1896) and it runs "The Banks family came on Sunday. The Ladies, as usual, visited Mrs Newton, and Sir Joseph and Papa the Wool Fair at Lewes on Monday . . . The Red Ribbon has made no alteration in Sir Jo. in any other respect than that there is a red ribbon across his waistcoat. He sprawls upon the Grass, kisses Toads, and is just as good humoured a nondescript of an Otaheitan as ever . . ." (Papa was Lord Sheffield, Gibbon's particular friend and a noted breeder of Southdown

*And only a little later they had a long conference on a present of plants to be sent to the Empress of Russia under the care of a German gardener called Noe, another of Banks's protected waifs.

sheep: it is not quite so easy to see Gibbon and Banks as friends, yet such was the case, and Banks was a witness to his will.)

For a young woman who had known Sir Jo since she was a little girl no doubt Banks *was* still a nondescript Otaheitan, but this was not necessarily the case with the Fellows of the Royal Society. Although the President assumed no new airs or graces he already possessed a massive dignity, and as he grew bulkier and more beetle-browed with advancing age, the addition of that broad red ribbon and the star, worn quite naturally, made him a more impressive figure still as he sat there in the high-backed Gothic chair, particularly to the younger Fellows. And most of the Fellows were junior to Banks by now. He had already lost many of his friends – older men of course like William Aiton of Kew, whose pall he had helped to bear not long since and whose place he had begged for Aiton's son, but also contemporaries like Lord Mulgrave, who had married the exquisite Miss Chomley when she was seventeen and he was forty-three – they were very much attached, but a year later she died in childbirth and he did not live long after. The ribbon should not perhaps have had much influence on a gathering of philosophers, but it did after all mark its wearer as one of a very small band: knighthoods were often given to mayors and rich tradesmen and for some time now there had been medical baronets, but even counting the Thistle and the recent order of St Patrick, there were not a hundred men in the two kingdoms who could sport a ribbon. It increased Sir Joseph's already considerable authority, and although at that time and later there was no lack of ambitious Fellows of greater family by far and sometimes of comparable ability – Lord Rosse, the Duke of Sussex, the Marquess of Northampton, for example – not one ever presumed to offer himself as an alternative candidate for the presidency at the annual elections.

The caricaturists, who had never quite abandoned Sir Joseph, were quick to seize upon this event, and as early as 4 July 1795 Gillray produced a Banks with wings, ribbon and star, his lower half dwindling into a sort of worm; he is straining up from a mudbank by the sea towards a sun with a crown upon it, and the legend reads: *The Great South Sea Caterpillar, transform'd into a Bath Butterfly – taken from the Philosophical Transactions for 1795 – This Insect first crawled into notice from among the Weeds and Mud of the South Sea; being afterwards placed in a Warm Situation by the Royal Society, was changed by the heat of the Sun into its present form – it is notic'd & Valued Solely on account of the beautiful Red which encircles its Body, & the Shining Spot on its Breast; a Distinction which never fails to render Caterpillars valuable.*

It is not likely that this would have vexed Sir Joseph much, but if it did he had plenty of other things to take his mind off it. For one, Miss Herschel discovered another comet of her own (she found eight altogether) and he had her communication, which was addressed to him, inserted in the Philosophical Transactions, which caused something of a sensation. Then there was the question of Labillardière's collections: it will be remembered that Captain de La Pérouse set out for the South Seas in 1785 with two ships, and that neither he nor any of his people ever came back; another expedition under Admiral d'Entrecasteaux was sent to look for him in 1791, and J.-J. de Labillardière, a friend of Banks's, went with it as naturalist. D'Entrecasteaux searched for two years and more, but although he discovered a number of islands, while Labillardière and his colleagues made splendid natural history collections, he did not find La Pérouse; nor did he ever see France again, for as he was approaching Java he died of scurvy. On 6 April 1794 Labillardière wrote to Banks from Samarang, telling him first of the scientific side of the voyage, then of the political: news of the later developments of the Revolution (though not of the war between England and Holland) had reached the Dutch East Indies before them and this produced grave conflict in both ships. There is no point in saying more than that Labillardière, like Broussonet and so many other scientific men, then favoured the Republic, because the Royal Navy captured all the Frenchmen, Royalist, Girondin or Jacobin, and their vessels: Labillardière's collections were brought back to England. The senior surviving French officer said that as he had entered a harbour in the Dutch East Indies without knowing about the war, they were not lawful prize. The British government agreed and placed them at the disposition of the Comte de Provence, the *de jure* King Louis XVIII of France; he was then in Russian Courland, and he told his ambassador in London to give them to the Queen of England as a present.

It was Banks of course who was asked to look at the collections. He found the "vast Herbarium", amounting to some ten thousand specimens a "testimony of an industry all but indefatigable in the Botanists who were employed, the chief of whom I am sorry to say was the principle fomentor of the Mutiny which took place in the ships built upon the strongest Jacobin Principles". (It is not clear whether Banks had received Labillardière's letter from Java by the time he wrote this: they were certainly friends somewhat later.) There were also about 1200 birds as well as many dried lizards, serpents, fishes and insects; and Banks thought that if Her Majesty did not "chuse to encumber herself with the stuffed animals" they would make a capital addition to the British Museum, of which he was so active a trustee.

Her Majesty agreed entirely: she would be happy to have a collection of one of each kind of plant, but nothing else – no serpents or insects at all – and was most grateful to Sir Joseph for his offer of choosing them. And Louis XVIII, by his representative, said that in that case all the other objects were to be a present to Banks, a token of the esteem in which he was held by the French refugees. But then another face of things was seen. The government of the Republic, having approached the British government in vain, wrote directly to Banks, representing to him that d'Entrecasteaux's expedition had not been the personal concern of Louis XVI like that of La Pérouse but had been fitted out and dispatched by the National Assembly, and that therefore the collections belonged to France as a whole.

If Banks agreed, and if his agreement was to have any effect, he would in the first place have to give up his own share of the spoil, then persuade the Queen to give up hers and finally convince the ministry that this was the right course to take. All these things he did, and on 10 August 1796 he wrote to Jussieu[5]

Sir,

The pleasure I received on seeing your hand writing after so long an interval of interruption, was, I assure you, very sincere. Heaven send that the agitations which have so long distressed your Country have at last finally subsided! the love of science which manifests itself with so much brilliancy among you is a good omen; may every thing good beside follow in due course, and rapid succession is my sincere wish.

I have infinite pleasure in telling you that our Government granted without, I believe, a moment's hesitation, a Passport to M. Baudin,* and that they have at last, after some months solicitation, acceded to my wishes respecting M. de Billardière's Collection. I hope within a few days to deliver to M. Charretie† the whole that I was able to gather together, I believe all that came to England; a monument to his indefatigable industry that does him immortal honour.

I confess I wish much to learn from his specimens some of those discoveries in the natural order of plants which he must have made, but it seemed to my feelings dishonorable to avail myself even of the opportunity I had of examining them: I of course did not look them over; all will be returned to him. I shall not retain a leaf, a flower, or a Botanical idea of his Collection, for I have not possessed myself of any thing at all of his, that fortune committed to my custody.

[He goes on to say that wartime in England, though less troubled than in

* Who wished to go on a scientific expedition to the West Indies.

† The French representative in England, chiefly concerned with the exchange of prisoners.

France, is not favourable to science: he sends the only recent book that might interest Jussieu, a botanical work published by the East India Company.]

Adieu, my dear Sir, think kindly of me; whatever the fortune of War may be, Science and those who possess the liberal views of it which you have ever done will be the nearest to the heart of one who is with distinguished consideration and unvaried esteem

Your most hble Servant,
J. Banks

In remaining on perfectly friendly and indeed affectionate terms with French men of science during the war Banks was following a tradition at least as old as the Royal Society itself, and Sir Gavin de Beer in his paper on the subject (*Notes and Records of the Royal Society of London* vol. 9) not only cites the correspondence between Sloane and Tournefort for example but names the twenty Frenchmen, including Voltaire, Montesquieu and Cuvier, who were elected to the Royal Society in wartime and the seventeen Britons, including Sloane, Banks and Maskelyne, who had the corresponding honours of the *Académie des Sciences* or its successor the First Class of the *Institut National*. He also gives instances of other botanical captures being returned, though never on such a heroic scale as this. Yet in Banks's case it was much more than the continuation of a pleasant, civilized custom: he for one understood that this was a war of a new kind, and as he said, writing to Lord Greville about the French government's request, ". . . the very application virtually offers during the horrors of a war unprecedented in the mutual implacability of the parties engaged, an unconditional armistice to science; surely, my Lord, such an offer should not be neglected; the ready acceptance of it may be the signal of the return of the dawnings of goodwill towards men and produce consequences, in the present position of Europe, valuable beyond appreciation to all the nations who inhabit it."[6]

In his letter to Jussieu Banks had spoken of the comparative calm in England. This was not to last. There had been two bad harvests and wheat, which in the last eighty-four years had only once exceeded fifty-five shillings a quarter, now rose to seventy-five. Other prices rose, and so did taxes; Pitt, the war, and even the King became unpopular, and as early as the state opening of parliament in the autumn of 1795 the windows of the royal coach were broken, the mob shouting "No Pitt – no war – no famine". In 1796 things grew worse. The government put this down to seditious republican notions, changed the law of treason, gagged the press and forbade unauthorized public meetings and political debates or lectures; there was some republican opinion, to be sure, and it is possible that the Corresponding Societies represented a certain danger, but general poverty and the rising price of bread certainly had a great deal more to do with the widespread and very real discontent. In Lincolnshire, for example, an awkwardly-phrased and misunderstood notice about service in the militia brought the country people out in a series of riots.

In spite of the efforts of various companies and private individuals, including three generations of Bankses, a great deal of fenland remained undrained and it was inhabited by a particularly fierce and independent race, the Slodgers, who lived by wild-fowling, fishing, cutting reeds, raising geese and digging turf. Many however had recently been displaced by reclamation, and many of their dry-land cousins had been reduced from the status of more or less self-sufficient peasants with considerable rights over the common-land to that of more or less casual labourers by the perhaps necessary but certainly very harsh enclosures, more and more frequent as the eighteenth century wore on. Here, therefore, there were particular causes for discontent, and the county called for an intelligent handling that it did not receive.

There had already been much confusion about drawing up the lists of men who might be called upon to serve in the militia, and the country people suspected bad faith on the part of the government – bad faith and perhaps something like an attempt at imposing general conscription, with the militiamen compelled to serve overseas: and now came this ambiguous notice.

The business was the responsibility of the Lord Lieutenant, the deputy-lieutenants and the magistrates; and apart from Thomas Coltman and Sir Joseph none of them behaved creditably when the rioting broke out. It began at Caister in Norfolk and quickly spread to Lincolnshire: early in November a huge crowd gathered in Horncastle, just to the north of Revesby, where the militiamen were to be chosen by lot from among those liable to serve. The people marched about shouting "God bless the King: no Pitt: no militia: oh the justices," and their attitude was so threatening that the magistrates decided that it would be impossible to hold the meeting. Two days later the same thing happened at Alford, but here things took an uglier turn: the demonstration swelled into a riot; people, including constables and a magistrate, were beaten and robbed, and the leaders of the crowd led excited bands about the countryside, demanding money.

The Lord Lieutenant, who was the fifth Duke of Ancaster, the grandson of the first Joseph Banks's friend, seemed quite incapable of dealing with the state of affairs and both Banks and Coltman wrote directly to the Under-Secretary of State, Banks saying that the military should be sent at once – the situation was potentially very dangerous.[7] The Under-Secretary agreed, thanked Sir Joseph for his exertions and told him that a regiment of cavalry had been ordered to march from Lincoln. Banks and Coltman, both of them large landowners with a great many tenants and a great deal of local information, together decided that immediate action was called for; apart from anything else the county was exceptionally well provided with firearms, so many of the fenmen having fowling-pieces and even punt-guns. Almost as soon as the troops reached Horncastle and Spilsby, therefore, they were called out, and under Coltman's direction they seized four prisoners: this was deliberately done on a Saturday night, so that the country people, having Sunday to reflect, might not attempt a rescue.

On Monday, market day at Spilsby and the day the magistrates sat, Banks and Coltman set out from Revesby, with an equally deliberate lack of weapons and attendants. Although the fenmen had been heard firing their guns before dawn and although there were persistent rumours of violence it was their intention "to carry on the business exactly as the customary justice meeting held in Spilsby on a Monday is conducted and unless disturbed by a mob, to show no particular anxiety on the occasion".

In the event this proved to have been the right decision. After an unhurried examination of all the prisoners, one, whose master gave him an excellent character and who was thought to be a mere fool, was lectured and discharged in floods of tears; the others were committed for trial and sent to Lincoln, surrounded by a strong cavalry escort with drawn swords. They set out "at a quick pace from the midst of a crowd who did not express a single murmur, or indeed anything but a quiet and astonished anxiety".

Banks and his intelligent colleagues (for he and Coltman had now been joined by Lord Gwydyr, another local landowner) had two great aims – first, to prevent the many foolish and the few wicked rioters from committing the irreparable and involving the county in a long-lasting sequence of outrage and repression, and then to have the official blunders about the militia put right in the most public way, thus calming the people's minds.

For the next few days they were very active, and although there were persistent rumours of a rising in the Fens and another in Lincoln itself, while information was hard to come by – when over two hundred crimes carried the death penalty men were unwilling to give names, and even one of the beaten constables could not remember who had attacked him – they took two of the three most dangerous leaders. By now the more stolid country gentlemen had recovered from their amazement and they offered to form a yeomanry or to serve as special constables, and now at last the Duke of Ancaster called a general meeting.

Banks however did not attend. The fit of gout that had been threatening now pinned him to his bed and in any case the crisis was over: besides, he had no opinion of the Lord Lieutenant.

Nor, it seems, had the ministry. On 19 November the Duke of Portland, Home Secretary, conveyed the government's thanks to Banks, with a marked lack of reference to the Lord Lieutenant. Sir Joseph was also desired to pass the thanks on to Mr Coltman. In his reply Banks offered his and Lord Gwydyr's services in the supplemental militia. Before the riots had grown violent, and when the people had confined themselves to tearing up the constable's lists and shouting about Pitt, they had said "that they had rather lose their lives than enter the new militia but that if the gentlemen would stand forward they would stand true to their King and country", and although Banks disliked the mob he had a strong fellow feeling for most of the countrymen who made it up: it seemed to him that their point was perfectly sound. His offer, with slight modifications, was accepted, and a few months later Sir Joseph was commissioned as lieutenant-colonel of the Lindsey Battalion, which was to include ten captains, ten lieutenants and ten ensigns.

Then, some time later, when the men came up for trial at the assizes and the most obviously guilty of them, a man with a long record of robbery, was sentenced to death, Banks used his influence to have Botany Bay substituted for the gallows.

All these last years since the sailing of the First Fleet in 1787 Australia had never been far from his mind: it was generally recognized that he had a discoverer's right to New South Wales and he certainly felt that he had a duty to the country. An isolated memorandum in his own hand,[8] dated February 1789, runs "I could not take office and do my duty to the colony. My successor would naturally oppose my wishes. I prefer, therefore, to be friendly with both sides." And in 1797, writing to Philip King (who had sent him so many botanical specimens, particularly from Norfolk Island) and telling him that membership of the Privy Council[9] had been added to the presidency of the Royal Society and his other responsibilities, he said that he hoped the position would enable him to be of service to his "favorite Colony", so neglected because of the war.

Certainly the infant community had need of all the support it could come by in England. It had started very badly indeed, with a large number of more or less criminal and largely urban people set down on a shore that was in no way whatsoever prepared to receive them, where the thin soil was by no means as fertile as Banks and Cook had supposed, and where even skilled farmers would have found it hard to overcome the droughts, floods, and invasions of caterpillars in countless millions. If they had not brought supplies with them and if they had not been able to send to Batavia and the Cape for more they must have died of famine in the first years, and as it was they had an exceedingly hard time of it, particularly when some of the supply ships were lost. Fortunately they had an admirable chief in Captain Arthur Phillip, RN, a fifty-year-old post-captain who had seen a great deal of service. It seemed natural in England that this remote possession, which might be assimilated to an island, should be run by a sailor, and Phillip was the first of a series of naval governors. He displayed all the qualities of resourcefulness, leadership and initiative usually associated with the Royal Navy, and although he shared the sea-officers' preoccupation with sodomy, putting it on a level with murder ("For either of these crimes I would wish to confine the criminal till an opportunity offered of delivering him as a prisoner to the natives of New Zealand, and let them eat him. The dread of this will operate much stronger than the fear of death."[10]) he was otherwise as kindly and humane as a man in charge of such a community could well be, and when food ran so low that starvation was not far away he followed the naval tradition of sharing the common lot, "wishing that if a convict complained he might see that want was not unfelt even at Government House".

Phillip, like all the subsequent naval governors, was a friend of Banks's, and as early as 1789 he sent him back fourteen kangaroo skins, a burrowing bird, a dingo, some black-lead, and a bottle of what may have been eucalyptus oil. He was also something of a gardener, and on the way out he took advantage of putting in at the Cape of Good Hope to take some vine cuttings. The parent plants had been used to the seasons of the southern hemisphere for generations and their offspring did well, unlike the northern seeds the ship had brought out or even the Cape corn, and they were a comfort to him in the midst of so many agricultural failures.

Yet Phillip had more to contend with than drought, pests, inverted seasons, the relative sterility of the soil, the ignorance and often the ill will of those who were to cultivate it, and his own indifferent health: he also had an uncommonly disagreeable set of soldiers. It is not surprising to find a want of harmony between the army and the navy: it occurs in our day and it was even more usual then, when the foremast jacks, masters of a hundred skills, naturally despised the private soldiers, whose talents were confined to neatness in drill and uniform, while the officers of the two services differed very widely in training, outlook and tradition. But what is surprising in this case is that the soldiers in question were Marines, a corps thoroughly accustomed to naval ways. Perhaps there was something in the air of New South Wales that made them perverse, sullen, litigious and unhelpful, for they had scarcely landed before they refused to help the Governor in even a very slight supervision of the convicts' labour; they also thought it a hardship to sit, unpaid, as members of the criminal court or to attend to the building of barracks for their own men, saying that as they saw it they had been sent out to do garrison duty and no more.[11] But if the captains and lieutenants were disobliging, the major-commandant and lieutenant-governor, Robert Ross, was downright impossible: he fell out with his own officers to such an extent that by February 1790, of the sixteen capable of duty no fewer than five were under arrest and would remain so until a general court martial could be assembled, while two more had been suspended. He was scarcely on speaking terms with the Governor and most of their intercourse was carried on by stiff formal letters. Presently Phillip dealt with the situation by sending Ross to command at Norfolk Island, a small dependency about 800 miles away in the Pacific, very difficult to land upon and very difficult to leave.

Under such officers as Ross and his subordinates the men could scarcely be expected to be exemplary, and indeed quite early in proceedings several of them were taken up for robbing the storehouses over a long period, and one of them having turned King's evidence the other six were hanged.

It was clear from Governor Phillip's early dispatches that the settlement could not possibly thrive with this kind of conflict going on, and in June 1789 the War Office set about raising a body of about three hundred men to be called the New South Wales Corps and to serve in the colony. The plan may have been sound enough, but the execution was lamentable, and if poor Phillip thought the new soldiers were going to be an improvement on the old Marines he was mistaken. The command of the corps was given to a Major Grose, and the first thing he did on going aboard HMS *Gorgon*, which was to carry him out, was to complain of his accommodation and then quarrel with her captain, William Harvey. He had enough influence to have Harvey superseded, but not enough to escape a very severe reprimand from the War Office for another thick-headed piece of conduct: he and his captains had three guineas for every man they could induce to enlist, and one of his recruits was a private soldier of the 12th Regiment who had been sentenced to death for a "heinous crime" but who had been reprieved on condition of serving in New South Wales. Grose gave this man leave to go ashore; he appeared at the 12th Regiment's parade, charmed to put a mock on his former officers. This was not to the taste of the general commanding and Grose was far more roughly handled for his want of military tact than ever he was for his very questionable dealings with land grants and rum in the colony.

The incident is worth mentioning only because it shows the wonderfully unpromising sort of colleagues Governor Phillip had to work with, and that at a time when his health was growing even worse. He asked for leave once in 1790 and twice in 1791 and he sailed for home at the end of 1792, leaving the colony in charge of Major Grose, who, with his enterprising factotum Lieutenant John Macarthur and most of the other officers of the corps, at once set about making their employment far more profitable than it would have been anywhere else.

This was possible because in spite of the difficulties he had to contend with, Governor Phillip had been remarkably successful. When his successor, Captain John Hunter RN, reached Sydney in October 1795 he found a viable colony, with farming and stock-raising moderately prosperous and promise for the future. The change was particularly impressive for him because he had known the country from the earliest days, having had the command of HMS *Sirius* when she first came out, staying in her until she was wrecked on the rocks of Norfolk Island in March 1790, carrying Major Ross to his new domain.

One of the first letters[12] that Governor Hunter wrote from Sydney was to Sir Joseph Banks: it ran in part

> To you, Sir, who have interested yourself so much in favour of this colony, it must be a pleasure to be told by a person who was concerned in its first establishment and whose opinions formed at that time of its success were not very sanguine, that many of the opinions formed in the early part of our time here were much too hastily fixed; we now see and know from pleasing experience that the Judgments of many individuals were too precipitately given and upon too limited an examination of the country. We now also know that there are extensive tracts of rich and fertile soil.

Somewhat later he had other pieces of good news. In the early days five cows and two bulls had escaped from the meagre band of those who had survived the voyage in the First Fleet: they were thought to have perished, but now, seven years later, a wandering convict said he had seen cattle far up the Hawkesbury river. Hunter rode out with a party and on the second day they not only heard mooing but on reaching the top of a hill they looked down "upon a herd of forty or more feeding in a beautiful meadow in the valley". The ruling bull came for them with such furious pertinacity that they were obliged to shoot him; but this did at least enable Hunter to make sure that the cattle were not native but of the Cape breed that he himself had brought out in the *Sirius*. He put the whole area out of bounds, making it a felony to harm the animals; and for many years Cowpastures, as it was called, remained inviolate. Another very welcome letter dated 20 August 1796 was brought by Captain Paterson, the most respectable member of the New South Wales Corps, a traveller in South Africa, a friend of Banks's and a candidate for the Royal Society (he was elected in 1798), and this one spoke of a wheat harvest of forty thousand bushels, with the maize also yielding well.

It is true that Hunter changed his opinion as a closer view showed him "a mere sink of every species of infamy . . . The state of profligacy is far, very far beyond my powers of description" (the treatment of the women convicts was unspeakably bad) and as he began to grapple with the New South Wales Corps. In an attempt at mollifying the soldiers Governor Phillip had most unfortunately granted them the privilege of buying rum at the cost price of four or five shillings a gallon: after his departure and during Grose's time as lieutenant-governor, the privilege had developed, under Macarthur's management, into a virtual monopoly not only of rum but of almost all imported goods; but at this stage rum was particularly significant, because it was the one thing the convicts would work for. They were comparatively indifferent to punishment and, since they could hardly spend it, to money; and as farm labourers, working for nothing, they were useless without perpetual supervision. The officers, particularly Macarthur, had large land grants, and although the thin sandstone soils were of little use without manure, scarcely yielding thirteen bushels an acre even in their first vigour, the alluvial soils gave twice as much and on the Hawkesbury sometimes even thirty-five bushels. The officers' farms, on carefully selected soil, and with plenty of willing, rum-paid labour, produced a great deal of wheat; and their owners had the comfort of knowing that if the colony had a surplus the soldiers' harvest would always be bought at the high government price whatever happened to the civilians, because Macarthur was the official purchaser.[13] Later the officers' cartel, buying up whole shiploads of goods at their own price and selling them to the settlers at an advance of five hundred or even a thousand per cent, grew to be an even more serious problem: but Hunter was unable to break their hold.

At first however the news travelling home was so cheerful that Banks replied with hearty congratulations.[14] He wished he could go out himself, he said, and settle on the banks of the Hawkesbury: "I see the future prospect of empires and dominions which cannot be disappointed. Who knows but that England may revive in New South Wales when it has sunk in Europe?" As for home news, "Pit rules, Fox grumbles, the French beat all they attack, and the King of Prussia threatens all who assist the Emperor . . . I am no politician." Yet even to one who was no politician the general picture was clear enough. Prussia and Spain had been knocked out of the war in 1795; Spain had joined France in 1796; and now in this year of 1797 the treaties of Leoben and then Campo Formio made Austria retire, leaving England quite alone, without a single ally.

The French did indeed beat everyone they attacked by land: but at sea it was quite another matter. Admiral Sir John Jervis and his fifth in command, Commodore Nelson, with fifteen line-of-battle ships, dealt with the Spanish fleet of twenty-five off Cape St Vincent, taking four of them and so shattering the rest that they were useless for a great while after. Yet the much more formidable French and Dutch fleets were still a very grave menace, for if they could combine an invasion of England might easily follow. And now in May 1797 the great naval mutiny broke out at Spithead, followed by another in July at the Nore – astonishing mutinies, provoked by intolerably bad pay, treatment, food and conditions, but accompanied, particularly at Spithead, by unwavering loyalty to the Crown and to respected commanders, the royal salute being fired on the King's birthday and no hard usage of even the most tyrannical officers. But mutinies for all that, and a fleet that would not leave harbour. The outlook can rarely have been blacker for England, and Lord Malmesbury, the ministry's confidential envoy, who was at Lille, trying for a second time to negotiate a peace treaty with France, had almost no room for manoeuvre at all.

But then within weeks of the seamen's grievances being at least in part removed, the Navy was itself again, and Duncan fought the stubborn, bloody battle of Camperdown off the coast of Holland, his sixteen ships of the line taking no less than nine of the enemy's fifteen as well as two of his frigates, thus doing away with the Dutch threat.

Some months later Bonaparte sailed from Toulon for his Egyptian campaign accompanied by a large number of savants, his transports escorted by thirteen line-of-battle ships, including *l'Orient*, a three-decker carrying 120 guns, and three eighty-gun two-deckers. He took Malta on his way to Alexandria, landed his troops in Africa, defeated the Mamelukes and marched on Cairo, leaving his ships in the bay of Aboukir. Here Nelson, with thirteen seventy-fours and a fifty-gun ship, came up with them on 1 August 1798: one of the seventy-fours ran aground, but with the fifty-gun ship taking her place in the line for this occasion, he so battered the French that only two escaped being taken, burnt or otherwise destroyed.

Bonaparte was cut off from home; the European nations rejoiced; and since France was now being abominably misgoverned by the Directoire they plucked up heart and formed the Second Coalition: Austria, Russia, England, Turkey, Portugal, Naples and the Papal States.

This may have relieved Sir Joseph's mind, though he had little opinion of foreigners unless they were scientists, but it did not make him any the less busy. The Privy Council was then a much smaller and much more active body: Banks served on the Coin Committee, which involved him in an immense correspondence with his old friend Charles Jenkinson, Master of the Mint and an authority on coinage, now no longer Lord Hawkesbury but Earl of Liverpool, and with his equally old friend Matthew Boulton, FRS, the engineer and senior partner of the great firm of Boulton and Watt. He had in fact corresponded with both on the subject of copper coinage long before this, but now his letters were much more frequent and they were official; they came not only from the President of the Royal Society but from the Right Honourable President, and when they were written so that they might be shown to some other person, such as a dealer who hoped to corner copper-ore or an official who hated Birmingham and all its ways, they therefore had an even greater weight. Joseph Banks had a remarkably good head for business, and these three between them made a resounding success of the new copper coinage in spite of the sullen obstruction of the old Mint inspectors, the difficulties caused by the fluctuating price of copper and the sudden strange interventions of the Treasury.

Being a Privy Councillor also entailed other duties, hardly to be expected. For example one day Sir Stephen Cottrell, the Clerk to the Council, wrote to ask Banks to receive the Prince of Württemberg and his minister of state, Count von Zeppelin. The idea was that the Prince, who was on his way to London to meet his future bride, Princess Charlotte Augusta, should pause at Spring Grove until the King's carriages came to carry him to St James's (the Prince's taste for a morning collation was chicken and ham and a bottle of hock). Cottrell had met His Highness and begged Sir Joseph to tell Lady Banks that he appeared affable, polite and pleasing.

During this same busy but less anxious time, that is to say in 1798, Banks very nearly persuaded Mungo Park to make an expedition to the inland parts of New South Wales, as an explorer and as a naturalist. Park was wonderfully gifted in both respects: James Dickson the botanist had introduced him to Banks in 1791 and Banks induced the East India Company to appoint him surgeon's mate in the *Worcester*, an Indiaman bound for Bencoolen in Sumatra, where he collected eight new fishes and a large variety of plants. Then in 1795 Banks and his associates in the African Association had sent him to discover the Niger, which he did, the journey being described in his classic *Travels in the Interior of Africa*.

At first Park was enchanted with the idea of New South Wales – indeed, it was he who first raised it – but then a strange reluctance came over him, and ten days before the ship was to sail he found that the salary was inadequate. Banks persuaded the Secretary of State to raise it from ten shillings a day to twelve and sixpence, which was roughly three times what Park would have had as the surgeon of a man-of-war; but still he would not go, and now it appeared that there was a Miss Anderson in the case. Yet Banks was never a man to bear ill will, and Mungo Park's last and most famous journey in 1805 was undertaken with his blessing and active help. In any event Sir Joseph's temporary impatience with Park was quite overcome by his far greater indignation at the treatment of Dolomieu.

Déodat de Gratet de Dolomieu, the geologist after whom dolomite is named, was one of the scientists who went to Egypt with Bonaparte. He fell sick and the ship that was carrying him back to France was obliged to put into Taranto, where the Neapolitans seized him. He had been a knight of Malta and it was said that he was involved in the tame surrender of the island to the French; it is unlikely that anyone believed in the charge but there was a sombre history of Italian revenge in the background and Dolomieu was kept in a filthy dungeon, lying upon straw, in conditions that might quite soon be his death.

As soon as Banks heard the news he did everything possible to have him released. The most obvious line of approach was through the Hamiltons. Sir William, who had a great deal of influence with King Ferdinand, was one of Banks's closest friends, so close that he not only listened without resentment to Banks's advice that he should marry Emma Lyon but followed it; and Lady Hamilton had even more influence with the Queen. Somewhat earlier Emma Hamilton had written to Banks[15] "I assure you Sir William loves you dearly, & as felt happy on hearing of any addition to your honner or comfort: . . . indeed I do not consider you as one of his common *friends*, and therefore love & esteem you more then you think I do . . ." Furthermore this was a time when the English were more popular in Naples than they had ever been before: the victory of the Nile had settled the King on his throne, and Nelson, who was there refitting some of his ships, was made Duke of Brontë with an immense estate on the lower slopes of Etna, while the King also gave him the famous diamond sword his father the King of Spain had left him to defend his kingdom. Banks therefore sent off his letters[16] with a fair amount of confidence: that to Sir William ended ". . . there is nothing I have ever ask'd of you in which I have taken a tenth part of the interest I now feel in the hopes of Dolomieu's being by your means restored to the service of science, and his Egyptian Observations being rescued from the Oblivion of an untimely grave . . ." while in the one to Lady Hamilton he said that although he had always been sure of her kindness he had never had to put her friendship to the test: "Now however a business has occurred which cannot, I am convinced, be effected unless both your influences are united in soliciting it. If it is possible to engage the Gallant Admiral to join the Trio, which is in the power of no one but yourself, what may I not hope in every thing from the warmth of your friendship? if the debilitating climate you have lately inhabited has not damp'd its ardor. What I wish for is the liberation of Dolomieu . . ."

The Hamiltons and perhaps Nelson did their best; and many, many letters from them and others passed to and fro. At one time seven of the most famous French scientists, including Jussieu, Laplace, Bougainville and Lacépède wrote to Banks in the name of the *Institut* and really of the learned world as a whole, adding the full weight of their reputation to his. Yet all these efforts were in vain. It is true that Banks's intervention caused the Neapolitans to treat Dolomieu a little less barbarously, to move him from his dungeon and to give him edible food, but it took the hammer-blows of Marengo and then Hohenlinden to bring him out of his prison. These two battles destroyed the Second Coalition; and in their peace treaty with Naples in March 1801 the French insisted upon a special clause providing for the release of Dolomieu, who, on reaching Paris, wrote a very graceful letter of thanks to London.

The collapse of the Second Coalition meant that England was alone again; more than alone, indeed, since the northern powers, offended by the British insistence on the right of search, formed the menacing "armed neutrality". Once more the outlook seemed very black, but with Abercromby's defeat of the French in Egypt and Nelson's victory at Copenhagen a better face of things was seen: by the later part of 1801 the confidential negotiators had worked out a reasonable peace treaty and it was signed at Amiens in March 1802.

But well before the signature, and when the countries were still at war, the *Institut* made Banks a member: it was a rarer distinction than being a Fellow of the Royal Society, since membership of the academies of which the *Institut* was formed was limited in number whereas that of the Society was not, and his letter[17] of thanks began

> Citizens,
>
> Be pleased to offer to the *Institut* my warmest thanks for the honour they have done me in conferring upon me the title of Associate of this learned and distinguished Body.
>
> Assure at the same time my respectable brothers that I consider this mark of their esteem as the highest and most enviable literary distinction which I could possibly attain. To be the first elected to be an Associate of the first Literary Society in the world surpassed my most ambitious hope, and I cannot be too grateful towards a Society which has conferred upon me this honour, and towards a nation of which it is the literary representative.

When it was published in the English papers this and some other passages excited the indignation of certain readers who thoroughly loathed all Frenchmen, learned or not; and letters appeared abusing Sir Joseph: one was by a man who signed himself Misogallus and who reprinted his words in a pamphlet. "Now Sir," said Misogallus, "notwithstanding my disgust at this load of filthy adulation I should trouble you with some calm remarks upon it." One of the calm remarks was to the effect that Banks's letter was "replete with statements which are a compound of servility, disloyalty and falsehood, sentiments which ought never to be conceived by an English heart, never written by an English hand and least of all by yours, distinguished as you are by repeated (out of respect to His Majesty I will not say unmerited) marks of royal favour". Lord Brougham, who had better means of knowing than most, says that the letter was afterwards acknowledged to have proceeded from the Bishop of St Asaph, Dr Horsley, the gentleman who was so very much against Banks in 1782 and who was so very much against the Peace of Amiens now. Yet even if that was true, and if Banks knew it to be true, it is improbable that he would have felt any lasting rancour; his was a remarkably forgiving nature, and in any case this was a happy time for him. Although he knew that the peace was only what he called "an armed truce", at least it did mean a halt in the bloodshed. Then, although his expressions of thanks do not have to be taken quite literally, being directed at a nation given to hyperbole, membership of the *Institut* did mean a good deal to him: and in the third place, between his increasingly frequent fits of gout and his many duties, he had succeeded in setting on foot an expedition for the thorough exploration of the coasts not only of New South Wales but of the continent as a whole, a matter very dear to his heart. The command of the *Investigator*, a sloop of 334 tons, was given to Matthew Flinders, the naval son of a Lincolnshire surgeon; as a senior midshipman and a lieutenant he had already charted considerable stretches of the eastern shores of what he (perhaps the first to do so) called Australia, as well as the Furneaux Islands and Tasmania. Captain Flinders was a navigator, explorer and hydrographer in Cook's own class, and Banks had the singular good fortune of being able to match him in the *Investigator*'s naturalist, Robert Brown. He had known the young man – Brown was twenty-seven – only since about 1798, but in those few years he and his friends had seen that he possessed quite remarkable powers. Brown was a Scotsman and his passionate love of botany had caused him to move from the university of Aberdeen to that of Edinburgh, where he studied under Banks's botanical friend Dr John Walker, the professor of natural history; like so many of his predecessors and contemporaries Brown combined botany and medicine, and when Sir Joseph's offer came he was assistant-surgeon to a regiment of Scots fencibles serving in Ulster. He accepted at once. For countless reasons – and the gout alone would have been sufficient – Banks could not possibly sail in the *Investigator*; as far as he was concerned exploration and the collecting of birds, beasts and flowers on a heroic scale had to be carried out vicariously; but at least he had picked upon a man who was to prove the country's most outstanding botanist and what with this and the prospect of peace the new century was full of promise.

Chapter 11

TROUBLE IN SYDNEY AND ICELAND: DECLINING HEALTH: THE END

TO SOME OBSERVERS it might have appeared that a new century could promise little to a man of Banks's age, weight and constitution. He was already sixty by the Peace of Amiens, at a time when the average expectation of life for men was little more than half of that figure; he weighed sixteen and even seventeen stone; and the gout which first attacked him in 1787 was growing steadily worse – as early as 1798 it had confined him for two months on end. Yet although he suffered much he did not see the future in this dismal light at all; after each spell in bed he arose with fresh zeal, taking the keenest interest in his remarkably active, varied life. He was deeply concerned with many things quite apart from the Royal Society and the Privy Council, and at this point in time there were two or three subjects that particularly engaged his mind, giving him very great satisfaction. One was of course the *Investigator*, which carried not only Flinders and Brown but also Ferdinand Bauer, next to his elder brother the best botanical draughtsman of his time; William Westall, the excellent topographical painter; an experienced gardener from Kew, Peter Good; and an astronomer engaged by the Board of Longitude.

The voyage began in July 1801, and although the astronomer fell ill and left the ship at the Cape, Flinders wrote to say that he and his naval brother would do their best to fill his place, otherwise the delay would be excessive. Flinders' next letter, dated from Port Jackson, New South Wales, in May 1802, brought a box of seeds from Robert Brown, who had already seen 750 new plants during the voyage along the virtually unknown south coast of Australia, while Bauer had made 350 drawings of vegetables and 100 of animals. The *Investigator* had reached Cape Leeuwin, the south-west tip of Australia, on 6 November and had worked slowly eastward, exploring the Great Bight and the islands, often putting the happy naturalists ashore. On the way, just east of Kangaroo Island, she met *Le Géographe*, Captain Baudin, which, in company with another French vessel, was in these waters on much the same errand, protected by much the same kind of pass, granted by the government on either side to the enemy's exploring ships – their botanist, by the way, was Leschenault de La Tour, a pupil of Banks's friend Jussieu. Both the French ships came into Port Jackson separately soon after the *Investigator*, *Le Géographe* with much of her sheathing gone, desperately short of food and water and so afflicted with scurvy that only twelve of her men could stand to their duty: they were well received and presently they sailed away sound in hull and crew.

By July 1802, when Flinders set sail for his circumnavigation of the entire continent, Good and Brown had added the seeds of some 500 more species to their store; but this was little in comparison with their eventual collection. In April 1803 Banks wrote to tell Flinders of his great pleasure at the success of the first part of the survey; and indeed if the northern and western coasts yielded unknown plants and animals in anything like the same proportion as the southern, then immense wealth was to be expected.

The next subject for deep inward pleasure was the King's merino flock. In spite of the great difficulty in getting conscientious or even reasonably competent shepherds the sheep had done much better than might have been expected: it had never been intended to build up a large, profitable population but to form a breeding nucleus from which pure-bred animals might go all over the country to improve the wool, either as crosses or as true merinos. By the turn of the century this had been accomplished and merinos from the main stock, which usually numbered between two and three hundred, had travelled far and wide, 259 as royal gifts and 83 as private purchases.[1] There was keen competition for the sheep and in 1804 it was thought fairer to sell them by public auction: those put up for the first of these sales were not a handsome group, for as Banks said in the catalogue, "they were in store condition, and as high Prices are not wished for, the usual means of preparing Stock for Sale by high keeping, have not been resorted to". For all that one ram fetched no less than forty-two guineas and a ewe twenty-four; and although the King's merino venture never had the slightest commercial aspiration at any time, these results could not but be gratifying to the man who had managed it from the start.

Yet the day was not without its cloud. Eleven of the sheep were bought by Captain Macarthur, that enterprising gent from New South Wales. Banks knew who he was – indeed, at the sale he warned Macarthur that it was illegal to export sheep – but he did not choose to be acquainted with him, although Macarthur had brought a letter of introduction and some boxes of natural history specimens from a traveller he met on St Helena. It was hardly to be wondered at:

Macarthur does not seem to have been an estimable character. He was certainly a somewhat aggressive one: he fought a duel with the captain of the ship that was carrying him out to New South Wales, and he had scarcely settled there before there was a question of sending him back again to be court-martialled for a disagreement with Captain Nepean. Then he fought another duel with an officer called Foveaux; after this he quarrelled with Governor Hunter, as he did with his successor Governor King, and now he was in England to be court-martialled for having fought yet again, this time with his own commanding officer, Lieutenant-Colonel Paterson, wounding him in the shoulder. Paterson was Banks's friend, a naturalist and now a Fellow of the Royal Society, and if this conflict was not enough to make Banks look sideways at Macarthur, these words of Governor King to the Under-Secretary (also called King and also a friend of Banks's) would have done so: they are taken from a letter[2] dated 8 November 1801 and they run: "He came here in 1790 more than £500 in debt, and is now worth at least £20,000 . . . His employment during the eleven years he has been here has been that of making a large fortune, helping his brother officers to make small ones (mostly at the publick expense) and sowing discord and strife. The points I have brought home to him are such that, if properly investigated, must certainly occasion his quitting the New South Wales Corps and the Army." But in any case Banks was closely in touch, both officially and unofficially, with New South Wales, and it is hardly conceivable that he was not aware of Macarthur's activities in the colony and his reputation there long before this.

The court-martial was soon dealt with: although Macarthur had behaved in a most offensive manner, trying to prevent the Colonel from living on good social terms with Governor King, it was Paterson who, in his exasperation, gave the challenge: from the military point of view Macarthur was therefore blameless and the case was dismissed. Now Macarthur could devote his time to his really important business in London, which was to persuade a number of wealthy and influential merchants to join with him in forming a company for the production of wool, fine wool, on a very large scale in New South Wales, on land to be provided by the government. When these proposals were put forward, Banks, who worked on almost all the active committees of the Privy Council, including that for Trade and Foreign Plantations, was of course consulted. Although he knew, particularly from the Rev. Samuel Marsden, the colony's chaplain and a successful farmer, that there were some sheep of more or less Spanish origin in New South Wales, imported from the Cape, and although he had seen some fairly good wool from them, his first report was unfavourable. He had seen fleeces from those parts, he said, but their quality was only that of the second or third pile Spanish, and

> I have no reason to believe from any facts that have come to my knowledge, either when I was in that country or since, that the climate and soil of N.S. Wales is at all better for the production of fine wools than that of other temperate climates and am confident that the natural growth of the grass of the country is tall, coarse, reedy and very different from the short and sweet mountain grass of Europe upon which sheep thrive to the best advantage.
>
> I had never heard of any luxuriant pastures of the natural growth of N. South Wales at all fitted for the pasturage of sheep till I read of them in Captain McArthur's statement, nor did I ever see such in that country. I confess therefore I have my fears that the Captain has been too sanguine in his wishes to give a favourable representation of the country and that it will be found on enquiry that sheep do not prosper well there unless in lands that have been cleared and prepared for their reception with some labour and expense.

He then went on to say that the carriage of the wool would no doubt be very costly, and ended

> From what I have stated above you will easily conceive that I am not inclined to advise their Lordships to recommend any special encouragement to be given at present either by grants of land or the sending out of shepherds to a prospect which as yet is a mere theoretical speculation.

Banks's attitude has been attributed to his dislike of Macarthur and perhaps in part it was. In any event the report reflects no credit upon Sir Joseph: it is unscientific, inaccurate, and based upon inadequate observation, insufficient information and a leap from the particular to the general. Yet not long after this, when Marsden had sent him a long, detailed and trustworthy communication about sheep in Australia, and when he had had time to spare from illness (three months' confinement in 1804) and from his other activities to reflect upon the subject, he changed his mind. And when it appeared that the land was to be granted to a company rather than to an individual of dubious reputation, he advised the allotment of no less than a million acres at a hundred thousand a time; but the land was not to be given away, and government might resume it, paying proper compensation for any buildings, when it was needed for other purposes such as agriculture; though he still maintained that the credit for the improvement of sheep-breeding in the colony belonged to Captain Kent and Captain Waterhouse, the first importers from the Cape, and not to Macarthur at all, who did "not merit reward". For the last century and more, however, the general opinion has been that Banks was mistaken, that the prodigious increase of sheep-raising in the colony was due in a very large part to Macarthur's enterprise, and that the King's merino experiment, which had no great lasting effect in England, succeeded far, far beyond all expectation in Australia.

The dislike has in its turn been attributed to Macarthur's lowly origin: he was the son of the keeper of a slop-shop in Gosport. But this is contradicted by Banks's whole way of life, his general behaviour and all his immense correspondence. Banks had many faults, but snobbery was not among them. The nearest approach to anything like a snobbish remark that I have ever come across is in a letter to Governor King:[3] on the subject of Caley he says "I feel a particular obligation to you for bearing with the effusions of his ill-judging spirit. Had he been born a gentleman, he would have been shot long ago in a duel." But he goes on "As it is, I have borne with much more than ever you have done, under a conviction that he acted under strong tho' mistaken feelings of a mind honest and upright." On the evidence Banks could scarcely feel the same kind of conviction about Macarthur. Then again, despising a man for humble birth was not only against Banks's style but against that of the Royal Society, which was so very much part of his life. The Fellows might elect kings, princes and peers in the hope (almost invariably disappointed) that these great men might further the ends of natural philosophy by even greater endowments; but in their real, their scientific, life they were utterly indifferent to family. Cavendish, the Duke of Devonshire's grandson, got along perfectly well with Herschel, the former bandsman; and d'Alembert, one of the Society's most valued foreign members, began life as a baby exposed in the street.

The true, the scientific Fellows' real delight was intercourse with minds of a like nature, and they were particularly happy when the peace made contact with their friends in Paris so much easier: Banks at once sent Cuvier a duck-billed platypus, and several Fellows crossed the Channel. Blagden, indeed, went over even before the signing of the treaty, and as early as April 1802 he told Banks how well he had been received by Laplace, Bertholet, Lalande, Lagrange and Broussonet, all of them Fellows of the Royal Society, as well as by Lacépède, Cuvier and many others; how he had attended a meeting of the *Institut* and how he had let his friends in Paris know that the President of the Royal Society wished to see the Rosetta Stone restored to France. Blagden, who was fluent in the language, thoroughly enjoyed himself in France, and as he was an exceptionally good correspondent his movements can be followed almost week by week: among other events there was his presentation to the First Consul, who invited him to dinner in May.[4] He "asked me very graciously whether I found myself well in Paris; and then inquired how you were. I replied that you were much better than when I left England. 'But,' said he, 'has he no thought of coming to France?' I answered that, undoubtedly, it would be your wish to do so; but I feared that your precarious state of health, and your lameness from the gout would prevent it." Bonaparte observed that at sixty Banks could not be called old, and then, Cuvier being at hand, they went on to speak of the duck-billed platypus. Blagden was sure that if Banks came he "would be treated with the most marked attention both by the Consul himself, and by the Nation at large". He continued, "It has occurred to me . . . that perhaps the most acceptable present which could be made to the first Consul, would be a pair of live Kangaroos. . . . The park of St Cloud, where he is going to reside, would be an excellent place for a little paddock of Kangaroos, like that of the King at Richmond."

Banks, who had his own views about Bonaparte (a little later he told James Forbes, FRS, that he would glory in the condemnation of "the cursed name of Napoleon") did not respond to the hint and Blagden returned to the charge a fortnight later. "As to the Kangaroos, it is entirely my own suggestion, and let it take its fate. Had I the honour of advising his Majesty, my counsel should be, to send a pair of them, as a present to the first Consul, without delay; and I should give this advice, not from a blind admiration of any man (for I am as sharp sighted in discerning faults as my neighbour) but from the conviction, that more is often gained by trifling personal civilities, than by great sacrifices. On the same principle I should recommend the choosing him a fellow of the R.S. in the most honourable manner that could be done, as it is evident that he prides himself on being a patron and protector of the sciences."

This denial of blind admiration would have been more convincing if in an earlier letter Blagden had not made it clear that Bonaparte had conquered him entirely: "He is indeed a very remarkable man. When he speaks to a person with whom he is pleased, there is an uncommon sweetness in his countenance . . . Strong volition seems the most prominent feature of his character at which I rejoice from a conviction that his intentions are good."

Bonaparte was not made a Fellow of the Royal Society, but even so things went on swimmingly between the scientists of either nation, with the interchange of astronomical information, plans to reward discoveries in galvanism, news of Egyptian papyri and so on until

May 1803, when what Banks had called the armed truce came to an end.

Perhaps Bonaparte had not supposed that a ministry so weak as Addington's would declare war, in spite of the fact that his conduct in Europe, particularly the reoccupation of Switzerland, and his aims in India absolutely required it, or perhaps some other circumstance angered him; but in either case he took violently against the English, and disregarding every civilized precedent he ordered the internment of all between eighteen and sixty who could be found in France. To this he presently added a decree forbidding the exchange of prisoners.

Already the conflict with revolutionary France had produced a new kind of warfare; and now this, against imperial France (for Bonaparte very soon crowned himself) added still another dimension of barbarity. With the renewal of the fighting Banks lost whatever hope he may have had of a long and fruitful exchange with his French colleagues; and at the same time these new and cruel restrictions not only destroyed his pleasure in the *Investigator* expedition but also involved him in endless negotiations for the release of natural philosophers and others detained in the bleak north-eastern town of Verdun.

The worn-out *Investigator*, having with great difficulty completed her circumnavigation of the continent, put into Port Jackson again in June 1803, her crew much reduced by disease, her captain sick, and her hull so battered and decayed as to be wholly unseaworthy. Brown and Bauer (poor Peter Good died of dysentery soon after landing) decided to stay in New South Wales to carry on with their botanical and mineralogical studies, but Flinders set out for home in the store-ship *Porpoise* to deliver his charts and Brown's collections and to obtain another ship for the exploration of those parts of the coast that the *Investigator*, in her crazy state, had been unable to survey. The *Porpoise*, with Brown's garden of growing plants aboard, sailed on 10 August 1803, in company with an Indiaman and the *Cato*, a trader. During the night of 17 August the *Porpoise* and the *Cato* struck a coral reef far out in the open sea, in about 22°S and 155°E, some 800 miles from Sydney. Fortunately they struck hard and high, for by daylight the Indiaman was nowhere to be seen; and although the ships soon went to pieces most of the people and a considerable quantity of stores, papers and specimens were saved. What is more they had a sandbank near at hand, three or four feet above high water, and there they stayed while Flinders went back in a six-oared cutter for help. On 8 October he returned in a small schooner, the *Cumberland*, together with a merchantman bound for China.

Some went home by way of Canton, but Flinders was determined to get back as quickly as possible and although the 29-ton *Cumberland*, old and worn, was only just capable of the voyage he and a crew of ten took her round the north Coast of Australia and so right across the Indian Ocean to the French island of Mauritius, which he reached in December 1803. Flinders did not know that the war had begun again, but even if he had known he would still have put in to repair her pumps and to obtain food and water: he carried not only the pass issued by belligerent governments to exploring vessels belonging to the other side, but also an open letter to the governors of Mauritius and La Réunion written by Captain Baudin expressing his gratitude for his treatment in New South Wales.

It so happened that *Le Naturaliste*, with all the collections of Baudin's expedition aboard, also returned to home waters soon after the declaration of war: she was taken by HMS *Minerve* on 27 May 1803 and carried into Portsmouth. On 31 May a Mr Cole forwarded a letter from her to Banks, his covering note observing that she had two black swans aboard, two emus, and a great many pots of plants. On 1 June Banks wrote to her captain, Jacques Hamelin, telling him that he had obtained the ship's release.

Governor Decaen's reaction was quite different. He affected to believe that Flinders was a spy, and claiming that his pass applied only when he was in the *Investigator* kept him prisoner, sometimes in close confinement, until 1810, the year the island was taken by the British. At no time would Flinders have submitted to this patiently, but now that there was a war to be fought, with the likelihood of active service and the step to post-captain (no prisoner could be promoted), the frustration was even greater. He wrote letter after letter to Banks, who from the very first set all his friends to work, both in London and in Paris. It took an immensely long time, partly because letters between France and Mauritius, clarifying various legal points, had to make the voyage by way of the Cape, which was held by the English, but much more because of the ill will on the part of Decaen who obviously loathed Flinders. But at last, in March 1806, the order for his release, obtained at the particular request of Bougainville, was signed in Paris; it reached Mauritius in July 1807; and Decaen refused to obey it. This and the want of exercise during part of his imprisonment preyed on Flinders' health, which had not been good even before he left Australia. When he was at last brought home in 1810, the company of the wife he had married only a few weeks before sailing on this expedition and of a daughter he had never seen did him some good; so did his promotion;

but he only just had health and strength enough to carry him through the writing of his splendid *Voyage to Terra Australis*. Indeed he died on the very day of its publication.

Eventually, it is true, the scientific side of the *Investigator*'s voyage was eminently successful, with the publication of Flinders' account and his volume of charts, and with the return of Brown and Bauer in 1805 with renewed collections and a great many drawings; but at the time in question, that is to say the beginning of the Napoleonic war, Banks could no longer take any pleasure in it.

These were cruel years for him. In 1804 he lost his mother; she had come to be with him and her daughter in Soho Square, and there she died. She was eighty-five and her end was peaceful, yet even so it was a most painful wrench: she was an exceptional woman and she had had great influence on him when he was young.

The next year he lost the friendship of the King. It was a case in which reflection on the natural course of events and upon their inevitability could do nothing to diminish the pain, for this particular loss could not have been foreseen; it was intensely personal and it hurt him very deeply. The unpleasantness arose from the merino auction of 1805,[5] a sale that aroused a great deal of interest and that attracted a large number of people – a financial success too, with one ram fetching sixty-four guineas. But neither this sale nor the last had drawn many of the great men of agriculture: Banks felt that their patronage would be of uncommon advantage to the breed, so when, a little while before the sale, Mr Coke of Norfolk asked for three ewes, Banks let him buy them by private treaty. At this period if Banks did not see the King at Kew or Windsor he usually communicated with him through Colonel Greville, and now he sent a note explaining what he had done and hoping the King would approve, as he had approved earlier in the case of the Duke of Bedford. This was twelve days before the sale. After it, the King being at Weymouth, Banks sent down a catalogue marked with the names of the buyers and the prices they had paid. He sent it expecting congratulations and he was extremely shocked and hurt by Greville's reply, telling him that on finding that Coke's ewes had been sold privately, the King, who up until now had been thoroughly pleased, burst into a violent passion, saying among other things that Banks had broken faith with the public. He was so angry that Greville had not been able to put in an appeasing word; nor obviously had Snart, the somewhat ambiguous person who had succeeded Robinson as superintendent of the parks.

The next day Greville wrote to say that all was calm again: "A little fret of Wind you know often flutters a sail, suddenly, but it soon fills again, & We glide away delightfully – So it has been with us here since I wrote to You yesterday – HM at the King's Lodge yesterday Eveng. came up to me in the Music Room, & in *great good humour* said, 'I now understand the business of the Sheep better'." But no other private sales were to be allowed.

Greville was no phoenix and he may have thought that this would heal the wound, the "very poignantly felt" wound; if so he was mistaken. After some reflection Banks replied.

Aug 20 1805

My dear Sir,

I enclose a justification of my conduct respecting the Sheep drawn up as concisely as I am able to do it. I hope it will not appear to you too long: whether you use it in the whole or in part, & the manner in which you introduce it, I must leave wholly to your Prudence & Friendship.

This Fret, as you call it, appears to me to lie deeper than meets the eye: the explosion was delayed from the time you first mentioned the circumstance till the Catalogue gave a proper opportunity for a vent: it was not the ebullition of a moment, but a concerted & contrived measure, or I am mistaken.

Great therefore as the misfortune will be to me to lose H.M. good will, I must make up my mind with fortitude to the event, whatever it may be; and, as I have the consolation of being certain that I do not deserve it, I trust I shall be able to bear it.

We have both observed that for some years past H.M. mind has been much more irritable & less placable than it formerly was.* I do not now recollect an instance of any one, of whom he has said so hard a thing as he has said of me, being restored to confidential favor; & it will be far better for me to be dismissed than to remain upon sufference only. I feel a friendship for the King, & if it is returned as it used to be, can never forego it; but coldness from a friend, tho' a King, I can never suffer.

The two remaining paragraphs only add some details to the justification, which was a plain statement of the facts.

Four days later, before leaving for Revesby by way of Derbyshire, Banks wrote to Snart saying that he wished to settle accounts for the 1804 wool, that his increasing infirmities prevented him from continuing his labours in perfecting the King's flock, that he wished to ask His Majesty to place the management in more able hands than his own, and that he would be obliged to Snart for telling the King of this.

*In 1801 the King had a mental relapse, caused, it was said, by Pitt's insistence that the Irish Catholics should no longer be penalized, which the King thought contrary to his coronation oath. The attack did not last long, but it was repeated for a short while in February 1804.

That was not in fact the end of the Spanish sheep, for in spite of abominable rudeness from Snart, who did not reply until July 1806, Banks did not wholly abandon the flock. Quite early there was a certain degree of reconciliation, with some very handsome words from the King conveyed by Greville, and in any case the merinos were very near to Banks's heart, so that although he would not resume the active management he remained closely associated with them until a little after the time of the King's final derangement in 1811.

But that was the situation in the early years of the Napoleonic war: the blessings, particularly the scientific blessings, of peace all gone; Flinders' expedition ending in his squalid, unjust imprisonment; the King's merinos in alien, inexpert hands and the King himself estranged; and all this against a background of poor harvest, dear bread and great rural hardship; Banks's own ill health; and the continual threat of invasion. Seasoned French troops, a hundred and fifty thousand strong, stood ready to step into the ship-rigged 110 foot 12-gun *prames*, the brig-rigged 80 foot 5-gun *chaloupes cannonières* and the large flat-bottomed landing-craft (2293 vessels in all, say the naval historians) that lay waiting in the Channel ports. "Give us eight hours of favourable weather one night," said Napoleon, "and the fate of the world will be settled," and he ordered a medal showing Hercules strangling a lion and the words *Descent on England. Struck at London, 1804*.

The invasion was possible; the illness was certain. Gout has always had faintly comic overtones, and now that the disease is so little known the overtones are almost all that is left; yet it was in fact a very grievous affliction. Sydenham, who knew from personal experience, described the acute stage, which might last from a week to ten days as "now a violent stretching and tearing of the ligaments, now . . . a gnawing pain, and now a pressure and tightening; so exquisite and lively meanwhile is the part affected that it cannot bear the weight of the bedclothes, nor the jar of a person walking in the room." Apart from this there is restlessness and extreme irritability, together with sadly disturbed digestion; while in time chalky deposits build up in various joints, stiffening and distorting them. As Banks told a friend, he had not had gout until he was nearly forty; but before he was sixty it had crippled him. For some fifteen years of his life (though with intervals) he had to move about in a wheeled chair, and there were times when he had to be carried in and out of his carriage.

Yet all this, though true, is not the whole truth; even at the darkest time there had been days of strong enjoyment. In 1804 for example he and a group of friends founded the Horticultural Society, which was soon to be called Royal and which was one of the few learned bodies apart from the Linneans and the much older Antiquaries that he thoroughly approved of; the others seemed to him likely to poach on the Royal Society's preserves and diminish its great influence. And then again even the most discouraging days had Soho Square, Spring Grove and Revesby as their background, with the affectionate companionship of his wife and sister, the comfort of a well-run house, and the presence of Dryander in the steadily growing library. Jonas Dryander might not be a Daniel Solander, but he was a sound scholar, a mine of information, and wholly reliable: a very great comfort to Sir Joseph.

Late in 1805 the tremendous news of Trafalgar lightened the scene (Bligh sent him an abstract of Collingwood's dispatch), and although modern historians say that by then Napoleon had already given up the idea of crossing the Channel, Banks and his contemporaries did not know it: what they did know was that the fear of invasion was gone for good. They mourned the loss of Nelson of course – Miss Banks filled one of her many albums with prints and cuttings about his magnificent state funeral – but the whole mood of the country was changed for the happier.

The day after the arrival of the Trafalgar dispatches Brown and Bauer reached the Admiralty; not surprisingly William Marsden, FRS, the Secretary, was too busy to receive them, and as Banks was then at Revesby, laid up with the gout once more, their homecoming may have seemed to them something of an anticlimax. But as soon as he could travel Banks was back in Soho Square, making a first quick inspection of Brown's collections and Bauer's drawings; and what a wealth he had to report in his official letter to his friend Marsden! A provisional estimate put the number of different species of plants at 3600, while there were also about 150 birds' skins, a case of insects and three boxes of minerals, all these being in addition to the puncheons brought by the *Calcutta*. And as for Bauer, "The quantity of sketches he has made during the voyage, and prepared in such a manner by references to a table of colours as to enable him to finish items at his leisure with perfect accuracy, is beyond what I thought possible to perform."[6] There were 2064 drawings in all, and Banks begged "leave humbly to suggest to their Lordships that the salaries of Mr Brown and Mr Bauer be continued to these gentlemen for such time as their Lordships shall think proper".

The Admiralty agreed, and the collections remained at Soho Square, where Brown worked on them for years, publishing the first volume of his famous *Prodromus Florae Novae Hollandiae* in 1810, a book in which the classification followed Jussieu rather than Linnaeus, which seemed a little heretical in one who had just been appointed librarian of the Linnean Society.

And to the happiness of their collections was added that of their account of New South Wales: not that all was well – far from it indeed, with the Rum Corps in such eager pursuit of wealth – but materially the colony was very much more prosperous, so prosperous that on his first visit Peter Good could say this about the Hawkesbury River district: "23 [of June 1802] Set out early in a boat for Portland head and returned to the Green hills about 12 at night – In these two days excursion we sailed on the River Between 30 & 40 miles for about 20 Miles of which distance the land is cleared and Cultivated on both sides and is probably as fertile and productive in wheat & maiz as any in the world as they have a Crop of each annually on the same ground and the general produce of wheat is 30 bushels an acre."[7]

Although Brown, Dryander, one or two sub-librarians and often Banks himself worked steadily in the big house in Soho Square, it was also an unusually hospitable place, and much frequented. Quite apart from Sir Joseph's famous breakfasts and Lady Banks's dinner parties, there were also his Sunday evening assemblies. Sir Benjamin Brodie, who later followed Banks as President of the Royal Society, went to one of these as a young, unknown medical man:

> It was during the period of which I am now speaking, and not very long after I had ceased to be house surgeon, that Mr [Everard] Home introduced me to Sir Joseph Banks. Sir Joseph took much interest in any one who was in any way engaged in the pursuit of science, and as I suppose partly from Home's recommendation and partly from knowing that I was occupied with him in making dissections in comparative anatomy, was led to show me much kindness and attention, such as it was very agreeable for so young a man to receive from so distinguished a person. He invited me to the meetings which were held in his library on the Sunday evenings which intervened between the meetings of the Royal Society. These meetings were of a very different kind from those larger assemblies which were held three or four times in the season by the Duke of Sussex, the Marquis of Northampton, and Lord Rosse, and they were much more useful. There was no crowding together of noblemen and philosophers, and would-be philosophers, nor any kind of magnificent display. The visitors consisted of those who were already distinguished by their scientific reputation, of younger men who, like myself, were following these greater persons at a humble distance, of a few individuals of high station who, though not working men themselves, were regarded by Sir Joseph as patrons of science, of such foreigners of distinction as during the war were to be found in London, and

> of very few besides. Everything was conducted in the plainest manner. Tea was handed round to the company, and there were no other refreshments. But here were to be seen the elder Herschel, Davy, Wollaston, Young, Hatchett, Wilkins the Sanskrit scholar, Marsden, Major Rennel, Henry Cavendish, Home, Barrow, Maskelyne, Blagden, Abernethy, Carlisle, and others who have long since passed away, but whose reputation remains, and gives a character to the age in which they lived.[8]

Indeed Banks led a remarkably full social life: it would have been considered active in a man of leisure; in the President of the Royal Society, a member of several committees of the Privy Council and of the Board of Longitude, a most conscientious trustee of the British Museum and a victim to chronic gout it was a most surprising proof of superabundant energy and appetite for life. He often attended his dining-clubs, presiding over that of the Royal Philosophers with remarkable constancy, wheelchair or no; he was a zealous Antiquary and member of his own Horticultural Society, to both of which he made painstaking and valuable contributions on such subjects as a breviate touching the order and government of a nobleman's house, the building of the steeple and the repairing of the church at Louth in the early sixteenth century, the forcing houses of the Romans, and the horticultural management of the Spanish chestnut tree. And then there were the many other associations such as the Merino Society (founded a little later than this) and the Lincolnshire Agricultural Society that required his presence: as far as Lincolnshire is concerned, his importance both as a man and (particularly since the massive enclosures and drainage operations of the last twenty years) as a landowner can hardly be overemphasized. When the Lord-Lieutenant, the Duke of Ancaster, died, the town of Boston chose Banks as his successor in the office of Recorder, an appointment that required no legal knowledge, no legal duties and no physical presence, but that was the highest honour in their gift. To all this must be added the ordinary invitations that a married man with a very wide acquaintance must both proffer and accept. Yet even more important, when social intercourse is considered, was letter-writing; and to those who puzzle for a whole morning over a couple of simple notes, even the scattered remains of Banks's correspondence are a deeply impressive sight: Warren Dawson, the great authority on the subject, thought the whole, that is to say those kept in London together with those at Revesby, might have represented the writing of no less than fifty letters a week throughout his active life, and virtually all of them by his own hand, since he never employed a secretary.

This flood of letters rose to a new height in the early years of the war, when he was so actively engaged in trying to obtain the release of scientists and others interned in France. Often he was able to exchange a French prisoner for a British one, as may be seen from this letter to Lacépède,[9] who like Cuvier had just been elected to the Royal Society:

Soho Square, London
Sir, May 24, 1806.

I had great pleasure in soliciting the liberation of your relation, M. de Rivaud, the Bearer of this: he wrote to me from the place where he was confined as soon as he arrived, and gave me reason to expect I should hear from you on his account, but, Sir, I did not think it necessary to wait for your Letter. I have therefore seized a fortunate opportunity of restoring him to his liberty and to his Friends.

If you, Sir, can procure for me in Exchange for him The Rev Francis Henry Egerton, now on his Parole at Paris, and well known to M. de Taleyrand, you will do me a particular favour, his brother, Lord Bridgwater, is a particular friend of mine, and I have other reasons for fixing upon him as the Man whose liberty I most wish for.

I have another request to make, which is that a young Man, the son of a Merchant of Boston near my estate, now only 18 years old, may be assisted in procuring a passport from the Grand Judge, without which he cannot leave the country, he was detained with the rest of the English when quite a boy, sent to France for his education, and has not tho' he has frequently attempted it yet been able to procure the proper Passport owing to his youth, his inexperience, and his want of friends. His name is Thomas Gee, he is under the care of M. Verdier at Rostrenen in the Department du Nord.

I have forwarded the Diplomas of yourself and M. Cuvier as F.R.S. by Col. Faujas, who has been exchanged by Gen Ernaud in the West Indies I conclude he will have delivered them before M. de Rivaud arrives.

I am, Sir
Your obt hble Servant
Jos: Banks

And as Lord Brougham says "His own countrymen, when detained by the arbitrary and perfidious policy of Napoleon, were in repeated instances indebted to Sir Joseph Banks for their permission to return home; and a learned friend of mine, one of the first Oriental scholars of the age, the late Professor Hamilton, must have perished at Verdun but for his generous interference. By his interposition the Institute exerted itself in various other cases; and whenever it could be made to appear that a man of science or of letters was among the detained, no very strict scrutiny being exercised either by Sir Joseph or his Paris colleagues, the order for his liberation was applied for and obtained."

This caused Sir Joseph great satisfaction, but most unhappily his work was cut short in 1806 by the jealousy of Lord Howick, a violent Whig and the newly-appointed First Lord of the Admiralty, who claimed that he and not Banks should have the credit for the liberation of Captain Millius, who had sailed *Le Géographe* back to home waters after Baudin's death and who was captured by HMS *Phoenix*, 36, after a stubborn resistance. It was William Marsden, "Sumatra" Marsden, FRS, who, as Secretary to the Admiralty had to write and tell his old friend that Lord Howick was "extremely surprised" that Banks had written to Lacépède stating that Millius was allowed to return to France as a result of his intervention. This was very close to giving Banks the lie direct, which he did not relish at all: in a private note[10] he said "I received a Letter from Lord H couched in terms that did his Lordship no credit, and that drew from me a reply not less unpleasant than his letter was to me."

The vast relief of Trafalgar persisted for the next two years, in spite of the terrible blows of Napoleon's victories at Ulm and Austerlitz, Jena and Friedland, in spite of Pitt's death, and the Continental System, until the extraordinary volte-face of Tilsit that changed the Russians from allies to enemies. Although the news of Austerlitz killed Pitt, that of the treaty of Tilsit seemed even graver, for it meant that the Baltic fleets of the northern powers – the twenty new Russian line-of-battle ships in Kronstadt and Revel, the eleven belonging to Sweden and the sixteen Danish – might be joined to the French and Dutch, making a fleet of sixty sail of the line in the North Sea and the Baltic. If England lost the command of the seas not only was there no hope of victory but invasion and defeat became possible once more, possible and even probable. The Royal Navy therefore proceeded to Copenhagen for a second time and although Denmark was a friendly power insisted upon taking the warships away: Admiral Gambier offered peaceable terms – the ships would be hired for a stated sum and restored undamaged at the end of the war. The Danes refused; the ships were taken by force, together with a great quantity of naval stores. The Danes declared war. This meant that their merchant ships might be seized as fair prize wherever they were found.

Iceland was a Danish possession: Icelandic ships were therefore Danish too, and shortly after this second battle of Copenhagen Banks received a letter from an Icelander he knew begging him to obtain the release of four merchantmen detained at Leith.

Iceland had never been far from Banks's mind since his visit in 1772. He had heard with great concern of the disastrous eruptions of 1783, which had destroyed the grazing over a vast area and diminished the population by perhaps a quarter; he had been in occasional touch with Governor Ólafur Stephensen, and he had been kind to the learned Grimur Thorkelin, the first editor of Beowulf, when he came to England. Kindness was indeed a most important element in Sir Joseph's attitude towards Iceland, though in time other elements came into being. They may be thought less sympathetic, particularly now that imperialism has such a bad name; but this is an attempt at showing Banks as he was rather than an unqualified eulogy. Banks was English, most decidedly and unmistakably English, and although he was kind to inoffensive foreigners, particularly scientists, his benevolence was not unmixed with pity, even for the most eminent of them: in this particular case, for example, he had occasion to speak of Count Trampe, the Governor of Iceland, in a confidential letter: ". . . a good man, as good I mean as Danes are, when they are good, which is by no means as good as a good Englishman". It followed then that if any country was to be ruled by a foreign power, it would be much, much better for all concerned that that power should be England.

Just when it occurred to him that Iceland ought to be one of the British Isles does not appear, but some of the Icelanders themselves suggested it at the time of his visit. "The bettermost people showed a predilection for England, and privately solicited the writer to propose to his government to purchase the island from Denmark."[11] At all events it was firmly fixed in his mind by 30 January 1801 when, as a Privy Councillor, he wrote a long, informed, carefully considered paper, presumably for the ministry, as a consequence of Denmark's joining the armed neutrality in the previous month. Five hundred men would be enough to take the island without any fighting, and, "in conquering Iceland and Ferroe, the United Kingdom would annex to itself the dominion of all the respectable islands in Northern Europe, a proud pre-eminence for the British Isles to obtain". It would not for the present be in any way a paying proposition, but it would emancipate the population "from an Egyptian bondage", a population that "would as the writer believes be much rejoiced in a change of masters that promised them any portion of liberty", and in time the fisheries and even perhaps the native sulphur would prove valuable. This paper must have been approved, for Sir Joseph then wrote a letter[12] addressed to Magnus Stephensen of Reykjavik, the son of the Governor Stephensen he had known, observing that "No one who looks upon the map of Europe can doubt that Iceland is by nature a part of the group of islands called by the ancients Britannia and consequently that it ought to be part of the British Empire." This would be of great advantage to the Icelanders, and they themselves could voluntarily bring the union about, a course that would avoid the horrors of war.

The letter was a clear invitation to Stephensen to take the initiative, but it was probably never sent. Pitt resigned in March 1801 and Addington was not a man to follow up his bolder strokes. In any event there is not the least reference to any earlier communication in this same Magnus Stephensen's letter of 17 October 1807 about the Icelandic ships held in Leith, for it was he who wrote to Banks. He was now Chief Justice of Iceland, a man of consequence, and he said very truly that if trade with Iceland was stopped the people must starve: all their corn was imported, and they had scarcely any vegetable food except Iceland moss, a kind of lichen.

At this time Lord Hawkesbury was Home Secretary: he was the son of Charles Jenkinson, first Lord Hawkesbury and now first Earl of Liverpool, Banks's old friend and colleague on the Coin Committee, and Banks had known him since he was a boy – what is more the present Lord Hawkesbury was also a Fellow of the Royal Society. Banks showed him Stephensen's letter, and the thought of occupation or annexation revived. Hawkesbury asked for a statement on the background and the present position in Iceland and Banks wrote a fuller version of his 1801 paper. But by this time he knew more about the conduct of troops in enemy or occupied territory and he added the paragraph[13] "However desirable the acquisition of an island circumstanced as Iceland is may be to the Imperial Crown of the British Kingdom (and that it is highly desirable no one who has the glory of the British Crown at heart can doubt), it is not certainly worth the expense of an expedition however small it may be; nor would it be conformable to the humane and generous disposition of Englishmen to subject such a country to the horrors of conquest, which, as it is unfortunately ever accompanied with plunder, would naturally where every one lives from day to day and where no accumulation of property can be met with, be succeeded by famine."

In his reply of 29 November 1807 Hawkesbury said "there will be no objection . . . in releasing the few Icelanders' ships which are at Leith"; but while the ministers were turning the plan over in their minds nothing was done and the ships lay there still, their cargoes of stock-fish and train-oil rapidly deteriorating. One at least of the skippers had his family with him – a pregnant wife and children sick with the measles, of which one died. In January 1808 three of the skippers came to London, but Banks was having a severe fit of gout and he could not see them;

they wrote him a long, remarkably dignified, eloquent, sorrowful letter in which they set out their case and said among other things that "we have namely learnt on very good authority, that an order has been given to discontinue the condemnation of Icelandic vessels, and not to proceed to the sale of such as have already been condemned. What may be the cause or the intention of this order, we have not been able to learn; but our sanguine hearts have not omitted to suggest to us, that this measure can only have originated in your benevolent representations, and may, most likely, prove the forerunner of a decision favourable to our interests; and we think in this instance to have another cause of blessing divine providence for throwing us under the protection of a man, who to the will unites also the powers of rescuing from misery."

Banks recovered in February and at once set about the various officials concerned. The King's Proctor was one of them and he could not or would not act on his own authority. Banks wrote a fine letter to Lord Castlereagh, Secretary for War and still another FRS and personal friend. Two days later the under-secretary replied in one of the shortest official letters known to man: "Dear Sir – Government decides to restore the Iceland ships and I have written to stop the cartel. Most truly and obediently E. Cooke."

By the same post Banks received another letter, this time from Bjarni Sivertsen, one of the leading Icelanders: "Sir: As you have before kindly supplied me with the means of conquering my present embarrassments and even offered me your further assistance, I again take the liberty . . . and solicit of you the loan of £30."

Banks sent the news and the money by return. The Icelander replied "For both, Sir, I am more infinitely bound to you, than I can express by words. Not only I, but all my compatriots too are infinitely bound to you for this favour, which, without your protection and interest, we could never have hoped to attain . . ."

There it might well have been supposed that the matter ended; but not at all, for in April the shipping agents wrote to say that the King's Proctor would not go into the case until he was shown a copy of Banks's memorial to the government on the Icelanders' behalf. Banks replied, "Sirs – The King's Proctor must not be in a state of sound mind, if he thinks it possible that I should lay open to any man the representations I made to HM Ministers on the subject of the Iceland ships, unless directed to do so . . ." and on the same day he wrote a letter quivering with indignation to the under-secretary.

The ships did sail away at last, all fourteen of them; yet their departure did not put a stop to Banks's connections with Iceland, and perhaps it would be as well to leave exact chronology to follow them through for a page or so.

The "revolution" in Iceland, a rather squalid little affair, has been treated at some length by Hooker[14] and others and it is not worth going into except as it affects Sir Joseph. At this time there was a prisoner of war on parole in London, the captain of a captured Danish privateer, a plausible fellow called Jörgen Jörgensen; he spoke English fluently and he had served in the Royal Navy, sailing with Flinders, who rated him midshipman. Returning from this voyage in 1806 he brought two Maoris and two Tahitians with him and presented them to Banks, thus forming an acquaintance. Banks confided them to a clergyman belonging to the Missionary Society before sending them to New South Wales with a recommendation to the governor. It was from this man that Phelps, a soap-boiler, learnt that quantities of tallow were to be had in Iceland: tallow and oil, everything a soap-boiler might covet, and dirt-cheap – Jörgensen knew the country well; he had an agent there. All that was necessary was a ship and a licence to trade, which he could certainly obtain through his friend Sir Joseph Banks.

Phelps's firm possessed or chartered a brig, the *Clarence*; they obtained the licence together with letters of marque, so that if she met an enemy she could overpower she might legally make prize of her. The *Clarence*, Jackson master, Savignac (Phelps's clerk) supercargo, and Jörgensen interpreter, reached Hafnafiord on 12 January 1809, with a trading cargo. The governor, Count Trampe, was in Copenhagen and his deputy said he had no power to let foreigners trade; the crew of the *Clarence* seized a Danish vessel in the harbour and Savignac sent to say that she should not be released until they had permission to trade. The permit was granted and Phelps's goods were carried ashore; but it was all in vain – there was no tallow, and no one wanted the goods. Jörgensen had been talking nonsense: he had never been to Iceland and he had no contacts there. It took more than that to make him lose countenance, however; apparently none of his companions understood a word of Danish, still less of Icelandic, and he was able to persuade them that all was well. They left their cargo under the care of Savignac and returned to England, where he managed to convince Phelps that a voyage in the early summer, when his agent would be back, would certainly put everything right; and what was perhaps more surprising he convinced Sir Joseph, who not only embarked a young botanical friend of his, William Hooker, in the *Margaret and Anne* letter of marque, the ship that replaced the *Clarence* for the summer voyage, but provided both him and Phelps, who was going too, with a letter of introduction to

"Dear Sir and my very old Friend" Ólafur Stephensen, the former governor and a most influential man.

On 21 June 1809 Phelps and Jörgensen reached Iceland, where they found that the governor, Count Trampe, had returned. On 25 June they landed with an armed party and took him back to the ship, a captive; they also seized the *Orion*, an Iceland vessel with a British licence. The next day Jörgensen proclaimed that Iceland was independent of Denmark, that a republican constitution was to be established, and that all debts to Danes were cancelled. Then having let the prisoners out of the gaol and seized the state treasury he said that he was the head of the government and that he was to be addressed as Your Excellency. He and Phelps carried on in the traditional way, halving taxes, increasing salaries, confiscating whatever they had a mind to and filling the *Margaret and Anne* with oil and tallow, most of it belonging to Danish merchants; and while they did so Mr Hooker botanized steadily, profiting by the midnight sun. There was no bloodshed, no overt resistance. The Danes had been unpopular and in any case Banks's introduction of Phelps gave him such an aura of respectability that people like the Stephensens temporized if they did not actively approve. But in August the sudden appearance of HMS *Talbot* put an end to these capers. Captain Jones restored the government to its former state and packed both the *Orion* and the *Margaret and Anne* off to England, Jörgensen in the one and very strangely Count Trampe in the other, for Jörgensen, as plausible as ever, had persuaded Captain Jones that he had charges to bring against the Danish governor.

Three days out from Iceland the *Margaret and Anne* caught fire: Jörgensen in the *Orion*, performing prodigies of seamanship and valour, rescued every soul, including Hooker; and although Hooker's botanical, ornithological and mineral collections and even his journal were lost, this endeared Jörgensen to him, so much so that for years Hooker tried to justify the Dane's conduct to Sir Joseph Banks. Jörgensen did the same, by word of mouth, letter, and written narrative. It was labour lost: after mature consideration of what everybody had to say Banks wrote "My mind is that Jorgensen is a bad man, Phelps as bad, and that Count Trampe is a good man . . ."

But his concern for Iceland did not end with Jörgensen's disappearance into the convict hulks at Chatham; he not only continued to take a lively interest in the country and its people but he used his great influence to bring into being a most exceptional Order in Council dated 7 February 1810 which among other things stated that Iceland "shall be exempted from the Attack and Hostilities of His Majesty's Forces and Subjects", that the inhabitants' ships might carry the island's produce to London or Leith without being seized and that the Icelanders should be considered "when resident in His Majesty's Dominions, as Stranger Friends . . . and in no case treated as Alien Enemies".

To return to 1808: this year, his sixty-fifth, was alas upon the whole an unhappy one for Banks. From the very beginning he was so tormented by gout that he was obliged to write to Marsden on 5 January to tell him that "the burden of the Royal Society's chair is likely to fall on you" for the meetings in the immediate future, and it was in this year that he wrote two letters whose grave melancholy stands out in marked contrast to the mass of his correspondence. The one was to Caley and it was dated from Soho Square on 25 August 1808:[15]

> I have been a long time prevented from writing to you by increasing age and infirmities principally by having the gout upon me with severity at the times when opportunity of letters offered.
>
> You have in general been an active, a diligent, and a useful assistant to me in your present situation; and I have found you on many occasions to possess a strong understanding. [But now follows a reproof because Caley stubbornly refused to entrust Brown's plants to Governor King when he returned to England.]
>
> I have grown of late years very infirm; my eyes fail me very much; and I have not of course the pleasure I used to have in the pursuits of Natural History. I have not, therefore, any longer occasion for your services in the extensive manner in which you have employed yourself of collecting great quantities of Articles. You deserve, however, some reward from me for your diligence and activity. [And the letter goes on to tell Caley about the annuity mentioned earlier, on page 251.]

The other was to Bligh (then, of course, the Governor of New South Wales) and it was written on the same day:

> My dear Sir,
>
> I beg you to be assurd that my long silence has not been owing to the least diminution of that friendship & respect to you, which I have for so many years been proud to acknowledge; it has arisen entirely from an increase of bodily ill health, & from my fits of the Gout having accidentally had possession of me at the very time when opportunities of writing to you presented themselves.
>
> [He then speaks at some length of the unhappy Captain Short and his court-martial.]
>
> My declining health & increasing infirmities prevent me from knowing so

much as I used to do of the circumstances of your Colony; & the immense pressure of business in the Privy Council, now the whole trade of England must be carried on by Licences, had delayd the settlement of your colony, which I have been anxiously promoting for some time past. A ray of light has just come upon us from Spain, which may increase to the liberation of Europe from French Tyranny.

[Then follow words about the political position, Governor King's return home, and Caley's obstinacy.]

I am much altered since you saw me, grown older & much more infirm, I think I shall not last much longer. I thank God I have had a long & a happy life, & that I am quite willing to resign it: at this moment I have no use of my left hand, & not much of my legs.

The ray of light that Banks perceived in Spain was in fact the dawn itself. The Spaniards had certainly risen against Napoleon, but perhaps even more important than a popular rising that lacked unity, discipline and material was Sir Arthur Wellesley's landing with nine thousand men on the coast of Portugal on 1 August 1808, with which the Peninsular War began, never to stop until, combined with the Russian disasters, it put an end to that particular tyranny.

Yet all this was far ahead and for the next six years life in Soho Square, Spring Grove and dear Revesby continued with war in the background, a war that had been going on with only one break since 1793, going on so long that it had become habitual, almost the natural atmosphere of life. Yet now as well as naval victories there were occasional triumphs by land: it is true that the Walcheren expedition was shamefully mismanaged, but these early years were brightened by the news of Vimiero, Talavera and Busaco. And from a purely domestic point of view, life was a little kinder to Sir Joseph. The gout, though still present, appears to have been less frequent and less severe; in 1810 there are only two letters in which he has to ask Marsden to take the chair for him at the Royal Society; and in these years, as in so many years both before and after, he had the intense personal satisfaction of being re-elected president of that illustrious body. In 1809, for example, he wrote to his particular friend John Lloyd on St Andrew's day itself, to tell him that he had been re-elected for the thirtieth time.

Then again Banks had a very great capacity for friendship, and since he never seems to have taken much notice of difference of age, any more than he did of class, the older he grew the greater number of friends he possessed very much younger than himself. William Hooker, born in 1775, was one of these; they were much attached, and when Hooker was writing his book on Iceland – a book he had to write from memory, of course – Banks lent him all his own notes and memoranda. Hooker dedicated his *Tour in Iceland* to Sir Joseph in the most graceful terms (My dear Sir – I feel a peculiar propriety in dedicating this little work to you, and, unworthy as it is in itself of the honor of being sent into the world under the sanction of a name like yours, I trust that you will not refuse to accept it as a proof of the esteem and respect of the author) yet even so Banks wrote him a severe, avuncular letter some time later, when it appeared that the Hooker family was persuading him not to go botanizing in Java, that desperately unhealthy place. (The letter is given on page 313.)

Hooker did not in fact go either to Java or Ceylon (which had also been planned) but he did botanize in the Alps, he did continue to cherish Sir Joseph, and when in 1841 he succeeded Aiton as director of Kew he did make improvements in the gardens that would have delighted Banks's heart, increasing the area from 11 to 75 acres with an arboretum of 270 acres and a museum of economic botany.

Another even younger friend was George Staunton, the Chinese scholar. He was the son of the Sir George Staunton, a medical man and diplomat, who accompanied Lord Macartney on his abortive embassy to China in 1792 and who wrote an excellent account of it. Young George went too, though he was only eleven, and there he laid the foundations of his quite exceptional knowledge of the language. He was a Fellow of the Royal Society by the age of twenty-two and he spent some eighteen years in Canton, perfecting his knowledge of Chinese. Apart from their strong mutual liking their chief points of contact were naturalists and porcelain: the naturalists included the Kew collector Kerr and John Reeves, FRS, who like Staunton was in the East India Company's service: Banks introduced them as well as several travelling friends and Staunton treated them all kindly. The porcelain was primarily Lady Banks's affair; she was as devoted a collector of china as her sister-in-law was of visiting cards; she was as her husband said "a little old-china mad" but as "she wishes to mix as much reason with her madness as possible" he often asked Staunton and his much older colleague David Lance, the superintendent of the factory at Canton, for information about methods, periods, dynasties, glazes and so on. His letters to them often carry her thanks for the advice and the splendid pieces they sent to her, and it is clear that Sir Joseph was almost as deeply engaged in her collecting as she was herself.

John Reeves was if anything an even more interesting young man. He was the East India Company's inspector of tea at Canton, and when he was not inspecting tea he inspected the gardens of his Chinese friends.

He found it difficult to answer Banks's questions about the figures on porcelain, but he did send tea, tea plants, different kinds of rice and the receipt for making Chinese ink, as well as a cake of ass-glue, said to be a specific for consumption. And since Sir Joseph was very well with the Company, who told the captains of the East-Indiamen to receive and tend his flowerpots, Reeves was able to send him azaleas, camellias, tree paeonies, chrysanthemums and roses, often of kinds that had never been seen in Europe before. These he established in pots long before the voyage, so that they often survived with remarkable success.

Another friend of these days, though neither so young nor so agreeable, was Everard Home, a surgeon. He too belonged to that remarkable freemasonry the Royal Society, but he does not seem to have been much more than an acquaintance until some time after 1804, when Banks consulted him professionally for his gout. Home put him on a diet of vegetables and milk for a while; this seemed to bring about an alleviation, and it certainly convinced Banks that Home was uncommonly gifted. Home had indeed worked under John Hunter, so he could not but be an accomplished anatomist and surgeon, and when Banks set out for his usual journey to Revesby in the late summer of 1810 he left Dryander in Home's hands with perfect confidence. Dryander was afflicted with a painful disorder that Banks had always feared was something much graver than piles; but Home reassured him – a simple operation would deal with the matter.

From Revesby Banks wrote a pleasant rambling letter to William Marsden (who was actively concerned with having the date of Flinders' promotion pushed back as far as possible) telling him among other things that "We are grown proud of heart . . . I never saw my neighbours in so high spirits. The Fens are drained and peopled, and agricultural industry is active among us." When Banks spoke of his neighbours he meant a very great many people; they fairly flocked to Revesby when he was there and he enjoyed their company. His idea of fishing, for example, was by no means a contemplative man's recreation: and it would have made a dry-fly purist stare. His version of the sport was a gregarious affair, carried out, usually in the river Witham, with nets both large and small; writing to Sir William Hamilton he says "We drew ten miles of fresh water, and in four days caught seventeen hundredweight of fish; dining always from twenty to thirty masters and mistresses with servants and attendants, on the fish we had caught, dressed at fires made on the bank; and when we had done we had not ten pound of fish left."

It is not sure that he was able to fish during that particular stay, but it is sure that he arranged for the bachelor Dryander to be housed in Soho Square and looked after there during the minor operation and his recovery from it. He wrote to Home on 11 October 1810 "I conclude that all our beds are at the wash or the scourer or somehow out of commission. What appears to me best is that my next neighbour Mr Marston should be applied to to lend a bed which may be put up in what we call the South Room, where my mother used to sleep, next to my sister's room, which is so full of her collections that I would not wish to have that used if it can be avoided, lest something should be displaced. If a bed could be put in the inner room of the Library or in the room above it, it might be more convenient. In short my wish is that every kind of accomodation the house can afford be given to my good friend and that the maid and porter should show him every attention."

At that time surgery was generally acknowledged to be a perilous business, but even so Banks was very deeply shocked at the news of Dryander's death. On 22 October he wrote "I was so stunned by the unlooked for Blow I received from the Perusal of your letter that I was utterly unable to answer by return of Post. I have lost my right hand & can never hope to provide a substitute that can at all make amends to me . . . If an unerring hand, guided by Skill, Practice and what is best of all superior Talents and a warm heart could have saved him he would still have been with us."[16]

Banks, in spite of his heavy, bull-like appearance and an expression that had by now taken on the cast of habitual pain or the expectation of pain, was an unusually affectionate man, and clearly it was impossible for him to replace anyone who had been so much of his life, even before the death of Solander; but he could replace his chief librarian, and this he did in the person of Robert Brown, the rising light in British botany.

Where botany was concerned Banks was strikingly modest; he had a great deal of practical experience and knowledge, he had turned over thousands of books and hundreds of thousands of plants in herbaria and in the field; but he did not possess inventive genius and he did not advance the science very much, apart from enabling others to do so by his vast collections and his intelligent support; but he was perfectly ready to acknowledge superior talents, and in botany if not in other cases (such as that of Bligh) he was ready to change his mind and to admit that he had been wrong. In 1784, when Banks was forty-one, Jussieu annoyed him and most other scientific men by supporting Mesmer's animal magnetism; and writing to Blagden Banks said "Jussieu must be more of a fool than even I (who never admired him) had an idea of to take part in so foolish a deception just at the moment when it is detected"; in 1817, when Banks was seventy-four, he wrote to J. E. Smith about his article on botany in the *Encyclopaedia Britannica*: he admired Smith's treatment of the Linnaean classification but observed that although Smith (the founder of the Linnean Society) would not agree, Jussieu's system of natural orders was far superior – "How immense has been the improvement of botany since I attached myself to the study." And no one was more heartily gratified than Banks at the almost universal applause that greeted Robert Brown's *Prodromus* and at the growing reputation of his librarian.

Yet soon after this momentous publication there were far greater excitements, greater joys. Napoleon's withdrawal of troops from Spain for his invasion of Russia made Wellington's task less impossibly difficult, and the victories of Badajoz and Salamanca, though very costly, brightened 1812, while that of Vitoria the next summer almost cleared Spain of the French, and by the autumn Wellington was north of the Pyrenees. Meanwhile Napoleon had lost the battle of Leipzig, and even before Wellington took Toulouse after very bloody fighting, Paris had fallen and the Emperor had abdicated.

It is true that he reappeared next spring and that for a hundred days he terrified Europe until Wellington and Blücher put a final stop to his career. But as Wellington himself said, Waterloo had been a damned near-run thing, and this time Lord Liverpool, who was now prime minister, sent Napoleon off to St Helena.

The Hundred Days, intensely dramatic though they were, did not seriously disturb the renewed intercourse between the Royal Society and the *Institut*: nor do I find any reference to them in Banks's letters until 1816.

Blagden settled in Paris almost as early as the returning King Louis XVIII and his exiled followers, and Banks wrote to him often, pleasant, discursive letters that give those who can read them – Banks was never much of a penman and now his poor knotted hand was very difficult except for his familiars – a remarkable view of his active, many-sided life and his unquenchable thirst for every kind of knowledge. Yet since Blagden was no great botanist these letters scarcely mention one of Banks's most important occupations, the revival of plant-collecting for Kew. As early as 1 September 1814 he sent the Treasury a long, considered statement[17] on the subject: he was of opinion that collectors ought to be sent out at once, particularly to the Cape and New South Wales; that the best were those who had been trained at Kew and who had there taken up the study of botany as well as that of mere horticulture; and that of these the most suitable were Scotsmen. "So well does the serious mind of a Scotch education fit Scotsmen to the habits of industry, attention, and frugality, that they rarely abandon them at any time of life, and I may say never while they are young." To begin with therefore he recommended Allan Cunningham and James Bowie, and suggested that they should be given £180 a year: "Out of this they may be expected to save £150 at the least, as £30 it is presumed will be sufficient to furnish them with clothes and pocket-money. A free passage in one of the King's ships is expected, and mess with the warrant-officers."

Since this letter, nominally for the information of the Lords of the Treasury, had already been discussed by Banks with Liverpool, who as prime minister was First Lord of the Treasury, it is scarcely surprising that in less than a fortnight the Treasury replied, agreeing to all the suggestions, and the two young men began their eminently successful travels that same year.

Banks and Blagden did share a very great many interests however and the letters between them cover a remarkable range of subjects. One of these of course was gout – Blagden was a medical man – and in almost the first letter Banks asked for a hundred two-drachm bottles of Busson's *Eau Médicinale*, a nostrum that he later identified with the Vinum colchici of the pharmacopœia, a potent but dangerously variable drug that sometimes gave him relief. Yet health is not often mentioned – a few of the many fits of gout, two carriage accidents, one in 1814 and another much more serious in 1818, a bout of jaundice in 1819 – and then only in passing: Banks was nothing of a hypochondriac. A list of the other subjects would take many pages, but a score or so may give some notion of their variety: the reclamation of the Fens, and Rennie's improved manner of drainage – Rennie's Strand Bridge (soon to be called Waterloo); König's printing presses; a request for information about the feeding of the geese that produce foie gras; Banks sends a present of kale seed; speaks of a thirteenth-century Greek medical writer; Young's paper on the Rosetta Stone; bad harvest and dear wheat in 1815; French men of science in London, Cuvier, Candolle, Arago, Biot, Gay-Lussac and others at various times, some of them not behaving quite as well as could be wished; Banks on the commissions for weights and measures and for the prevention of the forgery of banknotes; he sends a plant of the passion-flower from Revesby as a present for Countess Rumford; the death of Watt; Raffles' remarkable plant from Sumatra, drawn by Bauer, studied by Brown, but still unassignable to any known family; he thanks Blagden for *Don Juan* – has a low opinion of the book and its author; great success with a new kind of strawberry at Spring Grove in 1819 and so many grapes that wine is to be made; Pearce has reached Egypt from Abyssinia and the British Museum is to have his collection of birds; gas lighting; young Herschel's paper; the polarization of light; Luddites; the Arctic expedition; Newfoundland dogs. And all through the correspondence there is news of the Royal Society: in November 1819 when the elections were approaching "I always feel uneasy at again offering myself as a Candidate this year, if I am again elected it will be the 42nd time, enough I think to satisfy the ambition of any man." And then on 3 December he sent word that he had been re-elected unanimously: "I have now presided 41 years I hope not uselessly."

Certainly not uselessly. Banks may not have been a great reforming president – the times were utterly opposed to reform – but he left the Royal Society an even more respectable body than he had found it; he had been a most conscientious president, always taking the chair when his health would allow him and attending council meetings; and although he had not been able to make all the changes that he might have wished, the fellowship was now much more difficult to obtain, the number of foreign members had fallen from 120 in his first year of office to 40 in his last, and the Society was ready for the great change that came some years later, turning it into a purely scientific body.

Yet being the President of the Royal Society, the uncontested President for so long, was a dangerous distinction, one that conferred a kind of secular infallibility. No doubt his fellow botanists knew very well just where he stood in their particular hierarchy, but the difference would scarcely have been equally clear to mathematicians or astronomers, still less to the government departments that consulted him so often; while ordinary people would no more have questioned the President of the Royal Society's statement on any branch of science than that of the Archbishop of Canterbury's on any branch of theology. A man in such a position therefore grows unused to contradiction: then again if he happens to be rich and well acquainted with everybody of importance in the social, administrative and scientific world, a man whose patronage may be of the very first importance, the risk of contradiction becomes even less, while that of excessive deference increases. Since as Rousseau observes most members of any society consider themselves the most virtuous and intelligent people in it, this state of affairs, this lay papacy, may lead to resentment. Yet even quite strong resentment cannot, without an even stronger addition of ill-nature, account for Sir Humphry Davy's often-quoted remark after

Banks's death: "He was a good-humoured and liberal man, free and various in conversational power, a tolerable botanist and generally acquainted with natural history. He had not much reading, and no profound information. He was always ready to promote the objects of men of science, but he required to be regarded as a patron and readily swallowed gross flattery. When he gave anecdotes of his voyages he was very entertaining and unaffected. A courtier in character, he was a warm friend to a good King. In his relations to the Royal Society he was too personal and made his circle too like a court."[18]

There was everything to make Davy dislike Banks. Davy, intensely ambitious, was of humble origin and largely self-taught; all his life he remained socially inept – so remarkably inept that when he visited France his rudeness and arrogance gave great offence to those who entertained him, and he left a singular notion of English manners behind him. The *Encyclopaedia Britannica* speaks of his "ungainly exterior and peculiar manner", his occasional "petty jealousy", and concludes "Of the smaller observances of etiquette he was careless, and his frankness of disposition sometimes exposed him to annoyances which he might have avoided by the exercise of ordinary tact." A more complete contrast to Sir Joseph could hardly be imagined; but it is a pity that a man of such parts should have let himself down so far. And it may be added that Davy was in no way qualified to give an opinion on Banks's botanical knowledge.

This is not to say that Sir Joseph Banks was beyond criticism; he was at all times subject to the ordinary human failings and when great pain was added to the general unhappiness of old age he was capable, in spite of his deeply-engrained good manners, of giving a sharp answer or an over-emphatic contradiction. He was testy and more than testy at times, particularly after the splendour of victory had faded and the country awoke to the fact that it was very deeply indebted, that peace meant poverty and unemployment and, because of the corn laws, dear bread. Many great landowners' London houses were attacked during the Corn Law riots of 1815, and absurdly Sir Joseph's was among them – absurdly, because at considerable loss to himself he ran his estate on the basis of small farms, so that as many men as possible should be on their own holdings. The huge mob beat in the front door, broke windows and scattered some papers that were in the hall; although they did not come farther it must have been exceedingly frightening, and Banks was unusually pleased with the conduct of his ladies: as he told J. F. Smith, "They sat by me without any expression of extravagant fear till the door was burst open. I then requested them to retire which they did but not out of the house."

It is to this period that may be assigned his outburst against Lord Liverpool: writing to Davies Gilbert on 16 October 1816 he spoke of the general depression of trade caused by Napoleon, adding that he was astonished that a tyrant who had caused such universal misery should be permitted to live – "an instance of honourable feelings having gone mad". Much the same unhappy state of mind produced the curious statement about the *Resolution* voyage that he dictated to Robert Brown, a short, inaccurate statement in which he repeats his version of the affair, with an even greater sense of ill-usage. The fault that Banks's friends most deplored was his great difficulty in admitting that he was in the wrong; and this affair had obviously been rankling in his mind for more than forty years.

But pain, sleeplessness and heavy self-medication can answer for a great deal – the gout was very bad in 1816 – and it is clear that this rancorous tone was not habitual. Dr Lysaght quotes a letter that shows a very different picture, a very much more recognizable Banks: it was written in December 1817 by Edward Parry, later Admiral Sir Edward and a famous Arctic explorer but then only a junior lieutenant:

> My Dearest Parents,
>
> As I am sure you will be desirous to know the result of my introduction to Sir Joseph Banks, I begin my letter rather earlier than I have hitherto done. I dined very comfortably with Mr Maxwell yesterday, and of course enjoyed a great deal of pleasant and useful conversation. At ½ past 9 this morning, my Uncle called for me, and we went to Soho Square together. People who know Sir J. walk into his library without asking any questions, and we were there about a quarter of an hour before ten which is the breakfast hour. In the mean time, I was introduced to Mr Brown, his librarian, who is a *walking catalogue* of every book in the world, and of whom I asked several questions. At ten precisely Lady and Mrs Banks made their appearance, to whom I was introduced in form, and without waiting for Sir J. (who was wheeled in, five minutes after) we sat down to breakfast. Sir J. shook hands with me very cordially, said he was glad to become acquainted with a Son of Dr. Parry's, for whom he entertained the highest respect, and was glad to find I was nominated to serve on the Expedition to the North West. Having breakfasted, *I* wheeled Sir J. into an ante-room which adjoins the library, and, without any previous remark, he opened a map which he had just constructed, and in which the situation is shewn, of that enormous mass of ice which has lately disappeared from the Eastern coast of Greenland. It has been observed, by the Meteorological Journals of several years past (at least 10) that our summers have been decreasing in temperature. Everybody has remarked, in the common vague way, that the seasons have altered lately,

and Sir Joseph very confidently attributes this change to a breaking up of the Greenland ices, which are floated down to the more southern parallels of latitude, and impart a very sensible degree of cold to the atmosphere of the countries of Europe during the summer months. He says he has received accounts from Boston that for a year or two past, their crops of maize have not ripened, for which they are at a loss to account. *He* attributes this circumstance to the above cause also. Another very curious fact which he mentioned to me, and the no less curious speculation he has formed upon it, are worthy of remark. The oil of the whales of warm climates is so constituted by nature, that they are suited to a warm temperature, and freeze at a very high degree of the thermometer. That of the Greenland whale, on the other hand, requires a very low temperature to freeze it. Now, Sir J. has observed that the Greenland oil which he uses in his own lamp will never burn of late, (and *that*, without any great degree of cold) from which he thinks it possible that the constitution of the animal may have been so far changed by a change of temperature in the elements in which he lives, as, by warming his blood &c, to have affected a change in the nature of the oil he produces. The alteration in the temperature of the water he attributes to the clearing away of the mass of ice attached to the shores of Greenland. It is impossible, in the compass of a letter, to repeat to you half of what Sir Joseph Banks said to me upon the subject – much less, to give you any idea of his very affable, communicative manner; he desired that I would come to him as often as I pleased (the oftener the better) and read or take away any books I could find in his library that might be of service to me. He made me take his map with me, and I have it in Mr. Maxwell's office where I am now writing and where I shall keep it as the safest place. Having obtained a *Carte blanche* from Sir J., I shall of course go to his library without any ceremony, whenever I have occasions: for his invitations are not those of fashionable life, but are given from a real desire to do every-thing which can in the smallest degree tend to the advancement of every branch of science. . . . I am now going to the Hydrographical office, to copy some late information respecting Greenland, transmitted by a clever man by the name of Scoresby, Captn of a Greenland whaler. Even my visits to this office are more advantageous to me than I can express.

Adieu! my dearest Parents . . .

Ever affectionately yours

Banks's long correspondence with Blagden told a great deal, but it had some significant silences. For example, Banks did speak of the carriage accident in 1818, a most unpleasant accident best described in the letter to Home:

Spring Grove
August 27, 1818.

My dear Sir Everard, – I was overturned two days ago by a drunken

> coachman, but received no hurt. Lady Banks and my sister and I were driving home from dining with Sir A. Macdonald. We are all three rather heavy, and I, as you know, quite helpless. We were obliged to lie very uneasily at the bottom of the coach for half an hour before assistance could be got to lift us out. We all bore our misfortune without repining or any demonstration of the follies of fear; and we are all now quite recovered from the effects of our accident, except my sister, who has a cut on her head filled with lint and doing very well. But both ladies have gone everywhere since, without an hour's confinement.

And he did speak of the jagged great renal calculus he passed that night with the shocking agonies any sufferer from the stone can imagine; but he did not tell Blagden of his grief at Sophia's death. It was to William Scoresby, the scientific northern sailor, that he spoke of his affliction – affliction was the word he used. At first she had seemed quite recovered, and she even called on the princesses at Kew; but a month later she died. She was seventy-four and she had lived in her brother's house for fifty years, a fine tall upstanding woman with a deep voice and ways very much of her own. She dressed in the fashion of an earlier age and though some might think her eccentric – Gillray caricatured her – she was much loved and esteemed. Her brother gave all her collections to the British Museum, broadsides, visiting and invitation cards, coins, tokens, all of great sociological interest.

Another though much less important subject he did not mention to Blagden was the Board of Longitude. Banks, as President of the Royal Society, had belonged to it for more than forty years, and together with Dr Maskelyne, the Astronomer Royal, he was the most regular and most influential member. He and Maskelyne had disagreed upon many subjects, above all on the merits of chronometers made by Arnold and Earnshaw: although the President and the Astronomer had remained on perfectly civil terms, their disagreements had been violent enough for Banks to run into print with his *Sir Joseph Banks's Protest* in 1804, and now in 1818, having outlived his more pugnacious adversaries, he gained a final victory by causing Parliament to lay down that the President and Council of the Royal Society "should be empowered to elect from among the Fellows, five of those persons most conversant in those sciences upon which the discovery of the Longitude at sea most immediately depends".

After Sophia Banks's death her brother and sister-in-law stayed at Soho Square most of the year, though they did sometimes go to Spring Grove, where the gardens were doing remarkably well under the care of a new man, Isaac Oldaker, a "master of his profession" who had worked for the Tsar and who installed steam pipes in the greenhouses. But they did not go to Revesby again, for even at the gentle pace of their last visit, the four days' journey was too much: long-continued gout, it appears, affects not only joints but also heart, the great arteries, liver and kidneys; and now Sir Joseph, at 77, had been suffering for nearly forty years.

There was indeed a kind remission in 1819, wonderfully kind, and he presided at no fewer than twenty-seven of the Royal Philosophers' dinners,[19] and this year has almost as many letters as another, letters full of eager life and curiosity: he tells Mr Knight for example that at Spring Grove his bone manure "had exceeded his most sanguine hopes; while he had sent Knight's wasps and combs to the British Museum, which admitted the difference of the two species".

And even in January and February of 1820 he still took the chair at the meetings of the Royal Society: but on 16 March he sat there for the last time, and some weeks later Sir Everard Home told the Council that their President had sent his resignation.[20]

The Bishop of Carlisle, Dr Goodenough, a botanist and Banks's contemporary at Christ Church, was the officiating vice-president, and he and all those present unanimously voted the motion "That instead of accepting the resignation of the President, the Council do with one voice express their most cordial wishes that the President should not withdraw from the Chair of the Society, which he has filled so ably and so honourably during a period of forty-two years."

To this Sir Joseph replied:

> Sir Joseph Banks begs leave to inform the Council of the Royal Society that his motive for offering his resignation of the office of President was a conviction that old age had so far impaired his sight and his hearing as to render him by no means so well able to perform the duties of that respectable office as he has been. He is gratified in the extreme by finding that the Council think it possible for him to continue his services without detriment to the interests of the Society, and he begs leave to withdraw his resignation, assuring the Council that his utmost exertions shall never be wanting to conduct, as far as may be in his power, the affairs of the Society.

And so, eighteen days later, he died as he had lived so long, President of the Royal Society.

Yet to leave Joseph Banks on his deathbed, with the usual remarks about his will and his funeral, and extracts from the obituaries, would not only be sad but also misleading; there was such a fund of life there, such a zest and eager intelligent curiosity that no one who has dwelt with him long enough to write even a very small biography can leave him without wishing to show him in his vigour. So after the conventional last pieces of information I propose a few letters that will give the various sounds of his living voice again.

Chapter 12

HIS WILL, AND SOME LETTERS

JOSEPH BANKS had made his will in January 1820, and it was completed by two codicils at intervals of some weeks. The document has all the formality with which his lawyers could invest the "last Will and Testament of me The Right Honorable Sir Joseph Banks of Spring Grove in the Parish of Heston in the County of Middlesex and of Kings otherwise Soho Square in the same County one of His Majestys Most Honorable Privy Council Knight Grand Cross of the Most Honorable Military Order of the Bath and President of the Royal Society", yet even here his voice sometimes pierces through the legal phraseology and the no doubt necessary repetition.

He asked to be buried "in the most private manner in the Church or Church yard of the Parish in which I shall happen to die. I entreat my dear relatives to spare themselves the affliction of attending the ceremony and I earnestly request that they will not erect any Monument to my Memory."

Apart from some minor legacies he left almost everything to "my dear wife Dame Dorothea Banks", and after her death his great Lincolnshire possessions (apart from some leaseholds which appear to have formed a separate trust) were to be divided between Sir Henry Hawley and the Hon. James Hamilton Stanhope, cousins who descended from Joseph Banks II by his daughters Elizabeth and Margaret respectively. His other estates went to Sir Edward Knatchbull, Lady Banks's nephew; and the arrangement and settlement of all this property took a great deal of time, space, and legal acumen.

It is in the first codicil that the lawyers give way once more to the testator, and we read in plain English "I give and bequeath unto my indefatigable and intelligent Librarian Robert Brown Esquire an annuity of two hundred pounds . . . I also give the same Robert Brown the use and enjoyment during his life of my Library Herbarium Manuscripts Drawings Copper plates engraved" and everything else in the great Soho Square collections. After Brown's death they were to go to the British Museum, though they might go earlier if Brown agreed, as in fact he did. There was a condition that Brown should continue to help the superintendent of Kew, that he should accept no new post and that the library should be his chief place of study; but on the other hand Lady Banks was required to provide him with firing, candles and attendance of servants, while after her death Brown was to have the leasehold house itself.

In the same codicil he left "Mr Frederic* Bauer of Kew Green who has been employed by me as draughtsman for thirty years an annuity of three hundred pounds . . . to continue during his natural life or until he shall have been admitted into the Service of any other person . . . upon condition that he continues to reside at Kew Green and employ himself in making drawings of Plants that flower in the Collection at Kew in the same manner as he has hitherto done . . ."

Yet on reflection this did not seem quite clear enough to Sir Joseph and he returned to the matter in March with a second codicil which, after the usual preamble, reads "With every feeling of the dutiful homage and humble attention justly due from a Loyal Subject to a most gracious Sovereign I do hereby give and bequeath to His Majesty for the use of the Establishment of the Royal Botanic Gardens at Kew all those drawings and sketches of Plants that have grown in the said Gardens and have been made at my Costs and Charges by Mr Frederic Bauer of Kew Green . . . ." The codicil goes on to express the hope that Bauer may be made a member of the establishment; but "In case however of its being deemed inexpedient by His Majesty's advisers to make this small addition to the Royal Establishment of the Gardens", Banks's heirs would deal with the situation.

The parish "in which he happened to die" was that of Heston, and according to his wish he was buried in Heston church with nothing to show even the place of his grave (though in 1867 the then vicar set up a tablet stating that he lay there).

The obituaries were deeply respectful and naturally they were as solemn, if not as well-informed, as Cuvier's noble eulogy before the *Académie des Sciences*; yet when their first grief was over, it was surely the cheerful, eager, kind and hospitable Banks who lived on in his friends' memories, the Banks who can be seen in these letters.

The first[1] was written during his Newfoundland expedition, when he was twenty-three.

Dear Sister Chateau Bay 11 August [1766]

I received yours two days ago with newspapers &c: &c: which I must thank you all for as I can assure you they were the greatest Comfort you can Conceive – we all sat round the Fire & hunted out all the Deaths marriages &c: &c: as Eagerly as a schoolboy does Plumbs out of a Pudding.

* A mistake for Ferdinand.

How do you think I have spent my Leisure Time since I have been here Very Musically I can assure you I have learnt to play upon a new Instrument as I have Foreswore the Flute I have tried my hand upon strings what do you think it is now not a fiddle I can assure you but a Poor innocent Guittar which Lay in the Cabbin on which I can play Lady Coventries minuet & in Infancy &c: with Great success

Pray My Love to Coz Bate & tell her that she & I differ a little in opinion about Stamford races as I had rather be here Than at all the races in Europe – not but what I beleive she was at Least as happy there as I am here

I hope Mr Lee has been Very Civil & Given you Nosegays as often as you have been to him if not tell him he shall not have one of my Insects when I come home give my Compts to him also & tell him that if I did not think it might Endanger Cracking some of Your Ladyships teeth I would Let him know by you some of the Hard names of the things I have got

So Miss Frederick is going to be married to our countryman a dangerous Experiment I think he killed his Last wife in a hurry I hope he may keep her alive a little Longer but maybe she intends to Revenge Miss Pit & kill him I know you women are sad Husband killers in your hearts

I do not know what Else to say I am almost Exhausted thank you however for your ague receipt it has one merit however I think for if it would not Cure an ague I am sure it would kill a horse

We are here in daily Expectation of the Eskimaux Ladies here I wish with all my heart they would Come as I might have sent you a sealskin gown & Petticoat Perfumd with train oil which to them is as Sweet as Lavander water but more of them when I know them better at Present adieu only Beleive

Me Your very affectionate Brother

J Banks

P:S: Pray My Compts to all Freinds at Chelsea especialy our neighbours at the Garden I mean our Gardening uncle & aunt adieu

The second[2] is addressed to Sir William Hamilton, at Naples: and this time Banks was thirty-five.

Soho Square

Dear Sir, Decr 4 – 78

I have from time to time postpond an answer to your favor in the hopes that I should be able to pick up some literary news for your amusement but I fear our very Scientifick ones are too much involvd in contemplating the melancholy situation of poor Mrs Britain like the upholsterer to mind their own concerns

they did me the honer however last Monday to Elect me unanimously President of the Royal Society in the room of Sr Jno Pringle who resigned that office finding I suppose Newtons Chair not so easy a one as his own Fire side Elbow that I envy you your situation within two miles of an erupting Volcano you will easily guess I read your Letters with that Kind of Fidgetty anziety which continualy upbraids for not being in a similar situation I envy you I pity myself I blame myself & then begin to tumble over my Dried Plants in hopes to put such wishes out of my head which now I am tied by the leg to an arm chair I must with diligence suppress

So great is our real dearth of Philosophick news that I am obligd to have recourse to Politicks to amuse you but as I do not value myself upon my political performances I have chosen an abler Pen Mr Tickel* the Author of the Pamphlet you receive with this has livd a good deal with Mr Brummel Ld Norths secretary from that School he has got his knowledge & some do not scruple to say that the head master gave him lessons which have enabled him with so much real humor to Caricature the different styles of Eloquence which our Billingsgate senate affords certain it is that the laugh is so much with him that scarce a man for whom he has spoke can keep his speech clear of some expressions to be found in anticipation & the house no sooner hears them than a titter confounds the poor orator

Luttrel mentioned Egypt the other Day Mulgrave burst into a Horse-Laugh & Luttrel bore it so ill that he calld him a Bear

Do me the favor to make my respects acceptable to Lady Hamilton & beleive me at all times

Your affectionate & Obedient Hble Servant
Jos: Banks

Then comes another[3] from the still youthful Banks, unattacked as yet by weight or gout. It is dated from Revesby in October 1780, the year after his marriage, and it is addressed to Sir Edward Knatchbull, who married Dorothea Banks's sister Mary.

My Dear Brother,

I received your Obliging Favor on my return home from a Long Journey which business obliged me to take into Staffordshire in which my wife and Sister accompanied me Travelling stew through cross countrey roads in a mountanous countrey & sleeping at miserable ale houses without even a maid to Assist at their Toilets all which Hardship they voluntarily subjected to & chearfully endurd without a complaint I think they deserve a little eulogy for it.

The year has been (much to my dissatisfaction) most remarkable for publick meetings & dancing assemblys the races were no sooner finished than the interest I have in the neighboring burrough of Boston Call'd me there to exert myself in an opposition which ending in a victory produced a ball for the Freemen at which it was necessary that Mrs B should be present thank god she escaped pretty well as only one pot of Porter was thrown over

* This is Richard Tickell, a grandson of the poet: the pamphlet was called *Anticipation*.

her gown tho she danced between more Pots of porter & Bowls of Negus than Couples in the Countrey dance.

From Boston in three days we were hurried to Lincoln on fear of an opposition in the countrey this ended in two Balls *don't you pity me.*

Shooting has gone but ill what with business & Journey I have not for three weeks handled my Fire Lock but now I am returned the Pheasants must look sharp I walkd out yesterday & shot at but one who fell to the aim so at least I have not Miss'd a Pheasant this year.

I rejoice to hear of your being at Provender & shall always be happy to hear that you keep the old house warm . . . shall you be there at Christmas we would if you like it spend our Holidays with you I have three excellent spaniels Mab Tiney & Juno I do not think we should cut a bad figure in Put wood.

Adieu my dear Brother
give my affect Compts to my sister & believe me
your affect. Brother

Jos. Banks

The fourth letter[4] is from the President of the Royal Society to that most distinguished botanist Antoine-Laurent de Jussieu: it is more typical of Banks's kindness than it is of his highly individual way of writing, for very few of his editors have been able to resist the temptation of "touching him up" as Warren Dawson put it, and the young ladies who made the Dawson Turner copies for their father were no exception. The other letters however are taken directly from the originals.

Soho Square
June 29, 1788

Sir,

It is an unpleasant thing to be refused admittance to a Society to which one has been presented as a Candidate; but in your case I consider it as a matter which ought not in any degree vex or trouble you. I, Sir, who have had the misfortune to be rejected by the Academy of Paris, am now a member of it. Why then may not the same thing happen to you?*

Your literary character, I can assure you, never came into the contemplation of those who voted against you. That is highly respected here, as much as you could wish or expect. As far as I know, your enemies were guided by an antipathy to the doctrines of Mesmer; which, especially since Dr Franklin gave his opinion against them, is here very prevalent. And, good Sir, difference of opinion in matters of speculative nature have not the least influence on the respect which literary men owe to each other. I hope that, notwithstanding your disappointment, our correspondence will continue. Mine with my friends at Paris did not cease a moment on a similar occasion.

*Jussieu was elected to the Royal Society in 1829.

The son of Dr Hope, the late Professor of Botany, will shortly be with you at Paris. He brings you two plates which are intended for the new publication of *Hortus Kewensis*, coloured in the best style. They are intended as furniture, and pay compliments to the Queen, who studies Botany intensely, and really reads with perseverence Elementary Books; also Lady Tankerville, whose Lord has a very fine Botanic Garden, and who knows plants well and paints them exquisitely.* Accept these as a mark of my homage. Be assured of the continuation of that respect you have so justly inspired me with, and believe me at all times,

Your most faithful
Jos: Banks

Now comes a letter,[5] or perhaps it would be fairer to say the draft of a letter, to Henry Dundas, the Home Secretary. It was written from Soho Square in April 1794, at that unhappy time when Sir Joseph, having done very well for the administration as High Sheriff of Norfolk, found himself offered the Order of the Bath in such a way that it might be seen as a political reward.

S S April 5 1794

Sir,

It is now 5 years since the King was graciously pleased to tell me that from the manner in which I conducted the business of the Station I hold the opinions Foreigners have expressed of me in their books owing to the reception they have met with from me here and the correspondence I carry on with them abroad, as well as from the Satisfaction the RS appears to feel in the flourishing state they cry up under my Presidency it appeared to HM proper that a Red Ribband should be given to me and to this I answer with every humble expression of thankfullness which a heart penetrated with gratitude could suggest that I had long felt myself anzious to receive some mark of Royal approbation but that the intended one exceeded my warmest hopes for at that time I was sure I could receive it without suffering any diminution of my Pretentions to the character of an independent landowner.

From that time to the present I have never mentioned the Conversation to any Person whatever I watchd indeed every Red Ribband which was granted well knowing that no word has ever proceeded from the lips of my Royal Master has ever yet escaped his majesty's memory but observing that 4 were given to soldiers and 2 to foreign ministers I did not doubt that the Servants of the Crown had on each occasion urged as undoubtedly they had a right to do that the order was solely intended for these professions & I deduced from thence that my turn could not arrive till all persons of these two descriptions were satisfied.

* The plates were of *Strelitzia reginae* (Queen Charlotte came from Mecklenburg-Strelitz) and of *Limodorum tancarvilleae*.

had however my turn arrivd or rather had the Conversation which passd between you & me at the London Tavern on Wednesday last taken place early enough before the 6th of March when I set out to hold the assizes at Lincoln, for his M. gracious intention to have been made known to my friends before the 11th the day on which you received from me the subscriptions & resolutions of the Grand Jury I should have bowd with abundant gratitude to the minister who honord me with Tidings so highly acceptable because at that time I should have defy'd any man who had attempted to prove that my exaltation was the consequence of any Political operation.

but now sir the Case is changed I have collected with activity and success the Subscription proposed by government so much so as to have receivd from you sir a Letter thanking in the most Flattering terms my Countrymen for their conduct avowedly under the immediate guidance of my advice and sollicitation but the legality of the measure I have Carried is denied by the opposition and instead of being Confirm'd by the House of Commons is hung up by the majority there upon a previous Question

Thus circumstanced was I to receive a favor from government at this time is it not certain that all my enemies & all those of government would with one accord bellow forth that I am rewarded for conveying an illegal measure into execution and will not my friends no one of which is acquainted with HM previous intentions in my favor have reason to be certain that my Political and not my Literary character is the object of the distinction granted to me and will they not in Consequence of seeing me in their opinions take payment for the successful influence I have exerted over them withdraw from me the Confidence they have hitherto so liberaly granted to me which is founded to the best of my knowledge and belief solely on the opinion they hold of my incorruptible independence.

if I am right in these deductions it will be folly in you to grant & insanity in me to receive just now any favor from Government for by so doing I shall lose the whole of my present influence & you that assistance whatever it may be that Government has constantly received from active & not unsuccessful exertions on my Part to do them service ever since Mr Pits system of Prudence honesty & clean handed-ness has been adopted —* on my part without a wish for renumeration & till this moment without the least symptom of any pretention founded upon it even to thanks

I must then & with deeply seated greif do I state it decline now what a month ago was the main object of my ambitious hopes, so much is the nature of the gift altered by the Motives which will be attributed to the giver and with humble duty to my Sovereign who is not ignorant of the nature of my attachment both to his Person & his Government & sincere gratitude to his ministers for their good inclinations towards me I must cherish a hope that other Times & other situations will hereafter enable me to receive with

* There is a short word after adopted that I cannot make out.

pride and satisfaction a mark of Royal Approbation which I have saught after with diligence for years & now have obtained only as Tantalus did his Banquet to have it snatch'd from my Lips & teeth.

I am sir
with due respect
& real regard &c

The Rt. H. H. Dundas &c &c &c

The next letter[6] makes an agreeable pendant to the last: it was written to Sir Henry Hawley, one of his Lincolnshire cousins.

Soho Square
July 6 1795

My dear Sir

had I receivd any thing like the customary notice of the time when the honer I have newly receivd was to have been conferrd upon me I should not have suffered you to Read the first account of it in the Papers. I am too well aware of the kind interest you take in every thing that is agreable to us not to have taken great pleasure in communicating the news to you but from circumstances the Particulars of which I have not thought it necessary to enquire into I learnd only on Tuesday that I was to have my Ribband on Wednesday & Gen Abercrombie who was to have been my Companion in honer actualy did not receive his Time enough to take advantage of it

While I was kneeling on the Cushion before the King & the Sword of State which had me a Knight was still hanging over my Shoulders the King said to me in a low voice Sir Jos: I have for many years wishd to do this a mark of distinction so flattering has made me pleasd with an honer which as it came without sollicitation you may easily believe not to have been any object of my wishes, it had in the first instance been made palatable by coming in a direct course from the pure Fountain of honer without any portion of ministerial contamination but this latter instance of Gracious Condescention had made it inexpressibly valuable to my Feelings

Lady Banks my mother & sister desire to be rememberd in the kindest manner to you & to all yours I beg my dear sir you will beleive that I join sincerely in all good wishes & that I am with sincere affection & real Regard

most Faithfully yours
Jos: Banks

we shall all be happy if you can give us Good news respecting our cousin whose life was so long despaird of & whose cure if it is effected will not be owing to the skill of London Surgery

The last letter[7] from the 70-year-old Banks, tied to his wheelchair by gout but longing to be among the nondescripts of the East Indies if only by proxy, to the twenty-eight-year-old William Hooker, physically as free as the air but hampered by a possessive family, seems to me to give the very sound of Sir Joseph's living voice, not quite pleased, to be sure, but not at all rancorous either – it should be added that according to Edward Smith, who had sources of information that have now vanished, Banks had been to considerable pains to arrange an official, well-paid Eastern journey for his young friend, particularly to Java.

Spring Grove
June 19 1813

My dear Sir,

Tho I realy cannot think it Possible that your Relations and friends in Norfolk can consider an Island half as large as England to be of a deadly & unwholesome nature because one Town upon it is notoriously so, I see their objections are urgd with so much determination & eagerness that I am far indeed from advising you to despise them I have however no doubt that arguments or injunctions equaly strong will be urgd by them if you attempt to extend your views Further than the exhausted Azores originaly scarce worth the notice of a Botanist & now almost intirely transferd to Kew Gardens by the indefatigable Mason

From the Complexion of all that had Passd of Late in the Conduct of your Friends I have no doubt that they wish to force you to adopt Sardinapalus's advice to his citizens to Eat drink & propagate. how you will Like to be married & settled in the Countrey as Joe Miller wishd the dog had been who Flew at him & bit him I know not but that this Fate is prepared for you somewhat Earlier than the natural period of Renouncing an active Life is a matter of which I have no doubt but Pressd as you are I advise you to submit & sacrafice if you can your wish for Travelling to the importunities of those who think they can guide you to a more serene Quiet calm & sober mode of Slumbering away Life than that you proposd for yourself

Let me hear from you how you feel inclined to prefer Ease & indulgence to Hardship and activity I was about 23 when I began my Peregrinations you are somewhat older but you may be assured that if I had Listend to a multitude of voices that were Raisd up to dissuade me from my Enterprise I should have been now a Quiet countrey Gentleman ignorant of a multitude of matters I am now acquainted with & probably have attained to no higher Rank in Life than that of a countrey Justice of the Peace

adieu my dear Sir
Very Faithfully yours
Jos: Banks.

The Ladies beg to be Remembred to you. I get better daily but very Slowly

NOTES

I gratefully acknowledge the permission of the Royal Society, the British Library, the British Museum (Natural History), the Royal Botanic Gardens, the Lincolnshire Archives Office and Yale University to use material belonging to them. In these notes they are indicated by the following abbreviations: RS, BL, BM (Nat Hist), and Kew, while DTC stands for the Dawson Turner Copies in the Botany Library of the British Museum (Natural History), HR Aust for Historical Records of Australia, HR NSW for Historical Records of New South Wales, and PRO for Public Record Office.

CHAPTER 1 *(p. 13–p. 38)*

1 J. W. F. Hill *Letters and Papers of the Banks Family of Revesby Abbey 1704–1760* (Lincoln Record Society 1952).
2 RS Banks Papers, vol. III.
3 Hill, op.cit., p. XII.
4 Most of this information comes from P. M. Thornton's *Harrow School and its Surroundings* (London, 1885). Mr Thornton had access to John Lyon's papers, the governors' minutes and the school archives.
5 This is based on H. C. Maxwell-Lyte, *The History of Eton College* (London, 1911), C. Hollis, *Eton, a History* (London, 1960); and R. Ollard, *An English Education: a Perspective of Eton* (London, 1982).
6 It is now in the National Library of Australia, MS Branch, NK 73. A. M. Lysaght, *Joseph Banks in Newfoundland and Labrador 1766* (London, 1971), p. 234 gives it in full.
7 A. D. Godley, *Oxford in the Eighteenth Century* (London, 1908), quoting John James's correspondence.
8 Robert Brown, Correspondence, BM (Nat Hist) vol. 1 no. 20.
9 Arthur Young, *A General View of the Agriculture of the County of Lincoln* (London, 1799), p. 234.
10 Godley, op. cit.
11 Lysaght, op. cit., p. 44.
12 This is based upon R. A. Rauschenberg, *Daniel Carl Solander, Naturalist on the "Endeavour"* in the *Transactions of the American Philosophical Society* for November 1968.

CHAPTER 3 *(p. 59–p. 89)*

1 J. C. Beaglehole (ed.), *The Endeavour Journal of Joseph Banks* (Sydney, 1962), vol. I p. 17.
2 The same.
3 *The Dolphin's Return* from *Naval Songs and Ballads*, Navy Records Society, 1908.
4 J. E. Smith, *A Selection of the Correspondence of Linnaeus* (London, 1821), vol. I p. 230.
5 D. W. Freshfield, *Life of H. B. de Saussure* (London, 1920), p. 105.
6 This is from a German version of a Swedish translation of a letter written by Banks to Alströmer in 1784 and very kindly sent to me by Dr Rauschenberg of Ohio University, the authority on Solander.
7 J. F. Green, *Ocean Birds* (London, 1887).

CHAPTER 4 *(p. 90–p. 103)*

1 BL Add MS 33979 29–30.
2 Sydney Parkinson, *A Journal of a Voyage to the South Seas . . .* (London, 1773).

CHAPTER 5 *(p. 104–p. 141)*

1 Addressed to M. de Lauragais, December 1771: see Beaglehole, op. cit., vol. II p. 326.

2 This is from the surviving pages of the surgeon Monkhouse's journal in *The Journals of Captain James Cook* (ed. J. C. Beaglehole), vol. I, *The Voyage of the Endeavour 1768–1777*, p. 564.

3 Speaking of this incident in his journal Cook says, "I am aware that most humane men who have not experienced things of this nature will censure my conduct in firing upon the people in the boat nor do I my self think that the reason I had for seizing upon her will at all justify me, and had I thought that they would have made the least resistance I would not have come near them, but as they did I was not to stand still and suffer either my self or those that were with me to be knocked on the head."

4 William Dampier touched the northern coast of Australia in 1687 and the western in 1699. He wrote lively accounts of his voyages.

5 The plant is now called *Tetragonia expansa*, the New Zealand spinach: Banks it was who first brought it to Europe.

CHAPTER 6 *(p. 142–p. 167)*

1 BL Add MS 8094 33.

2 Quoted by Beaglehole, *Cook*, vol. I p. 652.

3 DTC, I 32. In Warren Dawson's opinion the Sunday of the date was 11 August 1771.

4 This is on the authority of Beaglehole, *Endeavour Journal*, I 73; but a footnote on the same page quotes Banks's list "*Resolution*, Zoffany, J. F. Miller and James Miller (draughtsmen) £100 a year each".

5 DTC, I 35.

6 Windsor, Royal Archives 1322.

7 Windsor, Royal Archives 1323.

8 Uno von Troil, *Letters on Iceland*, English translation in Pinkerton's Voyages.

CHAPTER 7 *(p. 168–p. 192)*

1 DTC, II 97/100.

2 R. A. Rauschenberg in ISIS, vol. 55 no. 179 (1964).

3 Lysaght, op. cit., p. 50.

4 Ann Savours on the Phipps expedition in *Arctic*, vol. 37 no. 4 (December, 1984).

5 Quoted in Beaglehole, *Endeavour Journal*, vol. I p. 115.

6 *Journal of Botany*, vol. 43 (1909).

7 M. Alexander, *Omai* (London, 1977), p. 71.

8 Alexander, op. cit., p. 83.

9 R. B. Peake, *Memoirs of the Colman Family* (vol. I p. 355), quoted by E. Smith.

10 DTC, I 94/5.

11 David Hume to W. Strahan, 10 May 1776, quoted by Beaglehole from *The Letters of David Hume* (ed. J. Y. T. Grieg, Oxford, 1932), vol. II.

CHAPTER 8 *(p. 193–p. 218)*

1 DTC, I 198.

2 DTC, I 199.

3 E. Smith, *The Life of Sir Joseph Banks* (London, 1911), p. 62.

4 The deer-park at Revesby covered 340 acres (about as much as Hyde Park) of moderate land, and in principle it carried 300 head, as well as some sheep, horses and cattle.

In 1803 Sir Joseph sent a detailed account of its economy to his friend Arthur Young for publication in the *Annals of Agriculture* (vol. 39), and he began by saying, "It has generally been supposed, that a deer-park is an expensive article of luxury; and, I confess, I was myself much impressed with that opinion: in order, therefore, to ascertain the amount of my annual expenditure, in that article, I directed an exact account to be kept of the profit derived from my small enclosure, setting it against the estimated rent of the land, taxes, cost of labour, people's wages, cost of maintaining the poles and temporary fences, &c. &c."

The account showed an expenditure of £516 5*s* 10*d* (including £209 7*s* 2½*d* for notional rent, £60 3*s* 9*d* for parish rates and £40 a year for the park-keeper) and an income of £568 4*s* 9½*d*, including £250 for venison at the London market rate of £18 a brace (10½ brace of bucks, 1½ brace of haviour bucks and 4½ brace of does) and smaller sums for the grazing of the various other animals, the wool from the sheep and the milk from the cows (19,600 pints at a penny a pint). This appears to have left a surplus of £51 18*s* 11½*d*, but perhaps it was more, for if the deer were really all sold at £18 a brace, they should have yielded £297: on the other hand there could easily be a misprint in the price of the does. Yet whether particular points of arithmetic were mistaken or not, a three years' trial convinced him that "I am regularly a gainer by holding it in hand".

5 B. Faujas de Saint-Fond, *Travels in England, Scotland and the Hebrides* (ed. A. Geikie, Glasgow, 1907), p. 51.

6 Arthur Young, op. cit., p. 234.

7 A. Kippis, *Observations on the late Contests in the Royal Society* (London, 1784).

8 Rauschenberg, op. cit. (1968).

9 W. M. Godschall to Banks, 30 December 1782: DTC, II 232/3.

10 Brougham, *Lives of the Philosophers of the Time of George III* (Edinburgh, 1872), p. 359.

11 RS Misc. MSS 1 30.

12 Letter dated 15 March 1846 to Sir Edward Knatchbull (Brown Correspondence in BM [Nat Hist]).

13 HR NSW, vol. I ii 1.

14 DTC, XIV 128.

CHAPTER 9 *(p. 219–p. 242)*

1 *The Diaries of Col. the Hon. R. F. Greville* (ed. F. McK. Bladon).

2 J. Sparks, *Memoirs of the Life and Travels of John Ledyard* (London, 1828).

3 RS Misc. MSS 6 60.

4 G. Mackaness, *Life of . . . Bligh* (Sydney, 1951), p. 37.

5 H. C. Cameron, *Sir Joseph Banks* (London, 1952), p. 65.

6 DTC, V 208.

7 R. T. Gould in *Mariner's Mirror*, vol. 14 no. 4, quoted by G. Kennedy in *Bligh* (London, 1978).

8 O. Rutter (ed.), *The Trial of the "Bounty" Mutineers* (Edinburgh, 1931), p. 8.

9 A. T. Gage, *History of the Linnean Society*.

CHAPTER 10 *(p. 243–p. 269)*

1 PRO (Chatham) III 129/130.

2 Preface to W. R. Dawson, *The Banks Letters* (London, 1958).

3 DTC, XIX 303.

4 B. Brodie, *Autobiography*, vol. 1 p. 45.

5 DTC, X(1) 63.

6 Brougham, op. cit., p. 378.

7 C. Lyte, *Sir Joseph Banks* (Newton Abbot, 1980) presumably referring to the Banks Papers in the Lindsey County Library 3, 1, 2/21.

8 HR NSW, vol. I ii 239.

9 This honour was more than Peter Pindar could forgive, and affecting to disbelieve the report he burst out into an ode which contains these lines:

From Joseph Banks unto Sir Knight,
Then Privy Counsellor in spite
Of nature, brain and education!
It, for the *last*, he hands *has* kiss'd;
There's not a reptile on his list
E'er knew a stranger transmutation.

10 HR NSW vol. 1, p. 53.

11 The same, p. 152.

12 DTC, IX 246.

13 HR Aust Ist Series, vol. II p. 96/7.
14 DTC, X(2) 93/5.
15 DTC, X(1) 4.
16 DTC, XI 313.
17 E. Smith, op. cit., p. 210.

CHAPTER 11 *(p. 270–p. 304)*

1 H. B. Carter, *His Majesty's Spanish Flock* (Sydney, 1964), p. 446.
2 HR Aust Ist series, III p. 321.
3 Mackaness, op. cit., p. 119.
4 DTC, XIII 101/6.
5 Carter, op. cit., deals with these happenings in the closest detail.
6 E. Smith, op. cit., p. 241.
7 *The Journal of Peter Good* (ed. Phyllis I. Edwards: Bulletin of the British Museum [Natural History] Historical Series vol. 9, London, 1981).
8 Brodie, op. cit., vol. I p. 42.
9 DTC, XVI 272.
10 DTC, XVI 331.
11 H. Hermannsson, *Sir Joseph Banks and Iceland* (Ithaca, 1928), p. 28.
12 DTC, XII 167.
13 Hermannsson, op. cit., p. 38.
14 W. J. Hooker, *Tour in Iceland* (London, 1813).
15 DTC, XVII 206.
16 DTC, XVIII 88.
17 DTC, XIX 56/63.
18 E. Smith, op. cit., p. 300.
19 Cameron, op. cit., p. 173.
20 E. Smith, op. cit., p. 325.

CHAPTER 12 *(p. 305–p. 313)*

1 Mitchell Library, Sydney: Banks Papers XVI 3, quoted by Beaglehole, *Endeavour Journal*, vol. I pp. 12/13.
2 BL Egerton MS, 2641 130/1.
3 From the Brabourne Papers in the Kent County Archives, quoted by Lysaght, op. cit., pp. 52/53.
4 DTC, VI 40.
5 From the Osborn Collection in the Library of Yale University.
6 From the Hawley Papers (Haw 6/3/4) in the Lincolnshire Archives.
7 From the Hooker Correspondence at Kew (vol. I no. 39).

BIBLIOGRAPHY

Aiton, W. *Hortus Kewensis*, 3 vols (London, 1789).

Alexander, M. *Omai* (London, 1977).

Anderson, J. *Letters to Sir Joseph Banks, Baronet, President of the Royal Society on the Subject of Cochineal Insects, discovered at Madras by James Anderson M.D.* (Madras, 1788).

Anonymous *An appeal to the fellows of the Royal Society, concerning the measures taken by Sir Joseph Banks, their president, to compel Dr Hutton to resign the office of secretary to the Society for their foreign correspondence.* By a friend to Dr Hutton (London, 1784).

[Banks, Sir Joseph] *The Propriety of Allowing a Qualified Exportation of Wool Discussed Historically* (London, 1782).

Banks, Sir Joseph

[Communications read to the Society of Antiquaries]

A Breviate touching the order and governments of a Nobleman's House (London, 1790).

Extracts out of an Old Book relating to . . . Louth Church. (London, 1800).

[Pamphlets]

A short Account of the causes of the disease in corn, called the blight (London, 1805).

Some remarks on mildew of wheat, and choice of seed corn (London, 1816).

[Articles in Arthur Young's *Annals of Agriculture* (1784–1809)]

A Report on Wool vol. IX

Instructions given to the Council against the Wool Bill vol. IX

Notes on Spinning vol. X

A New Hay-barn, and a New Rick-Cloth vol. X

On the Hessian Fly vol. XI

On the late Season, 1790 vol. XV

On the Hastings Turnip vol. XV

Account of Twelve Lincoln Sheep vol. XV

On the Musca pumilionis vol. XVI

Economy of a Park vol. XXXIX

[Papers in the Horticultural Society's Transactions, vol. I]

An attempt to ascertain the time when the Potatoe (Solanum tuberosum) *was first introduced into the United Kingdom*

Some hints respecting the proper mode of inuring Tender Plants to our climate

On the revival of an obsolete mode of managing Strawberries

An account of the method of cultivating the American cranberry (Vaccinium macrocarpum)

On the Horticultural Management of the Sweet or Spanish Chestnut-tree

A short account of a new Apple, called the Spring Grove Codling

On ripening the second crop of Figs that grow on the new shoots

Some Horticultural observations, selected from French authors

Desiderata bibliotheca Banksiana, 4th edition: text begins "I Aagaard, Nic. de nido Phoenicis. Hafn. 1647, 4to". Number of items required 1072 (London, 1794) (?).

Bauer, F. L. *Illustrationes Florae Novae Hollandiae* (London, 1813).

Beaglehole, J. C. (ed.) *The Endeavour Journal of Joseph Banks*, 2 vols (Sydney, 1962).

The Journals of Captain James Cook: The Voyage of the Endeavour 1768–1771 (Cambridge, 1952).

Beer, G. R. de *The Relations between Fellows of the Royal Society and French Men of Science when France and Britain were at War* (Notes and Records of the Royal Society vol. 9) (London, 1952).

Biswas, Kalipada *The Original Correspondence of Sir Joseph Banks relating to the Foundation of the Royal Botanic Garden, Calcutta* (Royal Asiatic Society of Bengal, Monograph series V 9) (Calcutta, 1950).

Blunt, W. *Captain Cook's Florilegium. A Selection of Engravings from the Drawings of Plants Collected by Joseph Banks and Daniel Solander on Captain Cook's First Voyage to the Islands of the Pacific* (London, 1973).

Bougainville, L. -A. de. *Voyage autour du Monde en 1766–1769* (Paris, 1771).

Brodie, Sir B. C. *Autobiography* (London, 1865).

Brosses, C. de *Histoire des Navigations aux Terres australes*, 2 vols (Paris, 1756).

Brougham, Lord *Lives of Men of Letters and Science who Flourished in the Time of George III*, 2 vols (London, 1846).

Lives of the Philosophers of the Time of George III (Edinburgh, 1872).

Brown, R. *Prodromus Florae Novae Hollandiae et Insulae van Diemen* (London, 1810).

Cameron, H. C. *Sir Joseph Banks, K.B., P.R.S., The Autocrat of the Philosophers* (London, 1952).

Carter, H. B. *His Majesty's Spanish Flock* (Sydney, 1964).

Sir Joseph Banks and the plant collection from Kew sent to the Empress Catherine II of Russia, 1795 (British Museum [Natural History]) (London 1974).

(ed.) *The Sheep and Wool Correspondence of Sir Joseph Banks, 1781–1820* (Library Council of New South Wales) (London, 1979).

Coke, M. *The Letters and Journals of Lady Mary Coke*, 4 vols (Edinburgh, 1896).

Collins, D. *An Account of the English Colony of New South Wales*, 2 vols (London, 1798–1802).

Dalrymple, A. *Account of the Discoveries made in the South Pacific Ocean before 1764* (London, 1769).

Dawson, Warren R. (ed.) *The Banks Letters: a Calendar of the Manuscript Correspondence* (British Museum) (London, 1958).

Supplementary Letters, 2 series (London, 1962–5).

Diment, J. A. (ed.) *Natural History Drawings Commissioned by Joseph Banks on the "Endeavour's" Voyage, 1768–71 Catalogue of the Part I: Botany, Australia.*

Dryander, J. *Catalogus bibliothecae historico-naturalis Josephi Banks, Baronetti*, 5 vols (London, 1796–1800).

Ellis, M. H. *John Macarthur* (Sydney, 1955).

Faujas de Saint-Fond, B. *Travels in England, Scotland and the Hebrides*, ed. A. Geikie (Glasgow, 1907).

Flinders, M. *A Voyage to Terra Australis . . . in . . . 1801–1803 in H.M.S. Investigator*, 2 vols (London, 1814).

Freshfield, D. W. *Life of H. B. de Saussure* (London, 1920).

Gage, A. T. *History of the Linnean Society* (London, 1938).

Godley, A. D. *Oxford in the Eighteenth Century* (London, 1908).

Good, P. *The Journal of Peter Good, Gardener on Matthew Flinders' Voyage to Terra Australia 1801–1803* ed. Phyllis Edwards (British Museum [Natural History] Historical Series vol. 9) (London, 1981).

Greville, R. F. *The Diaries of Col. the Hon. R. F. Greville*, ed. F. McK. Bladon.

Harris, J. *Navigantiaum atque Itinerantium Bibliotheca or, a Compleat Collection of Voyages and Travels: Consisting of above Four Hundred of the most Authentic Writers*, 2 vols (London, 1725).

Hawkesworth, J. *An Account of the Voyages undertaken . . . for making discoveries in the South Hemisphere and performed by Commodore Byrone, Captain Wallis, Captain Carteret and Captain Cook (from 1764 to 1771) drawn up from the Journals*, 3 vols (London, 1773).

Hermannsson, H. *Sir Joseph Banks and Iceland* (Islandica 18) (Ithaca, 1928).

Herschel, C. L. *Account of the discovery of a new comet, By Miss Caroline Herschel, In a letter to Sir Joseph Banks*, From the Philosophical transactions (London, 1796).

Hill, J. W. F. *The Letters and Papers of the Banks Family of Revesby Abbey 1704–1760* (Lincoln Record Society, 1952).

Historical Records of Australia 4 series

Historical Records of New South Wales, ed. F. M. Bladen, 8 vols (Sydney, 1895–1901).

Hollis, C. *Eton, a History* (London, 1960).

Hooker, W. J. *Journal of a Tour in Iceland in the Summer of 1809*, 2 vols (London, 1813).

Jussieu, A. -L. de *Genera Plantarum* (Paris, 1789).

Kennedy, G. *Bligh* (London, 1978).

Kippis, A. *Observations on the late Contests in the Royal Society* (London, 1784).

Knight, R. P. *An account of the remains of the worship of Priapus, lately existing at Isernia, in the Kingdom of Naples: in two letters; one from Sir William Hamilton to Sir Joseph Banks, and the other from a person residing at Isernia: to which is added, a discourse on the worship of Priapus* By R. P. Knight, Esq. (London, 1786).

Labillardière J. -J. de *Novae Hollandiae Plantarum specimen*, 2 vols (Paris, 1804–6).

Lyons, Sir. H. *The Royal Society 1660–1940* (Cambridge, 1944).

Lysaght, A. *Joseph Banks in Newfoundland and Labrador, 1766: His Diary, Manuscripts and Collections* (London, 1971).

Some eighteenth-century bird paintings in Sir Joseph Banks's library (in British Museum [Natural History] Historical Bulletin, Historical Series vol. 1) (London, 1959).

Lyte, C. *Sir Joseph Banks: 18th Century Explorer, Botanist and Entrepreneur* (Newton Abbot, 1980).

Mackaness, G. *Sir Joseph Banks: his Relations with Australia* (Sydney, 1936).

The Life of Vice-Admiral William Bligh, R.N., F.R.S. (revised edition), (Sydney, 1951).

Maiden, J. H. *Sir Joseph Banks, the Father of Australia* (Sydney, 1909).

Maxwell-Lyte, H. C. *The History of Eton College (1440–1910)* (London, 1911).

Miller, P. *The Gardener's and Florist's Dictionary* (London, 1724).

Ollard, R. *An English Education: a Perspective of Eton* (London, 1982).

Paget, H. *To the South there is a Great Land. Captain Cook, Sir Joseph Banks and Australia* (Sydney, 1970).

Parkinson, S. *A Journal of a Voyage to the South Seas in His Majesty's Ship the Endeavour.* Faithfully transcribed from the Papers of the late Sydney Parkinson (London, 1773).

Pennant, T. *A Tour in Scotland and Voyage to the Hebrides* (London, 1774–6).

Arctic Zoology, 2nd edition, 3 vols (London, 1792).

The Literary Life of the late Thomas Pennant, Esq., written by Himself (London, 1793).

Phipps, J. C. *A Voyage towards the North Pole* (London, 1774).

Pindar, P. *see* Wolcot, J.

Prévost d'Exiles, A. F. *Histoire Générale des Voyages* (Paris, 1746–61).

Rauschenberg, R. A. *Daniel Carl Solander, Naturalist on the "Endeavour"* (in *Transactions of the American Philosophical Society*) (Philadelphia, November 1968).

Roxborough, W. *Plants of the coast of Coromandel; selected from drawings and descriptions presented to the Hon. Court of directors of the East India Company, by William Roxborough, M.D.* Published, by their order, under the direction of Sir Joseph Banks, 3 vols (London, 1795–1819).

Rutter, O. (ed.) *The Trial of the "Bounty" Mutineers* (Edinburgh, 1931).

Rydén, Stig. *The Banks Collection* (Stockholm, 1963).

Savours, A. *The 1773 Phipps Expedition towards the North Pole* (in *Arctic*, vol. 37 no. 4, December 1984).

Schofield, R. E. *The Lunar Society of Birmingham: a Social History of Provincial Science and Industry in Eighteenth-century England* (Oxford, 1963).

Scott, E. *Australian Discovery by Sea* (London, 1929).

Smith, E. *The Life of Sir Joseph Banks* (London, 1911).

Smith, Sir J. E. *A Selection of the Correspondence of Linnaeus, and other Naturalists, from the Original Manuscripts*, 2 vols (London, 1821).

Solander, D. C. *An Account of the Gardenia: in a Letter to Philip Carteret Webb, Esq., F.R.S. from Daniel C. Solander, M.D.* (Philosophical Transactions 52, part II) (London, 1763).

Sparks, J. *Memoirs of the Life and Travels of John Ledyard* (London, 1828).

Suttor, G. *Memoirs of George Suttor, F.L.S., Banksian Collector* (1778–1859), ed. G. Mackaness (Sydney, 1948).

Thornton, P. M. *Harrow School and its Surroundings* (London, 1885).

Troil, U. von *Letters on Iceland: containing observations . . . made by Joseph Banks, Esq. F.R.S. . . . written by Uno von Troil. To which are added the letters of Dr Ihre and Dr Back to the author, concerning the Edda and the Elephantiasis of Iceland: also Professor Bergman's curious observations* (Dublin, 1780).

[Waring, J. S.] *An epistle from Oberea, Queen of Otaheite, to Joseph Banks, Esq.* Translated by T.Q.Z. Esq. Professor of the Otaheite language in Dublin. And enriched with historical and explanatory notes, London, 1774 (attributed to Major John Scott Waring).

Webster, M. *Johann Zoffany* (London, 1976).

Weld, C. R. *A History of the Royal Society* (London, 1848).

White, Rev. G. *The Natural History and Antiquities of Selborne* (1789), ed. Thomas Bell, 2 vols (London, 1877).

Wilkins, G. L. *A catalogue and historical account of the Banks Shell Collection:* Bulletin British Museum (Natural History) Historical Series 1.

Wolcot, J. *Sir Joseph Banks and the Emperor of Morocco.* A tale. By Peter Pindar, Esquire (London, 1788).

An Ode to the Livery of London. Also an Ode to Sir Joseph Banks on the Report of his Elevation to the important Dignity of a Privy Counsellor. By Peter Pindar, Esq. (London, 1797).

Young, A. *A General View of the Agriculture of the County of Lincoln* (London, 1799). *Autobiography*, ed. M. Betham-Edwards (London, 1898).

INDEX